ARISTOTLE

AN ATHENIAN CITIZEN OF THE FIFTH CENTURY BEFORE CHRIST.
FROM A GREEK VASE IN THE METROPOLITAN MUSEUM OF ART

ARISTOTLE

On Man In The Universe

METAPHYSICS · PARTS OF ANIMALS

ETHICS · POLITICS · POETICS

EDITED WITH INTRODUCTION
BY LOUISE ROPES LOOMIS

Published for the Classics Club by

WALTER J. BLACK · ROSLYN, NEW YORK

CONTENTS

INTRODUCTION
By Louise Ropes Loomis　　　　　　　　　xi

METAPHYSICS
Based on the translation of John Henry MacMahon　　3

PARTS OF ANIMALS
Based on the translation of William Ogle　　41

NICOMACHEAN ETHICS
Based on the translation of James E. C. Welldon　　85

POLITICS
Based on the translation of Benjamin Jowett　　246

POETICS
Based on the translation of Samuel Henry Butcher　　418

CONTENTS

INTRODUCTION
By Lewis Ropes Loomis

METAPHYSICS
Based on the translation of John Henry MacMahon

PARTS OF ANIMALS
Based on the translation of William Ogle

NICOMACHEAN ETHICS
Based on the translation of James E. C. Welldon

POLITICS
Based on the translation of Benjamin Jowett

POETICS
Based on the translation of Samuel Henry Butcher

ARISTOTLE

INTRODUCTION

EVERYONE WHO KNOWS anything about Plato knows that he had a pupil called Aristotle, who in time became almost, if not quite, as famous a philosopher as his master. They may know too that Aristotle in his turn had a pupil known as Alexander the Great, who, when hardly out of boyhood, became one of the world's most illustrious conquerors and empire-builders. An extraordinary line of men that little Greek corner of the earth could produce in the fourth century before Christ! But pupils do not always follow respectfully along the paths marked out for them by their teachers. Aristotle set up a school at Athens to rival and for long periods outshine Plato's. Alexander's empire spelled the downfall of the small, independent city-state that to Aristotle was the only possible form of civilized political community. For that empire was a vast conglomeration of races and kingdoms that stretched from Greece away eastward until it reached the mythical region of India, beyond the rising sun. In it the free Greek cities, to which Aristotle pinned his hopes for human progress, lost their pride and their liberties, never fully to get them back.

The story of Aristotle (384-322) is intertwined all through with the events going on in the half Greek, half barbarian country of Macedonia, to the north of Greece proper, and the adjacent shores of the Aegean Sea. He was not, like Socrates and Plato, an Athenian born. His father was a Greek physician at the court of the Macedonian king. As a boy he seems to have lived in an atmosphere of biological science and may even have been trained with a view to following his father's profession. At seventeen, however, his father being dead, he left his home country and went south to Athens, the capital of Greek culture, to enter the Academy of Plato and learn

what that renowned master could teach him. There he remained for a long twenty years, studying, writing, and eventually taking part in the teaching of philosophy, mathematics, ethics, politics, and esthetics. Plato is said to have called him the mind of the school. But on Plato's death another man was appointed head. Aristotle left Athens and went back north, this time to the coast of Asia Minor and the island of Lesbos. For a while he stayed at the court of an old fellow student, who had become ruler of a petty seaboard state, and married his niece. He picked up again his youthful interest in natural science, and made notes especially on the structure and habits of the marine creatures he observed along the shore.

At this time the king of Macedonia was Philip, a man of exceptional ability and driving will, who for some years past had been at work transforming his realm from a poor, backward country of untapped natural resources and a population of rude huntsmen and mountaineers into a rich and powerful kingdom with an invincible army, organized to fight after a new system in solid blocks of heavy armed infantry, known as the Macedonian phalanx. With this army and his freshly-acquired wealth behind him, Philip was now trying to induce the Greek cities in the south to join him in a concerted attack on the dangerous old empire of Persia, that was forever intriguing to divide and undermine Greek strength. The cities, however, were suspicious of the intentions of this upstart northern colossus. Nor could they bring themselves to forget their own mutual animosities and grievances and unite even against the ancient enemy. In Athens the great orator Demosthenes was passionately denouncing Philip as a wily tyrant, who under guise of helping his countrymen was plotting to make them all his slaves. Meanwhile, however, Philip was wanting a distinguished Greek to take charge of the education of his only son, the fair-haired, high-spirited boy Alexander, then thirteen years old. In 343 or 342, he offered the post to Aristotle, who accepted it. We know nothing of Aristotle's attitude to the political agitation then going on in Greece. We do not

even know how close became his relationship in Macedonia to Alexander.

In 340, Alexander, at fifteen, was made regent for his father, during the latter's absence in Greece, and apparently passed from Aristotle's surveillance. In 338, the armies of Athens and Thebes, which had been roused by Demosthenes to a futile defiance of Philip, were overwhelmed in the battle of Chaeronea. The rest of Greece succumbed gradually. Two years later, however, Philip was murdered, on the eve of launching his long-planned campaign against Persia, and Alexander, his son, reigned in his stead. He soon showed that he had inherited even more than his father's genius and ambition. He promptly reduced all Greece to complete submission, then invaded and conquered, one after the other, all the sumptuous old empires of the Eastern Mediterranean—Assyrian, Egyptian, and Persian. Everywhere he claimed to come as a delivering god, breaking down racial, caste, and political barriers and founding cities after the Greek pattern as centers of enlightened administration. There were Alexandrias planted as far east as modern Turkestan and the border of India. Then, in 323, he died of a fever and his generals divided his empire among them.

Not long after Alexander's assumption of power, Aristotle returned to Athens, now under Macedonian control. There he rented some buildings in a grove dedicated to Apollo Lyceius and opened a school known as the Lyceum. There too he collected one of the earliest reported libraries of manuscript books, and scientific specimens of many sorts as material for research and lectures. We hear of a botanical garden and a small menagerie of birds and other animals. One or more of his students accompanied Alexander on his expedition eastward and sent back accounts of the strange beasts and other things seen by the way. At the school, Aristotle directed investigations in well-nigh every known field of knowledge and lectured on many of them in a loggia or open-air porch looking on the garden. The name of such a porch is in Greek *peripaté*. Hence the title peripatetic given to his style of teaching. His remarkable learning and

force of intellect quickly made the Lyceum the center of fresh study and discussion both in natural science and in philosophy, politics, and other more familiar subjects. In size and activity it outstripped Plato's school, which continued working in general along the lines its founder had laid down.

But the premature death of Alexander put an abrupt stop to Aristotle's Athenian career. The patriotic anti-Macedonian feeling, that had smouldered underground in the city as long as the conqueror lived, blazed up after his death in an outbreak of hatred and bitterness against anyone with Macedonian connections or affiliations. Aristotle, as Alexander's old tutor, who had come back to Athens in the wake of the Macedonian victory, was inevitably suspect. A technical charge of impiety was lodged against him, as, eighty years before, it had been against Socrates. But before the case could be brought to trial, Aristotle had left once more for the North, refusing to let Athens "sin twice against philosophy." There, in Chalcis, a year later, he died, leaving a will in which he provided that several of his slaves should be freed. The Lyceum was carried on by his pupils and their successors for over eight hundred years, until it, like Plato's Academy, was closed by order of a Christian emperor in Constantinople.

The life of Aristotle coincides then with that confused and cheerless period when the proud Greek cities, that had once so valiantly defended their freedom against the countless hosts of Persia, now, through their inability to submerge their differences and co-operate with one another, were losing that freedom and sinking into the state of inglorious subjection that, but for a few short intervals, was to last until the nineteenth century. He lived in the thick of these events, knew personally some of the chief actors, left behind a mass of profoundly thoughtful writings on many topics, yet no word of comment on the fateful thing that was happening or on the men responsible for it. For all the information we get from him, we might suppose the state of Greece in his time to be as usual, with the customary petty wrangling going on between the cities, and the impe-

rial powers of Egypt, Persia, and Carthage lying off on the horizon, and no new cyclonic force crashing through the world, creating such havoc with the old order that nothing could ever bring it back. His discourse on politics has all to do with the management of the small, independent city-state, as if the day of that state were not already gone. Why, we wonder, this deliberate averting of the eyes, this refusal to speak of the earth-shaking revolution going on around him? Was it the detachment of a philosopher, who looked on the fall of Greece and Alexander's conquests as painful but passing incidents of no permanent significance, and aimed to keep his students' attention fixed on the eternally valid principles of nature and civilized human existence and art? Or was it the caution required of one coming from the enemy's habitat, who wished to live and study and teach safely in Athens? Not a syllable has survived the centuries to tell us. We have merely the notes of a number of highly impersonal lecture courses, delivered by him to the pupils of the Lyceum during the last thirteen years of his life.

It is true that about three-quarters of the works of Aristotle mentioned by ancient scholars were lost in the disasters that overtook libraries and literature during the wars that followed the division of Alexander's empire. Those lost include all the dialogues in the Platonic manner which he wrote as a young man, and everything else that he later composed and prepared for circulation and that was praised by other writers for its eloquence and beauty. The only exception is a short study of the Athenian constitution, discovered in 1890, in an Egyptian papyrus. By accident, however, a miscellaneous selection of notes and memoranda of his Lyceum lectures, written down at different times—some seemingly by himself, others by students for their own remembrance—were taken, perhaps for safekeeping, across to Asia Minor. There they were hidden away underground to save them from the kings of Pergamum, who were gathering in books from everywhere to fill their renowned library. For nearly two centuries the manuscripts lay forgotten, eaten by damp and worms, until, at the time of the Roman conquest of Asia Minor,

they chanced to be brought to light and someone carried them to Rome.

In Rome there were scholars who recognized the value of the little pile of moldering parchment. They made new copies, filling in the holes and illegible passages as best they could and combining blocks of notes on the same subject rather regardlessly into books. Only notes on topics that were not duplicated, such as the studies of sky and atmosphere, of animals and of psychological phenomena, were left in the form in which they had been found. Finally, about 70 B.C. a Greek, Andromicus of Rhodes, prepared a revised edition of all the material, which was thenceforth accepted as authoritative. It was his edition probably that Cicero knew and it is that which we use now. Nothing earlier than it has come down to us.

These remnants of a great man's teaching are all we have by which to judge him. They are at any rate enough to show the incredibly wide range of his speculations as to what makes up the universe we live in and how and why it comes to be as it is. His mind was naturally more methodical than that of his master Plato. These works are closely reasoned, learned treatises, each dealing with one definitely stated subject, unlike the Platonic dialogues that stray, as informal talk does, from one topic on to another, over creation and back again. Among these survivals are books on logic, metaphysics, astronomy, physics, biology, physiology, psychology, ethics, politics, rhetoric, and poetics. In almost every one of these fields they represent a notable advance in method, and often some epoch-making discovery in material.

Their scope may be explained, in part at least, by the two facts that Aristotle was, first, a physician's son, with an inherited taste for natural science and sharp observation of all living things, and, second, a pupil of Plato, who had imbibed from his teacher a broad philosophic view of the world as a whole, as also of human affairs. He may even be said to do over much of Plato's work, handling the same or similar questions but probing into them even more inquisitively and making greater use of data gathered from actual experi-

ence. Phases of existence, however, that Plato on his lofty eminence of thought had passed over slightingly or altogether ignored Aristotle must get down to earth to finger and explore. He could and did reason like Plato, from ideal, abstract principles, whenever the subject of his reasoning lay outside the field of observation possible to him, but he was also on the watch to reject or modify his theories when a closer examination of nature proved them wrong. He was both a great thinker and a great experimental scientist. Of certain of his own careful conclusions he said that the facts apparently supported them; but "I say apparently, for the actual facts are not yet sufficiently made out. Should further research ever discover them, we must yield to their guidance rather than to that of theory; for theories must be abandoned, unless their teachings tally with the indisputable results of observation."

Like Plato, Aristotle thought it necessary, first of all, to understand and explain the workings of the human mind and to show what kinds of reasoning were valid and could be relied on to give us sure knowledge of anything and what were not. This he did in a group of treatises, called together the *Logic,* or *Organon. Organon* is a Greek word meaning tool or instrument. Aristotle's *Organon* is an instrument for making clear the processes of logical, reasoned thinking and for proving the correctness of its conclusions. It aims to make plain the steps by which a science or body of trustworthy knowledge may be firmly built up from its starting point in certain fundamental axioms or obvious statements, perceived intuitively to be true.

Every science, Aristotle points out, must begin with a few of these necessary axioms or general truths. They cannot be logically proved, but our minds by simple intuition accept them nevertheless as obviously true to actual fact. Without some such assumptions as foundation stones we could never start to build anything. A student must accept the axioms of Euclid's geometry before he can go on to prove the theorems in the textbook. A doctor must believe there is such a thing as natural bodily disease before he can cure it by appropriate drugs and treatment. He cannot positively prove his assumption so

as to convince a savage, who is sure that all sick persons are possessed by devils. But, on the basis of his assumption, the doctor erects his system of medicine, while the savage, on his, resorts to exorcism and magic.

Beginning then in each case with certain assumptions that are to the holders so evident that they can dispense with logical proof, men proceed to construct their systems of knowledge and science. They add to what they already know something more that is both new and sure. To do this, they may reason in the pattern of what Aristotle calls the *syllogism*. By it "certain things being stated, something else follows of necessity," without need of any further testimony. It is what we call deductive reasoning, an arguing from previously established general rules or statements down to particular instances. The general rule is first laid down. All A are B, or, to borrow Aristotle's own illustration, all men must die. A second statement brings in some individual or group which unquestionably belongs under some head of statement number one. C, for example, is a part of A, or, Socrates was a man. Then, if all A are B, C, being part of A, must also be B. Or, Socrates, being a man, must have shared the fate of all men. He must have died. The same form of reasoning underlies a doctor's diagnosis. Such and such symptoms in my experience invariably indicate measles. My patient has these symptoms. Therefore, my patient has measles.

In all syllogistic or deductive reasoning, however, Aristotle warns us, we must make sure that the first or basic proposition is really comprehensive and covers every case. If A is only sometimes B, or if such and such symptoms indicate sometimes measles but at other times hives or scarlet fever, then C, though included in A, may not be B, and the patient with the red, spotted chest may have not measles at all but a bad attack of hives. Hence no exact conclusion is possible. Also we must be as certain as we can be that this basic proposition is true. One who starts with the conviction that all boys are bad and reasons therefrom that Johnny, being a boy, is necessarily bad and should be dealt with accordingly, has the form of his syllogism cor-

rect but the value of it to him or anyone else is nil. His basic statement is open to too much doubt and the conclusion drawn from it
may therefore be worthless, if not downright harmful. The danger
in all deductive reasoning is that one may build on a general principle that either does not cover the case or is itself unsound.

A second form of reasoning that may lead to valid conclusions,
Aristotle informs us, is what we call inductive argument, establishing, that is, a general rule on the evidence of many single, observed
facts or instances. It is the way in which universal propositions that
are not self-evident or axiomatic may be discovered to be true. If,
whenever we see an A it is always B, we decide in due course
that all A are B. We are sure that the sun will always rise in the east,
because this morning, yesterday morning and every morning without exception, as far as human memory has record, it has risen in the
east. We accept the law of gravity, because whenever we see an
object thrown into the air, it unfailingly falls to the ground. From a
multitude of such particular instances scientists have drawn the
conclusions we know as laws of nature or universal truths.

Here, however, Aristotle reminds us, we must be constantly on
guard against drawing conclusions too hastily. Unless the number
of instances on which we ground our generalization is large enough
to be thoroughly representative, there may be instances we have overlooked to which it does not apply. In which case the rule we are
trying to establish is false and perhaps dangerous. We may declare
of some one unpopular nation that it always has been a warmaker
and aggressor, responsible for whatever unrest existed in its part of
the globe. But unless we look far enough back into its history to learn
what have been the causes of most, at least, of the wars in which it
has been involved, and find that on all these occasions it has been the
unprovoked assailant and never the victim of attack and oppression,
our statement may sound well as propaganda but cannot be taken
seriously as truth. Nor, because one man who was out of work refused a job we offered him, have we a right to decide in exasperation
that every man out of work is so because he has refused a job. The

danger in all inductive reasoning is that we may draw too sweeping conclusions from insufficient data.

The *Organon* contains much more on the principles of orderly, analytical thinking and exact use of words, with instructions on how to avoid the self-deception that arises from inadequate definition of terms, failure to grasp the gist of the problem, begging the question, arguing in a circle, and other types of fallacious reasoning. At the end, Aristotle remarks: "On this subject of reasoning we found positively nothing said before us, but had to work it out by long and laborious research." You must therefore "for the shortcomings of this inquiry grant us your pardon and for the discoveries contained therein your grateful thanks." It is one of the rare passages in which he gives us an inkling of his own feeling about his work and his sense of opening up some hitherto unexplored field of human thought. No one of his writings made so wide an impression on later generations of Europeans, showing, as it did for the first time clearly how a mind might be turned back on itself to study the path of its own thinking.

As philosopher, Aristotle had of course to find his own answers to the fundamental questions of the causes and principles of the universe. In his *Metaphysics,* he reviews the theories of all the leading Greek thinkers down to his own day, including those of Plato and other contemporaries. But on one score or another he rejects them all. None is sufficiently analytical. All overlook points that should be considered and problems that should be solved. Take, to begin with, the matter of the *why,* the *causes* of things everywhere. Too many men thought they had explained the world when they said what it was made of. In fact they had barely begun to explain it. For every object that exists there must be certainly four causes or reasons to give for its existence before anyone can pretend to say why it is just as it is.

There is, first, the *material* cause, with which many older philosophers were content, thinking it enough to name the material of which an object was made. One reason for an oak tree is undoubtedly

the elements of earth, water, and air of which it is compounded
One reason for a statue is the bronze out of which it is cast. But,
second and more important, there is the *formal* cause, the form or
pattern assumed by the material in the object. The oak would not
be the sturdy, spreading tree it is, were it not for a natural form in it,
that keeps it from climbing up a wall like an ivy vine. What dis
tinguishes this statue from any other, or from a shapeless lump of
bronze, is its form, the graceful figure of a dancing faun. There is,
third, the *efficient* or moving cause, the agency or maker, whose activity produced the object. The efficient cause of the oak is the power
of nature in the acorn that kept it growing from seedling to mighty
tree. The efficient cause of the statue is the sculptor, who trans
lated the idea of the faun in his mind into terms of solid bronze.
Last and most important of all, there is the *final* cause, the purpose
or end for which the object was brought into being and now exists.
The final cause of the oak is nature's purpose to cover the earth
with rich and diversified vegetation, of the statue, the sculptor's
desire to create something beautiful or, perhaps, a piece of market-
able art to sell in order to pay his rent.

Each of these causes in its turn may be caused by something else.
Back of the acorn and its growth lies the parent oak from which it
fell. Back of the sculptor's idea lies, perhaps, some other man's carving
that gave him the idea. But no series of causes can run on forever.
Sooner or later we come to the end, to something for which we know
no reason. If bronze is the material cause of the statue, and copper
and tin of bronze, what is the cause of copper and tin? The atoms
of which they are made? Then what are atoms made of? Who or
what is their efficient cause? How did the oak's form come to be in
nature at all? For what final end is all existence? Somewhere there
must be an uncaused first principle from which everything else
starts, and a supreme and final end for the sake of which everything
else exists.

But before going on to the end we must consider what is meant
by existence or being. What is it to *be?* The problem of *being,* is not

when we stop to think it over, a simple one, and the beliefs people hold about it are often contradictory. Some even say that it does not matter what we believe, for we can never know anything absolutely certain about our world anyway. No knowledge of ours can be anything but relative, dependent on our unreliable senses. No two men can have precisely the same sense impressions and one man's impressions and the opinions he derives from them are as true as another's. Existence itself may be solely a matter of our impressions. Nothing perhaps exists except as we think it does. Against all such skeptical notions Aristotle argues stoutly that the world really *is*, has been, and will continue to be, regardless of human eyes and imaginings. We can learn too to distinguish between fluctuating sense impressions and a knowledge that is certain. To say of anything that it *is* so and so, may indeed be saying merely that it is of such and such a quality or quantity or in such and such a place or condition, naming just its changeable features. Or it may be saying *what it is*, naming, that is, its essential nature. To say, for example, of an animal, it is brown, it is large, it is here, it is hungry, is to give its accidental qualities at the moment. To say of it, it is a horse, is to state the one essential and permanent thing about it, which is its *substance*. What then is substance?

The substance of anything is that in it which gives it continuous and independent existence, which makes it more than a passing quality or quantity or other characteristic, that may exist in something else but never alone. Substance is then what *is*, the permanent core or substratum underlying the fleeting qualities. There must, however, be more to substance than purely material stuff or matter. For matter by itself, though permanent, is indefinite, inactive, characterless, chaotic, with merely a capacity latent in it to become something more, given the necessary, urging force. In everything we see or know there is something besides matter, that lends to it properties, dimensions, contour, makes it really *be*. Even a loose handful of dirt has shape, color, and other qualities of a sort. It is either hot or cold, wet or dry. It has a power of movement. If we

drop it, it can fall. Living substances have also powers of growth and reproduction, animals, of sensation. This something more that combines with matter as a shaping, purposive element and lifts it out of its state of non-being, Aristotle calls *form*. It is real and eternal and as much a part of every object as matter itself. It resembles Plato's *idea*, but it comes from no ideal world apart. It is always here, inseparable from matter, making our world *be*, giving it life.

The form in nature is what gives pattern and character to everything. In the act of reproduction, each plant and animal communicates a particular form to its descendant. That form becomes the efficient cause of the changes through which the young growth will pass, keeping it true to type and preventing it from turning into something else. The form is also its final cause, its purpose and end. All seedlings strive to become perfect plants, struggle toward the light to grow green and tall, each after its kind. Children tend to become like their parents. So in every species the forms travel on and on through endless generations, from mature individual to germ and foetus, to infant offspring, and on to youthful and finally mature individual again. The individual who has passed maturity grows old and perishes, but the forms in his descendants carry on the type undying into the future. In the world of man-made objects, the craftsman or artist who forges a tool, builds a boat, or carves a pillar, brings the form he has in his mind into a particular section of matter, and thus creates a new compound of matter and form. The iron, wood or marble he takes as material has already some more indefinite form of its own. It has color, density, smoothness, and other qualities. But it has not those definite qualities of outline, curve, polish, and adaptation to use which it will have when the new form is introduced into it.

All objects, even before they come into full being, are *potentially* whatever they have the capacity to become. The acorn has in itself the power of becoming an oak. The timber of the oak can be shaped to build a boat. A grain of corn cannot produce an oak, nor a

rock be hewn into a boat. The corn and the rock have other potentialities but not these. Because, however, an acorn can become
an *actual* oak, it does not follow that it will inevitably do so. External
conditions may prevent it. It may fall in a dry place, where it gets
no moisture but shrivels and dies. It may be eaten by a hog. The
timber for the boat may be left unused until it cracks or rots. So
potentiality does not ensure a thing becoming actual. It will only
become that if something outside does not prevent it. But actuality
is the end for which the thing exists. We human beings are born
unseeing and speechless but with powers of seeing and speaking, so
that in time we may see and speak. Potentiality and actuality are,
in reality, just another way of thinking of matter and form. "Matter,"
Aristotle says, "exists in a *potential* state just because it may come to
its form, and when it *actually* exists, then it is in its form."

As to which comes first, the potential or the actual, the child or
the father, the egg or the hen, Aristotle is sure that the father comes
before the child, the hen before the egg, the actual before the potential. For nothing can possibly be produced without something,
either parent or maker, actually existing and fully competent to
produce it. Moreover, there must be something eternal and imperishable to be the starting point of this whole world of forever
emerging and disappearing objects. Since it is eternal and imperishable, it must always have actually and perfectly existed. It can never
have been a mere potentiality, something that possibly might or
might not come to be.

With this we arrive at the first principle and final cause of all
the universe, Aristotle's God. He is not, however, like Plato's or the
Christian's God, the universe's creator. One of Aristotle's firmest
convictions is that nothing can ever be produced out of nothing, that
since matter and form now *are* and are continuously in motion, they
must always have been and must always be moving. Time too can
never have begun, "for there could not be a before nor an after, if
time did not exist." Nevertheless there must be somewhere a first
cause of all this activity and motion, something that keeps the

neavens revolving and life stirring on earth. That first something must be itself motionless, unaffected by any cause outside itself, a calm, immortal substance, pure form and intelligence, with no mixture of matter, for wherever there is matter there is change. While itself unmoved, it produces motion by being the object of the world's love and desire. Like the goal of a runner's race, it inspires the perpetual revolution of the outermost heaven, that keeps moving the spheres enclosed within it down to the low center which is our earth.

All lesser beings in their degree aspire, as we have said, to realize their potentialities. But the highest and best of forms, the supreme actuality, God, does not aspire. He is always in that state of serene, contemplative thought that is life at its pleasantest and fullest. Aloof and unknowable to us, he is rapt in himself, utterly beyond human reach. Yet of what that blessed state is like we catch a momentary glimpse when our lives are at their best. For man shares with God the divine power of thought and knows that "the act of contemplation is what is most of all pleasant and best." "The actuality of thought is life and God *is* that actuality. And God's essential actuality is life most good and eternal. We may say then that God is a living being, eternal and most good, so that life and duration, unbroken and eternal, belong to God; for this *is* God."

Having reached this point, we may pause to notice how Aristotle's view of the world differs from Plato's. Plato had two worlds in conflict, the terrestrial world of visible but unreal, transitory objects, and the celestial world of invisible but real and immortal spiritual existences. Making two worlds out of one, Aristotle insists, merely multiplies the things to be explained. Our present, visible world is the only one, and is itself real and eternal, an indissoluble combination of matter and form. There is conflict here, but conflict inherent in the nature of the constituent elements—sluggish, featureless matter and forceful, organizing form. No need to imagine visitors from a spiritual realm coming down to create the ferment, which has always existed. There is nothing indeed to show that a spiritual realm exists.

On the other hand, Aristotle is quite as keen as Plato to disprove the contention of the materialistic philosophers, that the world is a product of blind, mechanical force or necessity, operating on existent matter in such a way as to bring about by pure chance a sort of evolutionary survival of the fit. In his *Physics,* he has an excellent statement of a typical materialist's position. Why, he says, "should we look on the operations of nature as dictated by a purpose and intended to realize some desirable end? Why may they not be merely the results of necessity, just as the rain falls of necessity, and not that the corn may grow? For the vapor that is drawn up must cool and when cooled must become water and fall, and thus make the corn grow. If instead it spoils the farmer's crop on the threshing-floor, it does not rain in order to do that mischief, but the result happens to be that. Why may not the same be true of the parts of our body? Why, for instance, may not our teeth grow as they do of necessity—the front teeth sharp and fitted for cutting food and the back teeth broad for grinding—but not shaped for an end, merely as an accidental coincidence? And so with all other parts where there is an appearance of development for a purpose? In short, wherever natural parts came by accident to be just what they would have been, if they had been designed for an end, the resulting bodies survived, having developed spontaneously in a suitable way. But where this did not happen, they perished and continue to perish, as Empedocles says his monstrosities did."

No, declares Aristotle emphatically. Granted that our world is obviously faulty, because the matter which forms so large a proportion of it is constitutionally unstable and imperfect, we still have evidence everywhere of something working steadfastly within it toward a predetermined goal of goodness and perfection. Why otherwise does the usual season of rainfall come in time to bring on the farmer's crops? Why do our teeth normally take the shape most useful to us, and rarely grow out misshapen? The most important causes are in fact not the material, but the formal and final causes, the influence on substances of ends ahead, of purposes they are meant

to achieve, of potentialities they are trying to make actual. As a builder frames in his mind a picture of a house, and holds to it as the reason for each subsequent step he takes, so nature pursues a course set by "that which is yet to be." In order to have a man, it is necessary that a baby come into being first. The baby is born to make the man possible. Nor does any one portion of the universe exist for itself alone, unconnected with the rest. It is all intelligently ordered like one great household for the good of the whole, each member having his place, small or large, in the vast design. And like a general in an army, the supreme good in the universe is a presence that gives to all beneath it unity and direction, although how all are one "no man tells us at all nor can any man say, unless he says, as we do, that the Mover makes them one."

In his works on natural science Aristotle is constantly applying this same principle. Nature, he is sure, works ever in the best possible way with the elements she has to bring about the best possible world. Whenever he can, he supports this principle by concrete observation and fact. He will not, he says, be one of those who have "certain preconceived views and are resolved to compel everything to fall in line with them." The shape of the universe, for instance, he calls round both because the enveloping sky overhead looks round to us and because a sphere is a perfect shape and the shape of the universe must be perfect.

Our universe, he is also convinced, is the only one there is, since all matter by its weight must gravitate to it. The spherical shell that encloses it, which is to us the outermost or first heaven, revolves on its own axis, carrying with it the so-called fixed stars. Inside this heaven, the seven planets, including among them the sun and moon, swing in their orbits about the central earth. But the movements of the planets are not simple like those of the outermost heaven. They are seen traveling sometimes from east to west and again from west to east. Aristotle uses the computations of an older astronomer, Eudoxus of Cnidos, to fabricate a most elaborate scheme of fifty-five major and minor orbits, by means of which he contrives to ex-

plain the eccentricities of the planets. All the starry universe must be ageless and indestructible. "For in the whole range of time past, as far as our inherited records reach, no change appears to have taken place either in the general plan of the outer heaven or in any of its parts." Its substance must, therefore, be different from that of the objects that compose our earth, that are always changing and decaying. This celestial substance, rarer and purer than the substances of earth, Aristotle calls ether. For centuries after him people believed in the stainless, ethereal nature of the stars, until, in 1610, Galileo discovered through his telescope the dark, disfiguring spots on the sun.

Beneath the moon, in the middle of the whole universe, farthest removed from the high, first heaven, is our motionless, round and solid earth. Aristotle cannot agree with the followers of Pythagoras, who take the earth to be itself one of the stars, circling around a fire at the center of things and creating night and day by its own turning on its axis. Their reasoning, he declares, is not from facts to theory but a forcing of the facts to fit their preconceived theory. Because the center must be the most precious spot in the universe, therefore, they say, fire must be there to guard it. Plato, Aristotle adds, rightly put the earth in the center, though wrongly he had it rolling on an axis. Still other earlier philosophers had fancied the earth was flat and rested like a vast lid on the air beneath it. Against all these mistaken theories Aristotle brings his evidence of a variety of observed facts. All heavy objects, for example, fragments of stone and sod, if flung into the air, fall back in the direction of the earth's center. So the heavy earth itself must occupy the lowest and central point of the cosmos. In a lunar eclipse the earth throws a curved shadow on the moon, which it could do only if it were a ball.

But compared with the stars, the earth is of no great size. For a little change in an observer's position—from Greece, for instance, southward to Egypt—makes a noticeable difference in the station of the stars overhead, as would not be the case, unless the curve of the earth's surface were pronounced. "Hence one should not be too quick

to disbelieve the opinions of those who think there is no break between the regions beyond the Pillars of Hercules [Straits of Gibraltar] and the regions of India and that thus the ocean is one." The fact that elephants are found in both regions suggests some connection between them. Repeated in later centuries, this passage was one of the encouragements to Columbus to set out upon his voyage.

In his *Meteorology* and related works Aristotle tries, in a mixture of painstaking theory and such observations as he can collect, to account for the physical phenomena of sky and atmosphere, light, sound, shooting stars, the Milky Way, mist and snow, frost and dew, wind, thunder and earthquake. For light he has no definite explanation. Sound, however, he can prove to be vibration of the air, and a rainbow the effect of refraction of sunlight from aerial moisture. One book of the *Meteorology* treats of tangible substances such as water, oil, metals, and clays, and the results of applying to them varying amounts of heat and cold, with other similar experiments. Unfortunately, Aristotle had no dependable or accurate way of measuring or comparing heats and colds. So, though he makes here a beginning of the science of chemistry, he does not get far with it. In the field of mechanics, he describes an experiment by which he discovered the law of the lever, and others by which he attempted vainly to ascertain the relation of weight to speed in falling bodies.

This astronomical, physical, and chemical lore of Aristotle interests us today chiefly as showing the difficulties that beset any ancient pioneer in science with no technical apparatus for precise reckoning of time, space, weight, speed, or temperature, and no aids to the human eye like the microscope or the telescope. These things were not to be invented for eighteen hundred years after Aristotle's death. He himself is quite aware that his work is only a beginning, to be corrected and developed by the men who would come after him. For its deficiencies he makes his defense in words that render any further apology needless. "Inventions are either the elaboration by later workers of the results of previous labor handed down by others, or original discoveries, small in their beginnings but far more important

than what will later be developed from them. For in everything, as the saying is, the first step is what counts. First beginnings are hardest to make and as small and inconspicuous as they are potent in influence, but once they are made, it is easy to add the rest."

But while in his researches into inorganic nature, he goes wrong more often than not and draws conclusions that seem to us quite fantastic, in his studies of living or organic nature he works to somewhat better success. In that realm a keen eye and skillful hand can carry the owner farther without the aid of modern instruments, even though without them he is shut out from the innermost mysteries. In that realm, too, nature herself can be felt as a power presiding over the molding of her budding and growing creatures, suiting their physical structure to the lives they have to live, and endowing them with strength and soul proportionate to the tasks she intends them to perform. "To be," says Aristotle, "is better than not to be; to live than not to live; things with a soul than things without; the soul itself than the body." *Soul,* to him, is the vital energy in living things. In its most elementary form, as a nutritive soul, it inspires the whole vegetative life of plants and keeps all live bodies feeding, growing and reproducing their kind. In more advanced form, as a sensitive soul, it feels sensation and emotion and keeps memories of its experiences. As such, it is the mark of animals in varying degrees. Finally, as a reasonable soul, it thinks and judges and is the peculiar gift of man. Soul and body together, like form and matter, make the complete, living individual. When death dissolves their union, there is inevitably an end to the individual who was the product of that union.

Aristotle's writings on botany have disappeared, but we have several treatises of his on zoology—a *History of Animals, Parts of Animals, Generation of Animals,* and so on. From these we gather that he knew by sight or report some five hundred and forty species of animals, and had dissected and watched closely the habits of about fifty, especially mollusks, octopuses, sea anemones, bees, and others, mostly marine creatures and insects. He employs the comparative

method to interpret the structure and functions of animal bodies and the development of organs from more primitive forms. He is highly interested in modes of reproduction and what we now call embryology. His minute account of the day by day growth of the chick in the egg has been bettered only in very recent times. He has more difficulty with the anatomy of the higher animals, whose bodies he had less opportunity to dissect. The first requirement, as we now know, for any real comprehension of the working of their intricate mechanisms is some knowledge of the principle of the circulation of the blood. That neither Aristotle nor anyone after him was to discover for almost two thousand years. So the nature and business of the heart remain a riddle. It is, Aristotle thinks, the source of the blood and the seat of vital heat, feeling, and intelligence. The brain, on the other hand, is the bloodless, cooling, sleep-inducing organ, without sensation. The existence and function of the nervous system he never suspects.

But Aristotle, the zoologist, is more than a laborious student of physiological details. He devises the first rational scheme of animal classification, based on fundamental distinctions of type and use. He considers the bony skeleton as well as the covering flesh, and draws lines of truly significant division, that with some modification have been retained ever since, such as those between red-blooded vertebrates and white or clear-blooded invertebrates, and between mammals or viviparous and egg-laying or oviparous animals. Whales and dolphins he knows are mammals and rise to the surface of the sea to breathe.

Surveying next the spectacle of nature as a whole, he sees it as one immense, advancing process, a ladder of ascent from low to high. "Nature proceeds little by little from things lifeless to animal life, so gradually that it is impossible to detect the exact line of demarcation, or to tell on which side of it an intermediate form should lie. Thus, next after lifeless things in the upward scale comes the plant; and among plants one will differ from another in the amount of its apparent vitality. . . . Then in plants, as we just remarked, there is

observable a continuous scale of ascent toward the animal. In the sea there are things which it is hard to label as either animal or vegetable" [as, for example, sponges, which show little sensitiveness and live attached to rocks]. "The one function of plants that spring from seed is apparently the reproduction of their own species, and some animals have their sphere of action similarly limited. . . . Some animals, like plants, simply procreate their own species at set seasons. Other animals take pains to collect food for their young, but after they are reared, leave them and have no more to do with them. Others still are more intelligent and endowed with more memory. They live with their offspring for a longer time and on a closer footing." This conception of the entire natural world as a chain of graded links, stretching up from that which barely lives at all to that which lives most richly, was itself a momentous achievement that was to influence European thinking for centuries to come. As late as the nineteenth century, Charles Darwin wrote: "Linnaeus and Cuvier have been my two gods, though in very different ways, but they were mere schoolboys compared to old Aristotle."

Having thus put order and coherence into the picture of nature, Aristotle takes man into his purview, observing him, too, methodically from all angles. His anatomy and physical processes he has studied in connection with those of the other animals, to which he constantly compares him. To the phenomena of human consciousness he devotes several pyschological treatises—*On Sleep, On Dreams, On Sensation, On Memory*. Of what men, as reasoning, purposeful creatures, endeavor to get for themselves out of living, what ends they have in view in choosing to do the things they do, he writes in his two famous books on *Ethics*.

The end, he says, for which we all more or less consistently strive is happiness. Our differences in behavior are due to our different notions of what happiness is. He himself has little difficulty in proving that we are most happy when living a life of moral and intellectual virtue. Moral virtue is a state of character that "makes a man good and do his work well," or, in other words, that makes him

choose a golden mean of conduct between an excess and a defect, either one of which would involve him in wrongdoing and eventual unhappiness. Courage, for example, is a mean between the excess of foolhardiness and the defect of cowardice; temperance a mean between over self-indulgence and unfeeling austerity; liberality a mean between wasteful extravagance and crabbed miserliness. Justice is a fair balancing of claims between contending parties. Excesses and defects are the vices into which we fall when we deliberately choose to look for happiness in unworthy or evil ways. At other times, through sheer weakness of will we allow ourselves to be swept off our feet by passion or desire, and fail to act up to the good we really intend. Worse, however, than either of these ordinary vices or unintended lapses from goodness are the rarer and more bestial crimes that stamp the doers as men below the level of normal, civilized humanity, as sickminded or as savages.

Moral virtue demands of us more than a simple knowledge of what is right. All the knowledge in the world can have little effect on our acts, if we have not the will to choose and do our duty. Our wills, in Aristotle's judgment, are free, at least to start with, but habit can put chains on them and make them slaves. "Virtue depends on ourselves and vice likewise. For where it is in our power to do, it is in our power not to do. Where we can say no, we can say yes. . . . If then a man knowingly does things which must make him unjust, he will be voluntarily unjust. However, it does not follow that if he wishes it, he can stop being unjust and become just, any more than a sick man by wishing can become well. It may be that he is voluntarily sick through living incontinently and disobeying his doctors. At one time then it was open to him not to be sick, but not now when he has thrown away his health. Once you have flung a stone, it is too late to call it back. Nevertheless, the flinging of that stone rested with you, for the starting of its motion was in you. Just so, the unjust and profligate man at the beginning was free not to become a man of that kind, but now that he has become so, he can no longer cease being it."

Hence it is possible to make children good, even before they understand the reasons for being so, by steady training in good habits. "We learn by doing. For instance, men become builders by building and lyre-players by playing the lyre. So we become just by doing just deeds, temperate by acting temperately, brave by behaving bravely." And so moral virtue, as a matter of practical will and conduct, may be either the result of a conscious preference for goodness or of quite unthinking, implanted habits of goodness.

Intellectual virtue, on the other hand, is a state of our knowing and reasoning faculty, in which it perceives and grasps truth. The truth it perceives may be the truth of art, of science, of prudence, or right action, of philosophic wisdom or of pure intuition. But of this intellectual virtue it is impossible to have too much, for our reasons are the best and most divine element in us. Compounded, however, as we are of body as well as soul, our minds are necessarily affected somewhat by external things. Poverty, calamity and sorrow, like that which fell on Priam, King of Troy, will ruffle the best man's calm. We all need food and a moderate amount of physical comfort, even though "we can do noble acts without ruling earth and sea." Sincere friends too add a great deal to our joy, and the world's honor and esteem are gratifying to receive. None the less, a life of deep and lasting happiness he only can attain who is in his conduct brave, just, and good, and in his mind a lover of truth.

Hence "we must not follow those who advise us, being men, to think of human things and, being mortal, of mortal things, but must, as far as we can, make ourselves immortal and strain every nerve to live in accordance with the best thing in us; for even though it be small in bulk, in power and worth it much surpasses everything else. . . . That which is proper for each thing is naturally the best and pleasantest for it. For man, therefore, the life of reason is best and pleasantest, since reason more than anything else *is* man. So too this life is also the happiest." In it man realizes his potentialities to the full, reaches his end.

At the close of the *Ethics,* Aristotle speaks of the need of fair and

honest laws to govern the relations of men in communities and provide the environment each one requires to make his personal life
good. But student as he is of facts and conditions actually existing,
he is not interested in what seem to him visionary Utopias or in any
society "that is an aspiration only." In his *Politics,* as everywhere else,
he is on a search for things that really function in the world as it is,
and perform the service for which they were instituted. Here he is
after "a form of government which states in general can attain."
Accordingly, Plato's ideal, communistic aristocracy he rejects as totally impracticable. The experience of mankind is all against such a
scheme. It is dangerous to sweep aside the wellworn institutions of
family and private property, even though curbs should probably be
put on excessive private wealth and no one be allowed to suffer from
poverty. The *Politics* is essentially a critical case study of government
as it had been developed and practiced in the Greek cities of the
Eastern Mediterranean in the fourth century before Christ.

It begins, however, characteristically, with a discussion of the
origins, principles, and aims of human associations as such. Men are
by nature gregarious and join with other men in communities for
ends that seem to them good. The first community was, of course,
the family, consisting of man and woman, master and slave, persons
dependent on one another for their elementary, physical necessities.
Several families next combined to assist each other and form a village. But these simple communities alone were too small to be self-
sufficient or to furnish security. Ultimately, several villages united
in a third type of community and "the state came into existence,
originating in the effort to obtain the bare necessities of life but
continuing in existence for the sake of a good life." For the state is
the culmination and end of the social process. Men get from it not
only the material goods and safety they want but also the opportunity to develop a better and more satisfying life than the members
of smaller and more precarious groups could ever attain. "The state
is thus a natural creation and man is by nature a political animal."

Hence the proper definition of a state, understood, as everything

should be, by its purpose, is "not a mere society inhabiting a common locality and organized to prevent crime and carry on trade," to provide, that is, police protection and promote business. It must, of course, do these things as one part of its duty. But in addition it is or should be "a community of well-being, formed of families and aggregations of families for the sake of a perfect and self-sufficing life, . . . by which we mean a happy and honorable life." It should, in other words, be more than a mere defensive association, to keep persons and property safe. It should be a positive, creative institution, as the best Greek states for a time had seemed to be, actively assuming the function of helping to make the lives of its citizens good. The bond that holds men together in such states is not only physical necessity but the justice they establish there.

Who in states of this sort are counted citizens? Citizenship, says Aristotle, is bestowed in different states on different classes of the inhabitants. In his opinion, however, those have done best who have treated as citizens just the persons with means, ability, and leisure to attend and vote in the frequent popular assemblies, serve on court juries and local administrative boards, and by thus taking a hand in the workings of government learn how to rule and be ruled. Such a practice admittedly shuts out certain large classes of the population—children, women, slaves, farm laborers, and artisans. In the face of Plato's assertion of woman's right to an equal rôle in the state with man, Aristotle declares that he finds her unfitted for it. Her reasoning faculty is "inconclusive" and her nature for the most part inferior. "A man would be thought a coward who had no more courage than a courageous woman." As for slaves, they are usually servile by nature, their masters' contented tools. Some there are, unfortunately, free by nature and by accident of war unjustly enslaved, but the position of these debars them from citizenship. Laborers and artisans, though free, must toil for a living at the beck and call of others, and hence have no chance to acquire political sagacity or the art of command. One other class Aristotle would exclude for moral reasons that may appear to us singular. Tradesmen and "money-

makers" should not be accepted as citizens, for they have not the will to serve the public interest, as citizens should. They think only of how to pile up profits for themselves by any and every method. Their sole aim is to make themselves rich.

In Aristotle's day, Greek merchants had for some time been organizing commerce between the Black Sea countries and the Central Mediterranean on a large scale. Capital was being accumulated for this and for extensive industrial enterprises, and credit loans on interest were becoming common. To him it seemed an ominous movement, extending the influence of an ambitious and unscrupulous, materialistic class in the state, to the disadvantage of the old, sober, landholding citizen body, that had been satisfied to live moderately on more or less fixed limited incomes. Unquestionably some trade between states was essential, but not these concentrations of wealth and power in greedy, new hands. He now pitches on what he calls usury, the taking of interest for money loans, as the evil element in the situation, that makes possible the building up of excessive fortunes. Usury is wrong, he says, because it is a device for getting rich by unnatural means. Coined metal is not like grain, vines, flocks, and herds, which are things of inherent usefulness to man, and which he, working with nature, makes grow and multiply. They truly produce for a borrower more than he took from the lender. But money is a lifeless thing of purely conventional value. For a creditor to demand that his money loan bear fruit and increase is sheer robbery. Many later moralists, both pagan and Christian, troubled by similar phenomena, were to repeat Aristotle's condemnation of usury as a sin against nature. Shakespeare's upright merchant of Venice asks Shylock, the moneylender, reprovingly: "Is your gold and silver ewes and rams?" To which Shylock replies defiantly: "I cannot tell; I make it breed as fast."

As to forms of government, Aristotle has no one type to recommend as the best for all states under all circumstances. Monarchy, aristocracy, popular government—all have been administered to serve the public interest, and all perverted to serve the interest of the

ruler. To him, as to Plato, the word democracy has a calamitous association with oppression by a rough and ignorant mob, eager to pull everything down to its own low level. Like a one-man tyranny such a government is inimical to the good life.

But the choice of government for any people must always depend on their own character and intelligence, the quality of their leaders and the distribution of land, riches, and opportunity. Ideally a government by the best and noblest man or group of men might seem the best. But a state that has a large, middle clas, living mainly on the land, neither too rich nor too poor, and is governed by that class is probably the most fortunate in the long run. No single member of that class may be so brilliant or so cultivated as members of an aristocracy, but their total aggregate of judgment and experience excels that of any smaller group. They are less easily corrupted and more likely to decide fairly than either the very rich or the very poor. The mass, too, of average, responsible citizens are the best judges of the laws under which they live, as the best judges of a feast are not the expert cooks but the men who eat it, and of a house not the architect but the people who live in it. Their government is least apt to stir up dissatisfaction and resentment, for the principle of it is liberty. Yet it is liberty that goes along with obedience to law.

Since the final end of any true state is not to train its citizens to conquer and gain dominion over their neighbors but to give them the means of a good life, it should, as one of its first duties, undertake the education of its children in public, compulsory schools, as for years has been the custom in Sparta. In selecting the course of study, the chief point to bear in mind is that it should be liberal, calculated to enlarge and ennoble the child's intelligence and teach him how life may be enjoyed. Nothing should be allowed that vulgarizes, or sets up utility or mercenary profit as a serious aim. When grown, the child will, of course, some time go to war or engage in business, but "peace, as has often been said, is the end of war and leisure of toil." The real test then of a people's education is not so much the way they work or fight, but the way they use their leisure. "To show

excellent qualities in action and war but in times of peace and leisure to be no better than slaves" is to miss the happiness that is the end of human living. Hence the importance in schools of subjects like music, which is studied "solely with a view to leisure spent in intellectual activity" and "makes the hearts of men glad."

In one section of his long analysis of kinds and functions of governments, Aristotle discusses the question of their longevity. Ruling out overthrow by a foreign enemy, he asks how long may the various types of government be expected to last. What are the causes of revolutions and internal collapses in states? In general, he replies, they are social and economic, a sense of injustice produced either by "a desire for equality, when men think they are equal to others who have more than themselves, or a desire for inequality or superiority, when men who think themselves superior believe they are getting not more but the same or less than their inferiors." Under oligarchies, or governments by wealth, "the masses revolt in the conviction that they are unjustly treated, . . . and in democracies the notables revolt, because they are not equal and yet have only an equal share." The actual outbreak of revolution may be due to any irritating trifle, the insolent arbitrariness of a few officials, the flagrant avarice of a handful of rich men, or the spiteful rivalry of two or three popular leaders.

As a rule, monarchies and oligarchies are more shortlived than popular governments. However, "the more restricted the functions of kings, the longer their power will last unimpaired, for then they are more moderate and less despotic in their ways and less envied by their subjects." But a popular type of government is usually the most stable, "for the greater the number, the greater the strength, and when men are equal, they are more content." Yet even such a government must be alert to train its young people in democratic ideals, maintain in everyone the spirit of obedience to law, prevent inordinate accumulations of wealth, and keep its magistrates from graft and corruption. For "no government can stand that is not founded on justice." Yet Aristotle has advice for a despot who wants

to prolong his tyranny. He should either be so mild and benevolent a governor that his subjects will prefer his rule to any other, or else crush them so completely by craft, violence, and terror that they will not dare lift a finger against him. Machiavelli, in his time, read and pondered the *Politics* of Aristotle. He was learning by bitter experience with the Italian city-states of the Renaissance that there are periods when justice alone does not save a people but only a prince with power and the vigor to use it.

In his school Aristotle somehow found time to lecture on literature and esthetics. We have a treatise of his on *Rhetoric* as the art of verbal persuasion, with many a shrewd suggestion for the political speechmaker, the pleader in law courts, and the ceremonial orator on how to get audiences in a favorable frame of mind and keep them there. We have also an unfinished essay on *Poetics,* included in the present volume, in which are laid down rules for writing a good play, which, with a few modifications, are as sound today as they always have been.

It is hard, as the reader may be realizing by now, to give a brief account of Aristotle's work that does not degenerate into a mere table of contents. There are men who have gone farther than he along some particular line of thought or investigation and have achieved some one or two more famous discoveries. But no man, so far as we know, has ever started systematic exploration in so many fresh fields or has understood better the method by which knowledge might be pushed further. Theory, unsupported by fact and experience, he knew could be only tentative, liable to be later refuted by more observation. Plato's theories of creation, the father God, and human immortality he rejected because to him the facts seemed to point another way. For Plato's dream of women rulers, equal companions of men, he saw no justification in the cramped and confined minds of the Greek women he knew. A few facts indeed he could not apparently bring himself to recognize, such as the inevitable power of a rising commercial and moneyed class in state politics, which no amount of moral disapprobation could prevent, and, in an era of

battling empires, the doom of small states that had neither the military force to stand alone nor the wisdom to sink their jealousies and combine with their neighbors for the common safety. But as biologist, he could tell young Athenians not to be ashamed to grub in the slime after insects. In ethics and politics he could give wise, practical advice on how to make the most of life without expecting too much from men in the way of disinterested conduct or unworldly philosophy. Plato stirs us with the beauty, depth, and height of his imagination, Aristotle with his hard, intellectual grip and passion for exactitude and order. We see him, sharp-eyed and critical, turning over masses of unorganized, amorphous material, scrutinizing, sorting, classifying, and finally leaving it, all partitioned out, analyzed and accounted for, to pass on to something else.

As philosophers, the two men are often contrasted as if their views of the universe were diametrically opposed. Yet, with all their conspicuous differences, on certain fundamental points they always stood together. Both denounced the materialists and saw in the discords and contradictions of this present world a struggle between two principles, one intelligent, dynamic, and good, the other irrational, inert, and base. Plato's forces for good came from an invisible, spiritual world, Aristotle's were an inseparable part of this, yeast working eternally in our bread. But both men were sure that nature moved to a predetermined end, and that for each kind the end was the realization of its own impulse toward perfection. Both believed that man's reason made him in some degree akin to the God whose goodness was the cause of all goodness in the world beneath. At the end of his universal conspectus Aristotle agreed with his master perhaps almost as profoundly as he disagreed.

Centuries after his death, he was still what Dante called him, "the master of those who know." His *Logic,* translated into Latin, was the one work of classical Greek scholarship carried over into the crude monastic schools of the West, after the Roman Empire fell. When, in the twelfth and thirteenth centuries, learning revived in those parts of Europe, it came back in the form of more translations

and commentaries on Aristotle. In the universities of the later Middle Ages the undergraduate course was largely a course in Aristotle's science and philosophy. He was the final authority on things of this life, as the Scriptures were on things of the life to come, the man "in whom it pleased Nature to try how great a portion of reason she could admit into mortality." Eventually, the new astronomy, physics and anatomy of Copernicus, Galileo, Newton, and Harvey proved him mistaken on so many points that his credit as a natural scientist was destroyed and other authorities took his place in the schools. But as philosopher, moral and political thinker, and author of the earliest canons of literary criticism, he still commands the world's respectful attention.

One curious result of the veneration in which he was held so long was the ridiculous tales the people of medieval Europe invented about him. Students, it may be, started them in revenge for the labor and suffering he caused them. The great man, they said, was once bewitched by a malicious young flirt, whose joy it was to inveigle him into absurd and undignified situations, in which he was then surprised by his gloating pupil, Alexander. Tales of this sort, caricatures of his greatness, spread by word of mouth all over Europe. Not many years ago one was told by an old woman in Ireland to her grandson. It was, she said, a story of a man who lived once on a time, whose name was Harry Stottle.

His surviving works, as we have already said, are not, like the dialogues of Plato, designed and finished masterpieces of literary art. They are condensed and often disjointed summaries of academic lectures, which he certainly never expected would outlast him or the pupils for whom he intended them. It is possible to extract from them portions that are especially interesting and pertinent to us without each time breaking up a whole that is in itself a thing of beauty. In this present book then, where the limits of space required a choice between printing one or two works in full and selecting passages from several that would seem alive and valuable to a modern reader, we have preferred the second alternative. By giving parts of five very

different works, we can suggest to one who comes to Aristotle as a stranger something of the encyclopedic scope of his activity and the tireless power of his mind, that penetrated so far into so many subjects of human thought and knowledge, in the brief space of the thirteen years at the Lyceum.

The first work from which we take selections, the *Metaphysics,* is his study of the meaning and nature of being in the broadest sense. The second, the *Parts of Animals,* is one of his investigations into a particular phase of living nature. The third and fourth, the *Ethics* and *Politics,* have as topics the world of man's conscious endeavors to make his life happy and good. The last, the *Poetics,* is an essay in the field of art. From the first we have chosen just those passages that state most clearly Aristotle's ideas of the causes and character of all existence and of that one Cause that is the ultimate source and end of all. The selections from the second show both Aristotle's keenness as a naturalist and his unescapable mistakes and limitations. Of the last three we have given enough to enable the reader to follow the course of the discussion all the way through, omitting mainly the less important or more repetitious portions and the detailed illustrations from contemporary Greek life that to him would seem obscure. All translations have been thoroughly revised to make the English versions as clear as possible. Aristotle is not light reading, but anyone with a taste for pondering over the still unsolved problems of nature and human life will find himself more than rewarded for any effort he may make to understand the thinking of one of the great minds of history.

METAPHYSICS

METAPHYSICS

T HE READER who is not a philosopher and who has hitherto not
made Aristotle's acquaintance may do well to by-pass temporarily the *Metaphysics*. It is easier to understand him talking of the
usefulness of organs in animal bodies, or of the differences between
a brave man and a reckless one, or of the causes of revolution in
states, or of the structure of a good play, than discoursing on the
causes and nature of universal being and existence as such. But
after one has followed him for a while up and down and around
these more homelike fields, one can come back to the *Metaphysics*
and find it not so formidable. One may even find it throwing a new
and unexpected light on the studies already read of things better
known. One may reread them now with a deeper comprehension,
perceiving how each in its own way is in fact an illustration of the
all-embracing first principles of things laid down in the *Metaphysics*.

The word *Metaphysics* in Greek means simply *After Physics*. It
was, apparently, a title written by some ancient editor on certain
unnamed rolls of Aristotle's notes which he was placing next to
the treatise on physics. As it comes to us, the *Metaphysics* is a
compilation of a number of originally separate blocks of notes, all
dealing with the most fundamental problems of philosophy but put
together without much care to make them fit.

But the selections here given make up a fairly plain and coherent
whole. They open with Aristotle's first chapters explaining what
real wisdom is and how earlier men, having satisfied their most urgent physical needs, invented philosophy to appease their curiosity
as to *why* things on the earth were as they were, a knowledge they
wanted for its own sake, not for any utilitarian end. The first step
toward knowing anything, Aristotle continues, is always finding out

3

why it is or what caused it. So we have his famous doctrine of the *four causes,* which between them all account for everything that is and every event that happens.

Further on he comes to the question at the bottom of everything. What really do we mean by saying a thing *is* or is something or other? In what varying senses may the word *is* be understood? By the way he disposes of such puzzles as whether a thing can both be and not be at the same time, whether two contradictions can be simultaneously true, and whether we can assert positively of anything that it *is,* or whether all our knowledge is relative or subjective only, dependent on mere shifty, unreliable sense impressions that differ for each individual. After showing that we can say of an object some things assuredly true, the most important and essential thing to say of it, he declares, is not how big or how old or where it is or what it is doing, but *what* it is—in other words, what is its *substance.* So, at length, the inquiry comes down to this—what is *substance?* A combination, he now answers, of a blank, inert, limitless substratum or underlying something, which he calls matter, and a dynamic, purposeful, shaping principle or essence, he calls form. Everything that comes into any kind of being is a result of form entering into appropriate matter. Matter alone has potentiality, a capacity, that is, of becoming something. Marble can become a statue, a human seed can become a man. But Nature or the hand of man must seize and put form into it before it can realize its possibilities or the potential become actual. That actuality—the statue carved from the featureless marble, the man full grown from the feeble seed—is the thing's end or final cause, to realize which it exists.

Above and beyond this low earth, compounded of half-realized potentialities and perishable substances, is the starry realm of eternal beings, whose potentialities are always realized to the full. Over that again is the First Cause and Final Cause of all existence, the unmoving Mover, whose life is the highest actuality, pure form with no mixture of matter, pure thought in utter tranquillity thinking itself.

BOOK I

The wisdom for which all philosophers are in search is the knowledge of first principles and the causes of things.

CHAPTER I. All men by nature have a desire to know. A sign of this is the joy we take in our senses, for quite apart from their usefulness we love them for their own sake, and the sense of sight above all. For not only as a help in action but also when we have no intention of acting we value our sight above almost everything else. The reason for this is that of all the senses sight makes knowledge most possible for us and shows us the many differences between things.

By nature animals too are born endowed with sensation and in some of them memory follows sensation and in others not. The former are more intelligent and capable of learning than those who cannot remember. Animals who cannot hear sounds—as, for instance, bees and other similar tribes of creatures—are intelligent but cannot learn. Only those can learn that have hearing along with memory.

Thus animals live by impressions and memories but have little in the way of connected experience, whereas the human race lives by art and reasoning as well. In man, experience is a result of his memory, for many memories of doing the same thing end in creating a sense of a single experience. Experience seems almost the same as science and art. But in fact science and art come to men through experience; for, as Polus rightly said,[1] "Experience produces art but inexperience

---

[1] This statement, somewhat amplified, is made by one Polus in Plato's dialogue of *Gorgias*.

only luck." Art is produced when out of many ideas gained through experience we draw one general conclusion about some class of like cases. For to know that this particular remedy did Callias good when he was ill of this particular disease, and did the same for Socrates and various other individuals, is a matter of experience. But to know that it does good to all persons of a certain constitution, taken as a class, when ill of this disease—as, for instance, phlegmatic or bilious persons, when burning with fever—such knowledge is a matter of art.

For practical purposes experience looks to be not at all inferior to art; we even see men of experience succeeding better than those who have theory without experience. The reason is that experience is knowledge of individual instances and art knowledge of universals,[2] and that whatever we do or make is concerned with some individual. For the physician does not cure Man, except incidentally. He does cure Callias or Socrates or someone else with a name of his own, who happens to be a man. If then a physician without experience has the theory and knows the general principle but not the individual covered by it, he will often go wrong with his treatment, for the individual is what he has to cure. None the less we hold that knowledge and proficiency belong to art rather than to experience and hence regard artists as wiser than men of experience on the ground that wisdom depends always upon knowledge. And we think this because the former understand the cause and the latter do not.

For men of experience know that a thing is so but do not know why it is so, while the others know the why and the cause. Therefore we think that the masters in every craft deserve more honor and know more and are wiser than the handworkers, because they know the reasons for the things that are done. But the handworkers seem like certain lifeless things that act, but act without knowing what they are doing—as fire does when it burns. Lifeless things perform their functions because of some nature in them, and handworkers

---

[2] The universal, as contrasted with the individual, means the permanent type or class, of which the individual is a passing member; or the unchanging, general principle to which the shifting particular instance more or less conforms.

perform theirs through habit. But we call the masters wiser, not because they can do things but because they grasp the theory and understand the causes.

In general, the proof of a person's knowledge or ignorance is his
ability to teach. Hence we consider art more truly knowledge than
experience, for artists can teach and the others cannot. Also we do
not regard any of the senses as wisdom. They are indeed our most
authoritative sources of knowledge about individual objects, but they
do not tell us the why of anything—as, for example, why fire is hot—
but only that it is hot.

In the beginning, a man who invented any art that went outside
the ordinary range of the senses was naturally admired by other men,
not only because some of his inventions were useful but because they
considered him wise and superior to the rest. But as more arts were
invented—some to help in securing the necessities of life and others
for men's enjoyment—the inventors of the latter were always regarded as wiser than the inventors of the former, because their
branches of knowledge did not aim at mere utility. Then when all
inventions of this kind had been achieved, the sciences that aim
neither at giving pleasure nor at serving necessity were discovered
and first in the regions where men had some leisure. So the mathematical arts were first established in Egypt, for there the priestly
caste was granted leisure.

The difference between art and science and other related branches
we have explained already in the *Ethics*.[3] The theme of our present
remarks is this, that all men believe that what we call wisdom has to
do with first causes and principles of things. Accordingly, as we have
just said, the man of experience is considered wiser than those who
know only sensations of whatever kind, and the artist wiser than the
man of experience, the master than the handworker and the theoretical science than the practical. Patently then wisdom is knowledge of
principles and causes.

[3] See the *Ethics*, pp. 173-174.

CHAPTER 2. Since we are investigating this kind of knowledge, we must ask what are the causes and what are the principles the knowledge of which is wisdom. If we take our conception of a wise man, perhaps the answer to this question will seem clearer. In the first place, we expect a wise man to know all things, as far as that is possible, without, however, knowing each of them in individual detail. Secondly, we think he is one who understands difficult things, not easy for men to comprehend. (Sense perception is common to everyone and therefore easy and calls for no wisdom.) Furthermore, we think that in every branch of knowledge the wiser a man is, the more exact he is and the better able to teach the causes of things. Among the sciences too we call that one nearer to wisdom that is worth learning for its own sake and for the sake of knowing than the one that is desirable for the results to be got from it. A superior science also is nearer than one that is merely contributory. So too a wise man ought not to receive orders but to give them; nor should he obey another but the less wise should obey him.

Such and so many are the ideas we have about wisdom and a wise man. Now of these characteristics that of knowing everything must belong to him who to the fullest extent has a knowledge of the universal, for he knows in a sense all that is comprised under that head. But these things, the most universal, are perhaps the most difficult things for men to grasp, for they are farthest removed from the senses.[4] Again, the sciences that deal with first principles are the most exact of all, for those that employ few principles, like arithmetic, are more exact than those that employ more, like geometry. The science that investigates causes is also best for teaching, for our teachers are those who explain the causes of each thing. And knowledge and understanding desirable for their own sakes are found most in the science of that which is best to know. For one who desires knowledge for its own sake will desire above all what is most genuinely knowledge and that is the knowledge of what is best to know.

[4] That is, general laws, causes, principles, types, tendencies, etc., are all necessarily abstract. We cannot see or touch them.

And the things best to know are first principles and causes. For through them and from them all other things may be known but not they through the things covered by them. Supreme then among the sciences and superior to all subordinate science is that which knows the end for which everything takes place, which is the good for each thing and, as a whole, the highest good for all nature. According then to everything we have said, the name of wisdom belongs to this same science; for it must be that which investigates first principles and causes, since the good as the end and aim of things is one of the causes.

That this is not a science for producing things is plain from the story of the earliest philosophers. For it was wonder that made men first start to philosophize and still makes them today, wondering originally about the problems close at hand and then little by little advancing to strain their minds over the greater perplexities, such as the changes of the moon and sun, the stars and the origin of the universe. And a man who is puzzled and wondering sees himself as ignorant. (So a lover of myth is in his way a philosopher, for a myth is all about wonders.) Then as men framed systems of philosophy to escape from their ignorance, it is clear they were pursuing knowledge in order to understand and not for any practical use to which they might put it. The facts themselves support our statement, for it was not until after almost everything necessary for life, comfort, and recreation had been provided that this kind of knowledge began to be sought. Manifestly then we seek this knowledge for no utilitarian end but, even as we call a man free who lives for his own sake and not for another's, so we call this the only free science, for it alone exists for itself.

For this very reason mastery of this science may be justly regarded as beyond human power. For in many ways man's nature is enslaved, so that, according to Simonides,[5] God only can enjoy this

---

[5] Simonides of Keos was a most admired wit and poet, who wrote during the period of the Persian Wars. His terse and masterly lines were quoted by Greek writers long after his death. Plato and Aristotle often refer to him.

privilege and man ought by rights to try for just that knowledge that is suited to him. If, indeed, the poets were right and if God were by nature jealous, he would most probably be especially so on grounds of this kind and all men who excel in knowledge would be doomed to misfortune. But the Deity cannot be jealous and, as the proverb says, "The poets tell many a lie." Nor should any science be valued more highly than this. For what is most divine is also most valuable and this science alone is divine in two ways. A science which belongs peculiarly to God himself is a divine science. So also is one that deals with divine things. Now this science alone has both these characteristics. Everyone believes that God is one of the causes and a first principle of things, and either God alone or he above all others possesses this science. So every other science may be more necessary than this but none is more noble.

The acquiring of this science, moreover, should in a way bring us to something that is the opposite of our original questionings. For all men, as we remarked, begin by wondering that things are as they are, as they wonder at the motions of marionettes or at the solstices or at the incommensurability of the diagonal of a square[6] (for everyone who has not yet discovered the cause seems to find it amazing that there is something that cannot be measured by even the smallest unit). But we should end in a contrary and what is proverbially a better state of mind, as men do in the cases just mentioned when they learn to understand them. For nothing would so astonish a geometrician as to find a diagonal commensurate with the side.

We have explained now the nature of the science we are investigating and the end which our present inquiry and whole enterprise should strive to attain. . . .

[*In the remaining chapters of the first book Aristotle reviews and criticizes the doctrines of his predecessors, including Plato, regarding the causes and nature of the universe.*]

[6] An allusion, of course, to the well-known difficulty of expressing the length of a diagonal of a rectangle in terms of the length of a side.

BOOK II

The study of truth requires a study of causes. The causes through which everything comes to pass are four in number, not an infinite series.

CHAPTER 1. The study of truth is partly hard and partly easy. A proof of this is the fact that no one man is able to grasp it adequately. Yet they do not all entirely fail. Each says something about the nature of the world, and, though individually he adds little or nothing to our understanding of it, still from the combination of all something considerable is accomplished. Hence, as truth seems to be like the door which, the proverb says, no one can fail to hit, in that respect our study of it is easy. But the fact that we can have some notion of it as a whole, but not of the particular part we want, shows it is difficult. Perhaps too the difficulty is of two kinds and its cause is not so much in the things themselves as in us. For as the eyes of bats are to the brightness of daylight, so is the reason in our soul to the things that by nature are the clearest of all. . . .

It is right that philosophy should be called the knowledge of truth. For the object of theoretical knowledge is truth, whereas of practical knowledge it is action. (Even if practical men do ask *how* a thing is as it is, they are not trying to understand eternal being but only something relative and immediate.) But we do not know truth without some knowledge of its causes. And anything is whatever it is to a higher degree if, through it, other things are made to be like it. For example, fire is the hottest of things, because it is the cause of heat in everything else. So that is most true which causes everything depending on it to be true. Hence the principles of eternal things must always be most true, since they are not only sometimes true nor is anything else the cause of their being, but they are the causes of the

being of other things. And as each thing is as regards being, so it is as regards truth. . . .

[At this point we break temporarily the order of our text, and insert from Book V, chapter 2, the definition of the four causes of things, which is fuller and clearer than that given in Book II.]

"Cause" [7] means: (1) in one sense, that from which as present material something is made; as, for instance, the bronze of a statue, the silver of a cup, and the types of things that comprise these. (2) In another sense, the form or pattern, that is, the essential formula, and the types of things comprising this, and the parts of the formula. For instance, the ratio 2 : 1 and number in general are causes of the musical octave. (3) That by which a change is begun or stopped. For instance, the adviser is a cause of the act, the father of the child, and in general the maker is a cause of that which is made and the one who makes a change of the change. (4) Again, it means the final end, that is, that for the sake of which some thing else is. For instance, health is an end in walking. For why does one walk? "To be healthy," we say and in so saying think we have named the cause. We think the same of every means employed by some agent to bring about an end. For instance, flesh-reducing, purging, drugs and instruments are means that bring about health. All these are for the sake of that end, though they differ from one another in that some are instruments and others are actions.

These then are roughly all the meanings of "cause." But as the word is used with the various meanings, it follows that there may be several causes of the same thing, and not accidentally either. For instance, both the sculptor's art and the bronze are causes of the statue, not because it is something else too but because it is a statue. They are not, however, causes in the same sense; the one is the

---

[7] Briefly, the four causes are known as: (1) the material; (2) the formal; (3) the moving or efficient; (4) the final. For further discussion of them see Introduction, p. xx ff.

material and the other the source of the movements that made it. And things are causes of one another; as, for example, hard work is a cause of a sound body and a sound body of hard work. They are not, however, causes in the same sense, for one is the purpose or end and the other the source of movement. Further, the same thing is sometimes the cause of contrary results, for that which by its presence is the cause of something we sometimes blame for being by its absence the cause of the contrary. For instance, we call the absence of the pilot the cause of the shipwreck, when his presence was the cause of its safety. Both—his presence and his absence—are causes as sources of motion.

All the causes here mentioned fall under the four obvious headings. The letters that make up syllables, the material of manufactured objects, fire and earth and all such bodies, the parts of a whole, the premisses of a conclusion are causes in the sense that they are that out of which things are made. Of these some are causes as material, such as the parts. Others are causes as form or essence, such as the whole, the synthesis, and the formula. The seed, the physician, the adviser, and in general the makers, are all efficient causes of change or of rest. The remaining causes are the end and the good of things; for the final purpose tends to be the greatest good and end of the rest. Let it not matter whether we call it the good or what seems to be the good. . . .

[Book II, chapter 2, is here resumed.]

Plainly there is a first principle and the causes of things are neither an infinite series nor infinitely varied in kind. For in a material way, one thing cannot be made out of something else *ad infinitum;* as, for example, flesh out of earth, earth out of air, air out of fire, and so on without ever stopping. Nor can the source of motion be an infinite series: man moved by the air, the air by the sun, the sun by strife [8]

---

[8] Aristotle is referring here to the theory of the philosopher Empedocles, that the universe is composed of four primary material elements,—earth, air, fire, and water, continually acted upon by two opposing, creative and destructive powers, Love and Strife.

and so on endlessly. In the same way, the final cause cannot keep on receding indefinitely, walking for the sake of health, health for the sake of happiness, happiness for the sake of something else, one thing always existing for the sake of another. And the same with the formal cause. . . . Nor, on the other hand, can there be an infinite process downward from a start in something higher; as if, for instance, water were made from fire, earth from water and so forever something new being produced. . . .

Moreover the final cause is an end and the sort of end that exists not for the sake of something else but all other things exist for it. So, if there is a final cause of this kind, the process of change and becoming will not be infinite. But if there is no such terminus, there will be no final cause. Those who insist on the infinite series do not realize that they are destroying the nature of the good. No man would start to do anything, if he did not expect to reach some end. Nor would there be any intelligence in the universe, because an intelligent man certainly always does things for a purpose and that is their terminus, for the end is a terminus. . . .

Further, if the kinds of causes were infinite in number, then knowledge would be impossible for us; for only when we have discovered its causes, do we think we know a thing; but an infinite sum cannot be counted over in a finite time. . . .

BOOK IV

> *The meaning of "being." Words must be taken to have one clear meaning, and contradictions cannot be true of the same things at the same time. The changing sense world all that is? Appearances are not all true, nor are they all false. Not everything is at rest, nor is it all in motion.*

CHAPTER 1. There is a science that studies being as being and the properties characteristic of it.[9] It is not the same as any one of the so-called special sciences, for none of the others deals with being generally as being. They cut off a piece of it and study the character of that piece, as, for instance, the mathematical sciences do. But we are after first principles and ultimate causes and obviously there must be something to which they belong by virtue of its own nature. The men who in the past have looked for the elements of the existing world [10] have looked also for these first principles. Therefore it must be that these elements are elements of being, not incidentally but because it is being. Hence we too must find the first causes of being as being.

CHAPTER 2. There are various senses in which a thing may be said to "be," but all are in relation to some one central point and one particular kind of nature and not just vaguely so. Thus every-thing that *is* healthy has some relation to health; either it preserves health or creates health or is a sign of health or is capable of health.

[9] Aristotle is speaking here, of course, of the science we call Metaphysics, the subject of his book.

[10] A reference to Aristotle's predecessors in philosophy, the so-called Physicists, who tried to discover the material elements of which the world is composed and how it came into being.

. . . So there are several senses in which a thing is said to "be," though all have reference to the one principle. Some things are said to "be" because they are themselves substances, others because they are conditions of a substance, others because they are processes leading to substance, or destructions or privations or qualities of substance or formative or productive of substance or of things said to be connected with substance, or negations of one of them or of substance, itself. That is why we even say that non-being too *is* non-being. . . . In every case this science has to do with what is fundamental, on which other things depend and from which they get their names. If then substance is this fundamental thing, the philosopher must learn the first principles and causes of substances. . . .

CHAPTER 4.   There are some, however, who, as we have said, declare that it is possible for the same thing both to be and not to be and that such a belief is possible. Many even of the physicists hold this view. But we have hitherto assumed that a thing cannot at the same time be and not be, and therewith have proved that this is the most authentic of all principles. . . .

First, then, clearly this at least is true, that the phrase "to be" or "not to be" has a definite meaning, so that everything cannot be both so and not so. Next, if "man" means one thing, let that be "two-footed animal." . . . If, however, it should be said that "man" means an indefinite number of things, obviously all discussion would be impossible. For not to have one meaning is to have no meaning and if words have no meaning, all discussion with one another and even, strictly speaking, with ourselves, is over, since we cannot think at all if we do not think of one thing. . . . If "man" and "not man" mean nothing different, obviously "not being a man" will mean nothing different from "being a man" and so "to be a man" will be "not to be a man." They will be one. And to be one means to be, like wrap and cloak, that they have the same definition. And if "being a man" and "not being a man" are one, they too will mean the same

thing. But we have shown above that they mean different things. For if anything can be truly said "to be a man," it must be a "two-footed animal," since this is what "man" was said to mean. And if this must be so, it is impossible that that thing should not be a "two-footed animal." . . . Thus it cannot be true at the same time to say that the same thing is and is not a man. . . .

Again, if all contradictions are true at the same time of the same thing, palpably all things will then be one. For if it is possible either to affirm or to deny anything of everything, the same thing will be a ship and a wall and a man, as it must be for those who repeat the theory of Protagoras.[11] Then if anyone thinks that a man is not a ship, undoubtedly he is not a ship. But, in the same way, he is a ship, if the contrary is true. . . . I mean that if it is true to say that a man is not a man, then clearly it is also true that he is a ship and not a ship. . . . Then all things will be one, as we said before, and the same thing will be man and God and ship and their opposites. For if we can make all these assertions of everything, there will be no difference between any one thing and any other; if anything does differ, in this it will be true and unique. . . .

And if all men are equally wrong and right, a person like that can neither speak nor tell us anything, for he is saying at the same time both "yes" and "no." And if he has no opinion but both thinks and does not think together, how is he different from the vegetables? So it is very evident that no one, neither those who profess this theory nor any others, really abide by it. For why does a man who thinks he should walk to Megara actually walk there, instead of resting at home? Why, early one morning, does he not walk into a well or into a ravine, if he comes to one, instead of taking obvious care not to, just as if he did not think it equally good and not good to tumble in? Patently then he judges one thing better and the other worse. And

---

[11] Protagoras was a sophist or public teacher of the time of Socrates, who had taught that all knowledge was relative and that all appearances and opinions were equally true. Plato wrote a dialogue on him and his views.

if he does this, he must judge one thing to be a man and another not a man and one thing sweet and another not sweet. For when he wants and looks for a drink of water or a man to see, he does not go looking for everything and taking them all to be the same; and yet he should, if the same thing were equally a man and not a man. But, as we have remarked, there is no one who does not openly avoid some things and not others. Hence, as it seems, all men form unequivocal judgments, if not about everything, at least about what is better and what is worse. . . .

CHAPTER 5. . . . If, however, all beliefs and appearances are true, then everything must be at the same time both true and false. For many men hold opinions contrary to those of others and call deluded whoever does not think just as they do, and thus the same thing must both be and not be. Yet, if this is so, all beliefs must be true, since both those who are wrong as well as those who are right oppose the others' views. If then reality is like this, all are right in their beliefs. . . .

These questions come to persons who are perplexed by their observations of the world of sense. Their idea that contradictions and contraries are true at the same time comes from their seeing that contrary results do follow from the same thing. If, they say, nothing can come out of non-existence into being, the thing must have previously existed as two contraries together. . . . To those who base their ideas on these grounds we reply that in a sense they are right but in a sense they are mistaken. For to "be" has two meanings. In a sense it is possible that something should come out of what is not and in a sense it is impossible, and in a sense the same thing can at the same time both "be" and "not be," though not in the same way. For the same thing can at the same time "be" potentially two contraries [12] but not actually. And further, we suggest that these persons

---

[12] That is, it can at the same time have in itself the possibility of becoming either of two contraries, but when it actually becomes one, it then cannot also be the other.

conceive of another kind of substance among the things that are, in which neither movement nor decay nor generation ever occurs.[13]

Similarly, the view that all opinions are true has come to other persons from their observation of the sense world. For they think that the truth of an opinion should not be judged by the large or small number of those who hold it. And they say that the same thing seems sweet to some who taste it and bitter to others. So, if everybody were sick or everybody insane and only two or three were well or sane, the latter would be thought sick and insane but not the majority. Also, they say, to many of the other animals things seem the opposite of what they do to us. Even to the senses of one individual things do not always appear the same. Which then of these impressions are true and which false is hard to tell, for one is no more true than another but both are equally so. Hence Democritus [14] declares that either there is no truth or it is hidden from us. . . . Now if those who have seen most of the truth that is accessible to us (and those are they who search for and love it most), if those men hold such opinions and express such views of truth, is it not natural that beginners in philosophy should despair? For the hunt for truth would be the chase of a flying bird.

But the reason why these men held these opinions is that, although they did investigate the truth about things that are, they took the sense world to be all that is. In it there is much by nature indefinite, much that *is* in the anomalous sense we have described above.[15] . . . Again, because they saw the whole of this visible nature in motion and because no true statement is possible about what is forever changing, they concluded that nothing could truly be said about what was everywhere and in every respect being changed. . . .

[13] The first suggestion so far of the higher realm of immaterial being, beyond the world of sense, of which Aristotle will say more later.

[14] Aristotle refers often to Democritus of Thrace, the most famous of the materialistic philosophers of the preceding generation, known especially as the advocate of the atomic theory of matter.

[15] That is, perhaps, in the sense of being at the same time potentially both of two contraries.

But to their theory we shall make the reply that although they have some grounds in reason for supposing that a changing thing at the moment of change ceases to be, still the point is a debatable one. For that which is casting off a quality keeps something of that which it is casting off, and of that which is coming to be something must already exist. In general, even when a thing is ceasing to exist, there is something there which *is;* and when it is coming into being, the something that produces it or by which it is generated must *be.* Noi does the series go on *ad infinitum.* . . .

Again, we may find just fault with those who uphold such a theory for asserting about the whole of the universe what they have seen in only a minority of the objects of sense. For only the region of the sense world close around us is always in a state of birth and death and this is hardly a fraction of the whole. Accordingly, it would have been fairer to acquit this part for the sake of the other than to condemn that for the sake of this. Further too, we shall say plainly to these men what we alluded to before; for we must show and convince them that there is a nature beyond change. . . .

In general, if only the sense world existed, nothing would be at all, if living beings did not exist; for without them there would be no faculty of sense.[16] That neither the things we sense nor sensations would exist is probably true, for they both are impressions of the perceiver. But that the substances themselves, which produce our sensations, should not exist, even without our sensing them, is impossible. For certainly sensation is not sensation of itself, but there is something else beside the sensation, which must *be* prior to the sensation, since the thing that moves is prior in nature to that which it moves. . . .

CHAPTER 6. . . . Then if not everything is relative but some things do exist of themselves, not every appearance is true. For

---

[16] Aristotle is anticipating here the argument of Bishop Berkeley, the eighteenth century idealist, that things in our visible world exist because they are seen. They would cease to exist if no one observed them.

an appearance is what appears to someone, and whoever says that all appearances are true is making everything relative. So those who are looking for a powerful argument and expecting at the same time to maintain their own position should take the precaution to say that an appearance is true not in itself but for him to whom it appears, when it appears and in what way and form. And if they try to maintain their position without thus defining it, they will soon find themselves uttering contradictions. For it is possible for something to appear to one's sight to be honey but not to one's taste; and for things to seem different to each of a man's two eyes, if they do not match.

As to those who, for the reasons given above, declare that all appearances are true and therefore everything is alike both true and false, because they do not appear the same to everyone nor always the same to the same man, but often present contrary appearances at the same time (as our touch tells us, when we cross our fingers, there are two objects there and our sight tells us there is one)—to these persons we say: "Yes, but not contrary to the same sense, in the same way, under the same guise and at the same time." Subject to these conditions, every appearance is true. Thereupon those who are arguing, not because they feel the difficulty but for argument's sake, will be forced probably to say that appearances are not true in themselves but true to the perceiver. And, as we have said, they must make everything relative, depending on human opinion and sensation, so that nothing ever has been or will be without someone's first thinking of it. But if things have been and will continue to be without that, evidently not everything will depend on our opinion of it. . . . Enough has been said now to show, first, that the strongest of all our convictions is that two contradictory statements are not both true at the same time; and, then, what are the consequences of saying that they are true, and why people say they are. . . .

CHAPTER 8. . . . It is clear also that those who assert that all things are at rest are not right, nor are those who say that all things

are in motion.[17] For if all things are at rest, the same things will always be true and the same false; but obviously they change. For the very man who speaks of them once did not exist and again will not be. And if all things are in motion, nothing will be true; everything then will be false. But we have shown that this is impossible. Once more, being itself must change, for it changes from one thing into something else. Nor, on the other hand, is it true that all things are at some time motionless and again in motion, and nothing is so eternally. For there is something always moving the things that are being moved; and the first mover is itself unmoved. . . .

BOOK V

This book, which may not have been part of the original Metaphysics, *consists of definitions of terms*

CHAPTER 7. A thing is said to "be," sometimes in an accidental sense, sometimes by its own essential nature. In the accidental sense, we say that the man of honor is musical or the man is musical and the musician is a man. Similarly, we say that the musician is a builder, because the builder chances to be a musician or the musician a builder. In this sense, saying that one thing is another means that the one is an accident of the other. So in the examples we gave; for when we say that the man is musical and the musician is a man or that the pale man is musical or the musician is pale, the last two sentences mean that both predicates are accidents of that one person, and the first sentence means that its predicate is an accident of something that *is*, and "the musician is a man" means that being a musician is an accident of the man. . . .

[17] There were two famous schools of Greek thought, the first of which, headed by Heraclitus, taught that the whole universe was forever in a state of complete flux or change; the second, founded by Zeno of Elea, maintained that nothing really moved and change was only a delusion of our senses.

In how many senses a thing essentially *is,* is shown by the forms of the predicate we use in speaking of it, for to *be* has as many senses as there are forms.[18] Some predicates tell *what* the thing is, others its *quality,* others its *quantity,* others its *relation* to something else, others its *activity* or *passivity,* others its *place* and others its *time;* and for each of these predicates there is a corresponding sense of "being." . . .

Again, to "be" and "is" may mean that some statement is true, and "is not" that it is not true but false. This is so in both affirmation and negation. For example, "Socrates *is* musical" means that this is true; or "Socrates *is* not pale" means that this is true. But "the diagonal of a square *is not* commensurate with the side" means that it *is* false to say it is.

Furthermore, "being" and "is," in some cases we have mentioned, mean potential being and in others actual. For we say a thing *is* seeing, when either it can potentially see or actually does see. Likewise, we say a man knows, who either can use his knowledge or is actually using it, and a thing rests when either rest is already present in it or it is able to rest. In the same way too with substances, we say the Hermes is in the stone, and the half of the line in the whole, and we call "corn" what is not yet ripe. But when a thing is potential and when it is not must be explained later. . . .

---

[18] Aristotle is thinking here of his logical treatise on *Categories,* in which he had listed and explained the ten predicates or things to be stated of any object, when giving an exact definition of the kind of object it really is. These ten categories or predicates, to be used in an analysis of the object's essential nature, were the following: substance, quantity, quality, relation, time, place, position, state, activity and passivity. See Introduction, pp. xxii-xxiii.

BOOK VII

Discussion of substance, matter, essence, form and universal. Both natural and artificial objects are combinations of matter and essence, or form.

CHAPTER I. To "be" means any one of several things, as we pointed out earlier, in our chapter on its various senses.[19] For, in one sense, it "is" means telling *what* a thing is or what individual; and, in another, it means giving its quality or quantity or some other such characteristic. Now though "being" thus has many senses, manifestly the fundamental sense is that which tells the *what*, which means the *substance* of the thing. (When we speak of the *quality* of a thing, we say it is good or bad, but not that it is three cubits long or a man. But when we tell *what* it is, we do not say it is white or hot or three cubits long, but that it is a man or a god.) All other things are said to "be," because they are either quantities or qualities or states or something else of the kind.

Accordingly, one might ask whether *walking* and *being healthy* and *sitting* are each by itself something that *is* or not, and so as to other things of the kind. For none of them is either a thing that has any independent, natural existence or is capable of being separated from a substance. Rather, if anything, it is the *thing* that walks and sits and is healthy that exists. The *thing* seems really to exist because of something definite that underlies it, which is the *substance* and the individual that is clearly denoted by its category.[20] For "good" or "sitting" means nothing without the substance which it characterizes. Obviously then it is only through some substance

19 That is, in the chapter of Book V, just given.
20 That is by the class name that tells *what* it is—man or dog or stone.

that each of these latter things exists. Therefore that which primarily and absolutely *is* (not a quality) must be substance. . . .

Indeed the question that was raised in the beginning and is now and always being raised and never answered—namely, what is *being?* —is actually the question, what is *substance?* Some say it is one, others more than one. Some call it finite, others infinite. So we too have now to consider, foremost and chiefly and, I might say, solely, *being* in the sense of *substance*.

CHAPTER 2.   Substance seems to belong most obviously to bodies. Thus we call animals and plants and their parts substances, and also the natural bodies such as fire, water, earth and the like, and all things that are either portions of them or composed of them, either of parts of them or of them altogether, as are the heaven and its parts, the stars, moon and sun. We must ask then whether these are the only substances, or there are others beside, or whether only some of these are substances, or some and not others, or none of them at all but only some other things. Some think that the boundaries of bodies—namely, surfaces, lines, points, and dots—are substances and more truly so than body or anything solid.[21] Others do not believe anything is substance but the objects of sense;[22] still others say there are eternal beings, more numerous and more real than sense objects.[23] . . .

So on these questions we must consider which of the current statements is right and which wrong, and what substances are, and whether there are or are not any substances beside those we perceive by our senses, and how these last exist; also, whether there is any separate substance, and, if so, why and how it exists, or whether

[21] These would be the Pythagoreans, who believed that mathematical concepts, numbers, proportions, and ratios, were the true reality, making our universe what it is.

[22] The materialist philosophers already referred to.

[23] The followers of Plato taught that the invisible world of ideas was the only changeless reality.

there is no substance at all apart from those our senses know. But first we must frame some notion of what substance is.

CHAPTER 3. Now the name, "substance," is given to at least four, if not more, special things. The essence, the universal and the genus [24] are called the substance of an individual, and, fourthly, the underlying substratum. The substratum is the thing to which the rest are attached as predicates, but it itself is not a predicate to anything else. So we must first determine its nature, for that which underlies a thing as primary substratum seems most really to be its substance.

From one point of view we call the matter the substratum, from another the shape and from another the combination of the two. By the matter I mean, for instance, bronze, by shape the pattern assumed by the form, and by the combination of the two the complete thing, the statue. But if the form is prior to the matter and exists in a truer sense, by the same token it will be prior to the combination of the two. [25] . . .

By matter I mean something that by itself is not an individual object nor any definite quantity, and that possesses no other of the qualities by which existing things are identified. For there is a something to which every quality is said to belong, but which has an existence distinct from that of every quality; for all qualities are predicated of substance and substance is predicated of matter. So this ultimate thing in itself is neither an individual nor a quantity nor anything else. . . . But substance especially has both the power to exist separately and individually. Hence form and the combination of form and matter would appear to be substance more truly than matter alone is. . . .

[24] The essence, or form, is what gives its specific character to the individual. The universal, in the sense Aristotle means here, is the element that an individual shares with others of a great class. For example, in man, the universal is his animal nature. The genus is what he shares with a smaller class, with which he has more in common; in a man, it is the human nature he shares with all other men.

[25] The priority of the form, which is the actual, living power in the world, to matter, which, alone, is only potentially living, is proved later. See p. 30.

CHAPTER 4. . . . Since earlier in this book we listed the ways in which we define "substancc," and of these one was said to be "essence," we now must look into this. And first let us say something about the word. The essence of a thing is what it is said to be in its very self. Being you is not being musical, for you are not by your very nature musical. Your essence is what you are by your very nature. . . . The essence is the individuality; but whenever some quality is ascribed to something else, it is not always its individuality. For instance, "white man" is not an individual—if indeed individuality is an attribute of substance only. So essence is composed of those things the enumeration of which makes a definition. . . .

CHAPTER 6. . . . From this discussion it is clear that each individual thing is one and the same with its essence, and not accidentally so, but because to understand anything is to understand its essence. So by furnishing examples we may show that the two must be identical. . . .

CHAPTER 7. Of things that come into being, some are produced by nature, some by art and some spontaneously,[26] but every thing that comes into being is produced by something and from something and becomes something. . . . Now a natural coming into being is that of the objects produced by Nature, and that out of which they are produced is what we call matter, and that by which they are produced is something that naturally exists, and that which they become is a man or a plant or some other of the objects that we call particular substances. Everything produced by Nature or by art contains matter, for they all are capable of either being or not being, and this capacity is the matter in each of them. In general, both that from which they are produced and the manner in which they are produced is Nature, for the thing produced, such as plant or animal, has a nature. That further by which they are produced is

[26] As an example of something produced spontaneously Aristotle later mentions health.

the so-called form in Nature, which has the same form in the thing produced (though it is in something else); for man begets man.

In this way then natural products come into being. All other productions are called "makings." All makings are achieved either by art or by some power or thought. Some also take place spontaneously and by chance, much as natural productions do, for among them things are sometimes reproduced without seed as well as from seed.[27] These cases we will examine later. By art are produced the things of which the form is in the soul of the maker. By form I mean the essence of the thing and its primary substance. . . .

CHAPTER 8.   Whatever then is produced is produced by something (by this I mean the starter of the process), and out of something (and let this be matter . . .), and becomes something, which may be either a ball or a circle or whatever it happens to be. But just as we do not make the substratum—the bronze—so neither do we make the sphere, except incidentally, since a bronze ball is a sphere and we do make that. To make a particular object is to make that particular object out of the general substratum. I mean that to make the bronze ball is not to make the round or the sphere but something else, namely, to produce the form of the sphere in something different from it. For if we produce the form, we must make it out of something else, as already stated. For instance, we make a bronze ball. This we do as follows. Out of this thing that is bronze, we make this other thing that is a ball. . . . Obviously the form—or whatever we should call the shape of the sense object—we do not make, nor does it just come into existence, nor is that essence created. It is what is brought to be in something else, either by art or by Nature or by a potency. We do bring the bronze ball into existence. For we make it out of bronze and a sphere. We bring the form into this

[27] Aristotle believed that certain small and obscure plant and animal forms were produced by spontaneous generation out of slime and decaying matter, for without a microscope he could discover no apparatus in them for reproduction nor observe any reproductive activities.

particular matter and the thing is a bronze ball. . . . Clearly then, from what we have said, the thing in the sense of form or substance we do not make, but the so-called compound whole we make; and in everything that is made matter is present and one part of it is matter and the other form.

Is there then any sphere apart from these balls or any house apart from these bricks? Or if there were, would any of these concrete objects have come into being? Form means type. It is not a particular individual. But we produce or beget a type out of a particular material, and what is then produced is an individual of that type. The complete individual man is Callias or Socrates, as the individual object is this bronze ball; but "man" or "animal" is a type, like bronze sphere in general. . . . And the complete whole, such and such a form in these flesh and bones, is Callias or Socrates. Each differs from his father through his matter, because the matter in him is different; but in form he is the same, for form is indivisible. . . .

BOOK IX

> Being is either actual or potential. The actual comes before the potential.[28]

CHAPTER 6. . . . Actuality is the existence of a thing, but not in the way we mean when we call it potentially something. We say that potentially a statue of Hermes is in the wood and a half-line in the whole, because it could be separated out. We call even a man who is not studying a scholar, if he has the ability to study, though the opposite is actually true. What we mean can be plainly seen by inference from individual instances. (We should not

[28] Put in popular form, the problem Aristotle is discussing in the next few pages is, which came first, the hen or the egg? The egg is the potential hen, the hen is the bird actually existing.

look for a definition of everything but observe the analogies.) It is as one who is building to one who can build, and as one who is awake to one asleep, and as one who is seeing to one who can see but has shut his eyes, and as something framed out of matter to matter itself, and as something wrought and finished to the un-wrought material. Let actuality be defined as one member of each contrasted pair and potentiality as the other. . .

CHAPTER 7. What and what sort of thing the actual is should now be clear from these and similar considerations. But when a thing potentially exists and when it does not we must next determine, for that is not at any time or always. For example, is earth potentially a man? No, but only when it has previously become a seed and not even then perhaps. In the same way, not everything can be healed by medical art or by chance. But there is something with the capacity for being healed and this is what is potentially healthy. The requirement for that which by exercise of thought passes from being something potentially to being it actually is that, once the change is willed, nothing external must prevent its taking place. In the case of a person being healed, nothing in him must hinder the result. . . . In all cases where the principle of becom-ing actual is in the thing itself, it is already potentially whatever it will be, if nothing external prevents. For example, the seed is not yet potentially a man, for it must first undergo changes in another body. But when through its own moving principle it becomes what it needs to be, it is already potentially a man. . . . .

CHAPTER 8. From our discussion of the various meanings of "prior," it is plain that the *actual* is prior to the *potential*. . . . In time, actuality is prior in this way. The actual is prior to the poten-tial which is the same with it, in form though not in number. I mean that as far as this particular man, who now actually exists, and this corn and this seeing creature are concerned, the matter and the seed and the capacity to see, which were potentially man, corn, and seeing

creature but not yet actually so, were prior in time. But prior in time to these were other actually existing things, from which they came. For always something actual is produced from something potential by something actual, as a man by a man, a musician by a musician. Always there is a first mover and the mover *actually* exists. We said in our discussion of substance that everything that is produced is produced from something and by something of the same form as itself. . . .

The actual is also prior in substance, first, because things that are later in coming to be are really prior in form and substance, as, for example, man is prior to boy and human being to seed, since the one already has its form and the other has not. And everything that comes into being moves toward a principle, which is its end; for that for the sake of which it exists is its principle, and its coming into being is for its end. And actuality is its end, and it was to become actual that it acquired potentiality. For animals do not see in order to have the power of sight but have the power of sight in order to see. Similarly, men have the art of building that they may build, and theoretical method that they may theorize. But they do not theorize in order to have a theoretical method, save only those who are learning by practice; and those do not theorize in any but a small way, or on a subject they do not want to theorize about.

Matter too exists potentially, in order that it may come to a form. When it exists actually, then it is with its form. . . . Evidently then *substance* or *form* is *actuality*. By this reasoning too it is clear that the actual is prior in substance to the potential. As we have pointed out, something actual always comes in time before another, straight back to that actual which is the eternal first mover.

But in a deeper sense also the actual is prior to the potential, for things that are eternal are prior in substance to things perishable and nothing eternal exists potentially. The reason is this. Everything potential is at the same time a potentiality of contraries. For while that which is incapable of actual existence will not anywhere exist, everything that has the capacity may still not become actual. Ac-

cordingly, that which has the possibility of being may both be and not be. The same thing then is capable of both being and not being. And he thing that is capable of not being may possibly not be, and that which may possibly not be is perishable, either in the absolute sense of the word, or in the particular sense in which we say it may possibly not be, that is, in some place or quantity or quality. "In the absolute sense" means perishable in substance. Nothing then that is imperishable in the absolute sense is potential in the absolute sense, though it may be in a particular respect, as to quality or place. All imperishable things exist actually. Nor can anything that exists of necessity be potential. And these are the primary things, for, if they did not exist, nothing would. . . .

BOOK XII

A consideration of imperishable being, immovable and free of matter, the first mover and final cause, the good of the universe. Its life of tranquil thought. The world ordered for good.

CHAPTER I. . . . Now there are three kinds of substance. That which we know through our senses is in part eternal [29] and in part perishable. The latter, which includes plants and animals, is recognized by everyone. Of both these we should learn the elements, whether one or many. The third substance is immovable and, some say, has a separate existence apart. Some thinkers divide this substance into two classes, the forms and the objects of mathematics, others combine them in one class, and others identify the substance with just the objects of mathematics. [30] The first two kinds

[29] According to Aristotle, the heavenly bodies were made of some unchangeable, incorruptible substance, quite different from that of the corruptible bodies of earth.
[30] The allusions are to the views of Plato and other contemporary philosophers.

of substance belong in the sphere of physics, for they involve motion, but the last belongs to a different science, since there is no principle common to them all. . . .

CHAPTER 6.   There being three kinds of substance, two that are physical and one immovable, we must now consider the last named and show that there must be some eternal and immovable substance. For substances are the first of things that *are*, and if they are all perishable, everything is bound to perish. But it is impossible that motion should ever have begun to be or should ever be destroyed, for it always was. Time too can never have begun; for there could not be a before nor an after, if time did not exist. Motion then is forever continuing, as time is; for time is either the same as motion or a condition of motion. (But there is no continuous motion but motion in place, and of this only motion in a circle.)

If, however, there is something capable of moving or producing things, but which is not actually doing so, there may be no motion, because that which has the potentiality may not be making it actual. Nothing is gained then by supposing substances that are eternal, as the believers in ideas do,[31] unless there is in them a power to cause change. And even this would not be enough, nor would any other substance beside the ideas be enough; unless it actually exerted its power, there would be no motion. Furthermore, even if it were active, it would not be enough, if its essence were a potentiality, since in that case there would be no eternal motion. For a thing that exists potentially may perhaps not exist. There must therefore be a first principle of this kind, whose essence is actuality. Moreover, these substances must be free of matter, for they must be eternal—if anything is to be eternal. Thus they must actually *be*. . . .

For these reasons some thinkers, such as Leucippus [32] and Plato, believe in something forever actual, because, they say, motion is

[31] Another allusion to Plato's theory of the eternally existing ideas.

[32] Leucippus was a philosopher of the previous century about whom we know little but that he was apparently the author of the atomic theory of matter, which Democritus afterward developed and made famous.

everlasting. But why it is and what it is they do not tell, nor, if it moves in such and such a way, do they give us the cause. Now nothing is moved at random, but there must always be something there to move it, even as things are moved in one way by Nature and in another by force or by mind or something else. . . . Therefore there was no infinite age of Chaos and Night,[33] but the same things have always existed, either revolving in a cycle or moving in some other mode, as the actual is prior to the potential. If the same is constantly repeating itself in cycles, there must be something there always active in the same way. If there is birth and death, there must be something else always active in two different ways.[34] . . . And the first is the cause of what is permanent and the second of what is different and both together are the causes of perpetual variation. Now this is just the character of our motion. Why then need we look for any more principles?

CHAPTER 7. . . . There is then something that is always moving in a ceaseless motion, which is motion in a circle; and this is plain not in theory only but in fact. Hence the first heaven must be eternal. There is also something that moves it. For that which is moved while it moves others is but an intermediary. There is something that moves others without being moved, which is eternal and substance and actuality. It moves in this way. An object of desire and an object of thought move others without being themselves moved. . . .

That the final cause belongs among immovable things is proved by distinguishing between its different meanings. For the final cause is both the good for the sake of which something else is, and the

[33] The believers in the old tales of the gods, whom Aristotle called "theologians," said that the world had been divinely organized out of black Chaos and Night.

[34] In Aristotle's astronomy, the outermost or first heavenly sphere, that carried the fixed stars, rotated in one simple, unchanging motion on its axis and thus set moving the planets in all their more complicated courses enclosed within it. The sun, by contrast, had two different movements, one around its great yearly orbit, the other its daily revolution around the earth. Both had their influence on the constitution of the earth.

good which is the end of action. In the second of these senses it is among the immovable things, though in the first it is not. It produces motion by being loved, and what it moves moves all things else. Now whatever is moved is capable of being otherwise than as it is. So even if its actuality assumes the form of primary motion in space, then inasmuch as it is moved, it is capable of changing from what it is, in place, if not in substance. But there is something that moves others while itself unmoved, and that actually exists, and it can in no way be other than it is. For motion in space is the first beginning of change, and motion in a circle is the first kind of motion; and this is the motion the first mover produces.[35] This being then necessarily exists, and because it is necessary, its mode of being is good. It is thereby a first principle. . . .

On such a first principle depend the heavens and the natural world. And its life is like ours when for a brief moment it is at its best. This being lives forever in that state, as we cannot do, for its actuality is also pleasure. . . . Now pure thinking thinks of what is excellent in itself, and thinking in the highest sense of what is most excellent in the highest sense. And the mind thinks of itself, when it takes on the nature of an object of thought. It becomes an object of thought through its perceiving and thinking, and then thought and object of thought are the same. For that which is receptive of thought and essence is the mind. And when it possesses in itself these things, it is actual and active. And actuality, rather than potentiality, seems to be the divine feature in thought, and the act of contemplation is what is most of all pleasant and best. If then God is always in that happy state in which we sometimes are, this is wonderful; and if in a still more happy state, more wonderful still. And God is in that happier state. Life also belongs to God, for thought

[35] The reasoning here is that the first mover must exist to produce, through the love he arouses in things beneath him, the beginning of motion in the first heaven, from which all our diversified motions start. But if the first mover himself moved, we should then have to look behind him for the thing that made him move. As Aristotle has already said, we cannot run our series back indefinitely. We must make it begin somewhere.

as actuality is life, and God *is* that actuality. And God's essential actuality is life most good and everlasting. We say then that God is a living being, eternal, most good. And so life and unbroken and eternal existence are God's, for this *is* God. . . .

CHAPTER 9. The nature of the divine mind raises certain problems; for while it seems the most divine of all phenomena, the question of how it functions in that manner brings up difficulties. If it thinks of nothing, what is there majestic in that? It is like one asleep. . . . Then, whether its substance is thought or thinking, of what does it think? Either of itself or of something else. And if it thinks of something else, it thinks either of the same thing always or of something different. Does it matter or not whether it thinks of the good or of any casual object? Are there not some things of which it would be preposterous for it to think? Clearly it thinks of what is most divine and most to be prized and does not change; for the change would be for the worse, and anything like that would become at once a motion. . . . There still remains the question whether the object of divine thought is composite or not. For if it were, the thought would change, ranging from part to part of the whole. We reply that everything that is free of matter is indivisible. And as the human mind—that is, the mind of composite beings—is for a moment of time, . . . so is that thought that thinks itself throughout eternity.[36]

CHAPTER 10. We must consider also in what way the nature of the universe contains the good and the supreme good, whether as something existing apart and by itself or as the order in Nature. Perhaps in both ways, as an army does. For the excellence of an army lies both in its order and in its general, but principally in him, since he is not dependent on the order but the order depends on him. And all things in Nature are ordered and combined in some manner, though not all in the same manner—fishes and fowls and plants.

[36] A repetition of what Aristotle has already said, that the perfection of God's eternal state is known to man for only a brief space.

They are not so planned that nothing has anything in common with another, but there is a connection. For all are ordered together to one end. It is as in a household, where the free members are least at liberty to do what they happen to choose but all or most of their acts are prescribed, while little of the common interest is left to slaves and animals, who for the most part do whatever happens to come their way. The nature of each makes up his principle of action.[37] . . .

Then how numbers, or soul and body, or, in general, form and the object are one, this no one tells us at all, nor can any man say, unless he says, as we do, that the mover makes them one. . . .

[37] That is, obedience to duty and a sense of public responsibility are natural to the higher class, and aimlessness to the lower.

PARTS OF
ANIMALS

PARTS OF ANIMALS

T HE SCIENCE of biology was founded for us of the West by
Aristotle in four epoch-making books. The first, the *History of
Animals*, composed, perhaps, during his stay on the island of Lesbos,
is a detailed, descriptive account of the appearance, habits, and characteristics of the more than five hundred animals he knew, divided
into genera and species, beginning with the lowest types of marine
creatures, hardly more than plants, and going on through insects,
fishes, birds, and land beasts up to man. The second book, the
Parts of Animals, is an anatomical study, made in his school at
Athens, of the animal body in general as an organism composed of
parts, with an attempt to assign to each part its particular function.
The last two books on the *Generation* and *Movement of Animals*
are more specialized treatises on the organs and processes of reproduction and the mechanics of animal locomotion.

The following selections from the *Parts of Animals* may illustrate
for the reader both Aristotle's achievements and his failings as a
natural scientist. His aim, as he explains in the first chapter, is to
prove against the materialists, who believed in nothing but physical
necessity and chance, the presence of a purpose in Nature, working
with the material elements offered by the universe to produce living
and conscious bodies, capable of every kind and degree of pleasurable
activity. What Nature herself may be or what the source of her
power he does not say. But again and again he calls us to note how
wonderfully and beautifully she works, in even the humblest things,
and always for the best.

Throughout the book he is intent on making out his case with
arguments sometimes sound and sometimes purely fanciful. But
whenever possible he bases his contentions on the evidence of his

own observations or what seem to him reliably reported facts. He has his material ready organized. Within the body, he distinguishes between what he names the homogeneous and the heterogeneous parts, between, that is, what later men spoke of as tissues—flesh, blood, bone, sinew, marrow, hair, and so on—and the organs compounded of them. In the animal kingdom, he draws significant lines of demarcation between what he calls the blooded and the bloodless or what we call the warm-blooded and the cold-blooded animals, and again between the mammals and the egg-laying or oviparous species, as well as between the lesser groups and families. In a most interesting passage, however, he warns us of the impossibility of making his observations and comparisons as accurate as they should be. How, he asks, for instance, can one measure heat or tell which of two unlike hot substances, boiling water and red-hot iron, is the hotter?

The reader of this passage is perhaps a little less scornful than he might be later on when he discovers that Aristotle, having no microscope and no exact time-piece, as well as no thermometer and only limited opportunities for dissection, knows nothing of the nervous system or of the circulation of the blood and is entirely at sea about the character and function of the brain. He appreciates the more Aristotle's grasp of the main principles of bone anatomy, the general plan of the digestive apparatus, and the adaptation of parts like teeth, mouths, beaks, limbs, and hands to the uses of the animals possessing them. And he respects a mind that can lay down so broadly the outlines of comparative animal structure as a whole, marking not only the curious details but trying with untiring patience to read the pattern of it all.

BOOK I

Causes of the formation of animal bodies, their parts, and their adaptation to the functions they perform.

CHAPTER I. . . . The causes concerned in the generation of the works of nature are, as we see, more than one. There is the final cause and there is the moving cause.[1] Now we must decide which of these two causes comes first, which second. Plainly, however, that cause is the first which we call the final one. For this is the reason, and the reason forms the starting point, alike in works of art and works of nature. For consider how a physician or how a builder sets about his work. He starts by forming for himself a definite picture, in the one case mental, in the other actual, of his end—the physician of health, the builder of a house. This he keeps in mind as the reason and explanation of each subsequent step that he takes, and of his acting in this or that way as the case may be.

Now in the works of nature the good end and the final cause is still more important than in works of art, such as these, and necessity is a much less constant factor in their production; though it is to this that almost all writers seek to refer their origin,[2] though they do not distinguish the various senses in which the term necessity is used. For there is absolute necessity, manifesting itself in eternal phenomena; and there is conditional necessity, manifested in every-

---

[1] Aristotle's theory of the four kinds of causes he has described in his *Metaphysics*. See p. 12 and Introduction, p. xx. The moving cause is what starts a thing moving or being made. The final cause is the aim or end for which the act was performed or the thing made.

[2] A reference to the contemporary school of materialist philosophers, against whom Aristotle is arguing all the way through this book.

thing that is generated by nature,[3] as also in everything that is produced by art, be it a house or what it may. For if a house or other such final object is to be realized, it is necessary that such and such material shall exist; and it is necessary that first this and then that shall be produced, and first this and then that set in motion, and so on in continuous succession, until the end and final result is reached, for the sake of which each prior thing is produced and exists.

As with these productions of art, so also is it with the productions of nature. The mode of necessity, however, and the mode of reasoning are different in natural science [and in art] from what they are in the theoretical sciences; of which we have spoken elsewhere.[4] For in the latter the starting point is that which is; in the former that which is to be. For it is that which is yet to be—health, let us say, or a man—which, owing to its being of such and such a character, necessitates the pre-existence or previous production of this and that antecedent; and not this or that antecedent which, because it exists or is generated, makes it necessary that health or a man shall come into existence. . . .

The best course then appears to be that we should follow the method already mentioned, and begin with the phenomena presented by each group of animals, and, when this is done, proceed afterwards to state the causes of those phenomena, and to deal with their evolution. For elsewhere, as for instance in house building, this is the true sequence. The plan of the house, or the house, has this and that feature; and because it has this and that feature, therefore is its construction carried out in this or that manner. For the process of evolution is for the sake of the thing finally evolved, and not this for the sake of the process. Empedocles,[5] then was in error when he said that many of the characteristics presented by animals were merely

---

[3] Aristotle distinguished between what he thought were eternal phenomena, the apparently changeless sun, moon, and stars of heaven and the growing and perishing works of nature on this earth. See *Metaphysics*, pp. 32-33.

[4] What Aristotle called the theoretical sciences were the purely intellectual or abstract, that is, metaphysics, mathematics, and what he knew as physics.

[5] Empedocles of Sicily, a materialist philosopher, had made one of the earliest comparative studies of the bodily structure of man and animals. Unfortunately his book *On Nature* has not come down to us.

the results of accidental occurrences during their development; for instance, that the backbone was divided as it is into vertebrae because it happened to be broken, owing to the contorted position of the foetus in the womb. In so saying he overlooked the fact that propagation implies a creative seed endowed with certain formative properties. Secondly, he neglected another fact, namely, that the parent animal pre-exists, not only in idea, but actually in time. For man is generated from man; and thus it is the possession of certain characters by the parent that determines the development of like characters in the child. . . .

The fittest mode, then, of treatment is to say a man has such and such parts, because the conception of a man includes their presence, and because they are necessary conditions of his existence, or at any rate of his perfection; and these conditions in their turn imply other prior conditions. Thus we should say, "Because man is an animal with such and such characters, therefore is the process of his development necessarily such as it is; and therefore is it accomplished in such and such an order, this part being formed first, that next, and so on in succession"; and after a like fashion should we explain the evolution of all other works of nature.

Now that with which the ancient writers, who first philosophized about nature, busied themselves, was matter and the material cause.[6] They inquired what this was, and what its character; how the universe was generated out of it, and by what moving influence, whether, for instance, by strife or love, whether by intelligence or accident,[7] the substratum of matter being assumed to have certain inseparable properties. Fire, for instance, had a hot nature, earth a cold one; the former was light, the latter heavy. For even the genesis of the universe was thus explained by them. After a like fashion did they deal

[6] A material cause of anything was the material or substance out of which it had come to be made.

[7] Empedocles explained the universe as the result of two opposing forces, love and strife, acting on the elements of matter. Democritus, a younger man, thought it a conglomeration of invisible atoms brought together by chance. Anaxagoras and Plato called it the work of a creative intelligence.

also with the development of plants and of animals. They said, for instance, that the matter contained in a body caused by its currents the formation of the stomach and the other receptacles of food or of excretion; and that the breath by its passage broke open the outlets of the nostrils; air and water being the materials of which bodies are made. For they all represented nature as composed of such or similar substances.

But if men and animals and their several parts are natural phenomena, then the natural philosopher must take into consideration [not simply the ultimate substances from which they come, but also] their flesh, blood, bone, and all other homogeneous parts; [8] nor only these, but also the heterogeneous parts, such as face, hand, foot, and the like. He must examine how each of these comes to be what it is, and in virtue of what force. For to say what are the ultimate substances out of which an animal is formed, to state, for instance, that it is made of fire and water, is no more sufficient than would be a similar account of an inanimate object, such as a couch or the like. For we should not be content with saying merely that the couch was made of bronze or wood or whatever it might be, but should try to describe its design or mode of composition rather than its material; or, if we did deal with the material, it would at any rate be with the combination of material and form.[9] For a couch is such and such a form of this or that matter, or such and such a matter with this or that form; so that its shape and structure must be included in our description. For the formal nature is of much greater importance than the material nature. . . .

If now this something that makes up the form of a living being be the soul, or part of the soul, or something that without the soul cannot exist (as would seem to be the case, seeing at any rate that

---

[8] Aristotle thought of the animal body as built up of well distributed tissues of various kinds, which he called the homogeneous parts, and of combinations of these tissues in special organs, which he called the heterogeneous parts.

[9] For Aristotle's theory of form and matter see Introduction, p. xxiii ff. and *Metaphysics*, pp. 24-29.

when the soul departs, what is left is no longer a living animal, and that none of the parts remain what they were before, excepting in mere shape, like the animals that in the fable are turned into stone); if, I say, this be so, then it will come within the province of the natural philosopher to inform himself concerning the soul, and to treat of it, either in its entirety, or, at any rate, of that part of it which constitutes the essential character of an animal; and it will be his duty to say what this soul or this part of a soul is; and to discuss the attributes that attach to this essential character. . . . For just as human creations are the product of art, so living objects are manifestly the products of an analogous cause or principle, not external but internal, derived like the hot and the cold [and the other material elements of our bodies] from the environing universe.

And that the heaven, if it had an origin,[10] was evolved by such a cause, there is even more reason to believe, than that mortal animals so originated. For order and arrangement and constancy are much more plainly manifest in the celestial bodies than in our own frame; while change and chance are characteristic of the perishable things of earth. Yet there are some who, while they allow that animals were all generated by nature, nevertheless hold that the heaven was constructed to be what it is by chance and accident; the heaven, in which not the faintest sign of haphazard or of disorder is discernible!

Again, whenever there is plainly some final end to which a motion tends, should nothing stand in the way, we always say that such final end is the aim or purpose of the motion; and from this it is evident that there must be a something or other really existing, corresponding to what we call by the name of "nature." For a given germ does not give rise to any chance living being, nor spring from any chance one; but each germ springs from a definite parent and gives rise to a definite progeny. And thus it is the germ that is the ruling influence and fabricator of the offspring; for the offspring is that which in the course of nature will spring from it. . . .

[10] Aristotle himself believed that the heavens had no beginning but had existed from eternity.

There are then, as before said, two kinds of causation, and both of these must, so far as possible, be taken into account in explaining the works of nature. At any rate, it is plain that an attempt must be made to include them both; and that those who fail in this tell us in reality nothing about nature. For the main factor in the nature of an animal is much more the final cause than the necessary material. There are indeed passages in which even Empedocles hits upon this and, following the guidance of fact, finds himself constrained to speak of the final cause as constituting the essence and real nature of things. Such, for instance, is the case when he explains what a bone is. For he does not merely describe its material, and say it is this one element or those two or three elements or a compound of all the elements, but states the law or plan of their combination, and takes this to constitute the bone. As with a bone, so manifestly is it with the flesh and all other similar parts.

CHAPTER 4. Having laid this foundation, we proceed to the next topic, and by way of introduction we observe, that (Chapter 5) some members of the universe are ungenerated, imperishable, and eternal, while others are subject to generation and decay. The former are excellent beyond compare and divine, but less accessible to knowledge. The evidence that might throw light on them and the problems we long to solve respecting them is furnished but scantily by sensation; whereas respecting perishable plants and animals we have abundant information, living as we do in their midst, and ample data may be collected concerning all their various kinds, if only we are willing to take sufficient pains. Both departments, however, have their special charm. The scanty conceptions to which we can attain of celestial things give us, from their excellence, more pleasure than all our knowledge of the world in which we live; just as a half glimpse of persons that we love is more delightful than a leisurely view of other things, whatever their number and dimensions. On the other hand, in certitude and in completeness our knowledge of ter-

restrial things is better. Moreover, their greater nearness and affinity to us balances somewhat the loftier interest of the heavenly things that are the objects of the higher philosophy.

Having already treated of the celestial world, as far as our conjectures could reach,[11] we proceed to treat of animals, without, to the best of our ability, omitting any member of the kingdom, however ignoble. For if some have no graces to charm the sense, yet even these, by disclosing to intellectual perception the artistic spirit that designed them, give immense pleasure to all who can trace links of causation and are inclined to philosophy. Indeed, it would be strange if, while mimic representations of them are attractive, because they disclose the imitative skill of the painter or sculptor, the original realities themselves were not more interesting, to all at any rate who have eyes to discern the reason that presided over their formation. We therefore must not recoil with childish aversion from the examination of the humbler animals. Every realm of nature is marvelous: and as Heraclitus,[12] when the strangers who came to visit him found him warming himself at the fireplace in the kitchen, is reported to have bidden them not to hold back from entering, since even in that kitchen divinities were present, so we should venture on the study of every kind of animal without distaste; for each and all will reveal to us something natural and something beautiful. Absence of haphazard and adaptation of everything to a purpose are found in Nature's works to the highest degree, and the resultant end of her generations and combinations is a form of the beautiful.

If any person thinks the examination of the rest of the animal kingdom an unworthy task, he must hold in like scorn the study of man. For no one can look at the elements of the human frame—blood, flesh, bones, vessels, and the like—without much repugnance. But in every study, the examination of material elements and means

[11] Aristotle had written a treatise on astronomy, *On the Heavens*.
[12] The poet philosopher, Heraclitus, who lived at the beginning of the fifth century B.C., reverenced fire as the original substance from which everything else sprang.

is not to be regarded as final, but as preparatory to the conception of the total form. Thus the true object of architecture is not bricks or mortar or timber, but the house; and so the principal object of natural philosophy is not the material elements, but their combination and the totality of the form to which they contribute and independently of which they have no existence.

The course of the exposition must be, first, to state the attributes common to whole groups of animals and then to attempt to give their explanation. Many groups, as already noticed, present absolutely common attributes, that is to say, absolutely identical features, and absolutely identical organs—feet, feathers, scales, and the like; while in other groups the features and organs are only so far identical as that they are analogous. For instance, some groups have lungs, others have no lung, but an organ analogous to a lung in its place; some have blood, others have no blood, but a fluid analogous to blood and with the same office. To treat of the common attributes in connection with each individual group would involve, as already suggested, useless repetition. So much for this topic.

Every instrument and every bodily member serves some partial end, that is to say, performs some special action, and so the whole body must be destined to minister to some fuller sphere of action. Thus the saw is made for sawing, for this is its function, and not sawing for the saw. Similarly, the body must somehow or other be made for the soul, and each part of it for some subordinate function, to which it is adapted.

We have, then, first to describe the common functions, common, that is, to the whole animal kingdom, or to certain large groups, or to members of a species. In other words, we have to describe the features common to all animals, and to assemblages like the bird class of closely allied groups differentiated into grades, and to groups like Man not differentiated into subordinate groups. In the first case the common attributes may be called analogous, in the second generic, in the third specific.

When one function is subservient to another, a like relation manifestly obtains between the organs which discharge these functions; and similarly if one function is the end of another, their respective organs will stand to each other in the same relation. . . .

Instances of what I mean by functions are reproduction, growth, copulation, waking, sleep, locomotion, and other similar vital actions. Instances of what I mean by parts are nose, eye, face, and other so-called members or limbs, and also the more elementary parts of which these are made. So much for the method to be pursued. Let us now try to set forth the causes of all vital phenomena, whether universal or particular, and in so doing let us follow that order of exposition, which conforms, as we have indicated, to the order of nature.

BOOK II

Character and functions of the digestive organs, blood, brain, bones, and sense organs, especially in man.

CHAPTER 2. Of the homogeneous parts of animals, some are soft and fluid, others hard and solid; and of the former some are fluid permanently, others only so long as they are in the living body.

Among the fluids are blood, serum, lard, suet, marrow, semen, bile, milk when present, flesh, and their various analogues. For the parts enumerated are not to be found in all animals, some animals having only parts analogous to them. Of the hard and solid homogeneous parts, bone, fish-spine, sinew, blood vessel, are examples. . . .

The first question to be asked is what are the causes to which these homogeneous parts owe their existence? The causes are various; and this whether the parts be solid or fluid. Thus one set of homogeneous parts provide the material out of which the heterogeneous parts are formed; for each separate organ is constructed of bones

sinews, flesh and the like, which are either essential elements in its formation or contribute to the proper discharge of its function. A second set of parts are the nutriment of the first, and are invariably fluid, for all growth occurs at the expense of fluid matter; while a third set are the residue of the second. Such, for instance, are the feces and, in animals that have a bladder, the urine; the former being the dregs of the solid nutriment, the latter of the fluid.

Even the individual homogeneous parts show variations, which are intended in each case to render them more serviceable for their purpose. The variations of the blood may be selected to illustrate this. For different bloods differ in their degrees of thinness or thickness, of clearness or turbidity, of coldness or heat; and this whether we compare the bloods from different parts of the same individual or the bloods of different animals. For in the individual, all the differences just enumerated distinguish the blood of the upper from that of the lower half of the body; and in considering classes, we find one group of animals blooded, while another has no blood, but only something resembling it in its place. As regards the results of such differences, the thicker and the hotter blood is, the more conducive is it to strength, while in proportion to its thinness and its coldness is its suitability for sensation and intelligence. A like distinction exists also in the fluids which are analogous to blood. This explains how it is that bees and other similar creatures are of a more intelligent nature than many blooded animals; and why among blooded animals those are the most intelligent whose blood is thin and cold. Noblest of all are those whose blood is hot and at the same time thin and clear. For such are suited alike for the development of courage and of wisdom. The upper parts too of a body are superior in these respects to the lower, the male superior to the female, and the right side to the left.[1]

As with the blood, so also with the other parts, homogeneous and

[1] Aristotle, like Plato, believed that as a universal principle the upper was by nature superior to the lower, the right to the left, and the front to the back. He tried to prove the truth of this belief by observed facts, whenever possible.

heterogeneous alike. For here also such variations as occur must be held either to be related to the essential constitution and mode of life of the several animals, or, in other cases, to be merely matters of slightly better or slightly worse. Two animals, for instance, may have eyes, but in one of these they may be of fluid consistency, while in the other they are hard; and in one there may be eyelids, in the other no such appendages. In such a case, the fluid consistency and the presence of eyelids, which are intended to add to the accuracy of vision, are differences of degree.

As to why all animals must of necessity have blood or something of a similar character, and what the nature of blood may be, these are matters which can only be considered when we have first discussed hot and cold. The natural properties of many substances are referable to these two elementary principles; and it is a matter of frequent dispute what animals or what parts of animals are hot and what cold. For some maintain that water animals are hotter than such as live on land, asserting that their natural heat counterbalances the coldness of their medium; and, again, that bloodless animals are hotter than those with blood, and females than males. . . . If there is this endless disputing about heat and cold, which of all things that affect our senses are the most distinct, what are we to think as to our other sensory impressions?

The explanation of the difficulty appears to be that the term "hotter" is used in several senses; so that different statements, though in verbal contradiction with each other, may yet all be more or less true. There ought, then, to be some clear understanding as to the sense in which natural substances are to be termed hot or cold, solid or fluid. For it is plain that these are properties on which even life and death are largely dependent, and that they are, moreover, the causes of sleep and waking, of maturity and old age, of health and disease; while no similar importance belongs to roughness and smoothness, to heaviness and lightness, nor in short to any other like properties of matter. . . .

Is then the term hot used in one sense or many? [2] To answer this we must ascertain what is thought to be the special effect of a hotter substance, and if there are several such effects, how many these may be. A body is in one sense said to be hotter than another if it imparts a greater amount of heat to an object in contact with it. In a second sense, it is said to be hotter if it causes a keener sensation when touched, especially if the sensation is attended with pain. This criterion, however, would seem sometimes to be a false one; for occasionally it is the idiosyncrasy of an individual that causes the sensation to be painful to him. Again, when there are two hot masses of one and the same substance, the larger is said to have more heat than the smaller. Again, of any two things, that one is called the hotter which takes the longer time in cooling, as also we call something that is rapidly heated hotter than that which is long about it; as though the rapidity implied nearness and thus similarity of nature, while the want of rapidity implied distance and thus dissimilarity of nature. The term hotter is used in all the various senses mentioned, and perhaps in still more.

Now it is impossible for one body to be hotter than another in all these different fashions at once. Boiling water, for instance, though it is more scalding than flame, yet has no power of burning or melting combustible or fusible matter, while flame has. So, again, boiling water is hotter than a small fire, and yet gets cold much more rapidly and completely. For in fact fire never becomes cold, whereas water invariably does so. . . . Iron again and stones and other similar bodies are much longer in getting heated than water, but when once heated burn other substances with a much greater intensity.

Another distinction is this. In some of the bodies which are called hot the heat is derived from without, while in others it belongs to the bodies themselves; and it makes a most important difference whether

[2] The following passage is included in our selections, because it shows strikingly the difficulties under which an ancient scientist labored, who tried like Aristotle to be exact in his observations almost two thousand years before the invention of the thermometer made it possible to measure and compare heat by a single precise and universal standard.

the heat has the former or the latter origin. For to call that one of two bodies the hotter which is possessed of heat, we may almost say accidentally and not of its own essence, is very much the same thing as if, finding that some man in a fever was a musician, one were to say that musicians are hotter than healthy men. As between that which is hot in itself and that which is hot by accident, the former is the slower to cool, while not rarely the latter is hotter to the touch. The former again is the more burning of the two—flame, for instance, as compared with boiling water—while the latter, as boiling water, which is hot by accident, is the more heating to the touch. From all this it is clear that it is no simple matter to decide which of two bodies is the hotter. For the first may be hotter in one sense, the second hotter in another. . . .

In conclusion then, seeing that the terms hot and hotter are used in many different senses and that no one substance can be hotter than others in all these senses, we should, when we attribute this character to an object, add such further statements as that this substance is hotter in itself, though that other is often hotter by accident; or again, that this substance is potentially hot, that other actually so; or again, that this substance is hotter in the sense of causing a greater feeling of heat when touched, while that other is hotter in the sense of producing flame and burning. The term hot being used in all these various senses, it is plain to be seen that the term cold will also be used with like ambiguity. . . .

CHAPTER 3. Now since everything that grows must take nourishment, and nutriment in all cases consists of fluid and solid substances, and since it is by the force of heat that these are digested [3] and changed, it follows that all living things, animals and plants alike, must on this account, if on no other, have a natural source of heat. This natural heat, moreover, must belong to many parts, seeing

[3] Digestion, according to the old Greek physician, Hippocrates, whose opinion Aristotle adopted, was a process of cooking. In fact, the same Greek word, "pepsis," was used for both cooking and digestion. Hence our pepsin and dyspepsia.

that the organs by which the various changes in the food are effected are many in number. For first of all there is the mouth and the parts inside the mouth, on which the first share in the duty clearly devolves, in such animals at least as live on food which requires crushing. The mouth, however, does not actually digest the food, but merely facilitates digestion; for the breaking up of the food into small bits facilitates the action of heat upon it. After the mouth come the upper and the lower abdominal cavities, and here it is that digestion is effected through natural heat.

Again, just as there is a channel for the admission of the undigested food into the stomach, namely the mouth, and in some animals the so-called oesophagus, which is continuous with the mouth and reaches to the stomach, so must there also be other and more numerous channels by which the digested food or nutriment shall pass out of the stomach and intestines and into the body at large, and to which these cavities shall serve as a kind of food trough. For plants get their food from the earth by means of their roots; and this food is already prepared when taken in, which is the reason why plants produce no excrement, the earth and its heat serving them in the stead of a stomach. But animals, with scarcely an exception, and notably all such animals as are capable of locomotion, are provided with a stomachal sac, which is, as it were, an internal substitute for the earth. They must therefore have some instrument which shall correspond to the roots of plants, with which they may absorb their food from this sac, so that the proper end of the successive stages of digestion may at last be attained. The mouth, its duty done, passes over the food to the stomach, and there must then necessarily be something to take it in turn from there. This something is furnished by the blood vessels, which run throughout the whole extent of the mesentery from its lowest part right up to the stomach. A description of these will be found in the treatises on anatomy and natural history.[4]

---

[4] All we have left of Aristotle's special treatises on these subjects, beside the present work, is his *History of Animals,* and his two shorter treatises on *Motion and Progression of Animals.*

Now as there is a receptacle for the entire material taken as food, so there is also a receptacle, namely the blood vessels, which serve as such for the blood. It is plain that this blood must be the final nutritive material in such animals as have it; while in bloodless animals the same is true of the fluid which represents the blood. This explains why the blood diminishes in quantity when no food is taken, and increases when much is consumed, and also why it becomes healthy and unhealthy according as the food is of one or another character. These facts, then, and others of a like kind, make it quite plain that the purpose of the blood in animals that have it is to provide for the nutrition of the body. . . .

[*Aristotle describes briefly the fibers in blood that cause coagulation and then goes on to speak of body fats and marrow, all forms, he says, of hardened, digested blood.*]

CHAPTER 7. From the marrow we pass on in natural sequence to the brain. For there are some who think that the brain itself consists of marrow, and that it forms the commencement of that substance, because they see that the spinal marrow is continuous with it. In reality the two may be said to be utterly opposite to each other in character. For of all the parts of the body there is none so cold as the brain; [5] whereas the marrow is of a hot nature, as is plainly shown by its sheeny appearance, and by its fatness. Indeed this is the very reason why the brain and spinal marrow are continuous with each other. For wherever there is excessive action of any part, nature so contrives as to set by it another part with an excess of contrary action so that the excesses of the two may counterbalance each other. Now that the marrow is hot is clearly shown by many indications. The coldness of the brain too is manifest enough. For in the

[5] Aristotle's chief errors in his observations of the brain, namely, that it was cold to the touch and contained no blood, may be due to the fact that the brains he examined were mostly those of cold-blooded animals, fish, tortoises, etc. He may never have been able to dissect the brain of a warm-blooded animal, freshly killed. The blood vessels in the brain are also very minute. They might have seemed insignificant to him

first place it is cold even to the touch; and secondly, of all the fluids in the body it is the one that has the least blood; for in fact it has no blood at all in its proper substance. . . . Yet the purpose of its presence in animals is no less than the preservation of the whole body. How it effects this will be seen from what follows.

Some writers assert that the soul is fire or some such force.[6] This, however, is but a rough and inaccurate assertion; and it would perhaps be better to say that the soul is lodged in some substance of a fiery character. The reason for this being so is that of all substances there is none so suitable for ministering to the operations of the soul as that which is possessed of heat. For the functions of the soul are nutrition and motion,[7] and it is by heat that these are most readily effected. To say, however, that the soul is fire is much the same thing as to confound the auger or the saw with the carpenter or his craft, simply because the work is wrought by the two in conjunction. So far, then, this much is plain, that all animals must necessarily have a certain amount of heat.

But as all influences require to be counterbalanced so that they may be reduced to moderation and brought to the mean (for in the mean, and not in either extreme, lies the true and rational position), nature has contrived the brain as a counterpoise to the region of the heart with its contained heat, and has given it to animals to moderate the latter, compounding it of earth and water.[8] For this reason it is that every blooded animal has a brain; whereas no bloodless creature has such an organ, unless indeed it be, as in the octopus, by analogy. For where there is no blood, there in consequence is but little heat. The brain then tempers the heat and seething of the heart. In order, however, that it may not itself be absolutely without heat but may have a moderate amount, branches run from both blood vessels, that

[6] Democritus, a materialist philosopher of the generation before Aristotle, famed for his authorship of the atomic theory, had some such view of the soul.

[7] Aristotle is here speaking of what he called the animal soul.

[8] This means that though Aristotle made the heart the organ of sense and feeling, he yet made it dependent for healthy functioning on the cooling and moderating influence of the brain.

is to say, from the great vein and from what is called the aorta, and end in the membrane which surrounds the brain; while at the same time, in order to prevent any injury to the brain from the heat, these encompassing vessels, instead of being few and large, are numerous and small, and their blood scanty and clear, instead of being abundant and thick. . . .

It is the brain again, or, in animals that have no brains, the part analogous to it, which is the cause of sleep. For either by chilling the blood that streams upwards after food or by some other similar influences, it produces heaviness in the region in which it lies (which is the reason why drowsy persons hang the head), and causes the heat to escape downwards in company with the blood. It is the accumulation of this in excess in the lower part that produces complete sleep, taking away the power of standing upright from such animals as are able to assume that posture; and from the rest the power of holding up the head. These, however, are matters which have been separately considered in the treatises on sensation and on sleep.[9]

That the brain is a compound of earth and water is shown by what occurs when it is boiled. For when so treated it turns hard and solid, inasmuch as the water is evaporated by the heat and leaves the earthy part behind. The same occurs when beans and other fruits are boiled, for these also are hardened by the process, because the water which enters into their composition is driven off and leaves the earth, which is their main constituent, behind.

Of all animals man has the largest brain in proportion to his size; and it is larger in men than in women.[10] This is because the region of the heart and of the lung is hotter and richer in blood in man than in any other animal; and in men than in women. . . .

[9] Two of Aristotle's shorter treatises deal with the phenomena of sensation and of sleep.

[10] Man's brain is proportionately larger than that of almost all animals but not apparently larger than a woman's. Man is not so hot a creature as most birds or as many other mammals, but Aristotle, as we know, had no apparatus with which to measure temperatures exactly.

[In chapter 8 Aristotle discusses briefly flesh, which he calls the organ of touch, and the shells of hard-shelled animals.]

CHAPTER 9. There is a resemblance between the systems of bones and of blood vessels; for each has a central part in which it begins, and each forms a continuous whole. For no bone in the body exists as a separate individuality in itself, but each is either a portion of what may be considered a continuous whole or at any rate is linked with the rest by contact and by attachments; so that nature may use adjoining bones either as though they were actually continuous and formed a single bone, or, for purposes of flexion, as though they were two and distinct. Similarly, no blood vessel has in itself a separate individuality; but they all form parts of one whole. An isolated bone, if such there were, would in the first place be unable to perform the office for the sake of which bones exist; for if it were discontinuous and separated from the rest by a gap, it would be perfectly unable to produce either movement or extension; not only so, but it would actually be injurious, acting like a thorn or an arrow lodged in the flesh. Similarly, if a blood vessel were isolated, and not connected with the vascular center, it would be unable to retain the blood within it in a proper state. For it is the warmth derived from this center that hinders the blood from coagulating; indeed the blood, when withdrawn from its influence, actually becomes putrid.

Now the center or origin of the blood vessels is the heart, and the center or origin of the bones in all animals that have bones is what is called the spine. With this all the other bones of the body are in continuity; for it is the spine that keeps the body extended and straight. But since it is absolutely necessary that the body of an animal shall bend during locomotion, this spine, while it is one in virtue of the continuity of its parts, yet by its division into vertebrae is made to consist of many segments. It is from the spine that the bones of the limbs proceed, and with it they are continuous in those animals that have limbs. These bones form joints at the place where the limbs allow bending, being fastened together by sinews, and

having their extremities adapted to each other, either by the one being hollowed and the other rounded, or by both being hollowed and including between them a knucklebone as a connecting bolt, so as to allow of flexion and extension. For without some such arrangement these movements would be utterly impossible or at any rate would be performed with great difficulty. There are some joints, again, in which the lower end of one bone and the upper end of the other are alike in shape. In these cases the bones are bound together by sinews, and cartilaginous pieces are interposed in the joint, to serve as a kind of padding and to prevent the two extremities from grating against each other.

Round about the bones and attached to them by thin fibrous bands, grow the fleshy parts, for the sake of which the bones themselves exist. For just as an artist, when he is molding an animal out of clay or other soft substance, takes first some solid object as a basis, and round this molds the clay, so also has nature acted in fashioning the animal body out of flesh. Thus we find all the fleshy parts, with one exception, supported by bones, which serve, when the parts are organs of motion, to facilitate flexion and, when the parts are motionless, to act as a protection. The ribs, for example, which enclose the chest are intended to ensure the safety of the heart and neighboring viscera. The exception, of which mention has been made, is the belly. The walls of this are in all animals devoid of bones, in order that there may be no hindrance to the expansion which necessarily occurs in this part after a meal, or, in females, any interference with the growth of the embryo, which is lodged here. . . .

CHAPTER 10. Let us now make, as it were, a fresh beginning, and consider the heterogeneous parts,[11] taking those first which are first in importance. . . . Plants, inasmuch as they are without locomotion, present no great variety in their heterogeneous parts.

[11] That is, the separate organs.

For where the functions are but few, few also are the organs required to perform them. The organization of plants is a matter then for separate consideration. Animals, however, that not only live but feel, present a much greater multiformity of parts, and this diversity is greater in some animals than in others, being most varied in those to whose share has fallen not mere life but life of high degree. Now such an animal is man. For of all living beings with which we are acquainted, man alone partakes of the divine, or at any rate partakes of it in a fuller measure than the rest. For this reason then, and also because his external parts and their forms are more familiar to us than those of other animals, we must speak of man first; and this the more fitly, because in him alone do the natural parts hold their natural position; his upper part being turned towards that which is upper in the universe. For of all animals man alone stands erect.

In man then the head is destitute of flesh; this being the necessary consequence of what has already been stated concerning the brain. There are indeed some who hold that the life of man would be longer than it is were his head more abundantly furnished with flesh; and they account for the absence of this substance by saying that it is intended to ensure the perfection of sensation. For the brain they assert to be the organ of sensation; [12] and sensation, they say, cannot penetrate to parts that are too thickly covered with flesh. But neither part of this statement is true. On the contrary, were the region of the brain thickly covered with flesh, the real purpose for which animals are provided with a brain would be directly thwarted. For the brain would itself be heated to excess and so quite unable to cool any other part. As to the latter half of their statement, the brain cannot be the cause of any of the sensations, seeing that it is itself as utterly without feeling as any one of the excretions.[13]

These writers see that certain of the senses are located in the head,

[12] Plato had said this in his dialogue of *Timaeus,* and so before him had the philosopher-scientist Democritus and the physician Hippocrates.

[13] Aristotle had vivisected a chameleon, as he tells us in his *History of Animals,* II, ii. In that operation he may have noticed that the brain showed no sign of flinching from the knife.

and are unable to discern any other reason for this; they see also that the brain is the most peculiar of all the animal organs; and out of these facts they form an argument by which they link sensation and brain together. It has, however, already been clearly set forth in the treatise on sensation that it is the region of the heart that constitutes the center of sensation. There also it was stated that two of the senses, namely touch and taste, are manifestly directly dependent on the heart; and that as regards the other three, namely hearing, sight, and the centrally placed sense of smell, it is the character of their sense organs which causes them to be lodged as a rule in the head. Vision is so placed in all animals. . . . In many animals hearing too, as well as vision is lodged in the region of the head. Nor is this without a rational explanation. For what is called the empty space is full of air,[14] and the organ of hearing is, as we say, formed of air. Now there are channels which lead from the eyes to the blood vessels that surround the brain;[15] and similarly there is a channel which leads back again from each ear and connects it with the hinder part of the head. But no part that is without blood is endowed with sensation, as neither is the blood itself, but only certain parts formed of blood. . . .

CHAPTER 13. Men and birds and quadrupeds, viviparous and oviparous alike,[16] have their eyes protected by lids. In the vivipara there are two of these, and both are used by these animals not only

[14] Aristotle believed with Hippocrates that there was an empty space behind the brain in the skulls of all animals. There is actually some such space in the skulls of fishes and reptiles.

[15] By these "channels" Aristotle probably meant the openings or passages through which he thought the sense organ communicated with the membrane lining the inner brain cavity. From this membrane, he believed, ran the blood vessels connecting it with the heart, where the sensations were felt. The nervous system was yet to be discovered. Nerves had not yet been distinguished from tendons and ligaments.

[16] Viviparous animals, or the vivipara, are those who give birth to their young only after they have been fully formed within the mother's body. The ovipara lay their young as still undeveloped embryos in eggs, within which they grow until they are sufficiently developed to break the shell and emerge.

in closing the eye, but also in the act of blinking; whereas the oviparous quadrupeds,[17] and the heavy-bodied birds,[18] as well as some others, use only the lower lid to close the eye. Other birds blink by means of a membrane connected with the corner of the eye. The reason for the eyes being thus protected is that nature has made them of fluid consistency, in order to ensure keenness of vision. For had they been covered with hard skin, they would, it is true, have been less liable to get injured by anything falling into them from without, but they would not have been sharp-sighted. It is then to ensure keenness of vision that the skin over the pupil is fine and delicate, while the lids are super-added as a protection from injury. It is as a still further safeguard that all these animals blink, and man most of all. This action (which is not performed from deliberate intention but from a natural instinct) serves to keep objects from falling into the eyes and is more frequent in man than in the rest of the animals because of the greater delicacy of his skin. These lids are made of a roll of skin; and it is because they are made of skin and contain no flesh that neither they, nor the similarly constructed prepuce, unite again when once cut.

Oviparous quadrupeds do not blink in like manner as the birds; for living as they do on the ground, they are free from the necessity of having eyes of fluid consistency and of keen sight, whereas these are essential requisites for such birds as have to use their eyes at long distances. This too explains why birds with talons that have to search for prey by eye from aloft, and therefore soar to greater heights than other birds, are sharp-sighted; while common fowls and the like that live on the ground and are not made for flight have no such keenness of vision. For there is nothing in their mode of life which imperatively requires it. . . .

Fishes however have eyes of a fluid consistency. For all animals that move much about have to use their vision at considerable distances. If they live on land, the air in which they move is transparent enough.

---

[17] That is, crocodiles and frogs.
[18] Among these Aristotle classes partridges, quails. pheasants, and common fowls.

But the water in which fishes live is a hindrance to sharp sight, though it has this advantage over the air, that it does not contain so many objects to knock against the eyes. The risk of collision being thus small, nature, who makes nothing in vain, has given no eyelids to fishes, while to counterbalance the opacity of the water she has made their eyes of fluid consistency. . . .

[*In chapters 14 and 15 Aristotle describes the location and function of hair, eyebrows, and eyelashes.*]

CHAPTER 16. In most viviparous quadrupeds, there is no great variety in the forms of the organ of smell. In those of them, however, whose jaws project forwards and taper to a narrow end, so as to form what is called a snout, the nostrils are placed in this projection, there being no other available place; while in the rest there is a more definite demarcation between nostrils and jaws.

But in no animal is this part so peculiar as in the elephant,[19] where it attains an extraordinary size and strength. For the elephant uses its nostril as a hand, this being the instrument with which it conveys food, fluid and solid alike, to its mouth. With it too it tears up trees, coiling it round their trunks. In fact, it applies it generally to the purposes of a hand. For the elephant has the double character of a land animal and one that lives in swamps. Seeing then that it has to get food in the water and yet must necessarily breathe, inasmuch as it is a land animal and has blood; seeing also that its excessive weight prevents it from passing rapidly from water to land, as some other blooded vivipara that breathe can do, it becomes necessary that it shall be suited alike for life in the water and for life on dry land. Then just as divers are sometimes provided with instruments for respiration, through which they can draw air from above the water and thus remain for a long time under the sea,[20] so also have elephants

[19] It is doubtful whether Aristotle had ever actually seen an elephant. The information he displays here might all have come from travelers' reports.
[20] An interesting reference to divers' apparatus in Aristotle's time. In another work he speaks of something like a diver's bell.

been furnished by nature with their lengthened nostril; and when-ever they have to traverse the water, they lift this up above the surface and breathe through it. For the elephant's proboscis, as already said, is a nostril.

Now it would have been impossible for this nostril to have the form of a proboscis, had it been hard and incapable of bending. For its very length would then have prevented the animal from supply-ing itself with food, being as great an impediment as the horns of certain oxen that are said to be obliged to walk backwards while they are grazing.[21] It is therefore soft and flexible and, being such, is made, in addition to its own proper functions, to serve the office of the forefeet; nature in this following her wonted plan of using one and the same part for several purposes. For in quadrupeds with toes or fingers the forefeet are not intended merely to support the body but also to serve as hands. But in elephants, though they must be reckoned as having toes, since their foot has neither cloven nor solid hoof, the forefeet, owing to the great size and weight of the body, are reduced to the condition of mere supports; and indeed their slow motion and unfitness for bending make them useless for any other purpose.

A nostril then is given to the elephant for respiration, as to every other animal that has a lung, and is lengthened out and endowed with its power of coiling, because the animal has to remain for consider-able periods of time in the water and is unable to pass thence to dry ground with any rapidity. But as the feet are shorn of their full office, this same part is also, as before said, made by nature to supply their place, and give such help as otherwise would be rendered by them.

As to other blooded animals, the birds, the snakes, and the ovip-arous quadrupeds, in all of them there are the nostril-holes, placed in front of the mouth; but in none are there any distinctly formed

[21] The historian Herodotus was probably Aristotle's authority for this story. In a part of Africa, he had said, there were oxen whose horns were bent so as to stick in the ground in front of them, if they walked forward while grazing. Herodotus, IV, 183.

nostrils, nothing in fact which can be called nostrils except from a functional point of view. A bird, at any rate, has nothing that can properly be called a nose. For its so-called beak is a substitute for jaws. The reason for this is to be found in the natural conformation of birds. For they are winged bipeds; and this makes it necessary that their head and neck shall be of light weight, just as it makes it necessary that their breastbone shall be narrowed. The beak, therefore, with which they are provided is formed of a bone-like substance, in order that it may serve as a weapon as well as for nutritive purposes, but is made of narrow dimensions to suit the small size of the head. In this beak are placed the olfactory passages. But there are no nostrils; for such could not possibly be placed there. . . .

The use of the lips in all animals except man is to preserve and guard the teeth; and thus it is that the distinctness with which the lips are formed is in direct proportion to the degree of nicety and perfection with which the teeth are fashioned. In man the lips are soft and flesh-like and capable of separating from each other. Their purpose, as in other animals, is to guard the teeth, but they are more especially intended to serve a higher office, contributing in common with other parts to man's faculty of speech. For just as nature has made man's tongue unlike that of other animals, and, in accordance with what I have said is not her uncommon practice, has used it for two distinct operations, namely for the perception of taste and for speech, so also has she acted with regard to the lips, and made them serve both for speech and for the protection of the teeth. For vocal speech consists of combinations of the letters, and most of these it would be impossible to pronounce were the lips not moist, nor the tongue such as it is. . . . For some letters are formed by closures of the lips and others by applications of the tongue. . . .

[Chapter 17 contains some account of the tongue and mouth in birds, snakes, crocodiles, and fishes.]

BOOK III

Character and functions of other parts of the head and trunk—teeth, mouth, heart, lungs, liver, intestines, etc.

CHAPTER 1.   We have next to consider the teeth, and with these the mouth, that is, the cavity which they enclose and form. The teeth have one invariable office, namely, the crushing of food; but besides this general function they have other special ones, which differ in different species. Thus in some animals the teeth serve as weapons; but this with a distinction. For there are offensive weapons and there are defensive weapons; and while in some animals, as the wild carnivora, the teeth answer both purposes, in many others, both wild and domesticated, they serve only for defense. In man the teeth are admirably constructed for their general function, the front ones being sharp, so as to cut the food into bits, and the hinder ones broad and flat, so as to grind it to a pulp; while between these and separating them are the dog teeth, which, in accordance with the rule that the mean partakes of both extremes, share in the characters of those on either side, being broad in one part but sharp in another. Similar distinctions of shape appear in the teeth of other animals, with the exception of those whose teeth are one and all of the sharp kind. In man, however, the number and character of the teeth have been mainly determined by the requirements of speech. For the front teeth of man contribute in many ways to the formation of letter sounds.

In some animals, however, the teeth, as already said, serve merely for the crushing of food. When, besides this, they serve as offensive and defensive weapons, they may either be formed into tusks, as, for instance, is the case in swine, or may be sharp-pointed and interlock with those of the opposite jaw, in which case the animal is said

to be saw-toothed. The explanation of this latter arrangement is as follows. The strength of such an animal is in its teeth, and the efficacy of these depends on their sharpness. In order then to prevent their getting blunted by mutual friction, such of them as serve for weapons fit into each other's interspaces and are so kept in proper condition. No animal that is saw-toothed is at the same time furnished with tusks. For nature never makes anything superfluous or in vain. She therefore gives tusks to such animals as strike in fighting, and serrated teeth to such as bite. Sows, for instance, have no tusks, and accordingly sows bite instead of striking. . . .

In birds, the mouth consists of what is called the beak, which in them is a substitute for lips and teeth. This beak shows variations in harmony with the functions and protective purposes which it serves. Thus in those birds that are called crooked-clawed, it is invariably hooked, inasmuch as these birds are carnivorous and eat no kind of vegetable food whatever. For this form renders it serviceable to them in obtaining the mastery over their prey, and is better suited for deeds of violence than any other. Moreover, as their weapons of offense consist of this beak and their claws, the latter also are more crooked in them than in the generality of birds. Similarly, in every other kind of bird the beak is suited to its mode of life. Thus in woodpeckers it is hard and strong, as also in crows and birds of crow-like habit, while in the smaller birds it is delicate, so as to be of use in collecting seeds and picking up minute animals. In such birds, again, as eat herbage, and such as live on the edges of marshes —those, for example, that swim and have webbed feet—the bill is broad or adapted in some other way to their mode of life. For a broad bill enables a bird to dig into the ground with ease, as, among quadrupeds, does the broad snout of a pig, an animal which, like the birds in question, lives on roots. Moreover, in these root-eating birds and in some others of like habits of life, the tips of the bill end in hard points, which give them additional facility in dealing with herbaceous food. . . .

[*Chapters 2 and 3 describe animal horns and their use and the various organs of the throat, windpipe, larynx, oesophagus, etc.*]

CHAPTER 4.   In all blooded animals there is a heart, and the reason for this has already been given. For evidently such animals must necessarily have blood. And, as the blood is fluid, it is also necessary that there shall be a receptacle for it; and it is clearly to meet this requirement that nature has devised blood vessels. These, again, must necessarily have one primary source. For it is preferable that there shall be one such, when possible, rather than several. This primary source of the vessels is the heart.[1] For the vessels clearly are from it, and not through it. Moreover, since it is homogeneous, it has the character of a blood vessel. Again, its position is that of a primary or dominating part. For nature, when no other important purpose stands in her way, places the more honorable part in the more honorable position; and the heart lies about the center of the body, but rather in its upper than its lower half and also more in front than behind. . . .

From this it is quite evident that the heart is a part of the vessels and their origin; and for this it is well suited by its structure. For its central part consists of a thick and hollow body and is full of blood, while its wall is thick, that it may serve to protect the source of heat. For here and here alone in all the viscera and, in fact, in all the body, there is blood without blood vessels, the blood elsewhere being always contained within vessels. Nor is this but consistent with reason. For the blood is conveyed into the vessels from the heart, but none passes into the heart from without. For in itself it is the origin and fountain or primary receptacle of the blood. It is, however, from dissections

[1] From this passage one may learn Aristotle's theory of the heart as the seething fountain source of blood, the place where blood is made and from which it is poured as needed into the veins, arteries, and other vessels, through which it is distributed to feed all parts of the body. No blood ever comes into the heart from without. Neither he nor anyone before the 17th century worked out the principle of the circulation of the blood.

and from observations on the process of development that the truth of these statements receives its clearest demonstration.[2] For the heart is the first of all parts to be formed; and no sooner is it formed than it contains blood.

Moreover, the motions of pain and pleasure, and generally of all sensation, plainly start from the heart, and find in it their ultimate termination. This, indeed, reason would lead us to expect. For the starting point must, whenever possible, be one; and of all places the best suited for a starting place is the center. For the center is one and is equally, or almost equally within the reach of every part. Again, as neither the blood itself nor any part which is bloodless is endowed with sensation, it is plain that that part which first has blood and which holds it, as it were, in a receptacle, must be the primary source of sensation. And that this part is the heart is not only a rational inference but is also evident to the senses. For no sooner is the embryo formed than its heart is seen in motion like a living creature, and this before any of the other parts, as though it were the starting point of life in all animals that have blood. A further evidence of the truth of what has been stated is the fact that no blooded animal is without a heart. For the primary source of blood must of necessity be present in them all. . . .

The apex of the heart is pointed and more solid than the rest of the organ. It lies against the breast and entirely in the front part of the body, in order to prevent that region from getting chilled. For in all animals there is comparatively little flesh over the breast, whereas there is a more abundant covering of that substance on the back surface, so that the heat has in the back a sufficient amount of protection. In all animals but man the heart is placed in the center of the pectoral region; but in man it inclines a little toward the left, so that it may counter-balance the chilliness of that side.

The heart again is abundantly supplied with sinews, as might

---

[2] Aristotle had observed the growth of the heart in his first-hand studies of the development of the embryo of the chick.

reasonably be expected. For the motions of the body commence from the heart, and are brought about by contraction and relaxation. The heart therefore, which, as already said, is as it were a living creature inside its possessor, requires some such subservient and strengthening parts.

In no animals does the heart contain a bone, certainly in none of those that we have ourselves inspected, with the exception of the horse and a certain kind of ox.[3] In these exceptional cases, the heart, owing to its large bulk, is provided with a bone as a support; just as the bones serve as supports for the body generally.

In animals of great size the heart has three cavities; in smaller animals it has two; and in all has at least one.[4] The reason for this, as already stated, is that there must be some place in the heart to serve as a receptacle for the first blood, which, as has been mentioned more than once, is formed in this organ. But inasmuch as the main blood vessels are two in number, namely the so-called great vein and the aorta, each of which is the origin of other vessels; inasmuch, moreover, as these two vessels present differences, hereafter to be discussed, when compared with each other,[5] it is of advantage that they also shall themselves have distinct origins. This advantage will be obtained if each side have its own blood, and the blood of one side be kept separate from that of the other. . . .

[In chapter 5 Aristotle describes the distribution of blood through the body like that of water, carried by a network of channels from a central fountain through a garden.]

[3] In some large mammals, such as the ox, it is not uncommon to find ossification in the heart. In a horse such a thing sometimes appears as a sign of old age.

[4] Aristotle seems to have taken the right auricle of the heart as a part of the "great vein," and so to have counted only three cavities in the heart proper. The mere size of the animal has really nothing to do with this number. The mouse's heart has as many cavities as the ox's. But smaller reptiles and aquatic animals do get on with but three or two.

[5] Elsewhere Aristotle notes that the aorta and its branches, the other arteries, have heavier walls and contain blood of a brighter and lighter color than the veins. The "great vein," he seems to have thought, nourished the right side of the body and the aorta the left.

CHAPTER 6. The lung is an organ found in all the animals of a certain class, because they live on land. For there must of necessity be some or other means of cooling down the heat of the body; [6] and in blooded animals, as they are of an especially hot nature, the cooling agency must be an external one; whereas in the bloodless kinds the innate spirit is sufficient of itself for the purpose. The external cooling agent must be either air or water. In fishes the agent is water. Fishes therefore never have a lung, but have gills in its place, as was stated in the treatise on respiration.[7] But animals that breathe are cooled by air. These therefore are all provided with a lung.

All land animals breathe, and even some water animals, such as the whale,[8] the dolphin, and the spouting cetacea. For many animals lie halfway between terrestrial and aquatic. Some that are terrestrial and that breathe in air are nevertheless of such a bodily constitution that they abide for the most time in the water; and some that are aquatic partake so largely of the land character that respiration is for them an essential condition of life.

The organ of respiration is the lung. This derives its motion from the heart; but it is its own large size and spongy texture that afford amplitude of space for the entrance of the breath. For when the lung rises up the breath streams in, and is again expelled when the lung contracts. It has been stated, but incorrectly, that it is to the lung that the beating of the heart is due. That this is not so is shown by the phenomenon of palpitation, which occurs, I may say, in man alone, inasmuch as man alone is influenced by hope and expectation. Again, in most animals the heart is at a distance from the lung and placed above it, so that its beating can in no degree be brought about by the lung. . . .

[6] With the science of chemistry and chemical apparatus still practically non-existent, Aristotle could not possibly have understood the function of the lungs, as we do today. To him they were simply an organ to cool the blood vessels and the body at large, as the brain cooled the sense organs and the heart.

[7] Aristotle had composed a short treatise on respiration.

[8] Aristotle knew also that the whale and dolphin were mammals.

[*Chapters 7 through 15 deal especially with the lower organs of the body, such as the liver, kidneys, stomach, and intestines.*]

BOOK IV

> *Bodily structure and organs of the lower animals, especially marine animals and insects. Limbs and postures of all animals. [Chapters 1 through 4 continue the discussion of the lower organs, including now the gall bladder, as they appear in various animals. Chapter 5 takes up particularly marine animals.]*

CHAPTER 5. . . . The Ascidians [1] differ but slightly from plants and yet have more of an animal nature than the Sponges, which are in fact virtually plants and nothing more. For nature passes from lifeless objects to animals in such unbroken sequence, interposing between them beings which live and yet are not animals, that scarcely any difference seems to exist between two neighboring classes, owing to their close resemblance.

A sponge then, as already said, completely resembles a plant in that throughout its life it is attached to a rock and that when separated from this it dies. Slightly different from the Sponges are the so-called Holothuriae and Sea-lungs,[2] as also sundry other sea animals that resemble them. For these are free and unattached. Yet they have no feeling and their life is simply that of a plant separated from the ground. For even among land plants there are some that are independent of the soil and that spring up and grow, either parasitically upon other plants or even entirely free. Such, for example, is the plant which is found on Parnassus and which some call the epipe-

---

[1] A species of soft-bodied sea animals, like molluscs but enclosed in a tough, leathery skin instead of a shell.

[2] Just what animals Aristotle meant by these names is uncertain, though the Sea-Lungs are probably jellyfish.

trum.[3] This you may take up and hang from the rafters and it will go on living for a considerable time. Sometimes it is a matter of doubt whether a given organism should be classed with plants or with animals. The Ascidian, for instance, and things like it, so far resemble plants as never to live free and unattached, but, on the other hand, inasmuch as they have a certain flesh-like substance, they must be supposed to possess some degree of sensibility.[4] . . .

The animals which some call sea-nettles and others Acalephae [5] are not Testacea [6] at all nor included in their divisions. Their constitution brings them on one side to plants, on the other to animals. For seeing that some of them can detach themselves and can seize hold of their food, and that they are sensitive to objects which come in contact with them, we must consider them to have an animal nature. We are drawn to the like conclusion by the fact that they use the roughness of their bodies as a protection against their enemies. But, on the other hand, they are closely allied to plants, firstly, by the imperfection of their structure, secondly, by their ability to attach themselves to rocks with great rapidity, and, lastly, by their leaving no visible excreta, notwithstanding that they possess a mouth.

Very similar again to the Acalephae are the Starfishes. For these also seize hold of their prey and suck out its juices and thus destroy a vast number of oysters. At the same time they present a certain resemblance to such animals as the Cephalopods [7] and Crustacea,[8] inasmuch as they are free and unattached. The same may also be said of the Testacea.

Such then is the structure of the parts that provide for nutrition, and which every animal must necessarily possess. But besides these organs it is quite plain that in every animal there must be some part

[3] Probably a species of what we now call sedum. In his work *On the Generation of Animals* Aristotle mentions another parasite plant, the mistletoe.

[4] In Book II, chapter 8, Aristotle called flesh the organ of touch.

[5] Aristotle is naming here what are now called sea-anemones.

[6] What we commonly call shellfish, mussels, barnacles, etc.

[7] Cuttlefish, nautilus, etc.

[8] Shell-covered marine animals such as clams, lobsters, crabs, shrimps, etc.

or other which shall be analogous to what in blooded animals is the presiding seat of sensation. Whether an animal has or has not blood, it cannot possibly be without this. . . .

We have now done with the internal parts of animals and must return to the consideration of such external parts as have not yet been described. It will be better to begin with the animals we have just been describing, that is, with the bloodless animals, so that we may not be hampered with them hereafter, but may be free to deal in a leisurely way with the more perfect kinds of animals, those namely that have blood.

CHAPTER 6. We will begin with insects. These animals, though they consist of but few parts, are yet not without diversities when compared with each other. They are all many-footed, the object of this being to compensate their natural slowness and frigidity and give greater activity to their motions. Accordingly, we find that those which, like the Juli,[9] have long bodies and are therefore the most liable to chilling, have also the greatest number of feet. Again, in all insects, the body is made up of segments, the reason for this being that in these animals there is no one supreme and sovereign part but several. And the number of feet correspond to the number of segments. Should the feet fall short of this, their deficiency is supplied by the presence of wings. Of winged insects, some live a wandering life and are forced to make long expeditions in search of food. These have a body of light weight and four wings, two on either side, to support it. Such are bees and other insects akin to them. When, however, the insects are of very small bulk, their wings are reduced to two, as is the case with flies. . . .

The body of an insect is made of segments, not only for the reason already assigned, but also to enable it to bend in such a manner as may protect it from injury. For insects that have long bodies can roll themselves up, which would have been impossible

[9] Centipedes.

had they not been formed of segments. And even those which cannot do this can yet draw their segments closer together and so increase the hardness of their bodies. This can be felt quite plainly by putting the finger on any of the insects known as Canthari.[10] The touch frightens the insect and it remains perfectly motionless, while its body is felt to become harder than before. The division then of the body into segments has this final cause. It is also a necessary result of there being several supreme organs in place of one; and this again is a part of the essential constitution of insects and a characteristic that approximates them to plants. For as plants, though cut into pieces, still live, so also do insects. There is, however, this difference between the two, that the portions of the divided insect live for a very short space, whereas the portions of the plant live on and attain the perfect form of the whole, so that from one single plant you may obtain two or more.

Some insects are provided with another means of protection against their enemies, namely, a piercer or sting. In some, this is in front and connected with the tongue, in others, behind and connected with the tail. For just as the organ of smell in elephants answers several uses, serving alike for purposes of nutrition and for purposes of defense, so also does the lingual arrangement in some insects answer more than one end. For it is the instrument through which they derive their sensations of food, as well as that with which they suck it up and bring it to their mouths; and, when no such anterior piercer or sting exists, the mouth is furnished with teeth, which so far supply its place as to serve either for the mastication of food or for grasping and conveying it to the mouth. They serve this latter use, for instance, in ants and in all the various kinds of bees.

As for a tail sting, nature has given it to insects that are of a fierce disposition and to no others. Sometimes this instrument is lodged

[10] A species of beetle, perhaps the sacred beetle of Egypt, known also as the scarabeus.

inside the body, as in bees and wasps. This position is a necessary consequence of those insects being made for flight. For, were their piercer or sting external and of delicate make, it would very easily get hurt. If on the other hand, while still external, it were of stouter build, as in scorpions, its weight would interfere with flight. As for scorpions, they never rise from the ground, and their piercer or sting must therefore be placed in the way it is, as otherwise it would be of no use as a weapon. . . . For it is better, when possible, that one and the same instrument shall not be made to serve several dissimilar uses; but that there shall be one organ to serve as a weapon, which can then be very sharp, and a second distinct one to serve as a tongue, which can then be of spongy texture and fit to absorb nutriment. Whenever, therefore, nature is able to provide two separate instruments for two separate uses, without the one hampering the other, she does so, instead of acting like a coppersmith, who for cheapness makes a thing that is a spit and a candlestick in one. It is only when this is impossible that she uses one organ for several functions.[11]

The anterior legs are in some cases longer than the others that they may serve to clean off the dust or other matter which may fall into the insect's eyes and obstruct its sight, which already is not very distinct owing to the eyes being made of a hard substance. Flies and bees and the like may be constantly seen thus dressing themselves with crossed forelegs. Of the other legs, the hinder are bigger than the middle pair, both to aid in running and also to enable the insect when it takes flight to spring more easily from the ground. This difference is still more marked in such insects as leap, in grasshoppers, for instance, and in the various kinds of fleas. For these first bend and then extend the legs, and by so doing are necessarily shot up from the ground. The hindlegs of grasshoppers, though never the

[11] Aristotle has apparently forgotten that earlier in this same treatise he has remarked on Nature's skill in making one organ often fitted to perform two different operations.

front ones, resemble the two long stern oars by which a ship is steered. For it is essential that the joint shall be bent inwards, and this never occurs in the forelegs. The whole number of legs, including those used in leaping, is six in all these insects. . . .

[*Chapters 7 through 9 take up the organs and habits of shellfish, crabs, lobsters and cuttlefish.*]

CHAPTER 10. We must now go back to the animals that have blood, and consider such of their parts, already enumerated, that we before passed over. We will take the viviparous animals [12] first and when we have done with these, will pass on to the ovipara and treat of them in like manner.

The parts that border on the head and on what is known as the neck and throat have already been considered. As for the head itself, such a part is found in all animals that have blood. In some bloodless animals, however, in crabs for instance, there is no head distinctly separable from the trunk. As to the neck, it is present in all the vivipara but only in some of the ovipara; for while those that have a lung have also a neck, those that do not inhale the outer air have none. . . .

Continuous with the head and neck is the trunk with the upper limbs. In man the forelegs and forefeet are replaced by arms and by what we call hands. For of all animals man alone stands erect, in accordance with his god-like nature and essence. For it is the function of the god-like to think and to be wise; and no easy task were this under the burden of a heavy body, pressing down from above and obstructing by its weight the motions of the intellect and of the common sense. When the weight and bodily substance become excessive, the body must of necessity incline toward the ground. In such cases, therefore, nature, in order to give support to the body, has replaced the arms and hands by forefeet, and has thus converted

[12] These viviparous animals with blood, which Aristotle treats often as a group by themselves, are the mammals.

the animal into a quadruped.[13] For as every animal that walks must of necessity have two hinder feet, such an animal becomes a quadruped when its body inclines downwards in front from the weight which its soul cannot sustain. . . .

Let now a still further decrease occur in the elevating heat and a still further increase in the earthy matter, and the animals become smaller in bulk and their feet more numerous, until at a later stage they become footless and extended full length on the ground. Thus, by gradual small successions of change, they come to have their principal organ below; and at last their head part becomes motionless and destitute of sensation. Thus the animal becomes a plant that has its upper parts downward and its lower parts above. For in plants, the roots are the equivalents of mouth and head, while the seed, which is produced above at the extremities of the twigs, comes from the opposite extremity.

The reasons have now been stated why some animals have many feet, some only two, and others none; why, also, some living things are plants and others animals; and lastly, why man alone of all animals stands erect. Standing thus erect, man has no need of legs in front and in their stead has been endowed by nature with arms and hands. Now it is the opinion of Anaxagoras that the possession of these hands is the reason why man is of all animals the most intelligent. But it is rational to suppose that the possession of hands is the consequence rather than the cause of his superior intelligence. For the hands are instruments or organs, and the invariable plan of nature in distributing organs is to give each to the animals that can make use of it. Nature acts in this manner as any wise man would do. For to such a one it would seem much more appropriate to take a person who was already a flute player and give him a flute, than to take one who possessed a flute and teach him the art of flute play-

[13] Aristotle speaks here as if he thought of man, the highest animal, as the starting point and norm and the lower animals as descending down from him in a closely graded scale of increasing inferiority. Earlier, he starts from the bottom and climbs upward.

ing. For by the former plan something comparatively insignificant would be added to something of much greater importance; while by the latter the more valuable and the more important element would be superadded to the less valuable one.

Seeing then that it is a better plan to assign an instrument to a workman than to assign a workman to an instrument, and seeing also that of all available plans nature invariably adopts the best, we must conclude that man does not owe his superior intelligence to his hands but his hands to his superior intelligence. For the most intelligent of animals is the one which would put the most organs to the best use; and the hand is apparently not a single organ but many in one, for it is an organ that can serve in place of many. This instrument then, the hand, of all instruments the most variously serviceable, has been given by nature to man, the animal of all animals the most capable of acquiring the most varied handicrafts.

Much in error then are they who say that the structure of man is not only faulty, but inferior to that of every other animal, seeing that he is, as they point out, barefooted, naked, and without weapon of which to avail himself. For other animals have each but one mode of defense, and this they can never change; so that they must perform all the offices of life and even, so to speak, sleep with sandals on, never laying aside whatever serves as a protection to their bodies, nor changing such single weapon as they may chance to possess. But to man numerous modes of defense are open, and these, moreover, he may change at will; as also he may adopt such weapon as he pleases and at such times as suit him. For the hand is talon, hoof, and horn at will. So too is it spear and sword and whatsoever other weapon or instrument you please; for all these can it be from its power of grasping and holding everything.

Suited to its varied offices is the form which nature has contrived for it. For it is split into several fingers, and these are capable of separation. Such capacity for separation does not prevent their again converging so as to form a single compact fist, whereas had the hand been an undivided mass, separation would have been impossible.

Again, these parts may be used singly or together, and in various combinations. The joints, moreover, of the fingers are well constructed for grasping and for pressure. One of the fingers also—and this, not long like the rest but short and thick—is placed on the side. For were it not so placed all grasping would be impossible, as if there were no hand at all. For the pressure of this lateral thumb is applied from below upwards, while the rest act from above downwards; an arrangement which is essential, if the grasp is to be firm and hold like a tight clamp. As for the shortness of this lateral thumb, the object is to increase its strength, so that it may be able, though but one, to counterbalance its more numerous opponents. Indeed were it long it would be of no use. For this reason it is sometimes called the great digit, in spite of its small size; for without it all the rest would be practically useless. The finger which stands at the other end of the row is small, while the central one of all is long, like the center oar in a ship. This is rightly so, for in grasping an object, as a workman grasps his tool, it is the central part of the encircling hold which is of the most importance. . . .

[*The remainder of chapter 10 summarizes the general structure and character of the bodies of mammals as a class. Chapters 11, 12, and 13 do the same for oviparous quadrupeds, birds, and fishes respectively. Chapter 14 describes briefly the peculiarities of the ostrich, which seemed to Aristotle, according to what he had heard of it, to be something between a quadruped and a bird.*]

NICOMACHEAN

ETHICS

NICOMACHEAN ETHICS

THE BOOK from which we take the following selections is known as the *Nicomachean Ethics,* from an old tradition that Nicomachus, the son of Aristotle, collected and edited these notes from a set of his father's lectures. It certainly is not one of the books cobbled together out of originally separate fragments. It keeps to one style and follows one clear plan throughout. As a matter of fact, we have another work by Aristotle on the same subject, the so-called *Eudemian Ethics,* but the *Nicomachean* represents evidently his later and more mature thought. In his earlier years, under Plato's influence, he had taken a somewhat ascetic view of the relationship between the spiritual soul of man and his animal body. A truly good man, he said, would be entirely indifferent to matters of physical well-being and worldly station. In the *Nicomachean Ethics,* however, he has moved a long way from that earlier ideal standpoint. A life of some social activity, accompanied by a reasonable measure of pleasure, prosperity, and honor, seem to him now right and proper for a creature of composite nature like man's. Without some such gratifications, even a good man cannot be fully happy.

The *Nicomachean Ethics* is probably the most popular of all Aristotle's works. In its calm and searching analysis of human character and conduct every reader can find some picture of himself. The purpose of all ethics, we are told at the outset, is the search for that good that everyone aims to get out of living. That good is easily identified as happiness. What then is happiness and how do we reach it? Every creature, we presently hear, is most happy when fulfilling just the functions for which Nature designed him. In the case of man his unique function is activity of soul in obedience to reason. Virtues for us then are states of character in which we choose our

activities rationally and therefore aright. Through virtue we may arrive at the state of happiness we all so greatly desire.

How are these useful virtues to be acquired? Partly through early training in good habits and partly by deliberate will and choice. We become good by doing good things. What are these virtues, taken one by one? Some are moral and practical, such as courage, temperance, liberality, justice, good temper, and the like. Through them we govern our emotions and acts. All these, when we come to examine them, are means between certain ugly extremes of conduct that we call vices—cowardice, foolhardiness, licentiousness, meanness, greed, bad temper, and so on. In the same way, a work of art is a mean between deformities that are either too much or too little. Other virtues are intellectual and keep our minds looking straight at truth. They include prudence or good sense, that sees what needs doing at once here and now, and the more farsighted wisdom which we get from art, science, philosophy, and intuitive reason. Of no intellectual virtue can there be too much. Impediments in our way to possessing virtue, besides the vices already mentioned, are ignorance and the lack of self-control that is the failing of men of good intentions but weak will, who let their passions drag them into wrongdoing. More extreme types of inhuman brutality mark the morbid and sick-minded person and the barbarian.

After the chapters on virtues and vices come others equally penetrating on external influences that help or hinder our advance toward happiness—the blandishments of pleasure, the incentives of glory and honor, the distresses of pain and misfortune, the abiding comforts of sincere friendship, the transient values of friendship for amusement or profit. The book closes with a description of the happiness of those who arrive at a life in harmony with the best in themselves, honored of gods and men. But again we are reminded that every individual's character is bound to be affected by his training and environment, as determined especially by the laws under which he lives. So to complete our study of the good life we go on next to the *Politics*.

BOOK I

The end toward which men strive in life is happiness. Happiness for each creature is found in the best possible performance of the function for which he is peculiarly adapted. Man then finds his highest and most lasting happiness in the active life of his soul in accordance with virtue. Virtue may be either (1) intellectual, the excellence of the reasoning powers, that is, prudence and wisdom; or (2) moral, the control of emotions and desires in obedience to reason, that is, liberality and temperance.

CHAPTER I. Every art and every scientific inquiry, and similarly every action and purpose, may be said to aim at some good. Hence the good has been well defined as that at which all things aim. But it is clear that there is a difference in ends; for the ends are sometimes activities, and sometimes results beyond the mere activities. Where there are ends beyond the action, the results are naturally superior to the action.

As there are various actions, arts, and sciences, it follows that the ends are also various. Thus health is the end of medical art, a ship of shipbuilding, victory of strategy, and wealth of economies. It often happens that a number of such arts or sciences combine for a single enterprise, as the art of making bridles and all such other arts as furnish the implements of horsemanship combine for horsemanship, and horsemanship and every military action for strategy; and in the same way, other arts or sciences combine for others. In all these cases, the ends of the master arts or sciences, whatever they may be, are more desirable than those of the subordinate arts or sciences, as

it is for the sake of the former that the latter are pursued. It makes no difference to the argument whether the activities themselves are the ends of the action, or something beyond the activities, as in the above-mentioned sciences.

If it is true that in the sphere of action there is some end which we wish for its own sake, and for the sake of which we wish everything else, and if we do not desire everything for the sake of something else (for, if that is so, the process will go on *ad infinitum,* and our desire will be idle and futile), clearly this end will be good and the supreme good. Does it not follow then that the knowledge of this good is of great importance for the conduct of life? Like archers who have a mark at which to aim, shall we not have a better chance of attaining what we want? If this is so, we must endeavor to comprehend, at least in outline, what this good is, and what science or faculty makes it its object.

It would seem that this is the most authoritative science. Such a kind is evidently the political, for it is that which determines what sciences are necessary in states, and what kinds should be studied, and how far they should be studied by each class of inhabitant. We see too that even the faculties held in highest esteem, such as strategy, economics, and rhetoric, are subordinate to it. Then since politics makes use of the other sciences and also rules what people may do and what they may not do, it follows that its end will comprehend the ends of the other sciences, and will therefore be the good of mankind. For even if the good of an individual is identical with the good of a state, yet the good of the state is evidently greater and more perfect to attain or to preserve. For though the good of an individual by himself is something worth working for, to ensure the good of a nation or a state is nobler and more divine.

These then are the objects at which the present inquiry aims, and it is in a sense a political inquiry. . . .

CHAPTER 2.   As every science and undertaking aims at some good. what is in our view the good at which political science aims,

and what is the highest of all practical goods? As to its name there is, I may say, a general agreement. The masses and the cultured classes agree in calling it happiness, and conceive that "to live well" or "to do well" is the same thing as "to be happy." But as to what happiness is they do not agree, nor do the masses give the same account of it as the philosophers. The former take it to be something visible and palpable, such as pleasure, wealth, or honor; different people, however, give different definitions of it, and often even the same man gives different definitions at different times. When he is ill, it is health, when he is poor, it is wealth; if he is conscious of his own ignorance, he envies people who use grand language above his own comprehension. Some philosophers, on the other hand, have held that, besides these various goods, there is an absolute good which is the cause of goodness in them all.[1] It would perhaps be a waste of time to examine all these opinions; it will be enough to examine such as are most popular or as seem to be more or less reasonable.

CHAPTER 3. Men's conception of the good or of happiness may be read in the lives they lead. Ordinary or vulgar people conceive it to be a pleasure, and accordingly choose a life of enjoyment. For there are, we may say, three conspicuous types of life, the sensual, the political, and, thirdly, the life of thought. Now the mass of men present an absolutely slavish appearance, choosing the life of brute beasts, but they have ground for so doing because so many persons in authority share the tastes of Sardanapalus.[2] Cultivated and energetic people, on the other hand, identify happiness with honor, as honor is the general end of political life. But this seems too superficial an idea for our present purpose; for honor depends more upon the people who pay it than upon the person to whom it is paid, and the good we feel is something which is proper to a man himself and cannot be easily taken away from him. Men too appear to seek honor

[1] These were members of Plato's school of thought.
[2] A half legendary ruler of ancient Assyria, whose name to the Greeks stood for the extreme of Oriental luxury and extravagance.

in order to be assured of their own goodness. Accordingly, they seek it at the hands of the sage and of those who know them well, and they seek it on the ground of their virtue; clearly then, in their judgment at any rate, virtue is better than honor. Perhaps then we might look on virtue rather than honor as the end of political life. Yet even this idea appears not quite complete; for a man may possess virtue and yet be asleep or inactive throughout life, and not only so, but he may experience the greatest calamities and misfortunes. Yet no one would call such a life a life of happiness, unless he were maintaining a paradox. But we need not dwell further on this subject, since it is sufficiently discussed in popular philosophical treatises. The third life is the life of thought, which we will discuss later.[3]

The life of money making is a life of constraint; and wealth is obviously not the good of which we are in quest; for it is useful merely as a means to something else. It would be more reasonable to take the things mentioned before—sensual pleasure, honor, and virtue—as ends than wealth, since they are things desired on their own account. Yet these too are evidently not ends, although much argument has been employed to show that they are. . . .

CHAPTER 5.   But leaving this subject for the present, let us revert to the good of which we are in quest and consider what it may be. For it seems different in different activities or arts; it is one thing in medicine, another in strategy, and so on. What is the good in each of these instances? It is presumably that for the sake of which all else is done. In medicine this is health, in strategy victory, in architecture a house, and so on. In every activity and undertaking it is the end, since it is for the sake of the end that all people do whatever else they do. If then there is an end for all our activity, this will be the good to be accomplished; and if there are several such ends, it will be these.

Our argument has arrived by a different path at the same point as

[3] The discussion of the life of thought occurs in Book X.

before; but we must endeavor to make it still plainer. Since there are more ends than one, and some of these ends—for example, wealth, flutes, and instruments generally—we desire as means to something else, it is evident that not all are final ends. But the highest good is clearly something final. Hence if there is only one final end, this will be the object of which we are in search; and if there are more than one, it will be the most final. We call that which is sought after for its own sake more final than that which is sought after as a means to something else; we call that which is never desired as a means to something else more final than things that are desired both for themselves and as means to something else. Therefore, we call absolutely final that which is always desired for itself and never as a means to something else. Now happiness more than anything else answers to this description. For happiness we always desire for its own sake and never as a means to something else, whereas honor, pleasure, intelligence, and every virtue we desire partly for their own sakes (for we should desire them independently of what might result from them), but partly also as means to happiness, because we suppose they will prove instruments of happiness. Happiness, on the other hand, nobody desires for the sake of these things, nor indeed as a means to anything else at all.

If we start from the point of view of self-sufficiency, we reach the same conclusion; for we assume that the final good is self-sufficient. By self-sufficiency we do not mean that a person leads a solitary life all by himself, but that he has parents, children, wife and friends and fellow citizens in general, as man is naturally a social being. Yet here it is necessary to set some limit; for if the circle must be extended to include ancestors, descendants, and friends' friends, it will go on indefinitely. Leaving this point, however, for future investigation, we call the self-sufficient that which, taken even by itself, makes life desirable and wanting nothing at all; and this is what we mean by happiness.

Again, we think happiness the most desirable of all things, and that not merely as one good thing among others. If it were only that,

the addition of the smallest more good would increase its desirableness; for the addition would make an increase of goods, and the greater of two goods is always the more desirable. Happiness is something final and self-sufficient and the end of all action.

CHAPTER 6.   Perhaps, however, it seems a commonplace to say that happiness is the supreme good; what is wanted is to define its nature a little more clearly. The best way of arriving at such a definition will probably be to ascertain the function of man. For, as with a flute player, a sculptor, or any artist, or in fact anybody who has a special function or activity, his goodness and excellence seem to lie in his function, so it would seem to be with man, if indeed he has a special function. Can it be said that, while a carpenter and a cobbler have special functions and activities, man, unlike them, is naturally functionless? Or, as the eye, the hand, the foot, and similarly each part of the body has a special function, so may man be regarded as having a special function apart from all these? What, then, can this function be? It is not life; for life is apparently something that man shares with plants; and we are looking for something peculiar to him. We must exclude therefore the life of nutrition and growth. There is next what may be called the life of sensation. But this too, apparently, is shared by man with horses, cattle, and all other animals. There remains what I may call the active life of the rational part of man's being. Now this rational part is twofold; one part is rational in the sense of being obedient to reason, and the other in the sense of possessing and exercising reason and intelligence. The active life too may be conceived of in two ways,[4] either as a state of character, or as an activity; but we mean by it the life of activity, as this seems to be the truer form of the conception.

The function of man then is activity of soul in accordance with reason, or not apart from reason. Now, the function of a man of a

----

[4] In other words, life may be taken to mean either the mere possession of certain faculties or their active exercise.

certain kind, and of a man who is good of that kind—for example, of a harpist and a good harpist—are in our view the same in kind. This is true of all people of all kinds without exception, the superior excellence being only an addition to the function; for it is the function of a harpist to play the harp, and of a good harpist to play the harp well. This being so, if we define the function of man as a kind of life, and this life as an activity of the soul or a course of action in accordance with reason, and if the function of a good man is such activity of a good and noble kind, and if everything is well done when it is done in accordance with its proper excellence, it follows that the good of man is activity of soul in accordance with virtue, or, if there are more virtues than one, in accordance with the best and most complete virtue. But we must add the words "in a complete life." For as one swallow or one day does not make a spring, so one day or a short time does not make a man blessed or happy. . . .

CHAPTER 8. Goods have been divided into three classes: external goods as they are called, goods of the soul, and goods of the body. Of these three classes goods of the soul are considered goods in the strictest and truest sense. To the soul are ascribed spiritual actions and activities. Thus our definition must be a good one, at least according to this theory, which is both ancient and accepted by philosophers at the present time. It is correct too, inasmuch as we call certain actions and activities the end; for we put the end in some good of the soul and not in an external good. By a similar theory the happy man lives well and does well, and happiness, we have said, is in fact a kind of living and doing well. . . .

CHAPTER 9. . . . Our account accords too with the view of those who hold that happiness is virtue or excellence of some sort; for activity in accordance with virtue is virtue. But there is plainly a considerable difference between calling the supreme good possession or use, a state of mind, or an activity. For a state of mind may exist

without producing anything good—for example, if a person is asleep, or in any other way inert. Not so with an activity, since activity implies acting and acting well. As in the Olympic games it is not the most beautiful and strongest who receive the crown but those who actually enter the combat, for from those come the victors, so it is those who act that win rightly what is noble and good in life.

Their life too is pleasant in itself. For pleasure is a state of mind, and whatever a man is fond of is pleasant to him, as a horse is to a lover of horses, a show to a lover of spectacles, and, similarly, just acts to a lover of justice, and virtuous acts in general to a lover of virtue. Now most men find a sense of discord in their pleasures, because their pleasures are not all naturally pleasant. But the lovers of nobleness take pleasure in what is naturally pleasant, and virtuous acts are naturally pleasant. Such acts then are pleasant both to these persons and in themselves. Nor does the life of such persons need more pleasure attached to it as a sort of charm; it possesses pleasure in itself. For, it may be added, a man who does not delight in noble acts is not good; as nobody would call a man just who did not enjoy just action, or liberal who did not enjoy liberal action, and so on. If this is so, it follows that acts of virtue are pleasant in themselves. They are also good and noble, and good and noble in the highest degree, for the judgment of the virtuous man on them is right, and his judgment is as we have described. Happiness then is the best and noblest and pleasantest thing in the world; nor is there any such difference between these things as the inscription at Delos suggests:

> "Justice is noblest, health is best,
> To gain one's wish is pleasantest."

For they all are characteristics of the best activities, and happiness, we hold, is the same as these or as one and the noblest of these.

Still it is clear, as we said, that happiness requires the addition of external goods; for it is impossible, or at least difficult, to do noble deeds with no outside means. For many things can be done only through the aid of friends or wealth or political power; and there are

some things the lack of which spoils our felicity, such as good birth, wholesome children, and personal beauty. For a man who is extremely ugly in appearance or low born or solitary and childless can hardly be happy; perhaps still less so, if he has exceedingly bad children or friends, or has had good children or friends and lost them by death. As we said, then, happiness seems to need prosperity of this kind in addition to virtue. For this reason some persons identify happiness with good fortune, though others do so with virtue.

CHAPTER 10. The question is consequently raised whether happiness is something that can be learned or acquired by habit or training of some kind, or whether it comes by some divine dispensation, or even by chance.

Now if there is anything in the world that is a gift of the gods to men, it is reasonable to take happiness as a divine gift, and especially divine as it is the best of human things. This point, however, is perhaps more appropriate to another investigation than the present. But even if happiness is not sent by the gods but is the result of goodness and of learning or training of some kind, it is apparently one of the most divine things in the world; for that which is the prize and end of goodness would seem the best good and in its nature godlike and blessed. It may also be widely extended; for all persons who are not morally deformed may share in it by a process of study and care. And if it is better that happiness should come in this way than by chance, we may reasonably suppose that it does so come, since the order of things in Nature is the best possible, as it is in art and in causation generally, and most of all in the highest kind of causation. And to leave what is greatest and noblest to chance would be altogether unworthy. The definition of happiness itself helps to clear up the question; for happiness we have defined as a kind of virtuous activity of the soul. . . .

It is reasonable then not to call an ox or a horse or any other animal happy; for none of them is capable of sharing in this activity. For the same reason no child can be happy, since the youth of a

child keeps him for the time being from such activity; if a child is ever called happy, the ground of felicitation is his promise, rather than his actual performance. For happiness demands, as we said, a complete virtue and a complete life. And there are all sorts of changes and chances in life, and the most prosperous of men may in his old age fall into extreme calamities, as Priam did in the heroic legends.[5] And a person who has experienced such chances and died a miserable death, nobody calls happy.

CHAPTER 11.   Is it true then that nobody in the world may be called happy so long as he is alive? Must we adopt Solon's [6] rule of looking to the end? If we follow Solon, can it be said that a man is really happy after his death? Surely such a view is quite absurd, especially for us who define happiness as an activity. But if we do not call a dead man happy, and if Solon's meaning is not this, but rather that it is only when a man is dead that it is safe to call him fortunate, as being free at last from evil and calamities, this again is a view open to objection. For it seems that a dead man may be affected both by good and by evil, in the same way as one who is living but ignorant of them—by honors and dishonors, for instance, and by the successes or misfortunes of his children and his descendants generally. Yet here again a difficulty presents itself. For a person may live happily up to old age and die a happy death, and still his descendants may suffer many vicissitudes of fortune. Some of them may be good and enjoy the life they deserve; others may be bad and have a bad life. Obviously, these descendants may stand in all sorts of different degrees of relationship to their ancestor. It would be strange then if the dead man were to share the shifts in their fortunes and to become happy at one time and miserable at another, as they became either

5 The disastrous fate of Priam, king of Troy, was part of the well-known Homeric tales.

6 The historian Herodotus, I, ch. 32, is the authority for the celebrated warning which Solon is said to have addressed to Croesus, to call no man happy until he was dead.

happy or miserable. But it would be equally strange if the future of their descendants should not for a time affect the ancestors at all.

We would best return to our previous difficulty, for it will perhaps afford an answer to the present question. If it is right to wait for the end, and only when the end has come, to call a man happy, not for being happy then but for having been so before, surely it is an extraordinary thing that, at the time when he is happy, we should not speak the truth about him, because we are unwilling to call the living happy in view of the changes to which they are liable, and because we have formed an idea of happiness as something permanent and exempt from the possibility of change, while every man is liable to many turns of fortune's wheel. Unquestionably, if we follow the changes of fortune, we shall often call the same person happy at one time and miserable at another, making the happy man out as "a sort of chameleon with no stability." But to follow the changes of fortune cannot be right. It is not on these that good or evil depends; they are necessary accompaniments to human life, as we said; but it is a man's virtuous activities that constitute his happiness and their opposites that constitute his misery.

The difficulty we have now discussed proves again the correctness of our definition. For there is no human function so constant as virtuous activities; they seem to be more permanent than the sciences themselves. Among these activities too the most noble are the most permanent, and it is of them that the life of happiness chiefly and most continuously consists. This is apparently the reason why they are not likely to be forgotten.[7] The element of durability then which is required will be found in the happy man, and he will preserve his happiness through life; for always or chiefly he will pursue such actions and thoughts as accord with virtue; nor will anyone bear the

[7] Aristotle means that it is comparatively easy to forget scientific truths, when they have once been learned, but it is difficult, if not impossible, to lose the habit of virtuous activity. In other words, he means that knowledge is less stable, and therefore less valuable, than character.

chances of life so nobly, with such a perfect composure, as he who is truly good and "foursquare without a flaw." [8]

Now the events of chance are numerous and of different magnitudes. Small pieces of good fortune or the reverse do not turn the scale of life in any way, but great and numerous events make life happier if they turn out well, since they naturally give it beauty and the use of them may be noble and good. If, on the other hand, they turn out badly, they mar and mutilate happiness by causing pain and hindrances to many activities. Still, even in these circumstances, nobility shines out when a person bears with calmness the weight of accumulated misfortunes, not from insensibility but from dignity and greatness of spirit.

Then if activities determine the quality of life, as we said, no happy man can become miserable; for he will never do what is hateful and mean. For our idea of the truly good and wise man is that he bears all the chances of life with dignity and always does what is best in the circumstances, as a good general makes the best use of the forces at his command in war, or a good cobbler makes the best shoe with the leather given him, and so on through the whole series of the arts. If this is so, the happy man can never become miserable. I do not say that he will be fortunate if he meets such chances of life as Priam. Yet he will not be variable or constantly changing, for he will not be moved from his happiness easily or by ordinary misfortunes, but only by great and numerous ones; nor after them will he quickly regain his happiness. If he regains it at all, it will be only over a long and complete period of time and after great and notable achievement.

We may safely then define a happy man as one who is active in accord with perfect virtue and adequately furnished with external goods, not for some chance period of time but for his whole lifetime. But perhaps we ought to add that he should always live so and die

---

[8] The phrase is taken from Simonides. In a similar but not identical sense, a modern poet speaks of the great Duke of Wellington as

"that tower of strength
Which stood foursquare to all the winds that blew."

as he has lived. It is not given us to foresee the future, but we take happiness as an end, altogether final and complete; and, this being so, we shall call people happy during their lifetime if they possess and continue to possess these characteristics—yet happy only so far as men are happy. . . .

A serious doubt has been raised as to the participation of the dead in any good or evil. It is probable that if anything, whether good or evil, reaches the dead at all, it is feeble and insignificant, both in itself and in relation to them, or if not, is at least of no such magnitude and character as to be capable of making happy those who are not happy or of depriving of their felicity those who are. It would seem then that the dead are affected or influenced in some way by the prosperity and adversity of their friends, but that the influence is of such a kind and degree as not to make them unhappy, if they are happy, nor to have any similar effect. . . .

CHAPTER 13. Inasmuch as happiness is an activity of soul in accordance with perfect virtue, we must now consider virtue, as this will perhaps be the best way of studying happiness. . . . Clearly it is human virtue we have to consider; for the good of which we are in search is, as we said, human good, and the happiness, human happiness. By human virtue or excellence we mean not that of the body, but that of the soul, and by happiness we mean an activity of the soul.

There are some facts concerning the soul which are adequately stated in popular discourses, and these we may rightly accept. It is said, for example, that the soul has two parts, one irrational and the other rational. Whether these parts are separate like the parts of the body or like anything divisible, or whether they are theoretically distinct but in fact inseparable, like the convex and concave in the circumference of a circle, is of no importance to the present inquiry.

Of the irrational part of the soul one part is shared by man with all living things, and vegetative; I mean the part which is the cause of nutrition and growth. For we may assume such a faculty of the soul to exist in all young things that take food, even in embryos, and

the same faculty to exist in things full grown, since it is more reasonable to suppose it is the same faculty than something different.
Manifestly the virtue or excellence of this faculty is not peculiarly
human but is shared by man with all living things; this part or faculty
seems especially active in sleep, whereas goodness and badness never
show so little as in sleep. Hence the saying that during half their
lives there is no difference between the happy and the unhappy. And
this is only natural; for sleep is an inactivity of the soul as regards
its goodness or badness, except in so far as certain impulses affect it
slightly and make the dreams of good men better than those of ordinary people. Enough, however, on this point; we shall now leave
the faculty of nutrition, as it has by its nature no part in human
goodness.

There is, we think, another natural element of the soul which is
irrational and yet in a sense partakes of reason. For in continent and
incontinent persons we praise their reason, and that part of their
soul which possesses reason, because it counsels them aright and
directs them to the best conduct. But we know there is in them also
another element naturally opposed to reason that fights and contends
against reason. Just as paralyzed parts of the body, when we try to
move them to the right, pull in a contrary direction to the left, so it
is with the soul; the impulses of incontinent people run counter to
reason. But while in the body we see the part which pulls awry, in
the soul we do not see it. We may, however, suppose with equal certainty that in the soul too there is something alien to reason, which
opposes and thwarts it. The sense in which it is distinct from other
things is unimportant. But it too partakes of reason, as we said; at all
events, in a continent person it obeys reason, and in a temperate and
brave man it is probably still more obedient, for in him it is absolutely
harmonious with reason.

It appears then that the irrational part of the soul is twofold; for
the vegetative faculty does not participate at all in reason, but the
element of appetite and desire in general shares in it, in so far as it
is submissive and obedient to reason. It is so in the sense in which we

speak of "paying attention" to a father or to friends, but not in the sense in which we speak of "paying attention" to mathematics. All advice, reproof, and exhortation are witness that this irrational part of the soul is in a sense subject to influence by reason. And if we say that this part participates in reason, then as a part possessing reason, it will be twofold, one element possessing reason absolutely and in itself, the other listening to it as a child listens to its father.

Virtue too may be divided to correspond to this difference. For we call some virtues intellectual and others moral. Wisdom, intelligence, and prudence are intellectual; liberality and temperance moral. In describing a person's moral character we do not say that he is wise or intelligent but that he is gentle or temperate. A wise man, however, we praise for his mentality, and such mentality as deserves praise we call virtuous.

BOOK II

> *Moral virtues can best be acquired by practice and habit. They imply a right attitude toward pleasures and pains. A good man deliberately chooses to do what is noble and right for its own sake. What is right in matters of moral conduct is usually a mean between two extremes.*

CHAPTER I. Virtue then is twofold, partly intellectual and partly moral, and intellectual virtue is originated and fostered mainly by teaching; it demands therefore experience and time. Moral [1] virtue on the other hand is the outcome of habit, and accordingly its name, *ethike*, is derived by a slight variation from *ethos*, habit. From this fact it is clear that moral virtue is not implanted in

---

[1] A student of Aristotle must familiarize himself with the conception of intellectual as well as of moral virtues, although it is not the rule in modern philosophy to speak of "virtues" of the intellect.

us by nature; for nothing that exists by nature can be transformed by habit. Thus a stone, that naturally tends to fall downwards, cannot be habituated or trained to rise upwards, even if we tried to train it by throwing it up ten thousand times. Nor again can fire be trained to sink downwards, nor anything else that follows one natural law be habituated or trained to follow another. It is neither by nature then nor in defiance of nature that virtues grow in us. Nature gives us the capacity to receive them, and that capacity is perfected by habit.

Again, if we take the various natural powers which belong to us, we first possess the proper faculties and afterwards display the activities. It is obviously so with the senses. Not by seeing frequently or hearing frequently do we acquire the sense of seeing or hearing; on the contrary, because we have the senses we make use of them; we do not get them by making use of them. But the virtues we get by first practicing them, as we do in the arts. For it is by doing what we ought to do when we study the arts that we learn the arts themselves; we become builders by building and harpists by playing the harp. Similarly, it is by doing just acts that we become just, by doing temperate acts that we become temperate, by doing brave acts that we become brave. The experience of states confirms this statement, for it is by training in good habits that lawmakers make the citizens good. This is the object all lawmakers have at heart; if they do not succeed in it, they fail of their purpose; and it makes the distinction between a good constitution and a bad one.

Again, the causes and means by which any virtue is produced and destroyed are the same; and equally so in any art. For it is by playing the harp that both good and bad harpists are produced; and the case of builders and others is similar, for it is by building well that they become good builders and by building badly that they become bad builders. If it were not so, there would be no need of anybody to teach them; they would all be born good or bad in their several crafts. The case of the virtues is the same. It is by our actions in dealings between man and man that we become either just or unjust. It is by our actions in the face of danger and by our training ourselves to

fear or to courage that we become either cowardly or courageous. It
is much the same with our appetites and angry passions. People become temperate and gentle, others licentious and passionate, by behaving in one or the other way in particular circumstances. In a word,
moral states are the results of activities like the states themselves. It
is our duty therefore to keep a certain character in our activities,
since our moral states depend on the differences in our activities. So
the difference between one and another training in habits in our
childhood is not a light matter, but important, or rather, all-important.

CHAPTER 2. Our present study is not, like other studies,[2]
purely theoretical in intention; for the object of our inquiry is not to
know what virtue is but how to become good, and that is the sole
benefit of it. We must, therefore, consider the right way of performing actions, for it is acts, as we have said, that determine the character
of the resulting moral states.

That we should act in accordance with right reason is a common
general principle, which may here be taken for granted. The nature
of right reason, and its relation to the virtues generally, will be discussed later. But first of all it must be admitted that all reasoning on
matters of conduct must be like a sketch in outline; it cannot be
scientifically exact. We began by laying down the principle that the
kind of reasoning demanded in any subject must be such as the
subject matter itself allows; and questions of conduct and expediency
no more admit of hard and fast rules than questions of health.

If this is true of general reasoning on ethics, still more true is it
that scientific exactitude is impossible in treating of particular ethical
cases. They do not fall under any art or law, but the actors themselves have always to take account of circumstances, as much as in
medicine or navigation. Still, although such is the nature of our
present argument, we must try to make the best of it.

The first point to be observed is that in the matters we are now
considering deficiency and excess are both fatal. It is so, we see, in

[2] Such studies as generally occupied the attention of the Aristotelian school.

questions of health and strength. (We must judge of what we cannot see by the evidence of what we do see.) Too much or too little
gymnastic exercise is fatal to strength. Similarly, too much or too little
meat and drink is fatal to health, whereas a suitable amount produces,
increases, and sustains it. It is the same with temperance, courage,
and other moral virtues. A person who avoids and is afraid of everything and faces nothing becomes a coward; a person who is not afraid
of anything but is ready to face everything becomes foolhardy.
Similarly, he who enjoys every pleasure and abstains from none is
licentious; he who refuses all pleasures, like a boor, is an insensible
sort of person. For temperance and courage are destroyed by excess
and deficiency but preserved by the mean.

Again, not only are the causes and agencies of production, increase,
and destruction in moral states the same, but the field of their activity
is the same also. It is so in other more obvious instances, as, for example, strength; for strength is produced by taking a great deal of
food and undergoing a great deal of exertion, and it is the strong man
who is able to take most food and undergo most exertion. So too
with the virtues. By abstaining from pleasures we become temperate,
and, when we have become temperate, we are best able to abstain
from them. So again with courage; it is by training ourselves to despise
and face terrifying things that we become brave, and when we have
become brave, we shall be best able to face them.

The pleasure or pain which accompanies actions may be regarded
as a test of a person's moral state. He who abstains from physical
pleasures and feels pleasure in so doing is temperate; but he who
feels pain at so doing is licentious. He who faces dangers with pleasure, or at least without pain, is brave; but he who feels pain at facing
them is a coward. For moral virtue is concerned with pleasures and
pains. It is pleasure which makes us do what is base, and pain which
makes us abstain from doing what is noble. Hence the importance of
having a certain training from very early days, as Plato [3] says, so that

* *Laws,* II. 653.

we may feel pleasure and pain at the right objects; for this is true education. . . .

CHAPTER 3.   But we may be asked what we mean by saying that people must become just by doing what is just and temperate by doing what is temperate. For, it will be said, if they do what is just and temperate they are already just and temperate themselves, in the same way as, if they practice grammar and music, they are grammarians and musicians.

But is this true even in the case of the arts? For a person may speak grammatically either by chance or at the suggestion of somebody else; hence he will not be a grammarian unless he not only speaks grammatically but does so in a grammatical manner, that is, because of the grammatical knowledge which he possesses.

There is a point of difference too between the arts and the virtues. The productions of art have their excellence in themselves. It is enough then that, when they are produced, they themselves should possess a certain character. But acts in accordance with virtue are not justly or temperately performed simply because they are in themselves just or temperate. The doer at the time of performing them must satisfy certain conditions; in the first place, he must know what he is doing; secondly, he must deliberately choose to do it and do it for its own sake; and thirdly, he must do it as part of his own firm and immutable character. If it be a question of art, these conditions, except only the condition of knowledge, are not raised; but if it be a question of virtue, mere knowledge is of little or no avail; it is the other conditions, which are the results of frequently performing just and temperate acts, that are not slightly but all-important. Accordingly, deeds are called just and temperate when they are such as a just and temperate person would do; and a just and temperate person is not merely one who does these deeds but one who does them in the spirit of the just and the temperate.

It may fairly be said then that a just man becomes just by doing what is just, and a temperate man becomes temperate by doing what

is temperate, and if a man did not so act, he would not have much chance of becoming good. But most people, instead of acting, take refuge in theorizing; they imagine that they are philosophers and that philosophy will make them virtuous; in fact, they behave like people who listen attentively to their doctors but never do anything that their doctors tell them. But a healthy state of the soul will no more be produced by this kind of philosophizing than a healthy state of the body by this kind of medical treatment.

CHAPTER 4. We have next to consider the nature of virtue. Now, as the properties of the soul are three, namely, emotions, faculties, and moral states, it follows that virtue must be one of the three. By emotions I mean desire, anger, fear, pride, envy, joy, love, hatred, regret, ambition, pity—in a word, whatever feeling is attended by pleasure or pain. I call those faculties through which we are said to be capable of experiencing these emotions, for instance, capable of getting angry or being pained or feeling pity. And I call those moral states through which we are well or ill disposed in our emotions, ill disposed, for instance, in anger, if our anger be too violent or too feeble, and well disposed, if it be rightly moderate; and similarly in our other emotions.

Now neither the virtues nor the vices are emotions; for we are not called good or bad for our emotions but for our virtues or vices. We are not praised or blamed simply for being angry, but only for being angry in a certain way; but we are praised or blamed for our virtues or vices. Again, whereas we are angry or afraid without deliberate purpose, the virtues are matters of deliberate purpose, or require deliberate purpose. Moreover, we are said to be moved by our emotions, but by our virtues or vices we are not said to be moved but to have a certain disposition.

For these reasons the virtues are not faculties. For we are not called either good or bad, nor are we praised or blamed for having simple capacity for emotion. Also while Nature gives us our faculties, it is not Nature that makes us good or bad; but this point we have already

discussed. If then the virtues are neither emotions nor faculties, all that remains is that they must be moral states.

CHAPTER 5.   The nature of virtue has been now described in kind. But it is not enough to say merely that virtue is a moral state; we must also describe the character of that moral state.

We may assert then that every virtue or excellence puts into good condition that of which it is a virtue or excellence, and enables it to perform its work well. Thus excellence in the eye makes the eye good and its function good, for by excellence in the eye we see well. Similarly, excellence of the horse makes a horse excellent himself and good at racing, at carrying its rider and at facing the enemy. If then this rule is universally true, the virtue or excellence of a man will be such a moral state as makes a man good and able to perform his proper function well. How this will be the case we have already explained, but another way of making it clear will be to study the nature or character of virtue.

Now of everything, whether it be continuous or divisible, it is possible to take a greater, a smaller, or an equal amount, and this either in terms of the thing itself or in relation to ourselves, the equal being a mean between too much and too little. By the mean in terms of the thing itself, I understand that which is equally distinct from both its extremes, which is one and the same for every man. By the mean relatively to ourselves, I understand that which is neither too much nor too little for us; but this is not one nor the same for everybody. Thus if 10 be too much and 2 too little, we take 6 as a mean in terms of the thing itself; for 6 is as much greater than 2 as it is less than 10, and this is a mean in arithmetical proportion. But the mean considered relatively to ourselves may not be ascertained in that way. It does not follow that if 10 pounds of meat is too much and 2 too little for a man to eat, the trainer will order him 6 pounds, since this also may be too much or too little for him who is to take it; it will be too little, for example, for Milo [4] but too much for a be-

---

[4] The famous wrestler, Milo of Croton.

ginner in gymnastics. The same with running and wrestling; the right amount will vary with the individual. This being so, the skillful in any art avoids alike excess and deficiency; he seeks and chooses the mean, not the absolute mean, but the mean considered relatively to himself.

Every art then does its work well, if it regards the mean and judges the works it produces by the mean. For this reason we often say of successful works of art that it is impossible to take anything from them or to add anything to them, which implies that excess or deficiency is fatal to excellence but that the mean state ensures it. Good artists too, as we say, have an eye to the mean in their works. Now virtue, like Nature herself, is more accurate and better than any art; virtue, therefore, will aim at the mean. I speak of moral virtue, since it is moral virtue which is concerned with emotions and actions, and it is in these we have excess and deficiency and the mean. Thus it is possible to go too far, or not far enough in fear, pride, desire, anger, pity, and pleasure and pain generally, and the excess and the deficiency are alike wrong; but to feel these emotions at the right times, for the right objects, towards the right persons, for the right motives, and in the right manner, is the mean or the best good, which signifies virtue. Similarly, there may be excess, deficiency, or the mean, in acts. Virtue is concerned with both emotions and actions, wherein excess is an error and deficiency a fault, while the mean is successful and praised, and success and praise are both characteristics of virtue.

It appears then that virtue is a kind of mean because it aims at the mean.

On the other hand, there are many different ways of going wrong; for evil is in its nature infinite ɔ use the Pythagorean [5] phrase, but good is finite and there is only one possible way of going right. So

[5] The Pythagoreans who saw a mystical and moral significance in numbers, took the opposite principles of "the finite" and "the infinite" to represent respectively good and evil.

the former is easy and the latter is difficult; it is easy to miss the mark but difficult to hit it. And so by our reasoning excess and deficiency are characteristics of vice and the mean is a characteristic of virtue.

"For good is simple, evil manifold." [6]

CHAPTER 6.   Virtue then is a state of deliberate moral purpose, consisting in a mean relative to ourselves, the mean being determined by reason, or as a prudent man would determine it. It is a mean, firstly, as lying between two vices, the vice of excess on the one hand, and the vice of deficiency on the other, and, secondly, because, whereas the vices either fall short of or go beyond what is right in emotion and action, virtue discovers and chooses the mean. Accordingly, virtue, if regarded in its essence or theoretical definition, is a mean, though, if regarded from the point of view of what is best and most excellent, it is an extreme.

But not every action or every emotion admits of a mean. There are some whose very name implies wickedness, as, for example, malice, shamelessness, and envy among the emotions, and adultery, theft, and murder among the actions. All these and others like them are marked as intrinsically wicked, not merely the excesses or deficiencies of them. It is never possible then to be right in them; they are always sinful. Right or wrong in such acts as adultery does not depend on our committing it with the right woman, at the right time, or in the right manner; on the contrary, it is wrong to do it at all. It would be equally false to suppose that there can be a mean or an excess or deficiency in unjust, cowardly or licentious conduct; for, if that were so, it would be a mean of excess and deficiency, an excess of excess and a deficiency of deficiency. But as in temperance and courage there can be no excess or deficiency, because the mean there is in a sense an extreme, so too in these other cases there cannot

[6] A line—perhaps Pythagorean—of unknown authorship.

be a mean or an excess or a deficiency, but however the acts are done, they are wrong. For in general an excess or deficiency does not have a mean, nor a mean an excess or deficiency. . . .

CHAPTER 8. There are then three dispositions, two being vices, namely, excess and deficiency, and one virtue, which is the mean between them; and they are all in a sense mutually opposed. The extremes are opposed both to the mean and to each other, and the mean is opposed to the extremes. For as the equal if compared with the less is greater, but if compared with the greater is less, so the mean state, whether in emotion or action, if compared with deficiency is excessive, but if compared with excess is deficient. Thus the brave man appears foolhardy compared with the coward, but cowardly compared with the foolhardy. Similarly, the temperate man appears licentious compared with the insensible man but insensible compared with the licentious; and the liberal man appears extravagant compared with the stingy man but stingy compared with the spend-thrift. The result is that the extremes each denounce the mean as belonging to the other extreme; the coward calls the brave man foolhardy, and the foolhardy man calls him cowardly; and so on in other cases.

But while there is mutual opposition between the extremes and the mean, there is greater opposition between the two extremes than between extreme and the mean; for they are further removed from each other than from the mean, as the great is further from the small and the small from the great than either from the equal. Again, while some extremes show some likeness to the mean, as foolhardiness to courage and extravagance to liberality, there is the greatest possible dissimilarity between extremes. But things furthest removed from each other are called opposites; hence the further things are removed, the greater is the opposition between them.

In some cases it is deficiency and in others excess which is more opposed to the mean. Thus it is not foolhardiness, an excess, but

cowardice, a deficiency, which is more opposed to courage, nor is it insensibility, a deficiency, but licentiousness, an excess, which is more opposed to temperance. There are two reasons why this should be so. One lies in the nature of the matter itself; for when one of two extremes is nearer and more like the mean, it is not this extreme but its opposite that we chiefly contrast with the mean. For instance, as foolhardiness seems more like and nearer to courage than cowardice, it is cowardice that we chiefly contrast with courage; for things further removed from the mean seem to be more opposite to it. This reason lies in the nature of the matter itself; there is a second which lies in our own nature. The things to which we ourselves are naturally more inclined we think more opposed to the mean. Thus we are ourselves naturally more inclined to pleasures than to their opposites, and are more prone therefore to self-indulgence than to moderation. Accordingly we speak of those things in which we are more likely to run to great lengths as more opposed to the mean. Hence licentiousness, which is an excess, seems more opposed to temperance than insensibility.

CHAPTER 9. We have now sufficiently shown that moral virtue is a mean, and in what sense it is so; that it is a mean as lying between two vices, a vice of excess on the one side and a vice of deficiency on the other, and as aiming at the mean in emotion and action.

That is why it is so hard to be good; for it is always hard to find the mean in anything; it is not everyone but only a man of science who can find the mean or center of a circle. So too anybody can get angry—that is easy—and anybody can give or spend money, but to give it to the right person, to give the right amount of it, at the right time, for the right cause and in the right way, this is not what anybody can do, nor is it easy. That is why goodness is rare and praiseworthy and noble. One then who aims at a mean must begin by

departing from the extreme that is more contrary to the mean; he must act in the spirit of Calypso's advice,

"Far from this spray and swell hold thou thy ship," [7]

for of the two extremes one is more wrong than the other. As it is difficult to hit the mean exactly, we should take the second best course,[8] as the saying is, and choose the lesser of two evils. This we shall best do in the way described, that is, steering clear of the evil which is further from the mean. We must also note the weaknesses to which we are ourselves particularly prone, since different natures tend in different ways; and we may ascertain what our tendency is by observing our feelings of pleasure and pain. Then we must drag ourselves away towards the opposite extreme; for by pulling ourselves as far as possible from what is wrong we shall arrive at the mean, as we do when we pull a crooked stick straight.

In all cases we must especially be on our guard against the pleasant, or pleasure, for we are not impartial judges of pleasure. Hence our attitude towards pleasure must be like that of the elders of the people in the *Iliad* towards Helen, and we must constantly apply the words they use; [9] for if we dismiss pleasure as they dismissed Helen, we shall be less likely to go wrong. By action of this kind, to put it summarily, we shall best succeed in hitting the mean.

Undoubtedly this is a difficult task, especially in individual cases. It is not easy to determine the right manner, objects, occasion and duration of anger. Sometimes we praise people who are deficient in anger, and call them gentle, and at other times we praise people who

---

[7] *Odyssey* XII, 219, 220; but it is Odysseus who speaks there, and the advice has been given him not by Calypso but by Circe.

[8] The Greek proverb means properly "we must take to the oars, if sailing is impossible."

[9]
"No marvel that the Trojans and shining-greaved Achaeans
For such a woman year on year do suffer toil and woe;
Since fearfully is she in face like the deathless goddesses—
E'en so, in all her splendor, let the ships take her home,
Let her not stay, a curse to us and to our babes hereafter."

Iliad, III. See Classics Club edition. **p. 45.**

exhibit a fierce temper as high spirited. It is not however a man who deviates a little from goodness, but one who deviates a great deal, whether on the side of excess or of deficiency, that is blamed; for he is sure to call attention to himself. It is not easy to decide in theory how far and to what extent a man may go before he becomes blameworthy, but neither is it easy to define in theory anything else in the region of the senses; such things depend on circumstances, and our judgment of them depends on our perception.

So much then is plain, that the mean is everywhere praiseworthy, but that we ought to aim at one time towards an excess and at another towards a deficiency; for thus we shall most easily hit the mean, or in other words reach excellence.

BOOK III

A man is praised or blamed only for his voluntary acts. Involuntary acts, committed in ignorance or under compulsion, may be forgiven. Moral purpose is a deliberate desire to bring about something good within our power to be accomplished. Courage and temperance are moral virtues that represent means, the former a mean between the vices of cowardliness and foolhardiness in our attitude toward things terrifying, the latter between licentiousness and insensibility in our attitude toward bodily pleasure.

CHAPTER I. As virtue is concerned with emotion and action, and emotions and actions that are voluntary are objects for praise or blame, while those that are involuntary are objects for pardon and sometimes for pity, we must, I think, in a study of virtue distinguish the voluntary from the involuntary. It will also be useful

for lawmakers for its bearing on the award of honors and punishments.

Acts done under compulsion or from ignorance are generally considered involuntary. An act is compulsory if its origin is external to the doer or sufferer, that is, if it is one to which the doer or sufferer contributes nothing, as if, for example, the wind, or people who have us in their power, were to carry us in a certain direction. But if an act is performed for fear of some greater evil or for some noble end, as, for example, if a tyrant, who had our parents and children in his power, were to order us to do some shameful act on condition that, if we did it, their lives would be spared, and, if not, they would be put to death, it is questionable whether such an act is voluntary or involuntary. The act of throwing goods overboard during a storm at sea is of the same sort; for nobody would voluntarily make such a sacrifice in the abstract, yet every sensible person will make it for his own safety and that of his companions. Acts like these are of a mixed character, yet more like voluntary than involuntary acts, for they are the results of choice at the time, and the end of the act is a result of the choice made at the moment of performing it. When we speak then of an action as voluntary or involuntary, we must regard the occasion when it was performed. The person [1] whose acts we are here considering acts voluntarily; for in acts like his the power which sets the machinery of his limbs in motion is in himself, and when the origin of anything is in the person himself, it lies with him either to do it or not to do it. Such actions then are voluntary, although in the abstract they may be called involuntary; because nobody would choose any such act in itself.

Such acts are at times objects of praise, when men submit to something shameful or painful for the sake of gaining something great and noble; in a contrary case they are objects of blame, for only a bad man would submit to something utterly shameful, if his object were ignoble or only trivial. Some acts are pardonable, though not

[1] That is, the person who acts at the command of a tyrant or when he is at sea, under stress of stormy weather.

praiseworthy, as when a person is induced to do wrong by pressure too strong for human nature, that no one could resist. Yet there are acts, perhaps, we cannot be compelled to do; we should rather suffer the most dreadful form of death than do them. So the reasons which forced Alcmaeon in Euripides [2] to murder his mother are clearly ridiculous.

It is sometimes difficult to determine what ought to be chosen or endured in order to obtain or avoid a certain result. But it is still more difficult to abide by our decisions; for it generally happens that the consequence we expect is painful and the act we are forced to do is shameful; therefore we receive blame or praise according as we yield or do not yield to the constraint.

What class of acts then may rightly be called compulsory? Acts may be called absolutely compulsory whenever the cause is external to the doer and he contributes nothing. But when an act, though involuntary in itself, is chosen at a particular time and for a particular end, and when its cause is in the doer himself, then, though the act is involuntary in itself, it is voluntary at that time and for that end. Such an act is more like a voluntary than an involuntary act; for actions come under the class of particular things, and in the supposed case the particular act is voluntary. And what kind of acts should be chosen for what ends it is not easy to state, as particular cases admit of many differences.

Someone might argue that whatever is pleasant or noble is compulsory on us, because pleasure and nobleness are forces external to ourselves; but if that were so, every act would be compulsory, as these are the motives of all our acts. Also, if a person acts under compulsion and against his will, his act is painful to him; but if he is influenced to act by pleasure and nobleness, it is pleasant. It is absurd to lay the blame of our wrongdoings on external causes, rather than

<hr/>

[2] Euripides was the famous Athenian writer of psychological tragedies of the generation before Aristotle. Alcmaeon is said to have murdered his mother, Eriphyle, in revenge for the murder of his father; but as the play of Euripides is lost, it is impossible to say what "the reasons" alleged in it were.

on the facility with which we are caught by such influences, and take the credit of our noble actions ourselves, while laying the blame of our shameful acts on pleasure. An act then is compulsory if its origin is outside the doer, or if the person who is compelled contributes nothing to the act.

CHAPTER 2. An act committed in ignorance is never voluntary; but it is not involuntary, unless it is followed by pain and regret. For a person who does something, whatever it may be, from ignorance and yet feels no distress at his act, has not, it is true, acted voluntarily, since he did not know what he was doing, but on the other hand he has not acted involuntarily, so long as he feels no regret. If a person who has acted from ignorance regrets what he has done, he may be called an involuntary agent; but a person who does not regret it is in a different case, and he may be called a non-voluntary agent, for, since he differs from the other, it is better he should have a special name.

There is a difference too, it would seem, between acting from ignorance and acting in ignorance. Thus, if a person is intoxicated or enraged, he is not regarded as acting from ignorance, but as acting from intoxication or rage; yet he does not act consciously but in ignorance.

Every wicked person, we know, is ignorant of what he ought to do and what he ought not to do, and ignorance is the error which makes people unjust and generally bad. But when we speak of an action as involuntary, we do not mean merely that a person is ignorant of his true interest. The ignorance which causes involuntary action, as distinguished from that which causes wickedness, is not that which affects the moral purpose, nor again is it ignorance of the universal,[8] for that is blameworthy. It is rather ignorance of particulars, that is, of the particular circumstances and occasion of the act. Where this ignorance exists, there is room for pity and for-

---

[8] That is, of the universal laws of right and moral conduct.

giveness, since one who is ignorant of such particulars is an involun tary actor.

It will be well then to define the nature and number of these pai ticulars. They are

1. who is acting
2. what is the act
3. the occasion or circumstances of the act

Sometimes also

4. the instrument; for instance, the tool
5. the aim; for instance, safety
6. the manner of doing the act; for instance, gently or violently.

Nobody but a madman could be ignorant of all these particulars. Clearly too no one could be ignorant of the actor; for how could a person be ignorant of himself? But he might not know what he was doing, as when people say a word slipped from them unawares or they did not know something was secret, like Aeschylus [4] when he revealed the mysteries; or he might only have meant to show the working of a weapon when he discharged it, like the man who discharged the catapult. Again, a person might take his son for an enemy, like Merope,[5] or a pointed foil for one with its button on, or a solid stone for a pumice stone; or he might kill somebody by a drink that was meant to save him; or he might strike a fatal blow while only intending, as in a sparring match, to show how to strike. Since there may be ignorance in regard to all these particular circumstances of an act, a person may be said to have acted involuntarily, if he was ignorant of any one of them, and especially of the most important circumstances of the act and its end. But if an action is to be called involuntary because of such ignorance, it should be painful to the agent and excite in him a feeling of regret.

[4] The usual story, although it hardly suits the present passage, is that the great dramatist Aeschylus was accused before the Areopagus of having revealed the Eleusinian mysteries and defended himself by declaring that he had never been initiated in them.

[5] Merope, wife of Cresphontes, was on the point of murdering her son Aepytus by mistake, as Aristotle relates, *Poetics*, chap. 14.

CHAPTER 3. As an act is involuntary if done under compulsion or from ignorance, it would seem to follow that it is voluntary if the actor starts it in full knowledge of the particular circumstances of his act. It is probably wrong to call all acts of passion or desire involuntary. For on that principle, in the first place, none of the lower animals could be said to act voluntarily, nor could children; and, secondly, is it suggested that nothing we do from desire or passion is voluntary? Or are our noble acts done voluntarily, and our shameful acts involuntarily? Surely the latter view is ridiculous, if one and the same feeling is the cause of both kinds of act. It would seem strange to say that the things we ought to desire we desire involuntarily; there are things about which we ought to be angry, and things, such as health and learning, which we ought to desire. Again, we think the involuntary is painful; but what we do from desire is pleasant. Again, what difference is there as to involuntariness between errors committed in cold reason and errors committed in anger? It is our duty to avoid both; but the irrational emotions seem to be as truly human as reason itself. So the acts that spring from passion and desire are no less the acts of the man than his rational acts; it is absurd therefore to regard them as involuntary.

CHAPTER 4. Having thus distinguished voluntary from involuntary action, we must go on to discuss moral purpose. For moral purpose is evidently most closely related to virtue, and is a better test of character than acts are.

Moral purpose is clearly something voluntary. Still moral purpose and the will are not identical; the will is the broader term. For children and the lower animals have a share in will; they do not share in moral purpose. Also, we speak of acts done on the spur of the moment as voluntary, but not as done with a moral purpose.

Those then who define moral purpose as desire, or passion, or wish, or opinion of some sort are mistaken. For moral purpose is not like desire and passion, common both to irrational creatures and to

man. Again, an intemperate person acts from desire but not from moral purpose. On the other hand a temperate person acts from moral purpose but not from desire. Desire too is opposed to moral purpose, but desire is not opposed to desire. Desire too, though not moral purpose, is directed toward pleasures and pains. Still less can moral purpose be the same as passion; for no acts seem so little directed by moral purpose as those which spring from angry passion. Nor, again, is moral purpose the same as wishing, although it seems nearly allied to it. For moral purpose does not apply to impossibilities; anyone who said he had a purpose of achieving the impossible would be thought a fool. But there is such a thing as wishing for the impossible, as, for example, for immortality. Again, we may wish for things which could not possibly be won by our own efforts, as for the victory of a certain actor or athlete. But we cannot purpose such things; we only purpose what we think we can bring to pass by our own act. Again, a wish is directed rather to an end but a moral purpose to the means. Thus we wish to be healthy but we purpose or choose the means of keeping our health. Or, again, we wish to be happy and say so; but we cannot appropriately say that we purpose or choose to be happy. For in general our moral purpose seems limited to things that lie within our own power.

Nor, once more, can moral purpose be opinion; for the sphere of opinion is everywhere; we have opinions on things which are eternal or impossible as much as on things within our own power. Opinion too, unlike moral purpose, is distinguished as true or false, not as good or evil. Nobody, perhaps, maintains that moral purpose is identical with opinion generally; but neither is it identical with opinion of any particular kind. For according as we purpose or choose what is good or evil, and not according as we hold particular opinions, are we men of a certain character. Again, we choose to accept or avoid something and so on, but we have opinions as to what a thing is, or for whom or how it is beneficial. We have no opinion not to accept or avoid a thing. Again, moral purpose is praised more for being directed to a proper end than for being correct; opinion is

praised for being true. Again, we purpose or choose what we best know to be good; but we form an opinion of things of which we have little knowledge. Again, it is not the people who make the best moral choice who form the best opinions. Some, who form a better opinion than others, are prevented by vice from making the right choice. Opinion may precede moral purpose or follow it, but that is not the point; the question we are considering is simply this, whether moral purpose is identical with opinion of some kind.

What then is the nature and character of moral purpose, since it is none of the things we have mentioned? It is clearly voluntary, but there are things which are voluntary and yet not purposed. Is it then the result of previous deliberation, for moral purpose implies reason and thought? The very name seems to indicate something chosen deliberately in preference to other things.

CHAPTER 5. The question is, do we deliberate about everything? Is everything a matter for deliberation, or are there some things that are not subjects for deliberation? Presumably we understand by "a matter for deliberation" not that about which a fool or a madman would deliberate, but about which a sensible person would.

Nobody deliberates about eternal things, that is, the unchangeable, such as the universe or the incommensurability of the diagonal and the side of a square; or about things in motion that always follow the same course, whether of necessity or by nature or for some other cause, as the solstices and the risings of the sun; or about things which are wholly irregular, like droughts and showers; or about chance happenings, such as the finding of a treasure. Nor, again, are all human affairs matters of deliberation; thus no Spartan will deliberate about the best constitution for the Scythians. The reason we do not deliberate about these things is that none of them can be affected by our action. The matters about which we deliberate are practical matters, lying within our power. There is in fact no other class of matters left; for the causes of things are evidently nature.

necessity, chance, and besides these only intelligence and human agency in its various forms. Now different classes of people do deliberate about things that depend on their own efforts. The sciences which are exact and complete in themselves do not admit of deliberation, as, for example, writing; for we are in no doubt as to the proper way of writing. But a thing that depends on our own effort and is not invariable is a matter of deliberation, such as problems of medicine or finance. Navigation is more so than gymnastic, for it is less thoroughly systematized, and similarly all other arts. The arts are more matters of deliberation than the sciences, since we are in more doubt about them.

We deliberate over cases which fall under general rules, when it is uncertain what the issue will be, and when we can make no absolute decision. We invite the help of other people in our deliberations over questions of importance, when we distrust our own ability to decide them.

We deliberate not about ends but about means to ends. Thus a doctor does not deliberate whether he shall cure his patients, nor an orator whether he shall persuade his audience, nor a statesman whether he shall produce law and order; nor does anyone else deliberate about his end. They all set up a certain end and then consider how and by what means it can be attained; and if it apparently can be attained by several means, they consider what will be the easiest and best means of attaining it; and if there is but one means of attaining it, how to attain it by this means, and by what means the means can be attained, until they come to the first cause, which in the order of discovery is last. For deliberation, it seems, as we have described it, is a process of investigation and analysis. It is like the analysis of a geometrical figure.[6] Not all investigation, however, is deliberation; mathematical investigation is not; but deliberation is always investi-

[6] The point of the comparison is, that if we wish to learn how to construct a geometrical figure, the best way is often to assume the figure as already constructed and then to work backwards to the conditions necessary for constructing it.

gation, and that which comes last in the order of analysis is first in the order of action.

If in a deliberation we come on an impossibility, we abandon our task, as, for instance, if we need money and cannot get it. But if the thing appears possible, we set about doing it. By possibilities I mean things that may be brought about by our own efforts; for what is done by our friends we may call done by ourselves, since the origin of it lies in ourselves.[7] Sometimes the question is what tools are necessary and at other times how to use them. Similarly, in all cases it is sometimes the means of doing a thing and at other times the method or the agency that is the question. . . .

If the object of our moral purpose is that which, being in our power, is after deliberation the object of our desire, it follows that moral purpose is a deliberate desire for something in our power; for first we deliberate on a thing and, after reaching a decision on it, we desire it in accordance with our deliberation. Let us now leave this sketch of the moral purpose. We have shown what are the matters with which it deals and that it is directed to means rather than to ends.

CHAPTER 6.   We have said that wishing is directed to an end; there are people who hold that the end is a good, and others that it is what seems to be good. If the object of wishing is a good, it follows that where a person's moral purpose or choice is wrong, he wishes for something not in the proper sense an object of wish; for if it is an object of wish it will be a good, but it was perhaps an evil. If on the other hand, the object of wishing is what seems to be good, it follows that there is no such thing as a natural object of wish, but in every man's case it is that which seems good to him. Now different and it may be opposite things seem good to different people.

If these are unsatisfactory conclusions, it will perhaps be best to say that in an absolute or true sense it is the good which is the object of wishing, but that for each individual it is what seems to him

[7] The conception of a friend as "a second self" is thoroughly Aristotelian. See Book IX. p. 214

good. Hence the true good is good to the virtuous man, and something, we cannot tell what, is good to the bad man. The case is much the same with the body; when people are in good health, the truly wholesome things are wholesome to them; but when they are sick, other things are. The same with things that are bitter, sweet, hot, heavy, and so on. A good man is the right judge in every case and that which is true appears true to him. For every moral state has its own idea of honor and pleasure, nor is there perhaps any mark so distinctive of the good man as his power of seeing the truth in all cases, because he is, as it were, himself the standard and measure of things. Pleasure seems to be what most frequently deceives people, for pleasure seems to be a good, when it is not; as a result we choose what is pleasant as if it were good, and avoid pain as if it were evil.

CHAPTER 7.   The end then is the object of wishing and the means to the end the objects of deliberation and moral purpose. It follows that action concerned with the means will be guided by moral purpose and voluntary. Now the exercise of virtue has to do with means.

Virtue and vice are both alike in our own power; for where it is in our power to act, it is also in our power not to act, and where it is in our power not to act, it is also in our power to act. Hence if it is in our power to act when action is noble, it will also be in our power not to act when inaction is shameful; and if it is in our power not to act when inaction is noble, it will also be in our power to act when action is shameful. But if it is in our power to do, and likewise not to do, what is noble and shameful, and if this action or inaction means, as we have seen, being good or bad, it follows that it is in our power to be good or wicked. The saying,

"None would will to be wicked, none would not be blessed," [8]

[8] The line is of unknown authorship.

seems to be partly false and partly true; for while nobody would be blessed against his will, wickedness is voluntary.

Otherwise we shall have to dispute the statements we have just made and say that a man is not the originator or father of his acts as he is of his family. But if these statements are true and we cannot refer our acts to any other source than what lies in ourselves, then the act that has its sources in us must itself be in our power and voluntary. This view is apparently supported by the testimony both of private individuals and of lawmakers; for lawmakers punish and chastise evil-doers, unless they did wrong under compulsion or from ignorance for which they were not responsible; but they honor people who do noble acts, their object being to discourage the one class of deeds and encourage the other. Yet no one encourages us to do what is not in our own power or voluntary. It would be useless, for instance, to persuade us not to get hot, or to feel pain or hunger, or anything of that kind, for we should feel the sensations all the same. We do punish a person for mere ignorance, if it seems he is responsible for it. Thus punishments for drunken people who commit a crime are double, because the source of the crime lies in the person himself; it was in his power not to get drunk, and his drunkenness was the cause of his ignorance.

Again, we punish people who are ignorant of a point of law, if they ought to know it and could easily do so. Similarly, in other cases we punish people, whenever it seems that their ignorance was due to carelessness; for they had it in their power not to be ignorant, since they might have taken the trouble to inform themselves. But perhaps the man is the sort that cannot take trouble; even so, people are responsible for having made themselves persons of that kind by their dissolute lives, or for becoming unjust or licentious by acts of dishonesty, spending their time on drink and other such things. For a person's character is the result of the way in which he exercises his capacities. The rule is proved by those who train for any competition or action; for they never stop practicing.

Now only a fool does not know that moral states are formed by

the exercise of our powers in one way or another. It is absurd to say that a man who acts unjustly does not wish to be unjust or that one who acts licentiously does not wish to be licentious. If a man, acting not in ignorance, commits the acts that will make him unjust, he will be voluntarily unjust. However, it does not follow that, if he wishes, he may cease to be unjust and become just, any more than it follows that a sick man, if he wishes, will be well. It may be that he is voluntarily ill through living intemperately and disobeying his doctors. If so, it was once in his power not to be ill; but since he has thrown away his chance, it is no longer in his power. Similarly, once a man has thrown a stone, it is no longer in his power to call it back; still for all that, it was in his power to throw it, since the source of the act was in him. So too the unjust or licentious man had it in his power at first not to become so; hence he is voluntarily unjust or licentious; but once he has become unjust or licentious, it is no longer open to him not to be so.

Not only vices of the soul but vices of the body also are voluntary in some cases and in these cases blameworthy. For while nobody blames people who are born ugly, we do blame those whose ugliness arises from negligence and want of exercise. It is the same with bodily infirmities and defects. Nobody would find fault with a person who is born blind or whose blindness is the result of illness or a blow; he would rather be an object of pity; but if his blindness were the result of intemperance or licentiousness of any kind, he would be universally blamed. Such bodily vices then as depend on ourselves are blameable, and such as do not depend on ourselves are not. If so, it follows that the other vices, if they are blamed, must depend on ourselves.

We may say, however, that we all aspire after what seems to be good, only we are not masters of appearances, and the appearance which the end takes in the eyes of each of us depends on his character. But if each of us is in some degree responsible for his character, he will in some degree be responsible for the appearance; if not, nobody is responsible for his evil doing, everybody acts

as he does from ignorance of the end, under the impression that by this means he is gaining the supreme good, the aspiration after the true end is not a matter of our choice, and a man must be born with a sort of vision to enable him to form a noble judgment and choose what is truly good. He then who is endowed with this noble judgment is Nature's nobleman, for he possesses the greatest and noblest of all gifts, a gift which can never be received nor learned from anybody else, but must always be kept as Nature herself kept it. To possess this natural gift of virtue and honor is to have a perfect and true excellence of nature.

If this were true, how then would virtue be more voluntary than vice? But for both men alike, the good and the bad, the end is plain and fixed by Nature or whatever it is, and to these ends men direct all their acts, whatever they do. Whether the end then, whatever it be that any individual regards as his end, is not so presented to him by Nature but depends in part on himself, or whether the end is fixed by Nature, the good man uses voluntarily all means to gain the end; in either case virtue is voluntary and vice is voluntary as much as virtue; for in the bad man lies as great a power over his own acts, if not over his end.

If, as is generally allowed, the virtues are voluntary (for we are ourselves somehow in part responsible for our moral states; and because we possess a certain character, the end we set before ourselves is of such a kind), it follows that our vices too must be voluntary, for what is true of one is equally true of the other.

CHAPTER 8. We have now described in outline the nature of virtues in general. We have shown that they are the means between two vices, and they are moral states. We have explained what are the causes that produce them and how their natural result is the performance of acts by which they are further produced, that they are in our power and voluntary, and governed by the rule of right reason. But acts and states of character are not voluntary in the same sense. For we are masters of our acts from beginning to end, if we

know the facts in the case, but we are masters of only the beginning of our characters; we do not perceive the particular steps of their progress, as we do not perceive the particular steps in a disease. Yet because it was in our power to act in this way or that, our characters are voluntary.

CHAPTER 9.   Let us now consider the various virtues and discuss their nature, the matters with which they deal, and the way they deal with them. In so doing we shall ascertain their number.

We will begin with courage. We have already stated that courage is a mean state between sentiments of fear and confidence. It is clear too that the things we fear are frightful; and frightful things may be broadly described as evil. Hence fear is sometimes described as an anticipation of evil. Now, although we fear everything evil, such as disgrace, poverty, disease, friendlessness, death, they do not all give scope for a display of courage. Some things it is right and noble to fear and a shame not to fear, disgrace, for example; for to fear disgrace is to be virtuous and modest, and not to fear it is to be shameless. A shameless person is sometimes called brave by a twist of speech, because he looks something like a brave man; for a brave man too is fearless.

It is perhaps wrong to fear poverty or sickness or anything else that is not the result of vice or one's own fault. Still to be fearless of these things is not necessarily courage, though we speak of one who is fearless of them as brave by analogy; for some men who are cowardly in perils of battle are yet liberal and confident when losing money. Nor is a man a coward if he fears insults to his children or his wife, or envy or any such thing; nor is he brave if he swaggers before a flogging.

What then is the nature of the fearful things before which a courageous man is brave? Certainly the worst kind of fearful things, for nobody is better able to face dangers than he. Now nothing is so frightful as death, for death is the end, and when a man is dead, it seems that he is beyond the reach of good or evil. But on all occa-

sions does a man prove his courage even by facing death, whether facing death at sea or from disease? On what occasions then? Surely the noblest, that is, occasions such as occur in battle, for that is the greatest and noblest peril. For this reason special honors are paid, alike in free states and in monarchies, to citizens who die on the field of battle.

Strictly speaking then, we may call a man brave if he is fearless in face of a noble death, and in all such sudden emergencies as bring death near, especially therefore in face of the risks of war. Still the brave man is fearless in disease and at sea too, though not in the same way as seamen; for a landsman loses hope of safety and detests the prospect of a watery grave, while the experience of the seamen keeps them more sanguine. People display their courage better on occasions when they can show prowess or when death is glorious; but in death at sea or from disease there is scant room for courage or glory.

CHAPTER 10. People are not all terrified by the same things. Some things indeed we feel are beyond the power of human endurance, and such things therefore are terrible to every intelligent person. But terrors that are not beyond the power of endurance vary in magnitude and degree; the same is true of things that inspire confidence. The brave man is unshakable as far as a man may be. Hence, though he will fear terrifying things, he will face them in the right way and in a rational spirit for honor's sake, since this is the end of his virtue.

But it is possible to fear these things too much or too little; and also to fear things that are not frightful as if they were. A fault is committed when the fear itself is wrong or is wrong in manner of expression or in time or the like; the same with things which inspire confidence. Thus he who faces and fears the right things, for the right motive, in the right way, and at the right time, and whose confidence is similarly right, is a brave man; for the brave man in his emotions and his actions has a sense of fitness and obeys the law of reason. Now the end of every man's activity is determined by his

particular character. To the brave man courage is noble; therefore the end or object of his courage is also noble, and the nature of everything is determined by its end. For a noble end then the brave man faces and does all that his courage demands.

As for a man who goes to excess, there is no name for one whose fearlessness is excessive; it is one of the many states which, as we have already remarked, have no names. But he would be an insane or insensible creature who feared nothing at all, not even an earth-quake nor a storm at sea, as the Celts are said to do. A man excessively rash in facing frightful things is called foolhardy. The foolhardy person, however, may be thought an impostor, a boaster of courage that he does not possess. He wishes to seem to face frightful things in the spirit in which the brave man really does face them; there-fore he imitates him as far as he safely can. So most foolhardy people are cowards at heart; for although they show a foolhardy spirit where they safely can, they refuse to face real terrors.

One whose fear is excessive is a coward, for he fears the wrong things and fears them in the wrong way, and so on. He is lacking too in confidence, but he reveals himself more by his excess of fear in the presence of pain. The coward is a despondent sort of person, for he is afraid of everything. The contrary is true of the brave man; for a confident person is naturally sanguine. Thus the coward, the foolhardy person, and the brave man who face the same things, assume different attitudes toward them. For the two first go either too far or not far enough, and the third holds the middle position, which is right. Also, the foolhardy are precipitate and eager before the hour of danger, but fail in its presence, while the brave are keen in the height of action but quiet before the hour of action arrives.

CHAPTER 11. Courage then, as has been said, is a mean state with regard to things that cause confidence or fear in the circum-stances described. It chooses action or endures pain because it is honorable to do so or because the opposite course is disgraceful. But to die to escape from poverty or love or anything painful is the act

not of a courageous person but of a coward. For it is weakness to fly from troubles; nor does the suicide face death because it is noble, but because it is a refuge from evil. . . .

CHAPTER 13. We shall next consider temperance, for both courage and temperance, it seems, are virtues of the irrational parts of human nature.

We have said already that temperance is a mean state with regard to pleasures; for it is not in the same degree or manner concerned with pains. Pleasure is also the sphere in which licentiousness or intemperance displays itself. Let us therefore define now the character of these pleasures. We will accept the distinction commonly made between bodily and spiritual or intellectual pleasures, such as love of honor and love of learning; for he who loves either honor or learning finds pleasure in the object of his love, though his body is not affected but only his mind. However, people addicted to pleasures of this kind are not called either temperate or licentious. It is the same with all other pleasures that are not bodily. Thus people who are fond of talking and telling stories and spend their days on trifles we call gossips, but we do not call them licentious; nor do we call people licentious who are pained at the loss of money or of friends.

Temperance then is an attitude toward bodily pleasures only, and not toward all even of these. For people who delight in pleasures of sight, in colors, forms, and painting, are not called either temperate or licentious. Yet it would seem possible to take either a right or an excessive or an insufficient pleasure in these things as well as in others. It is the same with pleasures of the ear. Nobody speaks of people who take excessive delight in music or acting as licentious, or of people who take a proper delight as temperate. Nor again do we call people who enjoy the pleasures of smell licentious or temperate, except incidentally. We do not call them licentious if they are charmed by the fragrance of apples or roses or incense, but are more apt to do so, if they gloat over the odors of ointments and

sauces; for these are things a licentious person enjoys, because they remind him of the objects of his appetite. It is true we may see other people, when they are hungry, delighting in the smell of food; but it is only a licentious person who habitually gloats over such things, since they are the objects of his appetite.

The lower animals do not, in general, take pleasure in these senses, except incidentally. Dogs do not enjoy the scent of hare's flesh but only the eating of it, though the scent tells them the hares are near by. Again, a lion takes no delight in hearing an ox's lowing, but in eating the ox; however, the lowing tells him the ox is near and so he appears to delight in the lowing. Similarly, it is not the sight of a stag or a wild goat that gives him joy, but the prospect of a meal.

Temperance and licentiousness, however, have to do with the kinds of pleasures that the lower animals generally are capable of, which therefore appear slavish and brutish. They are the pleasures of touch and taste. But taste comes little, if at all, into question, for taste is a judgment of flavor, as when men taste wines or season dishes; but this judgment of flavors gives them no special pleasure, at least not those who are licentious. They want rather the full enjoyment which comes invariably through the sense of touch, both in meat and in drink and in what are called the pleasures of love. This was why a certain gourmand prayed that his throat might become longer than a crane's, showing that his pleasure was derived from the sense of contact. Thus the sense with which temperance is associated is the most universal of the senses. It would seem then right to disapprove of intemperance, since it is a mark not of our human but of our animal nature. To find delight and supreme satisfaction in such things is beastly. The most liberal and refined of the pleasures of touch, such as the comforts of rubbing and of taking a hot bath in the gymnasium, we do not count, because the sense as the licentious man cultivates it is not a matter of the whole body but only of certain parts.

Of appetites and desires some are universal and others peculiar to individuals and acquired. The desire for food is natural. Every-

body who is without it desires meat or drink, or perhaps both. A young man too in the springtime of life, says Homer,[9] desires the love of a woman. But not everybody wants one particular form of gratification or the same things. Hence such a particular desire is peculiar to ourselves as individuals. Nevertheless, there is something natural in it; for different people enjoy different things and some things are pleasanter to everyone than others.

Now in their natural desires few make a mistake, and their mistake is only on one side, that of excess. For to eat or drink anything to the point of surfeit is to exceed the natural limit, since natural desire does not go beyond the satisfaction of our need. Those persons, accordingly, are called gluttons who go beyond what is right in filling their stomachs. Only those who are exceedingly slavish behave in this way.

But with regard to pleasures peculiar to the individual there are many who go wrong and go wrong in many ways. For people who are said to be unduly fond of particular things either take pleasure in wrong things or take more pleasure than most people or take their pleasure in a wrong way, and the intemperate are guilty of excess in all these forms. For they both find joy in things which are detestable and wrong, and when they are things which it is right to enjoy, they enjoy them more than is right or than most people do.

It is clear then that excess in pleasure is licentiousness and blameworthy. When it comes to pain, however, a person is not, as in the case of courage, called temperate if he bears pain well, and intemperate if he does not; but the intemperate person is so called because he suffers more than he should at not getting his pleasures, his pleasure being the cause of his pain; and the temperate man is so called because he is not pained at the absence of pleasure and his failure to get it.

CHAPTER 14.   The intemperate man then wants all pleasures, or the greatest pleasures, and is led by his desire to choose them

---

[9] The reference seems to be to *Iliad*, XXIV, Classics Club edition, p. 375, the words addressed by Thetis to Achilles.

above everything else. He is pained, therefore, both when he fails to get them and when he is simply longing for them, for all desire involves pain. Yet it seems paradoxical to say that his pleasure is the cause of his pain.

We never find people with no love of pleasure or whose delight in it is less than it should be. Such insensibility is not human, for even the lower animals distinguish different kinds of food, liking some and disliking others. A being who took no pleasure in anything, nor made any difference between one thing and another, would be something far different from a man. There is no name for such a being, as he does not exist.

The temperate man keeps a middle position with regard to pleasure. He does not enjoy the things which the licentious man likes best; he rather dislikes them. Nor does he find any pleasure in wrong things nor too much in any pleasure. Nor is he pained at the absence of such things, nor has he a craving for them, except, perhaps, in moderation; not more than is right, and not at the wrong time, and so on. But in a moderate and right spirit he will want all things that are pleasant and that at the same time make for health and a sound bodily condition, and whatever other pleasures are not prejudicial to these ends, or opposed to what is noble, or costly beyond his means. For unless a person limits himself in this way, he indulges in pleasures more than he should, whereas a temperate man follows the guidance of right reason. . . .

BOOK IV

Liberality represents a mean between prodigality and greed in our attitude toward property, magnificence a mean between vulgarity and meanness in the conduct of great enterprises, good temper a mean between bad temper and phlegmatic apathy in affairs that may arouse our anger, and so on with other moral virtues.

CHAPTER 1.   Let us next consider liberality. Liberality seems to be a mean in our attitude toward property. For the liberal man wins praise, not in war, nor in the same sphere as the temperate man, nor again in matters requiring judgment, but in connection with giving and taking of property and particularly with giving it. By property we understand all things whose value is measured by money. Prodigality and stinginess are excesses and defects in connection with property. We apply the term "greedy" to people who care more than they ought for property; the term "prodigality" we use at times in a more complex sense, speaking of people who are intemperate and spend their money in licentious living as "prodigals." Prodigals therefore are taken to be utterly worthless people who combine in themselves several vices. But this is not a proper application of the term "prodigal"; strictly, it means a man with one particular vice, that of wasting his substance. For a prodigal is one who is ruining himself, and to waste one's substance seems a way of ruining oneself, since substance is our sole means of life. In this sense then we shall understand the term "prodigality."

Things for our use may be used either well or badly. Now riches are a useful thing. The person who makes the best use of anything is one who possesses the virtue appropriate to that thing. Accordingly riches will be best used by the man who possesses the virtue

appropriate to property, that is, the liberal man. Now the use of property seems to consist in spending and giving; taking and keeping are rather acquisition. Hence it is more truly the mark of a liberal man to give to the right people than to take from the right quarter and not to take from the wrong. For it is more characteristic of virtue to be a giver than a receiver of benefits, and to do what is noble than not to do something disgraceful. Clearly, giving implies doing good and acting nobly, and taking implies only being well treated and not behaving disgracefully. Gratitude too is the due of one who gives, not of one who does not take; and praise comes to him in a higher degree. It is easier also not to take than to give, for people are less ready to give away what is their own than to abstain from taking what belongs to somebody else. Again, people who give are called liberal, people who abstain from taking are not praised for liberality so much as for justice, whereas people who take are not praised at all. Of all good people none are so much beloved as the generous; for they are benefactors, and their benefaction consists in giving.

CHAPTER 2. Now virtuous actions are noble and have a noble motive. A liberal man then will give from a noble motive and in a right spirit; he will give the right amount, to the right persons, and at the right time, and satisfy all other conditions of right giving. He will do all this too with pleasure or without pain; for virtuous action is pleasant or painless; it is certainly anything but painful. But he who gives to the wrong people, or gives not from a noble motive but for some other cause, will not be called liberal but some other name. Nor is he liberal if giving is painful to him, since in that case he would prefer his wealth to a noble act, and such a preference is illiberal. Nor will a liberal man take from wrong sources; for such taking, again, is contrary to the character of one who is no admirer of wealth. Nor, again, will he be inclined to ask favors; for one in the habit of conferring benefits will not be ready at any moment to receive them. When he does take, it will be from right sources, such as his own possessions; and he will do so not as

if taking were noble, but because it is necessary, if he is to have the means of giving. Nor will he neglect his own property, since he wishes to employ it in aiding others. He will refrain from giving indiscriminately, that he may have wherewithal to give to the right people and at times and in places where giving is noble.

It is natural for a liberal man to go too far in his giving and reserve too little for himself; for disregard of self is a characteristic of liberality. In estimating liberality then we must take account of a person's own fortune; for liberality consists not in the amount of the money given but in the character of the giver,[1] and the liberality of a gift is its proportion to the fortune of the giver. It is quite possible that one who gives less may be the more liberal, if his means are smaller. People who have not made their own fortune, but inherited it, are thought to be the more liberal, for they have never known what want is; and all men are fond of their own creations—parents of their children, and poets of their poems.

It is hard for a liberal man to be rich, since he is not fond of getting or saving money, but rather of spending it; and he values wealth not for its own sake, but as affording him an opportunity of giving. Hence the reproach often leveled against Fortune, that the people who most deserve riches have the least. But the fact is easily explained; for no one can have wealth or anything else without taking trouble to have it. Still, the liberal man will not give to the wrong people, or at the wrong time, and so on; for to do so would be to cease acting in a liberal spirit, and if he spent money on these objects, he would have nothing to spend on the right objects. For a liberal man, as we have said, is one who spends in proportion to his substance and on the right objects. But one who spends beyond his means is a prodigal. Hence we do not call despots prodigals, because they cannot easily exceed by their gifts and expenditures the amount of their own possessions.

As liberality then is a mean with regard to the giving and taking

[1] As in the parable of the widow's two mites.

of property, a liberal man will both give and spend on the right objects and to the right amount, whether in small matters or in great, and will feel pleasure in doing so. He will also take from the right sources and to the right amount. For as the virtue is a mean with regard both to giving and taking, he will do both in the right way. For honorable taking is consistent with honorable giving; but the taking that is not honorable is incompatible with it. Thus consistent giving and taking are found together in the same person, but incompatible giving and taking obviously are not. If a liberal man happens to spend more or less than is right and noble, he will feel pain, but a moderate and proper pain, for virtue naturally feels pleasure and pain for just the right reasons and in the right way.

A generous man is easy to deal with in money matters. He can easily be cheated, for he does not care about money, and is more distressed at not having spent what he should than pained at having spent what he should not; in fact, he is a person who does not agree with Simonides.[2]

CHAPTER 3. The prodigal, on the other hand, is wrong in these respects as in others; for he feels neither pleasure nor pain for the right causes or in the right way, as we shall see more clearly when we proceed.

We have said that prodigality and greed are excesses and defects, and are so in two respects, in giving and in taking, for we count spending as a form of giving. Prodigality exceeds in giving and not taking, but is deficient in taking. Greediness is deficient in giving and exceeds in taking, but is deficient and exceeds in giving and taking on a small scale.

Now the two characteristics of prodigality, namely, giving and not taking, are seldom combined in one person. For it is not easy for a man who has no source of revenue to give to everybody; private persons, if they give in this way, soon find their property running

[2] There are several lines of the poet Simonides which show his appreciation of wealth.

short, and it is private persons who are commonly called prodigals. A prodigal of this kind, however, when he exists, would appear far superior to a greedy person; for his faults are easily cured by age and loss of property, and he is capable of attaining to the mean or middle state. In fact, he has the characteristics of a liberal man, for he gives and does not take, though in neither respect does he act right or well. If he were better trained or otherwise reformed, he would be liberal; for then he would give to the right people, and not take from the wrong sources. Plainly then his character is not a bad one; for it is neither vicious nor ignoble, but foolish, reckless in giving and too much abstaining from taking.

A prodigal of this kind seems far superior to a greedy person, not only for the reasons given but because he does good to many people, while the greedy man does good to no one, not even to himself. But most prodigals, as has been said, not only give to the wrong people, but take from the wrong sources, and are in this respect greedy. They grow grasping, because they are eager to spend and unable to do so easily, since their means soon give out and they are therefore obliged to get means from other sources. At the same time, as honor is a matter of indifference to them, they are heedless and indiscriminate in their taking; they are eager to give but care not at all how they give or how they get the means of giving. The result is that their very gifts are not liberal, because they are not noble in themselves or in their object or given in the right way. These prodigals sometimes enrich people who ought to be poor and refuse a penny to a decent man, while they heap presents on their flatterers and the companions of their various pleasures. Thus they are generally licentious; for, being fond of spending, they squander money on licentious living among other things, and since nobleness is not the rule of their lives, sink into being mere pleasure seekers. A prodigal then, left destitute of guidance, falls into these vagaries; yet by careful training he may come to the mean or right state of life.

Greed, on the other hand, is incurable; old age and disablement of any kind tend to make men greedy. Also it runs in human nature

more than prodigality; for most people are fonder of keeping money
than of giving it away. It is widely spread and assumes numerous
forms; there seem to be many kinds of greediness. For it consists of
two things, namely, deficiency in giving and excess in taking, and
is not always found in its entirety. Sometimes the two sides are
separated; some people go too far in taking, while others do not go
far enough in giving. Those who are described by words such as
"niggardly," "miserly," and "stingy," are all deficient in giving, but
they do not covet or wish to take other people's property. They are
influenced in some cases by a sense of honesty and desire to avoid
disgrace. There are people who hoard or profess to hoard their money
in order to protect themselves against ever being driven to disgrace.
This is the class of skinflints and all others whose names are taken
from their excessive unwillingness to give to anybody. Others again
are induced by fear to keep from taking other people's property,
knowing they would find it hard to take other people's property
without having their own property taken in turn; so they choose
neither to take nor to give.

Others again go too far in taking, for they take anything from
anybody. Such are people who follow low or degraded occupations,
keepers of brothels and the like, and usurers who lend small sums
of money at extortionate rates of interest. All these take money
from wrong sources, and take more than they ought. A sordid love
of gain is common to them all, since they all are willing to wear an evil
name for the sake of gain, and a petty gain at that; for people who
make great gains from improper sources or of an improper kind, we
do not call merely greedy. We do not so speak of despots, when they
sack cities and plunder temples; we call them rather wicked,
sacrilegious, and unjust. But cardsharpers, cutpurses,[3] and thieves
are meanly greedy people, who make money by sordid or shameful
methods; for love of gain makes them all ply their business and
consent to wear an evil name. Thieves run the greatest dangers for

[3] The Greek word means one who steals the clothes of somebody while he is
bathing.

loot; and cardsharpers make money out of their friends, to whom they ought to give. Both classes wish to get wealth from improper sources and have a sordid and disgraceful love of gain; all such forms of taking are illiberal and greedy.

It is reasonable then to regard greed as the opposite of liberality; for it is a greater evil than prodigality, and men are more likely to err on the side of greed than on the side of prodigality as we have described it. Enough then of liberality and of the vices opposed to it.

CHAPTER 4. We naturally discuss magnificence next, as magnificence is also a virtue that has to do with property. But it does not, like liberality, extend to all uses of property; it applies only to those that involve large expenditure, and here it exceeds liberality in scale; for, as the name suggests, magnificence means suitable expenditure on a grand scale. But the greatness is relative to the occasion; a person who fits out a ship does not bear the same expense as one who is head of a sacred embassy. What is suitable is relative to the person, the occasion, and the circumstances. A person who spends his money properly on merely small or unimportant occasions, who can say, in the poet's words,

"Oft to a vagrant gave I," [4]

is not called magnificent, but only one who spends his money adequately on great occasions; for though the magnificent person is liberal, it does not follow that the liberal person is magnificent.

Defect in such behavior is called meanness, excess vulgarity, bad taste, and the like, implying not so much excessive expenditure on right objects as ostentatious expenditure on wrong objects and in the wrong way. But of this we will speak later.

A magnificent man is like a connoisseur in art; he has the faculty of perceiving what is suitable and spending large sums of money tastefully. For, as we said at first, a character is determined by its

4 *Odyssey*, XVII, 420. It is Odysseus who speaks.

activities and its objects. The expenses of a magnificent man then are large and suitable; so too are his results; for in this way the large expenditure is suitable for the result. It follows that the result ought to be worthy of the expenditure, and the expenditure worthy of the result, or of an even greater result. The motive of the magnificent man in incurring this expense will be honor; for honor is a characteristic of all virtues. He will spend his money too in a cheerful and lavish spirit, for minute calculation of expense is a mark of meanness. He will consider how the work can be made most beautiful and most suitable, rather than how much it will cost, or how it can be done in the cheapest way. The magnificent man will necessarily be liberal as well; for the liberal man too will spend the right amount of money and will spend it in the right way. But here the greatness, the grand scale, of the magnificent man will appear, even though liberality has the same field as magnificence. With equal expenditure he will produce a more magnificent result. For the excellence of a piece of property is not the same as that of a work of art. The property which costs most is the most valuable, as, for example, gold; but the value of a work of art lies in its greatness and beauty. The contemplation of such a work excites admiration, and so does magnificence. In a word, magnificence is the excellence of a work of art on a grand scale.

CHAPTER 5. There is a kind of expenditure that we call honorable, such as expenditure on the gods, on votive offerings, temples and sacrifices, and similarly on all that belongs to divine worship; or on popular objects of patriotic rivalry, as when men think they must get up a chorus or fit out a warship or give a public dinner in handsome style.

Now in all these matters, as has been said, account must be taken of the spender and his resources. The expenditure should be worthy of him and his resources, and suitable both to the result and to its author. It follows that a poor man cannot be magnificent, because he has not the means to spend large sums of money suitably. He is

foolish if he makes the attempt, for his expenditure will be out of proportion to his means and inadequate in itself, and a thing that is not done in the right way cannot be good. But magnificence is becoming to people who possess the necessary means—either earned by their own efforts or inherited from their ancestors or relatives and also to persons of rank and reputation and the like, since all these advantages confer greatness and dignity.

Such, in general, is the character of the magnificent man, and such, as we have said, the expenditure in which his magnificence displays itself; it is the grandest and most honorable kind of expenditure. It displays itself also on such private occasions as occur once in a lifetime, weddings and the like, or on occasions of peculiar importance to the state or to the upper classes, or at receptions and farewells to foreigners, or in the exchange of presents; for a magnificent man spends money not on himself but on public objects, and gifts have a certain resemblance to religious offerings. Again, a magnificent man will furnish his house in a style suitable to his wealth; for even a private house may be an ornament to the city. He will prefer to spend his money on such works as are permanent, for none are so noble as these; and in all these instances he will observe the law of propriety; for the same things are not appropriate to gods and to men, or when building a temple and when setting up a tomb. In his expenditure too everything will be great of its kind; there is nothing so magnificent as great expenditure on a great occasion; and when that is impossible, the next thing is such greatness as the particular occasion allows.

There is a difference between greatness in result and greatness in expenditure. Thus the most beautiful of balls or bottles has a certain magnificence as a present for a child, though its price may be trifling and paltry. It is characteristic of the magnificent man that whatever the class of the thing he is producing, he produces it in a magnificent way; the result so produced cannot easily be surpassed, and it is worthy of the expenditure on it.

CHAPTER 6.   Such then being the character of the magnificent man, the man guilty of excess, or the vulgar man, exceeds in spending more than is right, as has been said; for he spends large sums on trifles and displays that are offensive to good taste, such as a dinner for members of his club as sumptuous as a wedding feast; or, when he provides a comic chorus, he brings the members on to the stage in purple robes, as the Megarians do. All this he will do not from a noble motive but merely for ostentation, and because he thinks it will win him admiration. Where he ought to spend a great deal, he will spend little, and where he ought to spend little, he will spend a great deal.

The mean man, on the other hand, will be deficient on all occasions, and after an enormous expenditure will ruin the beauty of his work for a trifle, never doing anything without hesitating over it, and wondering how he can keep expense down to a minimum, and grieving over it, and always imagining he is doing things on a bigger scale than necessary. Both these moral states, to wit, vulgarity and meanness, are vices, though they bring no disgrace on us, as they are not hurtful to others or exactly improper.

CHAPTER 7.   High-mindedness, as its name suggests, seems concerned with high things. Let us begin then by finding out what kinds of things. It makes no difference whether we consider the character or the man in whom the character appears. A high-minded man seems to be one who thinks himself worthy of high things, and is worthy of them. He who does so without being worthy is a fool, and no virtuous man is foolish or absurd.

Such then is the high-minded man. One who is worthy of small things, and thinks himself worthy of them, is temperate or sensible, but not high-minded; for high-mindedness can exist only on a large scale, as beauty exists only in a tall person. Small people may be elegant and well proportioned, but not beautiful. He who thinks himself worthy of high things but is unworthy of them is conceited, though not everyone who takes an exaggerated view of his own worth

is a conceited person. He who takes too low a view of his own worth is over-humble or mean-minded, whether it is high things or average things or little that he deserves, as long as he underrates his deserts. This fault would seem to be worst in one who deserves high things; for what would he do, it may be asked, if his deserts were less than they are?

The high-minded man then holds an extreme position by the greatness of his deserts, and a middle or mean position by the propriety of his conduct, since he estimates his own deserts aright, while others rate their deserts too high or too low. If then he thinks himself worthy of high things, and is so—especially if he deserves the highest things—he will have one particular object of interest. Desert has reference to external goods, and the greatest of external goods we should say is that which we offer to the gods, and which persons of lofty standing most desire, and which we award as prize for the noblest deeds. Now honor answers this description.

The high-minded man then bears himself in a right spirit towards honors and dishonors. We need not prove that he is concerned with honor; for it is honor more than anything else of which the great regard themselves worthy to match their deserts. But the mean-minded man underestimates himself both as regards his own deserts and in comparison with the professed deserts of the high-minded man. The conceited man overestimates his own deserts, even though he does not estimate them more highly than the high-minded man.

The high-minded man, since he deserves most, must be good in the highest degree; for the better man always deserves better things, and the best man the best. Therefore the truly high-minded man must be good. Apparently too the high-minded man possesses the greatness that belongs in every virtue. For it would be totally unlike a high-minded man to run away from danger in hot haste or commit a crime; for what would be his object in doing a disgraceful act, if nothing is great in his eyes? If we examine him, point by point, we shall find it thoroughly absurd to say that a high-minded man need not be good. Were he bad, he would deserve no honor at all; for honor

is the prize of virtue, and is paid to none but the good. High-minded-ness then seems, as it were, the crown of the virtues, for it enhances them, and does not exist without them. Hence it is hard to be truly high-minded, because it is impossible without a noble and good character.

A high-minded man is especially concerned with honors and dishonors. He will be moderately pleased at great honors conferred on him by good people, believing that he is getting his natural due, or even less than his due; for no one can devise an honor worthy of a perfect virtue.[5] Nevertheless he will accept the honor, since they have nothing greater to confer on him. But honor paid by ordinary people on trivial grounds, he will utterly despise, for he deserves something better than this. He will equally despise dishonor, believing it cannot justly attach to him.

The high-minded man then, as has been said, is principally concerned with honors. He will, at the same time, set moderate store by wealth, power, and good or evil fortune of all kinds, whatever may occur. He will not be over-elated by good or over-depressed by ill fortune; for he is not moved by honor itself, as if honor were anything very great. For it is honor which makes power and wealth desirable; the possessors, at all events, of power and wealth strive so to use them as to get honor. So he who looks on honor as a paltry thing will see them in the same light.

CHAPTER 8.   For this reason high-minded people seem to be proud.

The gifts of fortune too contribute to high-mindedness; for people of lofty birth or great power or wealth are considered worthy of honor, since they are in a position of superiority, and whatever is superior in any good is held in greater honor. Thus even the gifts of fortune enhance a person's high-mindedness, as in consequence of them he receives honor from certain quarters. But in truth the

[5] This sentence as showing Aristotle's exalted conception of "high-mindedness" throws light upon several remarks before and after.

good man alone deserves honor, though if a man possesses the gifts of fortune as well as goodness, he is thought still more worthy of honor. But people who possess such gifts, without goodness, are not justified in considering themselves deserving of great things, nor should they be called high-minded, since neither greatness nor high-mindedness is possible without complete goodness. The possessors of great advantages are indeed apt to become proud and insolent; for without goodness it is not easy to bear the gifts of fortune becomingly. Being unable to bear them, and imagining themselves superior to everyone else, such people treat others with contempt, and act according to their own caprices; for they imitate the high-minded man without being like him, and do so only so far as they have the power; for themselves they do no virtuous acts, but treat other people with scorn. The high-minded man is justified in despising others, because his estimate of them is true, but ordinary people have no such justification.

Again, the high-minded man is not eager to run into small dangers, or to run into danger at all, for he values few things enough to risk himself for them. But he will face great dangers and in the hour of danger is careless of his life, since he feels that life without honor is not worth living. He is ready to confer benefits but ashamed of receiving them, for in the one case he feels his superiority and in the other his inferiority. He will try to return with interest a benefit conferred on him, for then the original benefactor will actually become his debtor and will have been the gainer in the exchange. A high-minded person remembers those to whom he has done a service, but not those from whom he has received one; for the recipient of a service is inferior to the one who did it, and the high-minded man always aspires to superiority. Hence he is glad to be told of benefits he has conferred, but dislikes being told of those he has received. That is the reason (he thinks) why Thetis [6] does not mention to Zeus the services she has done him, and why the Spartans in negotia-

---

[6] *Iliad*, I, Classics Club edition, p. 18. It is where Thetis invokes the aid of Zeus on behalf of Achilles.

ting with the Athenians spoke not of their services to them but of their obligations.[7]

It is characteristic too of a high-minded man that he never, or hardly ever, asks a favor but is ready to do anyone else a service, and that, while his bearing is stately toward persons of rank and wealth, it is unassuming towards those of the middle class; for it is difficult and requires dignity to be superior to the former, but easy enough to be superior to the latter; and a dignified demeanor in dealing with the former is no mark of poor breeding, but among plain people it is as vulgar as a display of physical strength at the expense of a sick man.

A man like that too will not be eager to win popular honors or to dispute the supremacy of other people. He will not bestir himself or be in a hurry to act, except where there is some great honor to be won or some great work to be done. His deeds will be few, but they will be great and will win him a great name. He will, of course, be open in his hatreds and his friendships, for secrecy is a sign of fear. He will care for truth more than for reputation, will be frank in word and deed, since his pride will lead him to speak his mind boldly. He will tell the truth too, except when he speaks in irony in dealing with ordinary people. He will be incapable of planning his life to please anybody else, unless it be a friend, since such dependence on another would be slavish. That is why all toadies have the spirit of slaves, and persons of servile spirit are toadies.

Nor, again, will he be given to admiration, for nothing seems to him great. Nor will he bear grudges, for no high-minded person will dwell on the past, least of all past injuries; he will prefer to overlook them. He will not be a gossip; he will not talk much about himself or anybody else, for he does not care to be praised himself or to have other people blamed. On the other hand, he will not be given to praising other people. But not being a gossip, he will not speak evil of others, even of his enemies, except out of pride. He will be the

[7] To what incident Aristotle is referring here we do not know

last person to set up a complaint or a cry for help when something inevitable or unimportant happens, for to do so is to make much of it. He is one who would rather possess something beautiful, though it brought him no profit, than something profitable but not beautiful; and such a preference is a mark of his self-sufficiency.

The high-minded man will be slow too in his movements, his voice will be deep and his manner of speaking sedate; for a man is not likely to hurry, if there are not many things he cares about; nor will he be excited, if he regards nothing as important; those are things that make people's voices shrill and their movements rapid

CHAPTER 9. Such then is the character of the high-minded man, whose character is the mean; he who is deficient in pride is called mean-minded, and he who exceeds is called conceited.

It does not follow that these persons are bad. They are not evil-doers, they are only misguided; for the mean-minded or unduly humble man is one who is worthy of good things but deprives himself of the things he deserves, and prejudices his own position by self-depreciation and self-ignorance; since otherwise he would try to get what he deserves, for it would be good. Not that people of this kind are fools; they are timid rather. But their way of thinking is bad for their characters, for our aims always depend on our estimate of our deserts; and these people give up hope of performing noble acts and enterprises, as well as of external goods, from a feeling that they do not deserve them.

Conceited people, on the other hand, are fools, ignorant of themselves, who make themselves conspicuous by being so; they try for positions of honor under an impression of their own abilities, and then, if they get them, prove failures. They rig themselves up in fine clothes and pose for effect, and so on; they wish what good fortune they have to be known to the world, and talk about themselves, as if that were the road to honor.

Undue humility, rather than conceit, is opposed to high-mindedness; for it is a more common and a worse defect. . . .

CHAPTER 11. Good temper is a mean with respect to angry feelings; but there is no well recognized name for the mean, nor indeed, it may be said, for the extremes. We apply the term "good temper" to the mean, though, as understood, it leans toward the deficiency, which has no name. The excess may be described as bad temper of a sort or irritability. The feeling is anger, and the causes which produce it are many and various.

A person is praised who is angry for the right reasons, with the right people, and also in the right way, at the right time and for the right length of time; such a person is called good-tempered, since good temper is a term of praise. In effect, a good-tempered person is one who tends to be cool and not swept away by his feeling, but who will be angry in the way, for the causes, and for as long a time as reason may require. But he will probably err on the side of deficiency; for a good-tempered person is inclined to forgiveness rather than to revenge.

The deficiency, whether it is a sort of phlegmatic disposition or something else, is open to blame; for people look foolish, if they are not angry for the right reasons or in the right way. Then it looks as if they had no feeling or no sense of pain, and, since they do not get angry, as if they would be incapable of defending themselves. And it is a slavish nature that will submit to be insulted or let a friend be insulted unresistingly.

The excess may take any one of all the aforesaid forms. We may be angry with the wrong people, or for the wrong reasons, or more than is right, or too hastily, or for too long. I do not mean that all these faults are found in the same person; that would be impossible because evil is self-destructive, and, if it exists in complete form, becomes intolerable.

Quick-tempered people get angry quickly and with the wrong person, or for the wrong reasons, or more than is right. But they soon get over being angry; indeed this is the best point about them. It is because they do not control their anger; they are so quick-tempered that they retort bluntly and then have done. Hot-tempered people

again are excessively quick and get angry at every provocation and for every reason; hence their name. Sullen people are slow to make friends again and because they keep their temper down their anger lasts a long time. Retaliation brings them a feeling of relief; for their revenge makes them forget their anger by producing a state of pleasure instead of resentment. But if they do not retaliate, the burden remains; for since they do not reveal their anger, no one helps to reason them out of it, and it takes time for a person to digest his anger in his own soul. Sullen people are the greatest possible nuisance to themselves and to their best friends.

We call people bad-tempered if they get angry for the wrong reasons, and more than is right, and for too long a time, and if they will not make friends again without revenge or punishment. Such people are most difficult to live with. We generally regard the excess, that is, the irritable rather than the phlegmatic disposition, as the opposite of good temper; for it is more frequent, because it is more natural to men to want vengeance than to forgive. . . .

CHAPTER 12. Let this suffice for the moral states which have to do with anger.

In human society, with its common life and association in words and deeds, there are persons who seem obsequious. They are people who try to please us by praising everything we do and never opposing us, and who think they ought to take care not to annoy anybody they meet. There are others who take the contrary line of always opposing us and never give a thought to the pain they cause; these are called surly and quarrelsome people.

The characters thus described are patently wrong, and the middle state, in virtue of which a person will accept or object to the right things in the right spirit, is praiseworthy. No special name has been given to this mean, but it is most nearly like friendliness; for the person in whom it exists resembles our idea of a good friend, except that friendship implies affection as well. It differs from friendship in that it involves no emotion or affection for one's associates; for it is

not friendship or hatred that makes such a person accept things in the right spirit but his own character. For he will behave the same to strangers and to acquaintances and to people with whom he is and is not intimate, except that in each case his conduct will be suitable; for it is not natural to pay the same regard to strangers as to intimate friends, or to be equally scrupulous about causing them pain.

We have said in general terms that such a person will associate with other people in the right spirit, but should add that in his endeavor to avoid giving pain and to co-operate in giving pleasure, he will never lose sight of what is noble and expedient. He seems to be concerned with the pleasures and pains of human society. Yet whenever it is not honorable or is harmful for him to join in giving pleasure, he will refuse and prefer to give pain; or if his co-operation brings discredit and considerable discredit or injury on his companion, while his opposition causes him only slight pain, he will not join with him but oppose him. . . .

CHAPTER 13. . . . The people who make it their object to give pleasure or pain in the social intercourse of life have now been described. Let us speak next of those who are truthful and false, whether in word or in deed or in their pretensions.

The boaster is one who is fond of pretending to possess qualities which the world esteems, when he does not possess them, or does not possess them to the extent that he pretends. The falsely modest person, on the contrary, denies or disparages what he possesses. The person in between is a sort of "plain dealer," truthful both in life and in speech; he owns to having what he has; he neither exaggerates nor underrates it. Now it is possible to be boastful or falsely modest either with or without an ulterior motive. But every man speaks, acts, and lives in accordance with his character, if he has no ulterior object in view. Falsehood is base in itself and should be condemned, truth is noble and praiseworthy. So the truthful person, as he holds a mean or intermediate position, is praiseworthy and both kinds of untruthful persons are blameworthy, but especially the boaster.

Let us speak of them both, but first of the truthful man. We are not discussing one who is true to his legal contracts, or in the matters that fall in the domain of justice or injustice (for these things belong to a different virtue), but the man who, without any such important issue at stake, is truthful both in word and in life, because his character is truthful. Such a man would seem to be virtuous; for he who loves truth and is truthful when the matter is of no importance will be equally true when it is of great importance. He avoids falsehood as something disgraceful, for he avoids it in itself, apart from its consequences; and to avoid it so is admirable. He inclines by preference to understate the truth, for it seems in better taste than to overstate it, because exaggerations are irritating.

A person who pretends to greater things than he has, with no ulterior motive in doing so, is a fellow of low character, for otherwise he would not take pleasure in a falsehood; but he looks more foolish than bad. If, however, he has an object in view, if that object be glory or honor, he, like the boaster, is not to be blamed severely; but if it be money or a way to get money, he is a more discreditable character. It is no particular faculty but a particular state of character that makes a boaster; for he boasts because of his moral state and character, even as one man lies because he takes pleasure in a lie for its own sake, and another to win reputation or money. So boastful people, if their object is reputation, pretend to the qualities that win praise or congratulation, and, if their object is gain, pretend to qualities useful to their neighbors, their own lack of which cannot easily be proved, as, for example, a skill in prophesying or in healing. This is why most boasters claim qualities like these and boast of them.

Falsely modest people, on the other hand, in depreciating themselves show a more delicate character, for their object is apparently not to get something but to avoid pomp and show. They are particularly apt to disclaim the qualities the boaster claims, namely, the qualities which the world esteems; as was the way of Socrates. People

who deny things trivial and obvious are called humbugs; they deserve more contempt.

But false modesty appears sometimes as boastfulness, as it does in the dress of Spartans; for both exaggerated deficiency and excess are forms of boastfulness. But people who understate in moderation, and about matters that are not too obvious and self-evident, give an impression of refinement.

The boaster then seems to be the opposite of the truthful man, for he is worse than the too modest man.

CHAPTER 14.   Since life includes rest as well as business, and elements of rest are recreation and amusement, here too there is a form of intercourse which is in good taste. There are right things to say and a right way of saying them; and the same is true of listening. But the right way of speaking or of listening varies according to the class of people to whom one speaks or listens.

In this matter as in others, it is possible to go beyond or to fall short of the mean. Now those who carry humor beyond the proper limit are vulgar clowns, for their hearts are set on humor at any cost, and they aim rather at raising a laugh than at using decent language and not giving pain to the butt of their fun. On the other hand, those who never themselves make a joke and are indignant with everybody who does, are said to be boorish and crude. People whose fun is in good taste are called quick-witted, a name which implies the happy turns of their art, for their gay sallies seem like movements of their characters, and characters, like bodies, are judged by their movements. However, as subjects of ridicule are never far off and most men are more fond than they should be of fun and mockery, it happens that not only true wits but clowns are called witty, because they too are amusing. But from what we have said, it is clear that there is a difference, and a wide difference, between the two.

The characteristic of the mean is tact. A person of tact is one who will use and listen to such language as is suitable to a well-bred man.

for there are things a well-bred man may fitly say and listen to in the way of fun; and the fun of such a man is different from that of a vulgar man, and the fun of a cultivated person from that of an un-cultivated one. We may see this is so by a comparison of the old and the new comedy; in the former the obscenity of the language was meant to raise a laugh, in the latter it is rather innuendo, which makes a great difference from the point of view of decorum.

Shall we define a good jester as one who uses language that befits a man of breeding and who does not give pain or actually gives pleasure to his listener? Or on the latter points, is it probably impossi-ble to agree, for different things are detestable or agreeable to different people? But the language to which such a man listens will resemble the language he uses; he will make such jests as he can bear to listen to. There will be some kinds of joke then that he will not make, for joking is a kind of mocking, and there are some kinds of mockery which lawmakers prohibit. They ought perhaps to have prohibited certain kinds of joking as well.

Such will be, therefore, the character of the well-bred man; he will be, so to speak, a law unto himself. And such is the character of the mean, whether we call it tact or wit. But a clown is a slave of his own sense of humor; he will spare neither himself nor anybody else, if he can raise a laugh, and he will use language that no person of refinement would use or, sometimes, even listen to. A boor is useless for such social purposes; he contributes nothing and takes offense at everything. Yet relaxation and fun are indispensable ele-ments in life.

The means in life which we have now described are three, namely, friendliness, truthfulness, and wit. They are all concerned with social intercourse in words and deeds. They are different in that one is concerned with truth and the other two with what is agreeable; and, of the two which are concerned with agreeableness, one belongs to the sphere of recreation, the other to that of general intercourse in life.

CHAPTER 15. It would not be right to call shame a virtue, for it is more an emotion than a moral state; at least it may be defined as a kind of fear of disgrace. In its effects it is comparable to the fear of danger, for people blush when they are ashamed and turn pale when they are afraid of death. Both then seem to be bodily states, which are marks of emotion rather than states of character.

The feeling is not appropriate to all ages but to youth. The young, we think, should show a sense of shame, since their life is one of emotion and full of mistakes, and shame holds them in check. We praise young men for showing a sense of shame, but no one would praise an old one for shamefacedness, for we think he should not do anything to cause him shame. Neither will a good man feel shame, because shame is the result of misbehavior; and he ought not to misbehave himself. It makes no difference whether the behavior has been really disgraceful, or something regarded as disgraceful; people ought not to do either kind of thing, and therefore ought not to be ashamed. It is only a man of bad character who will be capable of doing something really disgraceful.

To have such a character as to feel shame when one has done anything wrong, but then on that score to imagine oneself to be good, is absurd; for shame is felt for voluntary acts, and a good man will never voluntarily do what is base. Still shame conditionally can be a good thing. If a good man should act in that way, he would be ashamed. But there is nothing conditional about the virtues. Granting that it is bad to be shameless and to feel no shame at doing disgraceful deeds, we need not conclude it is good to do them and then be ashamed of doing them.

Similarly, self-control [8] is not a virtue, but a sort of mixed state, as will be shown later on. But now let us proceed to consider justice.

[8] The point of similarity is that self-control implies the presence of a wrong desire, as shame implies the performance of a wrong action.

BOOK V

Justice in its most general sense is voluntary obedience to law. As such it includes all the moral virtues. In its limited or particular sense, it signifies taking no more than one's fair share of fortune's goods, which implies equality or due proportion in their distribution and in correction of injustices. Money is a measure of value that makes possible a fair exchange of goods and services in society. Can a man be unjust to himself?

CHAPTER I. We come now to investigate justice and in-justice. We have to consider the kinds of acts with which they deal, the sense in which justice is a mean, and the extremes between which it is a mean. In the investigation we will follow the same plan we have used with the virtues already described. . . .

Let us first then ascertain all the various meanings of the word "unjust." A man is unjust if he breaks the law of the land; he is unjust if he takes more than his fair share of anything. Clearly then the just man will be (1) one who keeps the law, (2) one who is fair. So what is just is (1) what is lawful, (2) what is fair; what is unjust is (1) what is unlawful, (2) what is unfair.

Now, as the unjust man in the second of these two senses is one who takes more than his share, he will be concerned with goods—not with all goods, but with all the goods of fortune, which in an absolute sense are always good, though not always good for the individual. They are indeed the objects of men's prayers and efforts; but men ought rather to pray that the things that are absolutely good may be good also for them, and to choose the things that are good for them.

The unjust man does not always choose more than his share; on

the contrary, he chooses less than his share of things absolutely evil. But the lesser of two evils may, it seems, in a sense be called a good. And to take more than one's share means to take more than one's share of something good; of this he is regarded as taking more than his share. Such a person is unfair; for unfairness is a general and comprehensive term.

CHAPTER 3. The lawbreaker being, as we saw, unjust and the law-abiding person just, evidently any lawful act is in some sense just; for all the acts prescribed by legislative authority are lawful, and we call them all just. Laws dictate on all subjects that which is to the interest of the community as a whole, or of those who are its best or leading citizens, either in virtue or in any other way. Thus in one sense we apply the term "just" to everything that tends to create and conserve happiness and the elements of happiness in the body politic. The law commands us to act as a brave man, that is, not to leave the ranks, or run away, or throw down our arms; to act as a temperate man, that is, to abstain from adultery and outrage; and to act as a good-tempered man, that is, to abstain from violence and abuse. And so with all the other virtues and vices, it prescribes some acts and prohibits others, and does all this in a right spirit, if it is a right law, or in a spirit not equally right, if it is a law passed in the heat of the moment.

Justice then in this form is complete virtue, though not in an absolute sense, still so in relation to one's neighbors. Hence it is often regarded as the supreme virtue, "more glorious than the star of eve or dawn"; [1] or as the proverb runs

"Justice is the summary of all virtue." [2]

It is in the fullest sense complete virtue, for it is the exercise of complete virtue. It is complete because he who possesses it can practice virtue not merely in himself but towards his neighbors, and many

---

[1] The expression is apparently a poetical quotation.
[2] A line variously attributed to Theognis, Phocylides, and other ancient poets.

people can be good at home but not in their relations with their neighbors. So there is truth in the saying of Bias that "office reveals the man," for a man in office is at once brought into relation and association with other men. For this same reason, justice alone of the virtues seems to mean the good of the other fellow, since it implies a relation to other people and works for the interest of someone else, whether our ruler or a simple fellow citizen. As then the worst of men is one who shows his depravity both in his own life and in his relation to his friends; so the best of men is one who shows his goodness not in his own life only but in his relation to others; for this is a difficult task.

Justice therefore, in this sense of the word, is not a part of virtue but the whole of virtue; its opposite, injustice, is not a part of vice but the whole of vice. If it be asked what is the difference between virtue and justice in this sense, the answer is clear from what we have already said. They are the same, but the idea of them is different; the state of character which, if regarded in its relation to others, is justice, if regarded absolutely as a moral state, is virtue.

CHAPTER 4. But we are now to investigate the justice which is only a part of virtue; for there is such a justice, we believe. Similarly, there is a particular injustice which we must inquire into. That it does exist we may infer from the following fact. A person may display other forms of wickedness in his conduct, and yet, though he acts wrongly, not take more than properly belongs to him. He may, for example, throw away his shield out of cowardice, or use abusive language out of bad temper, or refuse money to a friend out of stinginess. And one who takes more than his share may do no other act of vice—certainly not all of them—yet plainly he is wicked in some way, for we condemn his act; in other words, he is unjust. There is then an injustice which is a part of injustice in the broader sense, and a use of the word "unjust" in which it is a part of the wider field of injustice as lawbreaking.

Again, if one man commits adultery for the sake of getting some-

thing and makes money by it, while another suffers expense and loss for the sake of his passion, the latter would seem licentious but not grasping, and the former unjust but not licentious, the reason being clearly that his object was not the satisfaction of his passion but gain. Again, all other kinds of unjust act or crime may be ascribed to some particular vice—adultery to incontinence, desertion in battle to cowardice, and violence to anger; but an act committed for the sake of gain is ascribed to no other vice but injustice.

Evidently, then, besides injustice in the broader sense, there is another particular injustice, which has the same name because its definition falls under the same head, for both have to do with our relations to other people. But the latter is bent on getting honor or property or safety or whatever comprehensive name we may have for all these, and inspired by the pleasure of gain, whereas the former is concerned with the whole wide sphere of virtuous action.

CHAPTER 5.   We see then that there are different kinds of justice, and a kind that is different from complete virtue. We must, therefore, look into its nature and character.

The unjust has been defined in two distinct senses, namely, as what is unlawful and as what is unfair; similarly, the just is defined as what is lawful and as what is fair. The injustice we first described corresponds to unlawfulness. But since what is unfair and what is unlawful are not the same thing, but stand to each other in the relation of part to whole (what is unfair being always unlawful but what is unlawful not being always unfair), it follows that the words "unjust" and "injustice" when used in the sense of unfairness have a different meaning from the same words when used in the larger sense, standing to them in the relation of parts to wholes. For injustice in this limited sense is a part of injustice in the broader sense, and similarly justice in the sense of fairness is a part of justice in the broader sense. We must therefore speak now of particular justice and particular injustice, and similarly of the just and the unjust.

We may set aside then the justice and injustice which correspond

to complete virtue and vice, the former being the exercise of complete virtue and the latter of complete vice in our relations to others. We know too how just and unjust acts corresponding to universal justice and injustice are to be recognized. The majority of the acts the law prescribes are actions that belong to complete virtue; for the law bids us practice every virtue and forbids us to practice any vice. And the things that help to produce complete virtue are all prescribed in the laws that have been passed providing for an education of the individual which makes him not a good citizen but a good man in the absolute sense. We must decide later [3] whether this is a function of political art or of some other; for it may not in all cases be the same thing to be a good man and a good citizen. . . .

CHAPTER 6. As the person who is unjust and the thing which is unjust are unfair or unequal, there is evidently a mean between the inequalities. This mean is what is fair or equal; for any kind of action that takes too much or too little may also take what is fair or equal. If then the unjust is the unequal, the just is the equal, as indeed everyone sees without argument.

And since the equal is a mean between two extremes, the just will be a mean. But equality implies at least two persons or things. [4] The just then is a mean, and equal and relative to certain persons. Inasmuch as it is a mean, it is a mean between the extremes of too much and too little; inasmuch as it is equal, it involves at least two things; and inasmuch as it is just, it is so for certain persons. Justice then must imply four terms at least; because the persons for whom it is just are two, and the things with which it is concerned are two likewise. If the persons are equal, the things awarded them too should be equal; for one thing should be to the other thing as one person is to the other person. If the persons are not equal, they should not

---

[3] The promise is not fulfilled in the *Ethics,* but the question here raised is considered in the *Politics,* III, ch. 4. See p. 293. It must not be forgotten that Aristotle looks upon ethics as a branch of politics.

[4] Fairness in distribution cannot exist unless there are two recipients, nor equality unless there is a division of goods.

have equal shares. The cause of strife and complaints is either that
people who are equal are given unequal shares or that people who
are not equal are given equal shares. The same principle may be
seen applied in the idea of merit. For everybody agrees that justice
in distribution should be based on merit of some sort; only people
do not all understand the same thing by merit. Democrats take it to
mean freedom, supporters of oligarchy wealth or noble blood, and
aristocrats excellence.

Justice then is a sort of proportion; for proportion is not a property
of abstract number only, but of number everywhere. Proportion is
equality of ratios, implying four terms at least. . . .

CHAPTER 7.   The just then, in this sense, is the proportionate,
and the unjust the disproportionate. The disproportionate may take
the form either of excess or defect; which is what actually happens
when the doer of an injustice has too much of something good and
the victim too little. In the case of two evils, the contrary is the case;
for the lesser evil compared with the greater counts as a good, because
the lesser evil is more to be desired than the greater, and what is
desirable is a good, and what is more desirable is a greater good. This
then is one form of justice, that is, of particular justice.

The last form of justice is the corrective, which is shown in connection with private actions both voluntary and involuntary. This
justice is different in kind from the former. Distributive justice,
which deals with common property, always follows the rule of proportion we have described. When, for instance, distribution is made
to two or more people out of a common fund, it will be in accordance
with the ratio of the contributions which they have severally made
to that fund. The injustice too that is opposed to this form of justice
is a violation of proportion. But the justice that deals with private
acts, although in a sense it means fairness or equality, and the corresponding injustice means unfairness or inequality, follows not
that kind of proportion but the proportion of arithmetic. For it makes
no difference here whether it is a good man who has defrauded a

bad man, or a bad man who has defrauded a good man, or whether it is a good or a bad man who has committed adultery. The law looks only to the degree of the injury, it treats the parties as equal, and asks only if one is the author and the other the victim of injustice, or if one inflicted and the other sustained an injury.

Injustice in this sense too means unfairness or inequality, and the endeavor of the judge is to equalize it. For when one person deals a blow and the other receives it, or one person kills and the other is killed, the suffering and the action are divided into unequal parts, and it is the effort of the judge to restore equality by the penalty he inflicts, since the penalty is so much subtracted from the aggressor's profit. For the term "profit" is applied generally in such cases, though it is not always strictly appropriate. For example, the "profit" is his who strikes the blow, and the "loss" is his who suffers it; at any rate, when the suffering is assessed in a court of law, the one is termed profit, and the other loss. The fair or the equal then is the mean between excess and defect. And the profit and the loss are excess and defect, though in opposite senses. More of the good and less of the evil are profit, and more of the evil and less of the good are loss. The mean between them is, as we said, the equal, which we call justice. Hence corrective justice is a mean between profit and loss.

This is the reason why, when people dispute, they have recourse to a judge; and to go to the judge is to go to justice, for the judge is set up to be a sort of personification of justice. And people look for the mean in a judge, and sometimes call judges "mediators," which implies that, if they get the mean, they will get what is just. The just then is a mean, as the judge is a mean. . . . So the just in corrective justice is a mean between profit and loss of a particular kind in cases of voluntary action. It sees to it that the parties to an action have the same amount after it as before. . . .

CHAPTER 8. . . . People seek to return either evil for evil or good for good. It seems like slavery to them not to return an evil; and if they do not return a good, there is no interchange of services;

and it is this interchange that holds society together. Therefore men build a temple of the Graces in their streets to encourage reciprocity of services, for that is a characteristic of grace, to return the service of one who has been gracious to us, and take the initiative in being gracious ourselves.

Now, proportionate returns are brought about by cross-exchange. Thus let A represent a builder, B a shoemaker, C a house, and D a shoe. The builder then must get from the cobbler a part of his work and give him his own work in return. If there is, first, proportionate equality in the goods and then reciprocity follows, the result of which we are speaking is attained.[5] Otherwise the bargain will not be equal or permanent. For the work of one man may perhaps be superior to that of the other, and then they must be equalized. (This is equally true in all the arts; they would be ruined if the result for the receiver were not, in kind, quantity and quality, the same as the result for the doer.) For it is not two doctors who combine to exchange, but a doctor and a farmer, and in general people who are different and not equal and who need to be equalized.

Then the things they have to exchange must somehow be made comparable. This is why money was invented. Money is a sort of medium or mean; for it measures everything and consequently measures excess and defect, for instance, the number of shoes equivalent to a house or a meal. As a builder then is to a shoemaker, so must so many shoes be to a house; otherwise there would be no exchange and no intermingling. And the calculation will be impossible, unless the goods are somehow equalized. Hence the necessity of a single universal standard of measurement, as we said before. Actually this standard is the demand for mutual services, which holds society together; for if people wanted nothing of each other, or wanted it irregularly, there would be either no exchange or it would not be the same as it is now. But money is a sort of recognized representative

[5] The case here supposed is one in which two persons desiring to make an exchange of goods have goods of equal value to exchange; then the simple exchange of one good for the other satisfies the law of reciprocity.

of demand. That is the reason why it is called money (*nomisma*), because it is not nature but a law (*nomos*) that gives it existence, and it is in our power to change it and make it useless. . . .

The fact that it is demand which binds society together as a unit is evident. For if there is no mutual demand on the part of two persons, if neither of them or one only needs the services of the other, they do not exchange; whereas if someone wants what someone else has, they exchange, getting wine, for instance, and exporting corn in return. Here then the wine and the corn must be equated.

Money is useful too for future exchange; it is a sort of security which we possess that, if we do not want a thing now, we shall be able to get it when we do want it; for if we bring money, it will be in our power to get what we want. Money, it is true, is subject to the same laws as other goods; its value is not always the same; however, it tends to be more constant in value than anything else. All things then must have a money value to make exchange possible, and therewith the association of man and man. Money then is like a measure that equates things by making them commensurable; for association would be impossible without exchange, exchange without equality, and equality without commensurability. . . .

CHAPTER 9.   The nature of the just and the unjust has now been described. These definitions make it clear that just conduct is a mean between committing and suffering injustice, for the former is to have too much and the latter to have too little. But justice is a mean not in the same sense as the other virtues, but rather as aiming at a mean amount, while injustice aims at extremes in amount. Through justice a just man does deliberately what is just and acts as a divider, either between himself and somebody else or between two people, in such a way as not to give himself too large and his neighbor too small a share of something desirable (or conversely himself too small and his neighbor too large a share of something injurious). But he gives both himself and his neighbor a share proportionately equal, and the same when he divides anything between

two other people. Injustice, on the contrary, aims at the unjust; and the unjust is disproportionate excess and defect of something profitable or injurious. So injustice is excess and defect, because it aims at excess and defect. In one's own case, it aims at an excess of something absolutely profitable and a deficiency of something injurious; in the cases of other people, its behavior is generally similar, and the disproportion may take the form either of excess or of defect. In an unjust act the defect is the suffering of injustice, the excess is the infliction of it.

Let this be our account of the nature of justice and injustice, and similarly of the just and the unjust in general. . . .

CHAPTER 10. . . . Political justice is partly natural and partly legal. The part which is natural is that which has the same force everywhere and is independent of opinions. The part which is legal is that which, in the beginning, does not matter what form it takes but matters when it has been laid down; as, for instance, that the ransom of a prisoner shall be a mina,[6] or that a goat, and not two sheep, shall be offered in sacrifice. Such too are all laws made for particular cases, like the law for the sacrifice in honor of Brasidas [7] at Amphipolis and the provisions of popular decrees.

Some people think that all rules of justice are of this sort, because what is natural is changeless and has the same authority everywhere, even as fire burns equally here and in Persia, but the rules of justice, they see, are continually altering. Now this is not altogether true, though true to some extent. Among the gods indeed it is probably not true at all; but in this world, though there is such a thing as natural justice, still all justice is variable. Nevertheless there is a justice which is natural and a justice which is not. Within the sphere of possibility it is easy to see what kind of thing is natural and what

[6] That is, roughly, about twenty dollars.
[7] Brasidas, a brave Spartan general, died of his wounds in Amphipolis, during the Peloponnesian War. The citizens built him a tomb and decreed annual sacrifices and games in his honor.

is not natural but legal and conventional, though both kinds are alike variable. The distinction will apply in other cases; thus the right hand is naturally stronger than the left, yet everyone may acquire the power of using both hands alike.

Rules of justice based on convention and convenience may be compared to standard measures. For the measures of wine and corn are not everywhere equal but larger in wholesale and smaller in retail shops. Similarly, the rules of justice that exist not by nature but by the will of man are not everywhere the same; for governments themselves are not everywhere the same, although there is for every place only one naturally perfect government. . . .

There are three kinds of injury people may do to one another in society. An act done in ignorance is a mistake, when the person affected, or the thing done, or the instrument, or the result, is not what the doer expected. For instance, he expected not to hit, or not to hit with that particular instrument, or not to hit that particular person, or not to get that particular result from his blow; but the result turned out different from his expectation. He intended to prick a person but not to wound him, or the person was someone else, or the instrument not what he thought.

Now (1) when the hurt done is contrary to expectation, it is an accident. But (2) when, though not contrary to expectation, it does not imply malice, it is a mistake; for a person makes a mistake when the origin of the harm is in himself, but meets with an accident when it is outside himself. But (3) when a person acts knowingly but without deliberating, it is an act of injustice, like all human acts which spring from anger and other necessary or natural emotions; for in doing that harm, and making those mistakes he is unjust, and they are acts of injustice. Still it does not follow that he is an unjust or a wicked man, since the injury he does is not the consequence of malice. But (4) when the act is the result of deliberate purpose, the doer himself is unjust and wicked.

We rightly hold that acts that spring from anger are not done of malice aforethought; for not he who acts in anger, but he who pro-

voked the anger, begins the quarrel. Again, in most cases of anger, it is not whether a deed was done or not but whether it was just that causes the dispute; for anger starts at the appearance of injustice. It is not as in quarrels over contracts, where two parties dispute about a fact, and one of them must be a rascal—unless they are acting so in forgetfulness. Here they agree as to the fact, but dispute as to the side on which justice lies. The case of a deliberate aggressor is different; he knows on which side justice lies. But the person who acts in anger thinks he is injured, and his opponent does not think so.

If a man injures another of deliberate purpose, he acts unjustly. Such acts of injustice necessarily prove the man who does them to be unjust, if they violate the rules of proportion or equality. Similarly, a man is just who acts justly from deliberate purpose; but his act is just if he merely acts voluntarily.

Involuntary acts are either pardonable or not. They are pardonable if they are mistakes committed not only in ignorance but from ignorance; [8] but if they are not committed from ignorance but in ignorance, from some passion which is neither natural nor common to humanity, they are not pardonable. . . .

CHAPTER 12. We have still to discuss two of the questions we proposed. (1) Is it he who gives someone else more than he deserves or he who receives it that commits an injustice? (2) Can a person be unjust to himself? The questions are connected, for if the first of the two alternatives is possible, if it is the giver and not the recipient of the excessive share who commits the injustice, then, if a person knowingly and voluntarily gives more to another than to himself, he does an injustice to himself. This is what modest people seem to do; for a good man is inclined to take less than his share. Perhaps, however, the case is not so simple as it seems; for it may happen that in giving more of one good thing to another than to himself the man hopes to get more than his share of some other good,

[8] The distinction between acting in ignorance and from ignorance was explained earlier. See p. 116.

such as a fine reputation or pure nobility. The question may be answered by reference to our definition of an unjust act; for, in the case supposed, the giver suffers nothing contrary to his own wish; consequently he is not unjustly treated, at least not on this score, but at most is only damaged.

Still it is evident that the giver may commit the injustice, and not always the recipient of the excessive share. For it does not follow that if a person gets more than is just, he is acting unjustly, but only if he voluntarily does it; as does the person with whom the action originates, that is, the giver, and not the receiver. Again, there are various senses of the word "do." There is a sense in which lifeless things, such as a hand, or a servant who obeys his master's bidding, may be said to kill. But the receiver does not commit injustice, though he "does" something unjust.

Again, if the divider of goods gives his judgment in ignorance, he commits no injustice, nor is his judgment unjust in the eye of the law, though in a sense it is unjust, since there is a difference between legal justice and primordial justice; [9] but if knowingly he pronounces an unjust judgment, he is himself aiming to get an excessive share of popularity or of revenge. And if, induced by motives such as these, he pronounces an unjust judgment, he has got something unfairly, as truly as if he were to take a share of the booty, even though in such a case a judge who awards a plot of land unjustly will receive not land but money. . . .

CHAPTER 15. The foregoing remarks clarify the question whether a man can be unjust to himself or not. For justice, in one of its senses, means the exercise of the various virtues that are pre-scribed by law. Thus the law does not permit suicide and whatever it does not permit it forbids. Again, when a man in defiance of the law voluntarily hurts another, not by way of retaliation, he commits an injustice—"voluntarily" meaning "with knowledge of the person

[9] "Primordial justice" is natural or universal justice, independent of such legisla-tive or judicial enactments as exist in particular states.

affected and the instrument used." Now a man who cuts his own throat voluntarily in a fit of anger is acting in defiance of right reason, and this the law does not allow; accordingly he is acting unjustly. Yet unjustly to whom? Surely to the state, and not to himself. For he suffers voluntarily, and no one can call what he voluntarily suffers an injustice. That is why the state inflicts a penalty, that is, attaches a certain ignominy to the suicide, on the ground that he is doing an injustice to the state. . . .

Further, nobody commits injustice without committing some particular act of injustice; but nobody commits adultery with his own wife, or breaks into his own house, or steals his own property. . . .

[10] Plainly it is bad to suffer injustice and bad to commit it; for the one means having less and the other having more than the mean; and the mean corresponds to the healthy in medicine and good condition in gymnastic training. Still it is worse to commit injustice than to suffer it; for the doing of injustice is blameworthy and implies wickedness, either complete and absolute wickedness or something near to it (for not every voluntary unjust act implies injustice of character); but the suffering of injustice implies neither wickedness nor injustice in oneself. The suffering then is in itself the lesser evil, though it may turn out incidentally the greater. Theory, however, does not concern itself with such a possibility; it calls pleurisy a more serious mischief than a stumble, though the latter may become incidentally more serious than the pleurisy, as, for example, when the man who stumbles falls, and because of his fall is taken prisoner by the enemy and put to death.

Speaking metaphorically or by analogy, we may say there is a justice, not indeed between a man and himself, but between certain parts of himself. I do not mean justice in every sense, but the justice that appears in the relation of master and slave or of husband and wife. For these are the relations of the rational to the irrational parts of the soul. People have in mind this relation of parts when they

[10] The loose structure of this chapter is shown by the passage that follows, interrupting, as it does, the discussion of self-injury or injustice to oneself.

say a man can be unjust to himself, because the parts are liable to suffer something contrary to their desires. Hence there should be some such justice between them as between ruler and ruled.

We may take this as a sufficient description of justice and all the other moral virtues.

BOOK VI

The three faculties of the soul are sensation, which we share with the animals, appetite or desire, and reason. The five means by which reason arrives at truth and intellectual virtue are art, science, prudence, wisdom and intuitive reason. Art is a state of rational creation. Prudence is the activity of our practical reason or judgment in the field of human conduct. Wisdom is a union of science and intuitive reason in the fields of loftiest thought and purpose.

CHAPTER 2.   We divided the virtues of the soul between the moral virtues of character and the virtues of the mind. The moral virtues we have discussed [1] and may now consider the others; but there is a preliminary remark to be made on the soul itself.

We said before that there are two parts to the soul, the rational and the irrational. We must now make a division of the rational part. Let us assume then that the rational elements are two: (1) that with which we contemplate the existences whose principles are invariable and (2) that with which we contemplate variable things. For, when things are different in kind, there must be parts of the soul different in kind, to correspond naturally to each of them; since the knowledge these parts possess of things is due to a certain simi-

In Books II-V.

larity and kinship between the parts and the things. Let the former of these elements be called the scientific intellect and the other the calculating part. For deliberation and calculation are identical; but nobody deliberates on things that are invariable. The calculative then is one element of the rational part of the soul.

We must now discover what is the perfect state of each of these elements of the soul; for the perfect state will be the virtue of each. And its virtue will be relative to its proper function.

There are three faculties in the soul which determine for us action and truth: sensation, reason, and appetite or desire. Of these, sensation alone originates no moral action, as is plain from the fact that the lower animals have sensation but are incapable of moral action. Passing to the other faculties, we see that in appetite or desire pursuit and avoidance correspond to affirmation and denial in the intellect; so, as moral virtue is a state of moral purpose, and moral purpose is deliberate desire, therefore the deliberating must be true and the desire right, if the moral purpose is to be good, and the desire must pursue what the reason affirms. The intellect and truth so described are practical. But the good and evil of the speculative intellect, which is neither practical nor productive, are simply abstract truth and falsehood. For the function of the intellect generally is the apprehension of truth. But the function of the practical intellect is the apprehension of truth in order to promote right desire.

Moral purpose then is the origin of action, that is, the original motive, though not the final cause; and the origin of moral purpose is desire and reason directed to a certain end. Moral purpose then implies reason or intellect on the one hand, and a certain moral state on the other; for right action and its opposite are impossible without both intellect and character. Intellect in itself, however, has no power to move; it must be intellect directed to a certain end; in other words, it must be practical. For the practical intellect governs the productive, since every producer has an object in producing, and the thing produced is not an absolute end, but is relative or leads to something else. But action is an end in itself; and right action is an

end and the object of desire. Moral purpose then may be defined as desirous reason or rational desire; and it is this power of origination that is man.

Nothing in the past can be an object of moral purpose. Nobody, for instance, proposes to have sacked Troy; for we deliberate not on what is past but on what is future or possible, while the past cannot be undone. Thus Agathon [2] says rightly enough,

> "God himself lacks this power alone
> To make what has been done undone."

The understanding of truth then is the function of both the intellectual parts of the soul. Hence the state that will best enable each of these parts to arrive at truth will be that part's excellence or virtue.

CHAPTER 3. Let us go back then and resume the discussion of these virtues. We may take it that the means by which the soul arrives at truth in affirmation or denial are five in number: art, science, prudence, wisdom, and intuitive reason; for in what are merely thoughts and opinions we may be mistaken.

The nature of science, if we are to use exact language and not be led away by analogies, will be clear from the following considerations. We all believe that what we know, that is, an object of science, cannot possibly change. As to things that can change, they are no sooner out of our sight than we cannot tell whether they do or do not exist. It follows that the object of science is something necessary. It is therefore eternal; for all things necessary in themselves are eternal, and what is eternal admits neither of generation nor of corruption, that is, it has neither beginning nor end. Again, it is said that every science is capable of being taught, and an object of science is capable of being learned. . . .

Scientific knowledge then may be defined as a state in which the mind exercises its faculty of demonstration, with all such further

[2] On Agathon see p. 436, n. 24.

qualifications as we add to the definition in the *Analytics*.[3] For only when a person has a certain belief and is sure of the principles on which his belief rests, can he be said to possess scientific knowledge, since, if he is not more sure of his principles or premises than of his conclusion, his scientific knowledge will be only accidental. So much then for the definition of science.

CHAPTER 4.   Among things variable are included both things made and things done. But making is different from doing. On this point we may trust the popular view. The rationally active state of mind then is different from the rationally creative state. So neither of them is included in the other; for doing is not making and making is not doing. Architecture is an art, that is, in essence a rationally creative state of mind. There is no art which is not a rationally creative state of mind, nor any such state of mind which is not an art. Hence art must be the same thing as a creative state of mind under the guidance of true reason.

Again, all art has to do with creation. It has to contrive and consider how to create some one or other of the things whose existence is possible rather than necessary, and whose original cause lies in the creator, and not in the thing itself. For art is not concerned with things that already are or that come into being by necessity or by nature, for the original cause of these things lies in themselves. Creating and doing being different, the end of art must be creation and not action. In a sense, chance and art have the same object, as Agathon says,

> "Art loves Chance, Chance loves Art."

Art then, as we have said, is a creative state of mind under the guidance of true reason; and its opposite, poor art, is a creative state of

---

[3] In Aristotle's logical treatise known as the *Posterior Analytics*, I, ch. 2, he lays down the requirements for a sure and conclusive proof by reasoning of scientific truth—the student must, to begin with, be absolutely certain of the premises on which his reasoning rests.

mind under the guidance of false reason. Both are concerned with the variable or possible.

CHAPTER 5. As for prudence, we may learn its nature by considering who are the people we call prudent.[4] It is characteristic of a prudent man to be capable of deliberating well on what is good or expedient for himself, and that not in some restricted sense, as, for instance, on ways of keeping his health or strength, but on ways of achieving the good life in general. This is shown by the fact that we speak of people who deliberate well even along one particular line, as prudent, when their calculations bring them successfully to some good end that does not fall within the scope of art. In general then, a person who is successful in deliberation is prudent. Nobody, however, deliberates on matters that cannot be altered, or on such as lie outside his own power to accomplish. . . . Prudence then must be a rational and correct state of mind that is active in the field of human goods.

CHAPTER 6. Science is a mode of conceiving universal and necessary truths. Truth to be demonstrated and science in general depend on first principles, for science is impossible without reasoning. Now the first principles on which scientific truth is based, cannot themselves be the objects of science or of art or of prudence; for what can be scientifically known can be demonstrated, and art and prudence deal only with things variable. Nor, again, are these principles the objects of wisdom, since on many subjects the wise man too proceeds by way of demonstration. If then the means by which the soul apprehends truth and always apprehends it about things unchanging or even about things variable, are science, prudence, wisdom, and intuitive reason,[5] and if no one of the first three—prudence.

[4] In the *Metaphysics* Aristotle arrives at the meaning of wisdom by describing the kind of man who is thought wise. See p. 8.

[5] Aristotle here omits "art." On the need of apprehending by intuition the undemonstrable first principles or axioms on which any science is based, see Introduction, p. xvii.

science, and wisdom—is a means of apprehending first principles, our only possible conclusion is that they are apprehended by intuitive reason.

CHAPTER 7.   The term "wisdom" we apply in art to the greatest masters of the several arts. Thus we apply it to Phidias as a sculptor, and to Polyclitus as a carver of portraits, meaning no more by it than artistic excellence. But there are people whom we think wise generally, and not in one particular field or in any other limited sense, as Homer says in the *Margites*,

> "Him the Gods made not wise to delve or to plow
> Nor in aught else."

Clearly this general wisdom will be the most complete of the forms of knowledge.

If so, then the wise man ought to know not only what follows from his first principles; he should know also the truth about these principles. Wisdom therefore will be a union of intuitive reason and scientific knowledge; it may be defined as the complete science of the loftiest matters. For it would be absurd to call statesmanship or prudence the most excellent science, when man is not the best thing in the universe.

Now just as the words "wholesome" and "good" mean one thing for man and another thing for fishes, but the words "white" and "straight" have always the same meaning, so, it will be universally admitted, the word "wise" has always the same meaning, while the word "prudent" may have different meanings. For whatever has a keen eye out for its own interests may be called "prudent" and entrusted with the control of those interests; hence we actually speak of certain beasts as "prudent," if they seem to possess a faculty of forethought in regard to their own life. . . .

Hence too people call Anaxagoras, Thales, and men like them wise, but not prudent, seeing how ignorant they are of their own interests; and speak of their knowledge as extraordinary, marvelous,

difficult, and divine, but still useless, inasmuch as they expect no human goods to come from it.

CHAPTER 8. Prudence, on the other hand, deals with things of human interest that can be deliberated upon. For sage deliberation is, we conceive, the mark above all of the prudent man; but nobody deliberates on unchangeable things, or on those that have no definite object, or whose object is not some practicable good. And he who is thoroughly wise in deliberation is he who aims by a reasonable process at what is best for a man in practical life. . . .

CHAPTER 11. Again, intelligence and its opposite, in virtue of which we speak of people as intelligent or unintelligent, are not in general the same as scientific knowledge or as opinion. For if they were, everybody would be intelligent. Nor is intelligence one of the particular sciences, like medicine, that deals with matters of health, or geometry with magnitudes; for it is not concerned with things eternal and immutable, nor with everything and anything that occurs, but only with the natural subjects of human inquiry and deliberation. Hence intelligence has the same sphere as prudence, although intelligence and prudence are not identical. Prudence is imperative and issues commands; for its end or object is what ought or ought not to be done. Intelligence, on the other hand, merely forms judgments. There is no difference between intelligence and good intelligence, or between people of intelligence and people of good intelligence.

Intelligence is neither the possession nor the acquisition of prudence; but as a scholar is said to be intelligent when he turns his scientific knowledge to some use, so a prudent man may show intelligence in making use of his opinions to form a judgment and a sound judgment on what he hears from someone else about matters requiring prudence; for a wise judgment is the same thing as a sound judgment. . . .

What is called judgment or consideration, in virtue of which we

say some people are considerate or show consideration, is a correct appreciation of what is fair. A proof of this is the fact that we regard the fair man as especially disposed to exercise considerate judgment, and speak of considerate judgment in certain cases as being fair. And considerate judgment is correct judgment or consideration in deciding what is fair; and a correct judgment is a judgment of the truth. . . .

CHAPTER 12. . . . The intuitive reason deals with ultimates at both ends of the mental process; for both the first and the last terms, that is, both first principles and particular facts, are intuitively and not logically perceived. While on the one hand, as a basis for demonstrative reasoning, it grasps the immutable first principles, on the other, in considering matters of conduct, it grasps the ultimate or variable fact, which forms the minor premise of the syllogism; [6] for these variable facts are the starting points for arriving at the end in human life. As universals then are reached by way of particulars, these facts must be grasped by perception or, in other words, by intuitive reason.

The intuitive reason then is at once beginning and end. From the truths perceived by intuitive reason demonstration starts, and with them it is concerned. We should therefore pay no less attention to the undemonstrated assertions and opinions of old and experienced or prudent persons than to demonstrations; for their experience gives their eyes the power of correct vision.

Thus we have now explained the nature of prudence and of wisdom, the subjects with which they are each concerned, and the fact that each is a virtue of a different part of the soul. . . .

CHAPTER 13. . . . There is a faculty which is called cleverness. It is the faculty of hitting and acting on the means which lead to a given object. If then the object is noble, the faculty is admirable, but if ignoble, it is mere smartness; hence we even speak of prudent people as clever or smart.

[6] On the syllogism of Aristotle, see the Introduction, p. xviii ff.

Prudence is not cleverness, but neither can we have prudence without the faculty of cleverness. However, this eye of the soul, namely, prudence, does not attain its perfect condition without virtue, as we have already said, and as anyone may see. For all right syllogisms that relate to conduct start with this premise: "Since the end or the best good is so and so," whatever it may be (for the sake of argument it may be whatever we like). Now the best good is not perceived except by the good man, because vice distorts and deceives the mind when it comes to principles of action. Evidently, therefore, a man cannot be prudent unless he is good.

Let us resume once more the consideration of virtue. For the case of virtue is much the same as that of prudence in its relation to cleverness. Prudence, although not identical with cleverness, is akin to it; similarly, natural virtue is akin to virtue in the strict sense, but not identical with it. For the various moral qualities are in some sense innate in everybody. We are just, inclined to be temperate, brave and the like from our very birth. Nevertheless, when we speak of goodness in the strict sense, we mean something different from this, and look for these qualities in another form. For natural moral qualities exist even in children and the lower animals, but without reason they may clearly do harm. Yet this much seems evident, that, as a strong body moving without sight stumbles heavily, because it cannot see, so it is with natural virtue; but let it once acquire reason and it acts excellently. When that happens, the moral state which before resembled goodness will be goodness in the strict sense. . . .

It is clear then from what has been said that goodness in the strict sense is impossible without prudence, and prudence without moral virtue. Not only so, but this is the answer to an argument which will perhaps be offered, contending that the virtues exist apart from one another. The same person, it may be said, has not a perfect disposition for all the virtues; consequently he will already have acquired one before he has acquired another. The answer is that, though this may happen in the case of the natural virtues, it is impossible in the case of the virtues that entitle a person to be called truly good; for

if he has but the one virtue of prudence, he will have all the others with it.

Even if prudence had no practical value, we should need it as a virtue of its part of the soul, and because our moral purpose will not be right without both prudence and virtue. For prudence determines the right end, and virtue makes us act for the attainment of the end. At the same time, prudence is not superior over wisdom or over the better part of the soul, any more than medicine is superior over health. For prudence does not make use of wisdom, but aims at producing it; nor does it rule wisdom, but rules for wisdom's sake. To say that prudence rules wisdom is much the same thing as to say that the art of politics rules the gods, because it regulates all the institutions of the state.

BOOK VII

> *Three states of character are to be shunned: namely, vice, loss of self-control, and brutishness. The vices have been described in connection with the virtues. A man loses control of himself when he is drawn by emotion into doing what he knows to be wrong. It is neither so bad nor so hopeless a state as cold-blooded licentiousness. Brutishness is morbid or inhuman cruelty. Pleasure is the result of the unimpeded activity of some part of our nature. It may be either good or injurious. Bodily pleasures, being violent, are pursued by people who are incapable of any other.*

CHAPTER 1. It is time now to make one more start and state that there are three kinds of moral states to be avoided: namely, vice, lack of self-control and brutishness.

The opposites of the first two are clear. The one we call virtue and the other self-control. As the opposite of brutishness it is most

appropriate to name a virtue superhuman, what we may call heroic or divine virtue, as when Homer makes Priam say of Hector, that he was exceeding good,

> "nor seemed
> The son of mortal man, but of some god." [1]

If then it is true, as often said, that men are made gods as a reward for surpassing virtue, it is clear that the moral state opposite to brutish will be such a state of virtue; for as in a brute, so too in a god there is neither just virtue nor vice, but in the one something higher than virtue, and in the other something different from vice. But it is rare to find a "divine man," to use a phrase employed by the Spartans when they admire a person exceedingly, and so too a brutish man is rare in the world. Brutishness is found chiefly among barbarians, though it is sometimes the result of disease or deformity; and people who are extraordinarily vicious we call by the same opprobrious name.

This sort of disposition, however, we shall say something about later on,[2] and vice we have already [3] discussed. We must now therefore speak of loss of self-control and weakness on the one hand, and of self-control and steadfastness on the other; for it would be wrong to regard these moral states as identical each with a virtue or a vice, or again as altogether different from them. We must here state, as we have done elsewhere, the generally known facts of the case, and after discussing them thoroughly, establish the truth of all, or if not all, of most and the most important of the popular opinions in regard to these states of character; for if we solve the difficulties and show the justification for the popular opinions, they will be proved sufficiently for our purpose.

CHAPTER 2.   It is popular opinion then that self-control and steadfastness are virtuous and laudable, loss of control and weakness

---

[1] *Iliad*, XXIV. Classics Club edition, p. 378.
[2] See p. 185.
[3] In Books III. IV. V

wrong and blameworthy, and that the self-controlled man is one who abides by his own convictions, and the uncontrolled one who departs from them. Also that an uncontrolled man does what he knows to be wrong under the influence of emotion, but a self-controlled man, knowing his desires to be wrong, is kept by his reason from following them. Also that a temperate man is self-controlled and steadfast. And some people hold that a self-controlled and steadfast man is always temperate, but others do not. Some speak of a licentious man as lacking in self-control, and of an uncontrolled man as licentious indiscriminately; others make a distinction between the two. Again, it is sometimes said that a prudent man cannot be uncontrolled. and at other times that there are men who are prudent and clever but uncontrolled. And lastly, men are called uncontrolled in connection not only with sensual passion, but with anger, love of honor, and gain.

CHAPTER 3.   Such are the views generally expressed. But the question may be asked, How is it that a man whose ideas of duty are right loses his self-control? Some people say that loss of control is impossible, if one has knowledge. It seems to them strange, as it did to Socrates, that, where knowledge exists in a man, something else should master it and drag it about like a slave. Socrates wholly rejected this idea; he denied that control could be lost, arguing that nobody who knew what was best could act against it, and that, if he did so act, he must be acting in ignorance.

Now the Socratic view obviously contradicts the facts of experience. But if ignorance is the cause of what happens to the man, we must inquire what is the nature of his ignorance. For without a doubt a man who behaves in an uncontrolled manner, however he may act, does not think he is acting rightly until after he has got into a condition of no self-control. However, there are people who agree in part with Socrates' view and in part dissent from it. They admit that nothing can master or overcome knowledge, but not that nobody acts against what he imagines is best. Accordingly they hold that the

uncontrolled man, when he is mastered by pleasure, possesses not knowledge but only opinion. However, if he has opinion and not knowledge, if his resisting idea is not a strong but a feeble one, as in cases where we hesitate how to act, the man is pardonable for not remaining true to it in the teeth of strong desires; whereas neither vice nor anything else truly blameworthy admits of pardon at all. . . .

Again, if self-control means having strong and base desires, the temperate man will not be self-controlled nor the self-controlled man temperate; for it is inconsistent with the character of the temperate man to have extravagant and evil appetites. Yet the self-controlled man must. For if his desires were good, the moral character which prevented his following them would be bad, and therefore self-control would not always be good. If, on the other hand, his desires were feeble but not bad, there would be no great credit in resisting them; and if they were bad and feeble, it would be no great triumph to overcome them either. . . .

CHAPTER 4.   Such more or less are the difficulties which arise with regard to self-control. Some of them we must explain away, others we must leave standing; for the difficulty is solved by discovering the truth. We must inquire (1) whether uncontrolled people can be said to act with knowledge or not, and if so, what is the nature of their knowledge; (2) with what is the self-controlled or the uncontrolled man concerned—is it pleasure or pain in general, or certain definite pleasures and pains? (3) are the self-controlled and the steadfast person the same or different? We must deal similarly with all such other questions as are germane to the present inquiry. . . .

CHAPTER 5.   Now the word "knowledge" we use in two distinct senses; we speak of a person as "knowing" if he has knowledge but does not apply it, and also if he applies his knowledge. There will be a difference then between doing wrong when one has knowledge, but does not reflect on it, and doing so when one not only has

the knowledge but reflects on it. In the latter case the wrongdoing seems strange but not in the former. . . . For in a case where a person has knowledge but does not apply it, we see that "having" has a different meaning. In fact, in one sense he has knowledge and in another sense he does not have it, as, for example, in sleep or madness or intoxication. Now this is the very condition of people under the influence of passion; for fits of anger and craving for sensual pleasures and some such things do unmistakably produce a change in bodily condition, and in some instances actually cause madness.

Clearly then we should regard uncontrolled people as being in much the same condition as people who are asleep or mad or intoxicated. Nor is it any proof of their knowing anything that they use language that would seem to imply knowledge; for people who are mad or intoxicated repeat scientific demonstrations and verses of Empedocles,[4] and beginners in learning string phrases together before they know their meaning. To know a thing really it must become a part of oneself, and this takes time. We may suppose then that people in a state of no control use language in the same way as actors on the stage. . . .

CHAPTER 6. . . . If we look at bodily enjoyments, in relation to which we commonly speak of a man as either temperate or licentious, we note that one who pursues continuously excessive pleasures and avoids excessive pains, such as hunger, thirst, heat, cold, and the various sensations of touch and taste, and who does so not of deliberate choice but contrary to his own purpose and judgment, is called lacking in self-control and not merely so in certain respects, as, for instance, in respect to anger, but simply uncontrolled in general. We see this is so and that, similarly, people are called soft in connection with these same pleasures and pains, though not in connection with wealth, gain, honor, and the like.

[4] Empedocles of Sicily, a well-known scientific poet and philosopher who lived a century before Aristotle. See p. 44, n. 5, p. 45, n. 7.

For this reason we class together the uncontrolled man and the licentious man, and also the self-controlled and the temperate man, because they are concerned more or less with the same pleasures and pains, and we place no others in the same class with them. They are concerned with the same things, yet their attitude is different; the licentious act with deliberate purpose, but the uncontrolled do not. Hence we call a person licentious, who without appetite or any strong appetite pursues excessive pleasures and avoids moderate pains, rather than one who does so from a violent craving; for what (it may be asked) would the former do if a fierce craving came over him, and it was intensely painful to him not to gratify his natural appetites?

Now there are desires and pleasures which are noble and virtuous of their kind; for, by our previous definition, some pleasant things are by their nature desirable, such as wealth, gain, victory, and honor; others are the opposite of these, and others still intermediate. In regard to everything desirable or intermediate, people are not blamed for being stirred by them, feeling desire and affection for them, but for pushing it somehow to excess. And people are not always blamed who are unreasonably mastered by something naturally noble and good or who unreasonably pursue it, who, for example, are inordinately devoted to honor or to children or parents; for these all are good, and devotion to them is commendable. Yet even here it is possible to go too far, like Niobe,[5] vying with the gods themselves, or like Satyrus, who was nicknamed "the filial" from his overaffection for his father, which made him look exceedingly foolish. . . .

There are some things that are naturally pleasant, some of them pleasant in an absolute sense and others pleasant to particular classes of animals or of men. There are other things not naturally pleasant that owe their pleasantness to people's physical defects or acquired

---

[5] The story of Niobe, who matched her children against the children of Zeus, is well known. Satyrus may have been a king of Bosporus who deified his father.

habits or depravity of nature. We may now point out the states of character corresponding to each of these kinds of pleasure.

What I mean is that there are brutish states as, for example, in the female creature who is said to rip up pregnant women and devour their children, or in some savage tribes near the Black Sea that are said to delight in such practices as eating raw meat or human flesh, or in those cannibals who lend their children to one another to feast upon, or as once, the story tells us, in Phalaris.[6] These are brutish states. There are others produced in people by disease or madness, as in the man who sacrificed and ate his mother, or in the slave who ate the liver of his fellow slave. Other such states again are the results of a morbid disposition or habit, like the practice of pulling out one's hair, or biting one's nails, or eating cinders or earth, or committing unnatural vice. These habits come sometimes naturally and are sometimes acquired, by those, for example, who have been victims of outrage in childhood.

Now whenever nature is the cause of these habits, no one would call people who give way to them lacking in self-control, any more than we should call women the same for being not males but females; nor should we call people so in whom habit has produced a morbid condition. These various habits, like brutishness itself, lie beyond the pale of vice. But if a person in whom they exist becomes their master or their slave, his conduct may be called self-controlled or uncontrolled, though not in an absolute but in a metaphorical sense; just as a person who is mastered by his angry passions may be called uncontrolled in his anger, but not uncontrolled in an absolute sense.

All excess of either folly, cowardice, loss of control, or rage is either brutish or morbid. A person whose nature it is to be frightened at everything, even at the noise of a mouse, is such a coward as to be more like a brute than a human being; though it was disease which made the man afraid of the weasel. Again, foolish people who are naturally unthinking and live a life of mere sensation, like some

[6] The "story" is a tradition that Phalaris ate his son in infancy.

races of remote barbarians, are brutish; whereas foolish people whose folly arises from such diseases as epilepsy or insanity are in a morbid state. One of these tendencies a person may at times possess without being mastered by it. Phalaris, for instance, might have restrained his desire of eating a child or his unnatural passions. Again, he may not only possess it but be mastered by it. . . .

CHAPTER 7. . . . We must observe too that loss of control in anger is not so disgraceful as uncontrolled appetite. For it is as if anger heard reason more or less but misheard it, like hasty servants who run out before they have heard all that one says and so misunderstand their orders, or like dogs who bark at a person as soon as he knocks without waiting to see if he is a friend. In the same way, anger from its natural heat and impetuosity hears something, but does not hear the voice of command when it rushes to revenge. For when our reason or imagination tell us that an insult or slight has been imposed on us, anger jumps, as it were, to the conclusion that it must do battle with the person who imposed it, and therefore gets into a fury at once. Desire, on the other hand, dashes to enjoy a thing, when reason or sensation says merely that it is pleasant. Thus anger follows reason in a sense, but desire does not. Desire is therefore the more disgraceful; for the man of uncontrolled anger is in a sense the servant of reason, but the other is the servant of desire and not of reason.

Again, there is more excuse for following natural impulses, as indeed there is for following all emotions common to the whole world, and the more common they are, the more excusable they are also. Now anger and rage are more natural than a desire for excessive and superfluous pleasures, as was shown in the case of the man who defended himself for striking his father by saying, "Yes, but he struck his father once and his father struck his father," and, pointing to his child, "he too will strike me when he becomes a man; it is in our blood." So also the man who was being dragged out of his

house by his son told him to stop at the door, for he had himself dragged his father that far but not beyond it.

Again, the greater the slyness, the greater the wickedness of an act. Now an angry man is not sly nor is anger sly; it is open. Desire, on the other hand, is sly; thus Aphrodite is called the

> "Goddess of the Cyprian isle,
> Artisan of many a wile," [7]

and Homer says of her embroidered girdle that in it was

> "Guile that stealeth the wits of the wisest." [8]

Hence such a loss of control is more wicked and more disgraceful than uncontrolled temper, and may be called absolute lack of control; it is indeed a species of vice. . . .

Brutishness is not so wicked a thing as vice, though it is more terrifying, for in brutes there is no corruption of the best good, as there is in men. It does not exist. The comparison then of brutishness with vice is like the comparison of lifeless things with things living as regards wickedness; for the wickedness of that which has no inner spring of action is always less mischievous; and brutes lack the reason which is an inner spring of action. (It is much then like a comparison of injustice with an unjust man; there is a sense in which each of them is worse than the other.) A bad man will do ten thousand times as much evil as a brute.

CHAPTER 8. As to the pleasures and pains, appetites and aversions of touch and taste with which licentiousness and temperance, as already defined, are concerned, it is possible to be in such a state that one is a slave to things of which most people are masters, or again to be in such a state that one is master of things to which most people are slaves. According as a person's state is one or the other in respect to pleasure, he is self-controlled or un-

[7] The authorship of the lines is unknown.
[8] *Iliad*, XIV, Classics Club edition. p. 217.

controlled; in respect to pain, he is courageous or weak. The state of the large majority of mankind lies between the two, though they incline rather to the worse state.

Inasmuch as some pleasures are necessary and others are not, or necessary only up to a certain point, and as neither the excesses nor the deficiencies of these pleasures are necessary, and the same is true of appetites and pains, it follows that a person who pursues pleasures of an excessive character, or pursues any pleasures to an excessive degree, and does so by choice, for their own sake, and not for the sake of any result to be got from them, is licentious. He is necessarily disinclined to repentance and therefore incurable, since to be unable to repent is to be incurable. A man in the opposite state feels no pleasure; one in the mean is temperate. . . .

Everyone will agree that the man is worse who does something disgraceful with no appetite and no strong desire than one who does it at a time when his desire is violent; worse too, if he strikes a blow in cold blood than if he does it in anger; for what, it may be said, would such a person do if he were in a passion? Hence a licentious person is worse than one who has lost control of himself.

Of the characters we have described, the one that lacks self-control is a kind of weakness, the other licentiousness. The opposite of the uncontrolled character is the self-controlled, and of the weak the steadfast; for steadfastness consists in holding out against pain, and self-control in overcoming pleasure. It is one thing to hold out and another to overcome, as it is one thing not to be beaten and another to win a victory. Hence self-control is preferable to steadfastness. The man who gives in where people generally resist and are capable of resisting deserves to be called soft and self-indulgent; for self-indulgence is a form of softness. Such a person will let his cloak trail in the mud to avoid the trouble of lifting it up, and give himself the airs of an invalid, while knowing he is not suffering, though he imitates one who is suffering.

It is much the same with self-control and the loss of it. It is no wonder if a person is mastered by strong and overwhelming pleasures

or pains; rather, it is pardonable, provided he struggles against them,
like Philoctetes when bitten by the snake in the play of Theodectes,
or like Cercyon [9] in the *Alope* of Carcinus, or like people who try
to suppress their laughter and burst out in a loud guffaw, as happened to Xenophantus.[10] It is only unpardonable where a person
is mastered by things against which most people succeed in holding
out, and cannot resist them, unless his weakness is due to hereditary
constitution or to disease, as weakness is hereditary in the kings of
Scythia, or as a woman is naturally weaker than a man. . . .

CHAPTER 9.   A licentious person, as we said, is not disposed
to repentance, for he abides by his choice, but a man who loses self-
control is always so disposed. The difficulty which we raised does
not then exist.[11] The former is incurable, the latter can be cured;
for vice is like a disease such as dropsy or consumption, whereas loss
of control is like epilepsy, the one being a permanent, the other an
intermittent badness. There is in fact an absolute distinction of kind
between loss of control and vice; for vice may be, but the other cannot be, unconscious of itself. . . .

The uncontrolled man then is the kind who pursues bodily pleasures that are excessive and contrary to right reason, but not from
any conviction of their goodness; the vicious man, on the contrary,
is convinced of their goodness because he is the kind of person to
pursue them; hence it is easy to reform the former, but not the
latter. . . .

CHAPTER 10.   Some people are determined to stick by their
opinions at all costs; we call them obstinate. They are people, I mean,
who are hard to persuade and not easy to convert. Such people bear
some resemblance to self-controlled people, as do prodigals to liberal

9 The poet Carcinus may have represented in his *Alope* a struggle between a cruel
disposition and conscience in Cercyon.

10 The allusion is to something unknown.

11 That is, that the man who loses his self-control has not the power to stand by
his right convictions.

people, and foolhardy people to courageous, but there are many points of difference. For although the self-controlled person does not veer about in the gusts of emotion and desire, he is not immovable. It is easy to persuade him on occasion, but the obstinate person resists the persuasion of reason. As a matter of fact, such people may cherish their own desires and are frequently led away by pleasure. . . .

CHAPTER 11. There are the people too whose character it is to take less pleasure than is right in bodily gratification, and not to follow reason. A self-controlled man is midway between such people and the uncontrolled. For the reason an uncontrolled man does not follow reason lies in his excessive pleasure in such things, and the reason an insensible person does not follow it lies in his failure to feel any pleasure. But a self-controlled man does and is not swayed either way. Assuming that self-control is virtuous, we must conclude that both the moral states opposed to it are vicious, as in fact they clearly are. But because one of these states, insensibility, is seen only in few cases and on rare occasions, self-control is considered the opposite of no control, as temperance is of licentiousness. . . .

An uncontrolled person is not like one who has knowledge and power of reflection, but like one who is asleep or intoxicated. He acts voluntarily, for in a certain sense he knows both what he is doing and what is his object in doing it, but still he is not wicked, for his intentions are good; he may therefore be said to be only half wicked. Again, uncontrolled people are not wicked, because they are not sly. They are either incapable of abiding by the results of their deliberation or they are excitable and incapable of deliberating at all. An uncontrolled person then may be compared to a state which passes all the bills it ought to pass and has excellent laws, but does not enforce them, according to the taunt of Anaxandrides,[12]

" 'Twas the state's will; the state cares not for law."

[12] A poet of the so-called Middle Comedy, who is said to have satirized the Athenians.

A wicked man, on the other hand, may be compared to a state which enforces its laws, but whose laws are bad. . . .

We have now discussed the nature of self-control and the lack of it, of steadfastness and weakness, and the mutual relations of these states of character.

CHAPTER 12. Considerations of pleasure and pain belong to the political philosopher. He is the architect who builds the end which we have in view in defining good and evil in an absolute sense. There are reasons too why we must discuss them. We defined moral virtue and vice as having to do with pains and pleasures, and in the general opinion happiness implies pleasure. . . .

CHAPTER 14. Admittedly pain is an evil and should be avoided. It is an evil either absolutely or relatively, as causing some impediment to an individual. But the opposite of that which should be avoided, in the respect in which it should be avoided and is bad, is good. . . .

Nor does it follow that, because there are some vicious pleasures, there is not some pleasure which is the chief good, any more than it follows that, because there are vicious kinds of knowledge, some knowledge is not the chief good. Indeed, it is so, I think, necessarily; for since every state of mind calls for unimpeded activity, that activity, whether it be of them all, or of some one of them, which is happiness, is most desirable when unimpeded. And such unimpeded activity is pleasure. Hence the chief good will be pleasure of some kind, although most pleasures may in an absolute sense be bad. It is on this ground that everybody supposes a happy life to be pleasant, and happiness to involve pleasure. The idea is reasonable, for no activity is perfect if impeded, and happiness is in its nature perfect. It follows that the happy man needs bodily goods, worldly goods, and good fortune so that his activity may not be impeded. To say that a person on the rack, or plunged in the depth of calamities, is happy is either intentionally or unintentionally to talk nonsense.

The fact that good fortune is a necessary aid to happiness leads some people to hold that good fortune is identical with happiness; but it is not so. If excessive, it may be an actual obstacle to happiness, and then perhaps should rightly cease to be called good fortune; for its name depends on its relation to happiness.

Again, the fact that all brutes and all men pursue pleasure is a certain indication of its being in some sense a supreme good; for

"No voice is wholly lost that is the voice of many men." [13]

But inasmuch as it is not the same nature or condition that is, or is thought to be, best for everyone, so it is not the same pleasure that everyone pursues. Still it is pleasure. It may even be the case that all men really pursue not the pleasure which they imagine or would say they are pursuing, but some pleasure which is the same for all; for there is a divine instinct naturally implanted in all things. But bodily pleasures have usurped the name "pleasure," since they are what people most frequently look for, and in which everybody has his share. These then, because they are the only pleasures everyone knows, are therefore supposed to be the only pleasures that exist.

But it is evident that, unless pleasure or the activity which is pleasure is a good, the happy man will not live pleasantly. For why should he want pleasure if it is not a good, and if it is possible for him, as it then would be, to live painfully? For if pleasure is neither an evil nor a good, neither is pain. Why then should he avoid pain? Nor will the life of the good man be pleasanter than that of anyone else, unless his activities are pleasanter.

With regard to bodily pleasures, we may hold that some pleasures are highly desirable, that is, the noble pleasures, but not the bodily pleasures, that is, the pleasures of those who have no control of themselves. We must then ask why, if these pleasures are bad, the pains opposite to them are bad; for the opposite of things bad is good. Are the necessary pleasures good only in the sense that whatever is not evil is good? Or are they good up to a certain point?

[13] Hesiod, *Works and Days*, 761.

In all states and activities in which it is impossible to exceed the right limit of good, it is impossible also to exceed the right limit of pleasure; but where it is possible to go to excess, there is also a possible excess of pleasure. Now with bodily goods one may go to excess, and evil consists in pursuing that excess, but not in pursuing the necessary pleasures; for everyone finds some satisfaction in delicious food and wines and the pleasures of love, but not always just the proper satisfaction. The contrary is the case with pain. People in general do not avoid the excess of pain, but avoid pain altogether. So the opposite to excessive pleasure is not pain in general but only that felt by one who pursues that pleasure.

CHAPTER 15. We should explain not alone the truth but also the cause of error, since this explanation helps to produce belief. For understanding the reason why a thing is not true strengthens belief in the truth. We must therefore explain why it is that bodily pleasures seem more desirable than other pleasures.

It is then, firstly, that such pleasure drives out pain. The excessive pains that people feel make them pursue excessive pleasure and bodily pleasure generally, as a remedy. The remedies of severe diseases are themselves frequently severe, and people pursue them from their apparent contrast to the opposite pains. . . .

Bodily pleasures, too, are violent, and therefore pursued by people who are incapable of finding gratification in other pleasures. Thus people sometimes make themselves thirsty in order to enjoy the pleasure of satisfying their thirst. So long as these pleasures are harmless, there is no ground for disapproving of them (although when they are harmful they are wrong), for people who pursue them have no other way of enjoying themselves, and to many a neutral state of feeling is naturally painful. For all animals labor over something, as we read in books on natural science, where it is said that even seeing and hearing are painful, but that we have got used to them by this time. So in youth, people, because they are growing, are in much the same state as drunken men, and youth is pleasant. People of an

excitable nature also require constant outlet, for their temperament constantly frets their bodies away, and they are always in a state of restless desire. Now pain is extinguished either by the pleasure which is its opposite or by any other pleasure, if it be strong. This is why excitable people fall into licentiousness and wickedness.

Such pleasures, on the other hand, as involve no pains do not lead to excess; they are naturally and not merely incidentally pleasant. By "incidental pleasures" I mean those that are curative in their effects; for we are cured by the action of some part of our nature that remains healthy, and the process of cure is pleasant. By "natural pleasures" I mean those that stimulate the action of our nature in health.

The same thing is never always pleasant to us, for our nature is not simple, but there exists in us a sort of second nature, as we are mortal beings. Thus, when one element is active, it acts against the nature of the other; and when the two elements are in equilibrium, the action seems neither painful nor pleasant. If there were a being whose nature was simple, the same action would always be entirely pleasant to him. That is how God enjoys one simple pleasure everlastingly; for there is an activity not only of motion but of rest, and pleasure is found more in rest than in motion. But change, the poet [14] says, is "the sweetest thing in the world," because of the badness of our nature. For as the bad man is fond of change, so too the nature which calls for change is bad; it is not simple or good.

We have now discussed self-control and the lack of it, pleasures and pains, their nature and the reason why some of them are good and others bad. We have next to discuss friendship.

[14] Euripides. *Orestes*, v. 234.

BOOK VIII

> *Friendships are necessary and natural for men. They imply some likeness between the persons involved. The motives for a friendship may be its utility or its pleasantness for ourselves, or our love of our friend for his own sake and our desire for his welfare. Friendships of utility or pleasure and friendships between bad men will be less permanent than the true friendships of good men. Too much inequality between persons makes friendship impossible.*

CHAPTER 1.   It will be natural to discuss friendship next, for friendship is a kind of virtue or implies virtue. It is also indispensable to life. For without friends no one would choose to live, even though he possessed every other good. It even seems that people who are rich and hold official and powerful positions have the greatest need of friends; for what is the good of this sort of prosperity without some opportunity for generosity, which is never so freely or so admirably displayed as toward friends? Or how can prosperity be preserved in safety and security without friends? The greater a person's importance, the more liable it is to disaster. And in poverty and other misfortunes our friends are our only refuge. Again, when we are young, friends are a help to us, in saving us from error, and when we grow old, in taking care of us and doing the things for us we are too feeble to do for ourselves. When we are all in the prime of life, they prompt us to noble actions, as the line runs

"Two going together;" [1]

for two people are better than one both in thought and in action.

[1] *Iliad,* X, Classics Club edition, p. 149. Diomed is expressing his desire for a companion in invading the Trojan camp.

Friendship or love seems the natural instinct of a parent toward a child, and of a child toward a parent, not only among men but among birds and animals generally. It is felt by creatures of the same race toward one another, especially by men. For this reason we praise the lovers of their fellow men. In traveling we observe how near and dear every man is to his fellow man.

Again, it seems that friendship is the bond which holds states together, and that lawmakers set more store by it than by justice; for harmony is something like friendship, and it is harmony that they especially try to promote, and discord that they try to expel, as the enemy of the state. When people are friends there is no need of justice between them; but when they are just, they yet need friendship too. Indeed justice, in its supreme form, assumes the character of friendship.

Nor is friendship indispensable only; it is also noble. We praise those who love their friends, and to have many friends is thought to be a fine thing. Some people hold that to be a friend is the same thing as to be a good man.

CHAPTER 2.   The subject of friendship gives room for a good many differences of opinion. Some define it as a sort of likeness, and say people are friends because they are like each other. Hence the sayings, "Like seeks like," "Birds of a feather," and so on. Others, on the contrary, say "Two of a trade never agree." [2] So philosophical thinkers indulge in more profound physical speculations on the subject; Euripides asserting that

> "the parched Earth loves the rain,
> And the great Heaven rain-laden loves to fall
> Earthwards." [3]

Heraclitus [4] declares that "contending things draw together," that

[2] The Greek allusion is to the proverbial quarrelsomeness of two potters.

[3] The play from which these lines are taken is unknown.

[4] On Heraclitus of Ephesus, one of the most famous of the early Greek poet philosophers. See p. 22, n. 17.

"harmony most beautiful is formed of discords," and that "all things are by strife engendered." Others, among whom is Empedocles, take the opposite view and insist that "like desires like." . . .

It is possible, I think to shed light on the subject of friendship, by determining what is lovable or an object of love. For plainly not everything is loved, but only that which is lovable, which is what is good or pleasant or useful. A thing too is useful if it is a means of gaining something good or pleasant. If so, it follows that it is the good and the pleasant that are lovable because they are ends.

We may ask, then, do we love what is good in itself, or what is good for us? For there is sometimes a difference between them. The same question may be asked in regard to what is pleasant. It is said that everyone loves what is good for himself, and that, while the good is lovable in an absolute sense, it is what is good for each individual that is lovable in his eyes. It may even be said that a man loves not what is good for him but what seems good. But this will make no difference; for in that case, what is lovable will be what seems lovable.

Now there are three motives for love. We do not, it must be noted, apply the term "love" to our feeling for lifeless things. The reason is (1) that they are incapable of returning our affection, and (2) that we do not wish their good; for it would, of course, be ridiculous to wish good to the wine. If we wish it at all, it is only in the sense of wishing the wine to keep well, so that we may enjoy it ourselves. But everyone knows that we ought to wish our friend's good for his sake. If we wish people good in this sense, we call it good will, unless our good wishes are returned; reciprocal good will we call friendship.

We must add too that the good will must not be unknown. A person often wishes well to people whom he has not seen, but whom he supposes to be good or useful; and it is possible that one of these persons may entertain the same feeling toward him. Such people, then, it is clear, wish well to one another; but they cannot properly be called friends, so long as their feeling is unknown to each other.

If they are to be friends, they must feel good will to each other and wish each other's good for one of the motives aforesaid, and each of them must know that the other wishes him well.

CHAPTER 3. Now as the reasons for friendship differ in kind, so accordingly do the corresponding kinds of affection and friendship. The kinds of friendship therefore are three, being equal in number to the things which are lovable or the objects of friendship, for every such object may arouse a reciprocal affection between two persons.

People who love each other wish each other's good up to the point on which their love is fixed. Accordingly, those who love each other for reasons of utility do not love each other for themselves, but only as far as they get some benefit from one another. So with those who love for pleasure's sake. They are fond of witty people not for their character, but because they are pleasant to them. People then who love for utility's sake are moved to affection by what is good for themselves, and people who love for pleasure, by what is pleasant to themselves. They love a person not for what he is in himself, but only for being useful or pleasant to them. Such friendships then are friendships incidentally only; for the person loved is not loved for being what he is, but merely for being a source of some good or pleasure. Such friendships accordingly are easily dissolved, if the parties do not continue always the same; for they cease loving once they cease to be pleasant or useful to each other.

Now utility is not a permanent quality; it varies at different times. Hence when the reason for the friendship disappears, the friendship itself is dissolved, since it depended on that reason. Friendship of this kind seems to arise especially among old people, for in old age we look for profit rather than pleasure, and also among those in the prime of life or youth who have an eye to their own interest. Friends of this kind do not generally live together; for sometimes they are not even congenial. Nor do they want such companionship, except when they are of use to one another, since the pleasure they give

each other goes no further than the hopes they entertain of getting benefit from it. Among these friendships we may count the friendship which exists between host and guest.

The friendship of the young is based apparently on pleasure; for they live by emotion and are inclined to pursue most the pleasure of the moment. But as their age increases, their pleasures alter with it. They are therefore quick at making friendships and quick at abandoning them; for their friendships shift with the object that pleases them, and their pleasure is liable to sudden change. Young people are amorous too, amorousness being generally a matter of emotion and pleasure. Hence they fall in love and soon afterwards fall out of love, passing from one condition to another many times in a single day. But amorous people wish to spend their days and lives together, since thus they attain the object of their friendship.

CHAPTER 4. Perfect friendship is the friendship of people who are good and alike in virtue; for they are alike in wishing each other's good, inasmuch as they are good and good in themselves. Those who wish the good of their friends for their friends' sake are in the truest sense friends, since their friendship is the consequence of their own character, and not an accident. Their friendship therefore lasts as long as their goodness, and goodness is a permanent quality. So each of them is good in an absolute sense, and good in relation to his friend. For good men are not only good in an absolute sense, but helpful to each other. They are pleasant too; for the good are pleasant in an absolute sense, and pleasant to one another. For everybody finds pleasure in actions proper to him and in others like him, and all good people act alike or nearly alike.

Such a friendship is naturally permanent, for it unites in itself all the right conditions of friendship. For the aim of all friendship is good or pleasure, either absolute or relative to the person who feels the affection; and it is founded on a certain similarity. In the friendship of good men all the conditions just described are realized in the friends themselves; other friendships bear only a resemblance to the

perfect friendship. That which is good in an absolute sense is pleasant also in an absolute sense. They are too the most lovable objects of affection, and for this reason love and friendship in this highest and best sense are found most among such men.

Friendships of this kind are likely to be rare; for such people are few. Such friendships require time and familiarity too; for, as the adage puts it, men cannot know one another until they have eaten salt together; nor can they admit one another to friendship, or be friends at all, until each has been proved lovable and trustworthy by the other. People who are quick to treat one another as friends wish to be friends but are not so really, unless they are lovable and know each other to be so; for the wish to be friends may arise in a minute, but not friendship.

CHAPTER 5. This kind of friendship then is perfect as regards durability and in all other respects; and each friend receives from the other in every way the same or nearly the same treatment as he gives, which is as it ought to be. Friendship based on pleasure has a certain resemblance to it, for the good too are pleasant to one another. So also with friendship based on utility, for the good are useful too to one another. Here likewise friendships are most permanent when the two persons get the same thing, such as pleasure, from one another; and not only the same thing, but from the same source, as happens between two wits, though not between a lover and his beloved. For these do not find pleasure in the same things; the pleasure of one is in beholding the object of his love, and of the other in being courted by his lover.[5] Then when beauty passes away, the friendship sometimes passes away too; for the lover then finds no pleasure in the sight of his beloved, and the beloved is no more courted by his lover. On the other hand, lovers often remain friends, if their characters are similar, and familiarity has taught them to

[5] The reader must remember that in the time of Plato and Aristotle, the only love that was considered dignified in Athens and worth taking seriously was that between two men, not between man and woman. See on this subject the *Symposium* of Plato, Classics Club edition, pp. 159-216.

love each other's character. But those who give and receive not pleasure but profit are both less true and less constant friends. Friendships based on utility are dissolved as soon as the advantage comes to an end, for in them there is no love of a person, but only a love of profit.

For pleasure or profit then it is possible that even bad men may be friends to one another, and good people to bad, and one who is neither good nor bad to any sort of person; but clearly none but the good can be friends for the friend's own sake, since bad people do not delight in one another unless to gain something thereby.

It is only, too, the friendship of good men that cannot be destroyed by slander. For it is not easy to believe what anyone says about a person whom we have tested ourselves for many years, and found to be good. In the friendship of the good too there is confidence, and the assurance that neither of the two friends will do injury to the other, and whatever else is required by true friendship. But in other friendships there is no protection against slander and injury. . . .

CHAPTER 7. . . . Among austere and elderly people friendship arises less easily, because they are less good-tempered and less fond of society, and those are the qualities that seem to be the principal element in and causes of friendship. This is why the young form friendships quickly, but old men do not, for they do not make friends with anyone who is not delightful to them; nor do austere people. Such people, it is true, wish each other well; they desire one another's good, and help one another as needed. But they are not really friends, since they do not fulfill the principal condition of friendship by spending their time together and delighting in each other's society.

It is as impossible to be friends with a great number of people in the perfect sense of friendship as it is to be in love with a great number of people at once. For perfect friendship is in some sense an excess, and such excess of feeling is natural toward one individual, but it is not easy for a great number of people to give intense pleasure

to the same person at the same time, or, I may say, to seem even good to him at all. Friendship too involves experience and familiarity, which are very difficult. But it is possible to find a great number of acquaintances who are simply useful or pleasant or agreeable; for people of this kind are numerous and their services do not take much time.

Among such acquaintanceships one that is based on pleasure more nearly resembles a friendship, when each party renders the same services to the other, and is delighted with the other or with the same things, as they are in friendships of the young; for a generous spirit is especially characteristic of these friendships.

Friendships that rest on utility are for commercial characters. Fortunate people, however, do not want what is useful but what is pleasant. They want people to live with; and though for a short time they may put up with disagreeableness, nobody would stand it continuously. Nobody would stand the good itself continuously, if it were disagreeable to him. Hence they require their friends to be pleasant. They ought perhaps to require them also to be good, and not only so, but good for themselves; because then they would have all the qualities which friends ought to have.

People in positions of authority can make a distinction between their friends. Some are useful to them, and others pleasant, though the same people are not usually both useful and pleasant. They do not look for friends who are good as well as pleasant, or who will help them to attain noble ends; they want to be pleased and look partly for amusing people and partly for those who are clever at doing what they are told. These qualities are hardly ever combined in the same person.

We have said that a good man is at once pleasant and useful. But such a man does not become the friend of one superior to him in rank, unless he is himself superior to that person in goodness. Otherwise there is no equality, such as does occur when his superiority in virtue is proportionate to his inferiority in some other respect. Friendships of this kind, however, are exceedingly rare.

CHAPTER 8. . . . There is another kind of friendship that is based on inequality, such as the friendship of a father for his son, or of any elder person for a younger, or of a husband for his wife, or of a ruler for a subject. These friendships are of different sorts; for the friendship of parents for children is not the same as that of rulers for subjects, nor is even the friendship of a father for his son the same as that of a son for his father, nor that of a husband for his wife the same as a wife's for her husband. For in each of these there is a different virtue and a different function, and the motives of each are different; hence the friendships also are different. It follows that the services rendered by each party to the other in these friendships are not the same, nor is it right to expect they should be; but when children render to parents what is due to the authors of their being, and parents to children what is due to them, then their friendships are permanent and good.

In all friendships that involve the principle of inequality, the love also should be proportional; the better or the more useful party, or whoever may be the superior, should receive more love than he gives. For when the love is proportioned to the merit, a sort of equality is established; and this equality seems to be a condition of friendship.

CHAPTER 9. Equality in justice is apparently not the same as equality in friendship. In justice equality proportioned to merit is the prime consideration, and quantitative equality the second, but in friendship quantitative equality is first and proportion to merit second. This is clearly seen when there is a wide distinction between two persons as regards virtue, vice, wealth, or anything else. For persons so widely different cease to be friends; they do not even expect to be. And nowhere is this so conspicuous as in the case of the gods; for they are vastly superior to us in all good things. It is clear too in the case of kings; for people who are much their inferiors do not expect to be their friends. Nor again do worthless people expect to be friends with the best or wisest of mankind. No doubt in such cases it is impossible to define exactly the point up to which friendship may be

continued; it may suffer much from unevenness and yet keep on. But where the gulf is as wide as between a god and a man, it ceases to be.

This fact has given rise to the question whether friends do really wish the greatest good for their friends; whether, for example, they wish them to become gods. For then they would lose them as friends, and would therefore lose what are goods, for their friends are goods. That being so, if we were right in saying that a friend wishes his friend's good for the friend's sake, his friend will have to remain what he is. He will wish his friend the greatest good but only as a man. Yet perhaps he will not wish him every good, for each one wishes good in the highest sense to himself. . . .

CHAPTER 10.   Friendship seems to consist rather in loving than in being loved. This may be shown by the delight mothers have in loving; for mothers sometimes give their children to be brought up by others, and so long as they know about them and love them, do not look for love in return (if they cannot have both), but are content, it seems, to see their children doing well, and to give them their love, even if the children in their ignorance do them none of the services that are a mother's due. Then if friendship consists in loving rather than in being loved, and people who love their friends are praised, it is evidently the particular virtue of friends to love. Hence only where there is love in adequate measure, are friends permanent and their friendship lasting.

In this way, even people who are unequal can be friends, for they will be equalized. And equality and likeness make friendship, especially the likeness of the good; for the good, being constant themselves, remain unchanged in relation to one another, and neither ask others to do wrong nor do it themselves. They may even be said to prevent it; for good people do no wrong nor allow their friends to do it. But in wicked friends there is no stability; for they do not remain the same themselves for long. And if they become friends,

it is only for a short time, and for the satisfaction they take in each other's wickedness. . . .

CHAPTER 13. . . . Under perverted forms of government justice does not go far, and neither does friendship. Nowhere is its field so limited as under the worst of governments, for in a tyranny friendship does not exist, or hardly exists. Where there is nothing in common between ruler and subject, there cannot be friendship between them, as there cannot be justice either. The relation is like that between craftsman and tool, or soul and body, or master and slave. These latter get some benefit from the people who use them, but there can be no friendship or justice in our relation to lifeless things, or to a horse or an ox or a slave as slave. For there is nothing in common between a master and his tool, and a slave is a living tool and a tool a lifeless slave. One cannot therefore be friends with a slave as slave, though one can with a slave as man. For there seems a possibility of justice between a man and any other who is capable of taking part in a system of law and mutual agreements. Therefore one can be friends with him, so far as he is man. However, in tyrannies friendships and justice exist only to a slight extent and have only a narrow range. Their range is widest in democracies, because when people are equals they have most in common.

CHAPTER 14. All forms of friendship, as has been said, imply association. We may, however, properly distinguish the friendships of kinsmen and of comrades from other friendships. As for the friendships of fellow citizens, fellow tribesmen, fellow sailors and such, they are more like simple friendships of association, since they seem based on a sort of compact. We may class them with the friendship of host and guest.

The friendship of kinsmen appears to be of various kinds, but to depend all in all on the friendship of parent for child; for parents love their children as parts of themselves, and children their parents as the authors of their being. Parents know their offspring better

than the children know that they are their begetters; and the author of another's being feels more closely united to his child than the child to his parent; for the product of any person belongs to its producer, as a tooth or a hair or anything to its owner, but the producer does not belong to his product, or does not in the same degree. There is a difference between them too of time, for parents love their children as soon as they are born, but children do not love their parents until they have lived some time and gained intelligence or sense. From these considerations it is clear too why mothers love their children more than fathers do.

Parents then love their children as themselves, for their offspring are like second selves—second in the sense of being separate. And children love their parents as being born of them; and brothers love one another as being born of the same parents. For the identity of children with their parents constitutes an identity between the children themselves. Hence we use phrases like "the same blood," "the same stock," and so on, in speaking of brothers and sisters. They are therefore in a sense the same, though separate beings. It is a great help to friendship to have been brought up together, and to be of the same age; for "two of an age agree," as the saying is, and boys brought up together become comrades; hence the friendship of brothers resembles the friendship of comrades.[6] Cousins and all other kinsmen have a bond of union, as springing from the same source. They are more or less closely united according as their first common ancestor is near or remote.

The love of children for parents and of men for the gods is a love for what is good and higher than themselves; for parents are the authors of the greatest benefit to their children, since to them children owe their existence and nurture and education from the day of their birth. There is both more pleasure and more utility in such a friendship than in the friendship of strangers, for their lives have more in common.

[6] It is an instance of the part which comradeship played in Greek life that the mutual love of two brothers should be likened to the mutual love of two comrades.

The characteristics of friendship between brothers are the same as between comrades. They are intensified when brothers are good but exist always in consequence of their likeness; for brothers are more nearly related to each other and love one another naturally from birth. There is the greatest similarity of character among children of the same parents, who are brought up together and receive a similar education; and they have stood the strong and sure test of time. The elements of friendship between other kinsmen are in proportion to the nearness of their kinship.

Between husband and wife friendship seems to be a law of nature, since man is even more naturally inclined to contract a marriage than to set up a state. The household comes before and is more necessary than the state, and the procreation of children is the universal function of animals. In the case of other animals this is the limit of their married union; but men unite not only for the production of children but for other purposes of life. As soon as a man and a woman unite, a distribution of functions takes place. Some are proper to the husband and others to the wife; hence they supply one another's needs, each contributing his special gifts to the common stock. Accordingly, both utility and pleasure are found in this friendship. But its basis will be virtue too, if the husband and wife are good; for each has his or her own virtue, and both delight in that as right. Children too are seemingly a bond of union between them; hence marriages that are childless are more easily dissolved. For children are a blessing common to both parents, and this community of interest binds them together.

To ask how husband and wife and friends in general should live together is nothing else than to ask how it is just for them each to live. Justice is clearly not the same thing between one friend and another as between strangers or comrades or fellow travelers. . . .

CHAPTER 15. . . . Complaints and bickerings occur exclusively or most frequently in friendships based on utility, and it is reasonable that this should be so. For where the basis of friendship is

virtue, friends are eager to do good to each other as a sign of their goodness and friendship. Where rivalry takes this form, there is no room for complaint or bickering; for nobody finds fault with a person who loves him and treats him well. On the contrary, if he is a man of fine feeling, he returns the other's kindness. Nor will a superior person complain of his friend, for he is getting his desire; in such a friendship each friend desires the other's good.

Again, such quarreling hardly ever arises in a friendship of pleasure; for both parties there get what they want, if they enjoy living together. One would make himself ridiculous if he were to complain of the other for not giving him pleasure, when he has the power to stop living in his company. It is friendship based on utility that gives rise to complaints; for the parties to that in their dealings with each other have an eye out for profit. Each always wants the larger share, and imagines he is getting less than his due, and complains of not getting all he needs and deserves. No benefactor can supply all that such a recipient of his benefaction demands. . . .

CHAPTER 16. Differences occur also in friendships in which one party is superior to the other, when each party claims a larger share of the benefit; but when this occurs, the friendship is dissolved. The better of the two friends thinks he should have more, for his virtue deserves the larger share. So too does the more useful, as admittedly a person who is useless ought not to have so much as the one who is of use. His friendship (he says) ceases to be a friendship and becomes a public service if the proceeds of that friendship are not proportionate to the worth of the benefits he confers. For people think that as in a business firm the larger contributors get more of the returns, so it should be in friendship. But the needy or inferior person takes the opposite view. He argues that it is the part of a good friend to assist the needy; for what (he says) is the use of being a friend of a noble or powerful person if he is to get no benefit from it?

It would seem that each is justified in his claim, and that each ought to get more out of the friendship than the other but not more

of the same things. The superior person ought to get more honor, and the needy person more profit, for honor is the reward of virtue and generosity, and money is the relief the needy one wants. . . .

BOOK IX

> Questions for friends are: Should we pay our debts first or help a friend? Should we break off friendship with one whose character has deteriorated? Why are benefactors better friends to the recipients of their bounty than the latter are to them? Should a man love himself more than anyone else? Should we have all the friends we can get?

CHAPTER 2. There are still certain questions that present problems. For instance, is the respect and obedience due to a father unlimited or ought a person, if he is ill, to obey his doctor instead? Ought he to vote for the best soldier as general, rather than for his father? Similarly, ought he to serve a friend rather than a good man, and pay a debt to a benefactor rather than make a present to a comrade, if he cannot do both?

It is difficult perhaps to decide all such questions precisely, as cases vary indefinitely in importance or dignity or urgency. But it is obvious at once that no person can be entitled to unlimited respect. As a general rule, we ought to repay services which have been done to us rather than confer favors on our comrades. We should pay our debts to our creditors before we make a gift to our comrade. However, even this rule is possibly open to exceptions. Suppose a person has been ransomed from the hands of brigands; is it his first duty to ransom his ransomer in turn, whoever he may be, or repay him, if he has not been taken prisoner but demands repayment? Or ought he first to

ransom his own father? It would seem that he ought to ransom his father.

As a general rule then, as we have said, we should pay our debts, but if honor or an urgent need of making a gift outweighs such considerations, we should decide in favor of the gift. For it sometimes happens that there is an actual unfairness in returning what we have received, as when A has done a service to B, knowing him to be a good man, and B is called on to repay A, whom he believes to be a rascal. There are times when it is actually not right to lend money in return to one who has lent money to us. For A may have lent money to B, who is an honest man, sure of getting it back again, but B may know A to be bad and therefore would not expect to get his money back. If this is the true state of the case, the claim A makes for a loan in return is not a fair claim. Or even if this is not the case, but people think it is, B's conduct cannot be called unreasonable. We can only repeat then the remark we have made several times before, that arguments relating to human emotions and human actions admit of neither greater nor less precision than the subjects with which they deal.

It is clear enough that all people cannot rightly claim the same respect; nor can a father claim unlimited respect, as Zeus himself does not receive unlimited sacrifices. But since the claims of parents, brothers, comrades, and benefactors are all different, it is our duty to render to each class the respect that is natural and appropriate to them. This, in fact, is what we seem to do. We invite our relatives to a wedding because they have an interest in the family and therefore in all events that affect the family; for the same reason we look on relations as having the best right to meet at funerals.

It would seem to be our especial duty to provide our parents with the means of livelihood, for we owe our own living to them, and it is more honorable to give support to the authors of our being than to ourselves. Honor, too, we should pay to parents, as to the gods, but not pay it indiscriminately. The same honor is not due to a father and to a mother; nor again should they receive the same honor as

a philosopher or a general, but just the honor of a father or a mother, as the case may be. Again, we should pay all our elders the honor due their age, by rising to receive them, giving them the seat of honor at the table and so on. To our comrades and brothers, on the other hand, we should speak our mind frankly, and share with them everything that belongs to us. Again, to our kinsfolk, fellow tribes-men, fellow citizens, and all other persons, we should try to render their due, estimating their claims on us by considering the nearness of their connection with us, their character, and the services they have done us. It is easy to make this comparative estimate where people belong to the same class, and more difficult where they belong to different classes. Still that is no reason for giving up the attempt; we must make our distinctions as best we can.

CHAPTER 3. Another question that presents a problem is whether we ought or ought not to break off friendships with people whose character is no longer what it once was. If the motive of the friendship was utility or pleasure, then when the utility or the pleasure comes to an end, there is nothing unreasonable in breaking off the friendship. For it was the utility or the pleasure that we loved, and when they have ceased to exist, it is only reasonable that our love should come to an end too.

But a man would have ground for complaint, if a friend who had loved him for his usefulness or pleasantness had pretended to love him for his character. For, as we said at the outset, differences arise between friends most often when the actual grounds of the friendship are not what they suppose it to be. Now if a person, A, has deceived himself into imagining it was his character which won him B's affection, although there was nothing in B's conduct to warrant such an idea, he has only himself to blame. But if he was deluded by pretense on B's part, he has a right to complain of him as an impostor and to denounce him more bitterly than he would a man who counter-feits money, inasmuch as this felony affects something more precious than money.

But suppose we take a person into our friendship, believing him to be a good man, and he turns out and is recognized as a rascal, is it still our duty to love him? Love, it would seem, is now an impossibility, because not everything, but only the good is lovable. Evil neither can nor ought to be loved; for it is not our duty to love the wicked, or to make ourselves like bad men. We have said already that like loves like. Is it right then in such circumstances to break off the friendship at once? Or, perhaps, if not in all cases, at least where the vice is incurable? If there is any possibility of reforming the friend who has gone wrong, we should indeed come to the help of his character even more than of his property, since character is a better thing than property and enters more closely into friendship. Still a person who breaks off a friendship under these circumstances is not thought to be acting at all unreasonably. He was not a friend of the person as that person is now; therefore, if his friend has altered and it is impossible to reclaim him, he lets him go.

Again, suppose A stays as he was but B becomes better and vastly superior to A in virtue. Ought B then to treat A still as a friend? It is, I think, impossible. The case becomes clearest when the distance is wide between the two friends, as happens with childhood friendships, when one of two friends remains a child in mind and the other is a fully developed man. How can they be friends, when they sympathize with each other neither in their ideas nor in their pleasures and pains? There will be no personal understanding between them, and without understanding it is impossible, as we saw, to be friends, for it is impossible for two people to live together. But this point has been already discussed.

Is it right then, when two friends cease to be sympathetic, for one to treat the other exactly as if he had never been his friend? Surely we must not entirely forget the old intimacy, but even as we think we should oblige friends rather than strangers, so for old friends we should show some consideration for the sake of the past friendship, provided that the break in the friendship was not caused by some extraordinary wickedness.

CHAPTER 4. The origin of our friendly relations with our friends and of the marks that characterize friendship seems to lie in our own relation to ourselves. For a friend may be defined as one who wishes and does what is good, or what seems to be good, to another for that other's sake, or who wishes his friend to live and be safe for that friend's sake. This is the feeling of mothers for their children, and of friends, even if they have quarreled, for each other. Or, again, a friend may be defined as one who lives with another and shares his tastes, or as one who sympathizes with another in his sorrows and joys, as mothers above all do with their children. It is by one or other of these characteristics that we define friendship.

Now these all are found in the relation of a good man to himself, and in the relation of other men to themselves, in so far as they aspire to be good. For, as we have said, virtue and the virtuous man are, seemingly, the measure of everything; because a virtuous man is at one with himself, and desires the same things with his whole heart. He therefore wishes for himself what is good or what appears to be good, and makes it happen. For a good man naturally works for what is good and does so for his own sake, that is, for the sake of the intellectual part of his nature, which seems to be in every man his true self. Also, he wishes for himself to live in safety, especially that part of himself by which he thinks. For life is a good thing for a good man, and everybody wishes for himself what is good; and no one desires to win everything else at the price of losing himself. Though God now possesses the supreme good, he desires it only on condition of remaining whatever he now is. And manifestly the thinking faculty is a man's true self, or more nearly his true self than anything else is.

Such a man wishes to live with himself. He enjoys doing so, for his memories of the past are pleasant and he has good hopes, that is, pleasant hopes, for the future. His mind is full of subjects for thought, and he sympathizes more than another would do with himself in pain and pleasure. For the same things are pleasant or painful to him always; they do not vary, and he has, it may be said, few regrets. As then all these things are characteristic of the relation of

a good man to himself, and as he has the same relation with a friend as with himself (for his friend is a second self), it looks as if friendship consisted of one or other of these characteristics, and that those in whom they are realized are friends.

But whether or not it is possible for a man to be a friend to himself is a question which may be left for the present. It would seem to be possible in so far as two or more of the specified conditions exist, and because an extraordinary friendship of one man for another is compared to that of a man for himself. On the other hand, it seems as if these conditions existed in the majority of people, even when they are not good. Perhaps then we may say that the conditions are found in such people as far as they are pleased with themselves and suppose themselves to be good. For in a person who is utterly bad and impious, these conditions do not exist; they do not even appear to exist. And practically they do not exist in any badly behaved people; for such people are at war with themselves. While desiring madly one kind of thing, they wish too for something different. They are perhaps uncontrolled people, choosing not what they know is good but what is pleasant, though harmful, or they are cowardly or lazy people, shrinking from doing what they believe is best for themselves; or they are people whose moral depravity has led them to commit terrible crimes; and they hate and dread living and put an end to themselves.

Wicked people seek companions to spend their days with and try to escape from themselves; for when they are alone, they recall too many disagreeable things, and anticipate more, but when they are with other people they forget. There is nothing lovable in them, so they have no love for themselves. Nor do such people sympathize with themselves in joy or sorrow; for their soul is divided against itself. One part is pained out of viciousness at having to refrain from certain acts, and the other part is pleased. One part pulls this way and the other that way, as if they would tear the man asunder. Or, if he does not feel pain and pleasure simultaneously, at all events he is soon displeased at having been pleased and could wish that he had

not felt that pleasure; for the wicked are full of regrets. It appears then that the wicked man has no friendly feeling even for himself, since there is nothing lovable in him. So, if to be thus is to be in deep misery, we must strain every nerve to avoid wickedness and strive hard to be good, since only then can we be friends with ourselves and become the friends of others.

CHAPTER 5.   Good will resembles friendship, but is not the same thing; for good will, unlike friendship, we may feel for people unknown to us, who do not know that we wish them well, as we have already said. Again, good will is not the same as love; for it does not imply intensity of feeling or desire, which are the signs of love. Again, love implies familiarity, but good will may start in a moment, as when we feel good will towards competitors in the games. We wish them well and sympathize with them, but we should not think of doing something for them; for, as we said, good will starts in a moment and implies no more than a superficial regard.

Good will then may be called the germ of friendship, as the pleasure we feel in looking at a person is the germ of love. No one falls in love unless he has first felt delight in the aspect of the person he loves. Yet it does not follow that one who feels delight in a person's aspect loves him, unless he also longs for him in absence and yearns for his presence. So too it is impossible for people to be friends who have felt no good will to each other, but it does not follow that, if they feel good will, they are friends. For to those to whom we feel good will we merely wish well; we should not think of doing something for them or of taking serious trouble in their behalf. It may be said then, figuratively, that good will is unproductive friendship, which in course of time and familiarity may become friendship, but not a friendship based on utility or pleasure; for neither utility nor pleasure is the basis of good will. It is true that if A has received a kindness from B, he feels good will towards B in return for the service done him, and it is right he should make such a return. But if A wishes to bestow a kindness on B in the hope of gaining some

advantage by it, he is not wishing well to B, but rather to himself; as in fact he is not B's friend, if his motive in courting him is the desire to get something out of him. On the whole, it may be said that good will, when it arises, is prompted by some sort of virtue or goodness. It arises when we regard someone as noble or brave and so on, as we said in the case of competitors in the games. . . .

CHAPTER 7.   Benefactors are thought to be better friends to those they have helped than the latter are to their benefactors. This is a puzzling fact, and people try to account for it. The usual explanation is that benefactors are creditors and the receivers of their kindness debtors. Hence, as in the case of loans, the debtors would be glad if their creditors ceased to exist, whereas the creditors look anxiously to the safety of their debtors, so here the benefactors desire the existence of the receivers of their bounty in hopes of a return in gratitude, but the receivers are not eager to make that return. As to this explanation, Epicharmus would perhaps say that it takes too low a view of mankind; yet it seems true to human nature, for people generally have short memories, and are more eager to receive benefits than to confer them.

The true reason, however, seems to lie deeper down in the nature of things. It is not the same reason that makes creditors care for their debtors; for creditors have no affection for their debtors, and if they feel a wish for their safety, it is only in hopes of recovering the debt. But those who have done a kindness to others feel love and friendship for the people they have helped, even if the latter do not and cannot do anything for them. The same thing happens with craftsmen. Every craftsman loves his own handiwork more than it, if it were alive, would love him. And nowhere, I think, is this so true as with poets; they have an extraordinary affection for their own poems, and are as fond of them as if they were their children. It is much the same with benefactors. The person they have helped is their handiwork, and they feel a greater affection for their work than it feels for its author. The reason is that life is something we

all desire and love, and we live by activity, that is, by living and acting. The author of a work then lives by virtue of his activity in his handiwork; he therefore loves his work because he loves living.

This love then of an author for his handiwork is a law of nature; for what he is potentially is shown in his work living actually.[1] It is also true that in the eyes of the benefactor his is a deed of nobility; he therefore delights in the person who gives him the opportunity of displaying nobility. . . .

Again, we are all most fond of the things that have cost us trouble. Thus men who have made their money are always fonder of it than men who have inherited it. Accordingly, as it takes no trouble to receive a kindness but a good deal to confer it, benefactors are more affectionate than the recipients of their generosity. For this reason mothers are more devoted to their children than fathers; they suffer more in giving them birth and are more certain that they are their own. This last is also true of benefactors.

CHAPTER 8.   The question is also asked whether a man should love himself or someone else most. We criticize people who are exceedingly fond of themselves, and call them "self-lovers" by way of reproach; for a bad man has an eye to his own interest in all that he does, and the more so the worse he is. So we accuse him of doing nothing except for his own advantage. A good man, on the other hand, is moved by a feeling of honor, and the better he is, the more strongly he is so moved. He acts in his friend's interest, disregarding his own. . . .

It is therefore reasonable to ask, which of these two views we should follow, since there is something plausible in both. Perhaps then we ought to analyze them and determine how far and in what sense they are each right. The truth will, I think, become clear if we make plain the meaning of the word "self-love" in them both When people use it as a term of reproach, they give the name "self-

[1] On the difference between potential and actual being, see the *Metaphysics*, p. 23.

lovers" to men who grasp for themselves a larger share of money, honors, and bodily pleasures than belongs to them. These things are what men in general desire. These they believe to be the best goods, on these they set their hearts, and for these they compete. So the men who work to get an unfair share of these things are gratifying their appetites and emotions generally, or, in other words, the irrational parts of their souls. Most men are like this and therefore most self-love is bad. Hence the term "self-love" has come to be used in a bad sense. It is right then to disapprove of men who love themselves in this sense. People ordinarily apply the term "self-love" to those who snatch for themselves an unfair share of these things.

But a man who sets his heart always on doing above all what is just or temperate or virtuous in any respect, and who always and in every way chooses for himself the noble part, is never accused of self-love or blamed for it. Yet such a man, more than the other, would seem a lover of himself. At all events, he takes for himself what is noblest and best, and gratifies the highest part of his nature and yields it unqualified obedience. And as the highest element in a state or any other corporation seems to be in the truest sense the state or corporation itself, so with a man. He is then in the truest sense a lover of himself, who loves and gratifies the higher part of his being. . . .

Now when any persons are especially intent on doing noble acts, we all approve and applaud them. If all people were eager to do what is noble and exerted themselves to the utmost in the noblest deeds, then the state would have every need supplied, and the individual too would have the greatest of all goods, since virtue is the greatest good. We conclude then that a good man should be a lover of self, for by his noble deeds he will benefit himself and serve others, but that a wicked man should not be a lover of self, for he will injure himself and other people too by following his evil passions. . . .

It is true of the good man that he will act often in the interest of his friends and of his country, and, if need be, will even die for

them. He will give up money, honor, and all the goods for which the world contends, reserving only nobility for himself, because he would rather enjoy an intense pleasure for a short time than a moderate pleasure for long, have one year of noble life than many years of ordinary existence, and perform one great and lofty act than many trifling ones. It is true of one who dies for another that he chooses a great nobility for his own. Such a man will spend his riches gladly to enrich his friends; for while his friend gets money, he wins nobility, and so obtains the greater good for himself. The same with honor and offices of state. All these he will surrender to his friend, for the surrender is noble and laudable for himself.

It is right to call such a man good, for he chooses nobility above everything. He may give up even the opportunity for a good act to a friend. It may be nobler for him to inspire his friend to act than to act himself. In whatever field men deserve praise, a good man assigns to himself the greater share of noble conduct. In this sense then a man should be a lover of self, but not in the sense in which ordinary people love themselves.

CHAPTER 9.   Another question for discussion is whether a happy man needs friends or not. It is said sometimes that people whose lives are happy and independent have no need of friends, since they already have every good thing. Being independent they need nothing more, whereas a friend, like a second self, supplies what is not in our power to provide. Hence the saying,

"Let but God bless us, what's the good of friends?" [2]

But it looks strange to assign all good things to a happy man, and yet not grant him friends—the greatest it seems, of all external goods. If it is more a friend's part to do good than to receive it, if acts of generosity are part of a good man and of virtue, and if it is nobler to do good to friends than to strangers, the good man will need someone to do good to.

[2] Euripides, *Orestes*, 667.

So the question is asked whether we need friends more in prosperity or in adversity, the idea being that while an unfortunate man needs someone to help him, a fortunate man needs someone to do good to. It is, I think, absurd to place the happy man in solitude, as no one would choose to possess the whole world by himself. For man is a social being, and disposed to live with others. It follows that a happy man must live in society, for he possesses all that is by nature good. And clearly it is better to spend one's days with friends and good people than with strangers, who may or may not be good. It follows, therefore, that the happy man has need of friends. . . .

And if we look more deeply into the nature of things, we find that a good friend is naturally desirable for a good man; because that which is naturally good, as we have said, is good and pleasant in itself to the good man. Now life among animals is defined by the faculty of perception; among men it is defined by the faculties of perception and thought. But a faculty is intelligible only with reference to its corresponding activity. It is for the activity that the faculty essentially exists. Our life seems then to consist essentially of perception and thought.

Life is a thing that is good and pleasant in itself, for it possesses definiteness,[3] which is part of the nature of the good; and that which is naturally good is good also to the good man. It is as a natural good that life seems pleasant to everybody. But in speaking of life as pleasant, we must not think of a wicked or corrupt life, or a life of pain; for such a life is indefinite, as are its attributes. The subject of pain we will make clearer later. Life in itself, however, is good and pleasant. It seems to be so from the fact that all men desire it, and especially the good and happy; for to them life is most desirable, as theirs is the happiest life.

Now one who sees perceives that he sees, and one who hears that he hears, and one who walks that he walks; similarly in all our activi-

---

[3] The idea of "definiteness" or "limitation" as a characteristic of the good and of "indefiniteness" or "infinity" as a characteristic of evil is Pythagorean. See p. 108, ʰ 5.

ties there is something in us that perceives that we are active; and if so, it follows that we perceive that we perceive, and perceive that we think. But to perceive that we perceive or that we think is to perceive that we live; [4] for life consists, as we said, of perceiving and thinking. Thus perception of life is a pleasure in itself; for life is naturally a good, and it is pleasant to perceive good existing in oneself.

Life then is desirable and to none so desirable as to the good, because mere existence is to them good and pleasant; for they feel a pleasure in their consciousness of the presence of something good in itself. And a good man stands in the same relation to his friend as to himself; for his friend is a second self. Since then he desires his own existence, so or nearly so he desires the existence of his friend. But the desirableness of existence, as we saw, lies in a perception of goodness in oneself, such a perception being pleasant in itself. He requires therefore a consciousness of his friend's existence, and this he gets by living with him and associating with him in conversation and thought. For this is what we mean when we speak of men's living together; we do not mean, as when we speak of cattle, merely occupying the same feeding ground.

If the happy man then finds existence desirable in itself, as being naturally good and pleasant, and if a friend's existence is much the same as his own, it follows that a friend will be a desirable thing. And that which is desirable he ought to possess, or he will be so far deficient. We conclude then that if a man is to be happy he will need good friends.

CHAPTER 10. Should we then have as many friends as possible? Or is it with friendship generally as with hospitality, of which it has been neatly said,

"Give me not many guests, nor give me none." [5]

[4] This statement of "the absolute unity of existence with thought" may be taken as anticipating the formula of Descartes, "I think, therefore I am."

[5] Hesiod, *Works and Days*, 713.

That is, should a man neither be friendless nor again have an excessive number of friends?

In the case of friends whose friendship we make from motives of utility, the saying is perfectly applicable, for to return the services of many people is a laborious task and life is not long enough. A larger number of such friends then than one needs for one's own life would be superfluous and an obstacle to noble living. We therefore do not want them. As for friends made because they seem pleasant or sweet to us, a few are enough, as a little sweetening is enough in our diet.

But taking only good friends, we may ask, "Should we have as many as possible, or is there a limit fixed to the size of a circle of friends, as there is to the size of a city state? [6] For although ten people would not be enough to compose such a state, still if the population rose to a hundred thousand, it would cease to be a city state. The number of citizens, however, cannot probably be precisely fixed, but may be anything within certain definite limits. So too to the number of friends there will be a limit, namely, the largest number with whom one can live. For the sharing of life together, we saw, was a special characteristic of friendship. Obviously a person cannot live with many people and distribute himself among them.

Again, a person's friends must be friends of one another, if they are all to pass their days together; and this condition can hardly be carried out by many people at a time. It is hard too for one person to sympathize fittingly with many people in their joys and sorrows; for probably at the very time he is called on to rejoice with one he will be summoned to sorrow with another.

Perhaps then it is well not to try to have the largest number of friends possible, but only as many as suffice for a life together, since apparently no one can be a devoted friend to many people at once. So too no one can love several people at once; for love is in idea a

[6] To Aristotle's way of thinking, a population of over 100,000 would be too unwieldy to organize and govern in the free and civilized way a Greek city state was conducted. Big empires and cities were barbaric.

sort of exaggerated friendship and no person can feel this friendship for more than one individual. So too one cannot be a devoted friend of more than a few people. This seems actually to be the case. We do not find people having many friends as intimate with themselves as comrades. The classical friendships [7] of story too have all been friendships between two persons. People who have a host of friends and take everybody to their arms seem to be nobody's friends, unless indeed in the sense in which all fellow citizens are friends. If they have such a host of friends we call them easily suited.

Although then one may simply as a fellow citizen be a friend of many people, and yet not be too easygoing but truly good, one cannot have with many people a friendship based on virtue and on the merits of our friends themselves. We must be content if we find a few such friends.

CHAPTER 11. We have yet to ask whether we need friends more in prosperity or in adversity? We need them at both times; for in trouble we need assistance, and in prosperity we need people to live with and to do good to; for presumably we wish to do good. Friendship is more necessary in times of trouble; and in trouble we want friends able to help us; but it is nobler in times of good fortune. So in prosperity we look for good people, since we like better to do them services and to live in their society. For the mere presence of friends is pleasant in good fortune, and also in bad, for our distress is lightened by the sympathy of friends. Accordingly it is a question whether they take part of the burden as it were upon themselves, or whether it is rather the pleasure of their presence and the thought of their sympathy that softens our pain. . . .

On our side, we should, I think, go to our friends when they are in trouble, even if they do not send for us, and make a point of going. For it is the part of a friend to be helpful, especially to friends in need who have made no claim on us; it is the nobler and pleas-

[7] Such as the friendship of Achilles and Patroclus, or of Damon and Pythias.

anter way for both. We should too be quick to join them when they are enjoying themselves—for this again is something friends can do —but be less quick in looking for enjoyment for ourselves, since there is nothing noble in being eager to receive benefits. Still we must, I think, be on our guard against seeming churlish in rejecting their gifts, as people sometimes do. The presence of friends then is evidently always desirable.

CHAPTER 12.   Nothing is so welcome to people who are in love as the sight of one another. There is no sense they would choose in preference to sight, since on this more than on anything else depends the existence and origin of their love. Thus there is nothing friends desire so much as living together. For the essence of friendship is companionship. . . . And whatever people regard as the purpose of existence, whatever it is that makes them desire life, this they wish to share with their friends. So some people are companions in drinking, others in gambling, others in athletics, or in hunting or in the study of philosophy. Each class spends its days on that which it loves most in life. For as they wish to live with their friends, they do and participate together in the things that seem to them to mean a common life.

Thus the friendship of the bad turns out to be vicious; for they are unstable and combine to do evil, and become more wicked by growing like one another. But the friendship of the good is good. It grows as their intimacy grows, and they seem to become better by acting together and correcting each other's faults. For each models himself on the attractive features of the other's character; whence the saying,

"From good men learn good life." [8]

Enough then of friendship. We will next discuss pleasure.

[8] A saying of Theognis.

BOOK X

> *Pleasure intensifies every activity it accompanies, and is complete in itself while it lasts. It varies in goodness and badness with the activity it accompanies and with the individual who feels it. The good man's activities produce the most perfect pleasure. Happiness is the leisurely activity of the most divine part of man's nature, that is, his reason, which is his true self. Perfect happiness consists in the life of thought or contemplation of truth, in which we approach the life of God. But, with his composite human nature, man finds a secondary happiness in external things and in the practice of the moral virtues in his relations with other men. Education and training in virtue should be provided for all citizens by the laws of the state in which they live.*

CHAPTER 1. It is right, I think, to discuss pleasure next; for there is, it seems, a close affinity between pleasure and our human nature, which is the reason why, in educating the young, we steer their course by the rudders of pleasure and pain. There is too no more important element in the formation of a good character than a rightly directed sense of pleasure and pain. For pleasure and pain go with us through life, and exert a powerful influence for virtue and happiness in life, since we choose what is pleasant and avoid what is painful.

Considering then the importance of these questions, it is clearly our duty not to pass them over, especially since they admit of much dispute. For some people say that the good [1] is pleasure. Others, on

---

[1] When Aristotle in this tenth book speaks of "the good," he means usually the highest good open to man.

the contrary, insist that pleasure is something utterly bad, whether because possibly they are convinced that it really is so, or else they think it better in the interest of morals to represent pleasure as an evil, even if it is not. Men, they seem to think, are generally inclined to pleasure and slaves of their pleasures, and it is therefore their duty to lead them in the contrary direction, since thus they will arrive at the mean or proper state.

But I venture to think they are wrong. For in matters of emotion and action theories are not so trustworthy as facts. And when theories clash with the facts, as we perceive them, they fall into contempt, and involve the truth itself in the same discredit. Thus, if a person who condemns pleasure seems for once to be pursuing it, people think he is aiming at something that is altogether desirable; for it is beyond the power of ordinary persons to make distinctions. True theories, however, are exceedingly useful, not only as aids to knowledge but as guides of life. Being in harmony with the facts, they are believed, and being believed, they encourage those who understand them to shape their lives in accordance with them. . . .

CHAPTER 2. . . . The truth perhaps may be stated thus: Pleasures are desirable, but not if they are immoral in their origin; just as wealth is pleasant, but not as a reward for turning traitor to one's country, or as health is, but not at the cost of eating any food, however disagreeable. Or we may say that pleasures are of different kinds, those which are noble in their source are different from those whose source is dishonorable; and it is impossible to enjoy a just man's pleasure without being just, or a musician's without being musical, and so on. The difference between a friend and a flatterer shows clearly the truth that mere pleasure is not a good, and that there are pleasures of different kinds. For the object of a friend in his intercourse with us is good, while that of a flatterer is to give us pleasure. The flatterer is condemned, but the friend for his disinterestedness is praised.

Again, no one would choose to live all his life with the mind of a

child, even though he enjoyed extremely the pleasures of childhood. Nor would he like doing something utterly disgraceful, even though he were never to suffer pain for doing it. There are many things, on the other hand, for which we should keep on caring, even if they brought no pleasure with them, as, for example, our sight, memory, knowledge, and the virtues we possess. Even if it be true that these are necessarily accompanied by pleasure, it is no matter, for we should desire them if no pleasure came with them. It seems clear then that pleasure is not the good, nor is every pleasure desirable, that some pleasures are desirable in themselves, and that they differ in kind or in sources from the others. So much for the views people hold of pleasure and pain.

CHAPTER 3.   What the nature or character of pleasure really is will be seen more clearly if we take up our discussion again from the beginning. It seems that the act of sight is perfect or complete at any moment of time; it does not need anything that will be produced later to make it perfect in its form. Pleasure appears to resemble sight in this respect; it is a whole. At no time shall we find a pleasure that will be made more perfect in form if it lasts longer.

It follows that pleasure is not a motion; for every motion takes a certain time, and aims at a certain end and, like a builder's work, is complete only when it has accomplished its object. It is complete only in the whole time which the building took, or at the moment when it was completed. But in their various parts and in the time they take all the various motions are incomplete and different in kind from the whole motion and from one another. The setting of the stones is different from the fluting of the column, and both from the building of the temple as a whole. The building of the temple is complete, lacking nothing for the end proposed, but the carving of a base or a triglyph is incomplete, for each is only the building of a part. These motions are different in kind, and it is impossible at any time when the building is going on to find a motion which is

complete in form. Such a motion, if found at all, will be found only over the whole time. . . .

Motion is evidently not complete at any and every point of time. On the contrary, most motions are incomplete and different in kind, inasmuch as their starting point and goals give them different forms. Pleasure, on the other hand, seems to be complete in its form at any and every point of time. It is clear then that motion and pleasure must be different from one another, and that pleasure is something whole and complete. Another reason for maintaining this view is that motion is impossible except over a period of time, but pleasure is not; for the pleasure of a moment is itself a whole. . . .

CHAPTER 4.   Again, every sense is active on its own object, and the activity is perfect when the sense itself is in sound condition, and when the object is the most beautiful that falls within the realm of that sense. Such seems to be the character of its perfect activity. It makes no difference whether we speak of the sense itself or of the organ in which it resides as active. In every instance the activity is perfect when the part which acts is in the best condition, and the object on which it acts is the finest of the objects which fall within its realm. Such an activity is both the most perfect and the most pleasant. For whereas there is pleasure in all sensation, and similarly in all thought and speculation, the activity is pleasantest when it is most complete; and the activity of an organ in sound condition acting on the most excellent of its objects is the most complete. Pleasure then completes the activity, but not in the same way in which the excellence of the sense or of the object of sense completes it; just as health is the cause in one sense of our being healthy and the doctor is the cause in another.

Every sense has clearly its proper pleasure; for we speak of pleasant sights, pleasant sounds and so on. Clearly too the pleasure is greatest when the sense is at its best and its object is best. When both perceiver and object perceived are at their best. there will al-

ways be pleasure, so long as there is something that acts and an object to be acted upon. . . .

How then is it that nobody feels pleasure continuously? It is probably because we grow weary. Human beings are incapable of continuous activity, and as the activity comes to an end, so does the pleasure; for it is an accompaniment of activity. For the same reason some things give pleasure when they are new, but give less pleasure afterwards. The mind is called into play at first, and applies itself to the object with intense activity, as when we look a person full in the face in order to recognize him. But afterwards our activity ceases to be so intense and becomes casual and consequently the pleasure also fades away.

Everyone is supposed to desire pleasure, for everyone clings to life. And life is a species of activity and everyone is active about the things and with the faculties he enjoys most. Thus a musician uses his ears to listen to music, a student his intellect to speculate, and so on. Pleasure then makes our activities complete; it therefore completes life, which is the aim of human desire. It is reasonable therefore to aim at pleasure, since it makes life complete for each of us; and life is our object of desire.

CHAPTER 5. Whether we desire life for the sake of pleasure or pleasure for the sake of life, is a question we may dismiss for the moment. For pleasure and life are manifestly yoked together and do not admit of separation, since pleasure is impossible without activity and every activity is completed by pleasure.

This being so, it follows that pleasures are of different kinds, for things different in kind are completed by things themselves different in kind. This, we see, is the rule in works of nature or of art; for example, in animals, trees, pictures, statues, a house, or a piece of furniture. Similarly, we say that activities different in kind are completed by things also different in kind. Now activities of the mind differ from activities of the senses, and these again differ in

kind among themselves. Hence the pleasures that complete them will also be different.

The same may be shown by the intimate connection of each pleasure with the activity it completes. For an activity is intensified by its proper pleasure, since if the activity seems pleasant to us, we are more likely to arrive at a true judgment or an accurate result in it. People, for example, who like geometry make better geometricians and understand the various problems of geometry better than other people. It is so too with people who enjoy music or architecture or any other subject; their progress in their particular subject is due to the pleasure they take in it. Pleasure then intensifies activity, and whatever intensifies a thing must be closely connected with it. Where things then are different in kind, things closely connected with them will also be different in kind.

This becomes still clearer when we observe that pleasures that spring from one activity are hindrances to the exercise of another. Thus people who are fond of playing the flute are incapable of attending to an argument, if they hear someone else playing a flute, because they take a greater pleasure in flute playing than in the activity in which they are engaged at the moment. Hence the pleasure of flute playing destroys their activity in argument. Much the same result happens in other cases when a person is active on two enterprises at once. The pleasanter of the two activities eclipses the other—especially if it be much pleasanter—until all activity on the other ceases. So if we take intense delight in one thing, we cannot do anything else at all. It is only when we do not care much for a thing that we can do something else at the same time; as people who eat candy in the theater do so most when the actors are bad. . . .

Again, as activities differ in goodness and badness, some being desirable, some undesirable, and some neither one nor the other, so it is with pleasures, since every activity has its proper pleasure. Thus the pleasure proper to a virtuous activity is good, and that proper to a low activity is bad, just as the desire for something noble is itself laudable and the desire for something base is disgraceful. The pleas-

ures which are felt in the activities are even closer to them than the desires for them; for the latter are distinct from the activities in time and in nature, but the former are intimately connected in time with the activities, and so difficult to distinguish from them that it is a question whether the activity is not identical with the pleasure. Pleasure, however, is not the same as thought or sensation; it would be strange if it were. But the impossibility of separating them makes some people regard them as the same.

As activities then are different, so are their pleasures. Sight is superior to touch in purity, and hearing and smell to taste; there is a corresponding difference therefore in their pleasures. The pleasures of the intellect are superior to these; and some pleasures of the senses and of the intellect are superior to others. There is apparently a pleasure, as there is a function, proper to every living thing, namely, the pleasure inherent in its own activity. If we consider the animals one by one, we see this is so; for the pleasures of a horse, a dog, and a man are different. As Heraclitus says, "a donkey would prefer a bundle of hay to gold," for fodder is pleasanter to donkeys than gold.

Though the pleasures then of beings different in kind are themselves different in kind, we might suppose that there would be no difference between the pleasures of beings of the same species. But there is a wide difference, at least in the case of men. The same things charm some people and pain others; some find them painful and odious, others pleasant and lovable. This is true of sweet things; the same things do not seem sweet to a man in a fever and to one in good health. Nor does the same thing seem hot to an invalid and to a person in robust physical condition. It is much the same with other things as well.

But in all such cases we think that a thing really is what it appears to a good man to be. And if this is as true a statement of fact, as it seems, if virtue or the good man as such is the measure of everything, it follows that the pleasures that seem pleasures to the good man are really pleasures, and the things he enjoys are really delightful. If the things he finds disgusting seem pleasant to someone else,

we should not be surprised, for men are susceptible to corruption and defilement. But such things are not pleasant except to such people, and to them only when they are in that condition. Pleasures then that are admittedly disgraceful should not be called pleasures, except for people of depraved tastes.

But among those that are good, what pleasures or kinds of pleasure deserve to be called the proper pleasures of man? It is plain, I think, from a consideration of his activities; for activities bring pleasures in their train. Whether there is one activity or several that mark the perfect and the happy man, it is the pleasures which complete these activities that are strictly the proper pleasures of man. All other pleasures are so only in a secondary or partial sense, as are all other activities.

CHAPTER 6. Now that we have discussed the virtues, friendship, and pleasure, we have yet to give a brief account of happiness, since happiness, we said, was the end of human life. We shall shorten our account by summing up first our previous remarks.

We said that happiness is not a state of mind; for, if it were, a man who spends his whole life in sleep, living the life of a vegetable, or one who is thoroughly unfortunate, might be called happy. If then we reject this view, if we should rather call happiness an activity of some kind, as we said earlier, and if activities are either necessary and desirable as a means to something else or else desirable in themselves, then clearly we must count happiness among those activities that are desirable in themselves, and not as means to something else; for happiness has no want beyond itself; it is self-sufficient. Now activities are desirable in themselves, if nothing is expected from them beyond the activity. This is the case with good actions, for the practice of nobility and goodness is a thing desirable in itself. It is the case also with pleasant amusements. We do not desire them as means to other things; for they often prove hurtful rather than advantageous to us, making us careless about our persons and our property. Such pastimes are generally the resort of those whom the

world calls happy. Accordingly people who are clever at them are highly popular in the courts of tyrants, for they make themselves pleasant company to the tyrant in the occupations he likes; and what he wants is to pass his time pleasantly. These things are supposed to constitute happiness, because people who hold high positions devote their leisure to them.

But such people are not, I think, a criterion. For a high position is no guarantee of virtue or intelligence, which are the sources from which virtuous activities spring. And if these people, who have never tasted a pure and generous pleasure, take refuge in the pleasures of the body, we must not infer that these pleasures are more desirable; for children too think that the things that they value are the best. It is natural then that, as men and children differ in their estimates of what is valuable, so should good and bad people. As, therefore, we have often remarked, it is the things which are valuable and pleasant to a good man that are really valuable and pleasant. To everybody the activity that harmonizes with his own moral state is most desirable; to the good man, accordingly, activity in accordance with virtue is most desirable.

Happiness then does not lie in amusement. It would be strange indeed to believe that the end of life is amusement, and that we should toil and suffer all our lives for the sake of amusing ourselves. For seemingly we desire everything as a means to something else, except happiness, for happiness is our end. To take great trouble and pains then for the sake of amusement is foolish and utterly childish. However, to amuse oneself in order that one may work is right, as Anacharsis says; for amusement is a kind of relaxation, and since we cannot work forever, we need relaxation.

Relaxation then is not an end. We enjoy it as a means to activity; but the happy life is a life of virtue, and such a life is serious, not one of mere amusement. We call serious things too better than ridiculous and amusing things, and the activity of the better part of man's nature or of the better man always the more serious. Now the activity of the better is necessarily higher and happier. Anyone

can enjoy bodily pleasures. A slave can enjoy them as much as the best of men. But no one would grant that a slave can be happy without granting him a man's life,[2] for happiness consists not in the amusements I have been speaking of, but in virtuous activities, as we have already said.

CHAPTER 7. If happiness consists of virtuous activity, it must be the activity of the highest virtue, or in other words, of the best part of our nature. Whether it is reason or something else that seems to exercise rule and authority over us by natural right and to reach up to things noble and divine—because it is itself either divine or the most divine part of us—the activity of this part in accordance with its proper virtue will be perfect happiness.

This, we have already stated,[3] is an activity of thought or contemplation. Such a view would agree with our previous arguments and with the truth itself; for thought is the highest of our activities, as reason is the highest of our faculties, and the objects with which reason is concerned are the highest that can be known. Thought is also the most continuous, for it can more easily be continuous than any kind of action. We consider pleasure too an essential element of happiness; and we know there is no virtuous activity so pleasant as the activity of wisdom or philosophic reflection. Certainly philosophy is thought to offer pleasures of wonderful purity and certainty; and it is reasonable to suppose that people who know pass their time more pleasantly than people who are only searching.

Self-sufficiency too, of which we hear, is particularly a characteristic of thought activity. For while a philosopher, a just man, and everyone else needs the necessaries of life, after they are adequately provided with these things a just man still needs people to whom and with whom he may do justice, and a temperate man, a brave man, and everyone else needs others too. But the philosopher can contem-

[2] That is, the life of a free Athenian citizen.
[3] The reference is not clear, but the general drift of Aristotle's argument in Book VI has tended to show the intellectual nature of happiness.

plate truth by himself, and the wiser he is, the better he can do so. It is perhaps better for him to have fellow workers; nevertheless he is of all the most self-sufficient. It would seem too that this activity is the only one loved for its own sake, since it has no result but thinking; whereas from all practical action we gain something more or less besides the action itself.

Again, happiness seemingly requires leisure; for the object of our labor is to gain leisure, as the object of war is to enjoy peace. Now the activity of the practical virtues is displayed in politics or war, but actions of this sort seem the contrary of leisurely. This is entirely true of military action, and nobody desires war or prepares to go to war for its own sake. A man would be regarded as absolutely bloodthirsty if he were to make enemies of his friends for the mere sake of fighting and killing. But the activity of the statesman too is far from leisurely. Its aim is to secure something beyond and apart from mere politics, namely, power and honor, or at least the happiness of the statesman himself and his fellow citizens. This happiness is different from political activity and they search for it as something different.

If then political and military actions are distinguished among virtuous actions for nobility and grandeur, but if they allow no room for leisure and aim at some other end and are not desired for their own sakes; if too the activity of reason is superior in seriousness and aims at no end beyond itself and has its own pleasure, and if this pleasure intensifies the activity; and if whatever self-sufficiency and power of leisure and absence of fatigue as are possible to man and all other attributes of felicity are found in this activity, then this will be the supreme happiness for man, provided he is allowed a perfect length of life for it, since in happiness there is no imperfection. But such a life would be too lofty for man. He will live it not in virtue of his humanity but in virtue of a divine element within him. And the superiority of this activity to the activity of any other virtue is proportionate to the superiority of the divine element in man to his composite or material nature.

If then reason is divine in comparison with the rest of man's nature, a life in accordance with reason is divine in comparison with human life in general. Nor must we follow the advice of those people who say that the thoughts of men should not be too high for humanity or the thoughts of mortals too high for mortality. For a man, as far as in him lies, should make himself immortal, and do all in his power to live in accordance with the highest part of himself. That part, although it is small in size, yet in power and authority is far superior to all the rest. It would seem too to be the true self of everyone, if a man's true self is his supreme or better part. It would be strange then if a man should desire not the life of his own self but that of some other being. A statement we made before belongs here also. What is proper to everyone is by nature best and pleasantest for him. The life which accords with reason then is best and pleasantest for man, for a man's reason more than all else is himself. This life therefore will be the happiest.

CHAPTER 8. But in an inferior sense the life which accords with other kinds of virtue is happy; for the activities of such virtues are human. Our just and brave acts or the virtuous acts of any kind we perform in relation to one another, as when we fulfill our mutual obligations in contracts and services and other fields of conduct and in our emotions—and all these acts are naturally human. Such moral virtues seem actually the outgrowth of our physical organisms and in many respects closely tied up with our emotions. Prudence too is indissolubly linked to moral virtue and it to prudence, since the principles of prudence are dictated by these moral virtues, and moral uprightness is dictated by prudence. And the moral virtues, being inseparably connected with the emotions, must belong to our composite nature, and the virtues of our nature are human. So therefore is the life which accords with these virtues; so too is the happiness that comes with them.

But the happiness that lies in reason is a thing apart. Suffice it to say so much about it; for to describe it in detail would take us beyond

our present limit. It would seem to require few external aids or less than moral virtue does. Granted that both do need the sheer necessaries of life and need them equally, even though the statesman's labors have more to do with the body and bodily welfare than the philosopher's, that difference will not be important. But in what more they need for their activities there will be a great difference. The liberal man will want money for the practice of liberality, and the just man to return the services which have been done him; for our wishes, unless they are manifested in acts, will always remain obscure, and people who are not just pretend they wish to act justly. The brave man too will want physical strength if he is to perform any fine deed, and the temperate man an occasion; for otherwise it will be impossible for him or the other to show his character.

Now when the question is asked whether it is the will or the deed that is more essential in moral virtue, since that virtue requires both, palpably both are necessary to perfection. But for deeds, various conditions must be met; and the greater and nobler the deed, the more numerous will the conditions be. But for contemplation of truth, no such conditions need to be met, at least for the activity; rather they would be actual obstacles to thought; however, as a human being living in society, a man will choose to do virtuous deeds. Such conditions then must be fulfilled if he is to live as a man.

But that perfect happiness is an activity of thought will appear from the following consideration also. We think of the gods as happy and blessed. Then what kind of activity should we attribute to them? Just acts? But it would make them ridiculous to suppose they draw up contracts, return deposits, and so on. Brave acts? Do the gods face dangers and alarms for honor's sake? Or liberal acts? But to whom should they give money? To suppose they have a currency or anything of the kind would be absurd. Or what would their temperate acts be? Surely to commend the gods for temperance is to degrade them; they are free from cheap desires. We may go through the whole category of virtues, and whatever bears on moral action is petty and unworthy of the gods.

Yet the gods are universally conceived as living and therefore as active; we certainly do not imagine they sleep like Endymion.[4] If then one who is living is neither to act nor to produce, what is left him but thought? Therefore the activity of God, which surpasses all others in bliss, will be contemplation. If so, then the human activity which comes closest to it will be most like happiness. It is evidence of this that the other animals, who have no share in such activity, are without this happiness. For the whole life of the gods is happy and blessed, and the life of men is blessed in as far as it resembles their contemplative activity. But no other animal is happy, for none of them thinks.

We conclude then that happiness reaches as far as the power of thought does, and that the greater a person's power of thought, the greater will be his happiness; not as something accidental but in virtue of his thinking, for that is noble in itself. Hence happiness must be a form of contemplation.

CHAPTER 9. Man, nevertheless, being human, needs some external prosperity. His nature alone is not sufficient to support his thinking; it needs bodily health, food, and care of every kind. We must not however suppose that, because one cannot be happy without some external goods, a great variety of such goods is necessary for happiness. For neither self-sufficiency nor moral action demands excess of such things. We can do noble deeds without being lords of land and sea, for moderate means will enable a person to act virtuously. We may readily see this is so; for private persons are known to do good acts not less but actually more than their rulers. It is enough to have just as much as is needed for virtue. The man who lives in the active exercise of virtue will be happy. . . .

The opinions of philosophers seem to accord with our theories and such opinions possess a sort of authority. However, it is the facts of life that are the tests of truth in practical matters, for they are our

[4] Endymion was the beautiful shepherd boy whom the goddess Artemis kept sleeping in a cave.

final authority. We should then consider the theories we have been advancing in the light of the facts of life, accept them if they harmonize with those facts, and discard them as empty theories if they run contrary to them.

A man whose activity is governed by reason and who cultivates his reason is in the best, that is, the most rational state of mind and is also, as it seems, the most beloved of the gods. For if the gods have any care for human affairs, as it is believed they do, it would be only reasonable for them to delight in what is best and nearest akin to them, that is, in reason, and to reward with kindness those who love and honor it most, as loving what is dear to themselves and acting rightly and nobly. Obviously these are the characteristics above all of a philosopher. He will therefore be the most beloved of the gods, and in that undoubtedly he will be the most happy. If so, it is another reason for thinking a philosopher the happiest of men.

CHAPTER 10. If now our account of these subjects, of the virtues, and of friendship and pleasure too has been adequate, shall we regard our purpose as achieved? Or are we to say, in the old phrase, that in practical matters the end is not to examine and learn about them but to act? It is not enough to know what virtue is; we must strive to have and use it, and try whatever ways we may to become good.

If theories were enough in themselves to make men good, they would deserve any number of handsome rewards, as Theognis said, and we should have seen to providing them. But as a matter of fact, though they have the power to encourage and stimulate the youths who are generous-minded, and can bring a soul that is magnanimous and a lover of honor under the spell of virtue, they are impotent to inspire the mass of men to upright action. Such men are not naturally influenced by honor but by fear and refrain from evil not in dread of disgrace but of punishment. For they live by feelings, pursue their own pleasures and the means of getting these pleasures, and shun the opposite pains. But of what is noble and truly pleasant

they have not so much as an idea, because they have never tasted it. Where is the theory or argument that can reform such people? It is hard to change by argument the settled features of character. We must perhaps be content if, after supplying all the means by which to become good, we get in return some particles of virtue.

Some people think men are made good by nature, others by habit, others again by teaching. Now clearly the gifts of Nature are not in our power to control, but are bestowed through a divine providence on those who are truly fortunate. As for argument and teaching, it is probably true that they are not universally efficacious. The soul of the pupil must first have been cultivated by habit to a right spirit of pleasure and aversion, like earth that is to nourish the seed. For one whose life is swayed by passion will not listen to a voice of reason dissuading him, or even understand it. How, in such a state, can we convert him? Passion seems never to submit to reason but only to force. We must then find characters already prepared and with some kinship to virtue, that love what is noble and hate what is base.

But it is difficult to get from youth up a right training in virtue, unless one is brought up under good laws; for a life of temperance and steadfastness is not pleasant to most people, least of all to the young. Hence the nurture and activities of the young should be regulated by law, for they will not be painful when he grows used to them. Still it is not enough, I think, that the young should receive right nurture and guidance; we must practice what is right, even when we have come to man's estate, and get accustomed to doing it. We shall need laws then to teach us too what is right and all the duty of life; for most people are controlled by necessity rather than by reason and by fear of punishment rather than by love of nobility.

For this reason it is sometimes said that lawmakers should urge and exhort men to virtue because it is so noble, and those who have been already trained in virtue will heed them. They should also impose penalties and punishment on the disobedient and degenerate, and banish altogether those who are hopelessly incurable. So the good man, who lives by rule of honor, will obey reason, and the bad man,

whose sole aim is pleasure, will be chastened by pain like a beast of burden. So too, it is said, the pains should be such as are opposed to those men's favorite pleasures.

If then, as we have said, a man who is to be good must needs receive a noble nurture and training and then live worthily in virtuous pursuits and never voluntarily or involuntarily do evil, this result will be attained only if he lives in accordance both with reason and with some sort of right order resting on force. Now the authority of a father does not possess such force or compulsion, nor indeed does that of any individual, unless he is a king or some such potentate. But the law has compulsory power, and is itself at the same time a product of prudence and reason. And whereas we hate men who oppose our desires, even when they are right in doing so, we do not resent the law for its insistence on virtue.

It is only in Sparta and a few other states that the lawmaker seems to have undertaken to control the nurture and occupations of the citizens. In the great majority of states there is an absolute neglect of such matters, and everybody lives as he chooses, "being lawgiver to his wife and children" like the Cyclops.[5] The state would do well then to undertake control of these matters and exercise it rightly, and it should have the power of making its control effective. But if the state entirely neglects them, it would seem the duty of every citizen to further the cause of virtue in his own children and friends, or at least to attempt to do so.

It would seem too from what has been said that he can do this better if he has learned the principles of legislation; for public control is exercised through laws, and is good if the laws are good. Whether, however, the laws are written or unwritten, and whether they apply to the education of individuals or of groups, is apparently a matter of indifference, as it is in music or gymnastics or other fields. For as in a state law and custom are supreme, so in a household the father's commands and habits are binding, and all the more so be-

[5] Homer's description of the life in the Cyclops' cave, to which Aristotle frequently refers, is found in the *Odyssey*, IX, 114, 115.

cause of his paternal relationship to his family and the benefits he confers on them; for children are naturally affectionate and obedient to their father from the first. There is an advantage, moreover, in private as against public methods of education. It is much the same as in medicine, where, though it is the general rule that a feverish patient should be kept quiet and take no food, there may be individual exceptions. Nor does a teacher of boxing teach all his pupils to box in the same style. It would seem then that a study of individual characters is the best way of making education perfect, for then each has a better chance of receiving the treatment that suits him.

But the separate subjects, whether medicine or gymnastics or any other, may be best handled by one who knows the general rules applicable to all people or to people of some one kind; for the sciences are said to deal, and do deal, with general laws. At the same time there is no reason why even a person without scientific knowledge should not be successful in dealing with a particular case, if throughout his experience he has accurately observed the results which follow a particular course of action, just as there are doctors who are excellent in their own cases, though they cannot cure anyone else.

Nevertheless a man who wishes to go far in art or science, must, I think, proceed to universal principles and make himself acquainted with them, as far as possible; for sciences, as we have said, deal with universals. So also must anyone who wishes to make people, whether few or many, better by his efforts, try to learn methods of legislation, if laws are the natural means of making us good. And in education not everybody—but at best only the man who knows—can create a noble disposition in all who are sent to him; and the same in medicine or any other art which demands care and prudence. . . .

As previous writers have failed to investigate the subject of legislation, it will perhaps be well to study it ourselves, and indeed survey the whole subject of politics,[6] in order to complete as far as we can, our philosophy of human nature. First then we shall try to review the

[6] Aristotle here paves the way for his *Politics*, a treatise published later than the *Ethics*.

particular opinions of our predecessors that were sound, and then in the light of the constitutions we have collected,[7] to consider the causes of the preservation and destruction of states and of particular constitutions and the reasons why some constitutions are good and others bad. For when we have studied these, it will perhaps be easier to see what kind of constitution is best, and what is the best way of ordering it, and what should be its laws and customs.

[7] Aristotle made a collection of over one hundred and fifty constitutions of states of his day. Unfortunately it is one of his many works that are lost.

POLITICS

POLITICS

THE *Politics* of Aristotle is a work that at various times has had much influence on posterity. Machiavelli on the one hand and champions of popular government on the other have drawn ideas and arguments from its sagacious pages. Yet it, like the *Metaphysics*, is a patchwork of pieces not very well fitted together and not always representing consistent points of view. Other pieces, which should have been a part of it and to which Aristotle tantalizingly refers, are lost or else were never finished. Scholars now disagree as to the proper order of the books of which it is composed. Some put the last two, on the building of a successful state, immediately after Book III, and Book V, on the breakdown of states, at the end. But one who does not worry too much about the occasional repetitions, discrepancies, and omissions, but reads the *Politics* for all there is in it, will find plenty in the way of reward.

The opening books are controversial in tone. The first aims to show how wrong are those people who refuse to take politics and government seriously but treat them as merely conventional institutions of secondary importance. Actually they are as indispensable for the satisfaction of man's basic creature needs as the family and the village community, and far superior to them as a means for providing "the good life." The second book starts with a long argument to prove that the communism, advocated by Plato in his *Republic*, cannot work, and goes on to describe several efficient non-Athenian governments with which Aristotle was acquainted.

Book III contains Aristotle's definitions of certain stock political terms—citizen, state, monarchy, tyranny, aristocracy, oligarchy, democracy, and constitutional government or commonwealth. Which of these well-known forms of government does he consider the best?

Which, that is, of these forms offers to the people living under it the best chance to make their lives good? His ideal here seems to be a perfect kingship or aristocracy, in other words, government by the noblest element in the community. But in Book IV he admits that the man or group of men noble enough to govern solely for the best interests of the people at large is rare and hardly to be found. He recommends now a government by the body of free citizens, excluding the classes—women, slaves, manual laborers, and trades-men—whose dispositions and occupations do not, in his judgment, fit them for a share in the ruling. The arguments of Book IV are strong weapons in the hands of all defenders of democracy, and even stronger when the democracy they defend is less restricted than was Aristotle's.

The same book contains much detailed study of the actual work-ing of contemporary Greek states. Aristotle, we may remember, made a collection of one hundred and fifty-eight city constitutions as materials for his analyses and comparisons. It is a great mistake, he says, to oversimplify the classification of governments. There are all shades of variation and compromise possible between, for in-stance, a pure democracy and a pure oligarchy or government of wealth. Such mixed types of government are, in fact, the common-est of all. In Book V his subject is the causes of revolutions and the overthrow of governments. These, he thinks, can usually be re-duced to either too much equality or too much inequality between citizens. His advice on how to prevent discontent and uprisings and keep a state stable, including some realistic suggestions to tyrants on how by craft or by terror to maintain themselves in the saddle, is still worth any statesman's reading. In Book VI he considers espe-cially how either a liberty-loving democracy or a property-owning oligarchy may stay functioning securely, and discusses such topics as the best kind of population for a democracy, practical franchise qualifications, distribution of wealth, effects of official graft and dis-honesty on popular temper, and so on. In the last two books he describes the building and organization of a sound and happy state

from the ground up. He breaks off abruptly in the midst of a program for compulsory public education.

It is always, of course, a miniature city-state of which Aristotle is thinking. The empire that presaged the state of the future, that his willful pupil Alexander was constructing at an amazing pace in the East, while Aristotle lectured peacefully away in Athens, seemed to him too huge and heterogeneous and uncivilized to hold any promise of "the good life." Such a sprawling mass of men and lands might be subjugated by a despot and his armies, but its inhabitants could never be free citizens of any true state. Yet the *Politics* is full of suggestiveness even for us, members of a republic vaster than Alexander's empire. We may even ask ourselves, as we finish it, how far we have gone beyond the Greeks in devising governments that give to their people what Aristotle thought governments existed to give, namely, "the good and honorable life."

BOOK I

The origin of human associations—households, villages, states. The free members of the household. Its property, slaves, and the getting of household wealth.

CHAPTER I. Every state is a community of some kind, and every community is established with a view to some good; for mankind always act in order to obtain that which they think good. But, if all communities aim at some good, the state or political community, which is the highest of all, and which embraces all the rest, aims, and in a greater degree than any other, at the highest good.

Now there is an erroneous opinion that a statesman, king, householder, and master are the same, and that they differ not in kind but only in the number of their subjects. For example, the ruler over a few is called a master; over more, the manager of a household; over a still larger number, a statesman or king, as if there were no difference between a great household and a small state. The distinction which is made between the king and the statesman is as follows: When the government is personal, the ruler is a king; when, according to the principles of political science, the citizens rule and are ruled in turn, then he is called a statesman.

But all this is a mistake; for governments differ in kind, as will be evident to anyone who considers the matter according to the method which has hitherto guided us.[1] As in other departments of science, so in politics, the compound should always be resolved into the

---

[1] That is, the method of analysis, breaking a complex idea into its simple parts, as described in the succeeding sentence. Aristotle uses that method in all the treatises in this book.

simple elements or least parts of the whole. We must therefore look at the elements of which the state is composed, in order that we may see in what they differ from one another, and whether any scientific distinction can be drawn between the different kinds of rule.

CHAPTER 2. He who considers things in their first growth and origin, whether a state or anything else, will obtain the clearest view of them. In the first place (1) there must be a union of those who cannot exist without each other; for example, of male and female, that the race may continue; and this is a union which is formed, not of deliberate purpose, but because, in common with other animals and with plants, mankind have a natural desire to leave behind them an image of themselves. And (2) there must be a union of natural ruler and subject, that both may be preserved. For he who can foresee with his mind is by nature intended to be lord and master, and he who can work with his body is a subject, and by nature a slave; hence master and slave have the same interest. Nature, however, has distinguished between the female and the slave. For she is not niggardly, like the smith who fashions the Delphian knife for many uses; she makes each thing for a single use, and every instrument is best made when intended for one and not for many uses.[2] But among barbarians no distinction is made between women and slaves, because there is no natural ruler among them: they are a community of slaves, male and female. Wherefore the poets say,

"It is meet that Greeks should rule over barbarians," [3]

as if they thought that the barbarian and the slave were by nature one.

Out of these two relationships, between man and woman, master and slave, the family first arises, and Hesiod is right when he says,

"First house and wife and an ox for the plow," [4]

[2] See the same idea expressed in the *Parts of Animals*, p. 78.
[3] Euripides, *Iphigenia in Aulis*, 1400.
[4] *Works and Days*, 405.

for the ox is the poor man's slave. The family is the association established by nature for the supply of men's everyday wants, and the members of it are called by Charondas "companions of the cupboard," and by Epimenides the Cretan, "companions of the manger." But when several families are united, and the association aims at something more than the supply of daily needs, then comes into existence the village. And the most natural form of a village appears to be that of a colony from the family, composed of the children and grandchildren, who are said to be "suckled with the same milk." And this is the reason why Greek states were originally governed by kings; because the Greeks were under royal rule before they came together, as the barbarians still are. Every family is ruled by the eldest, and therefore in the colonies of the family the kingly form of government prevailed because they were of the same blood. As Homer says [of the Cyclopes]:

"Each one gives law to his children and to his wives." [5]

For they lived dispersedly, as was the manner in ancient times. Wherefore men say that the Gods have a king, because they themselves either are or were in ancient times under the rule of a king. For they imagine, not only the forms of the Gods, but their ways of life to be like their own.

When several villages are united in a single community, perfect and large enough to be nearly or quite self-sufficing, the state comes into existence, originating in the bare needs of life, and continuing in existence for the sake of a good life. And therefore, if the earlier forms of society are natural, so is the state, for it is the end of them, and the [completed] nature is the end. For what each thing is when fully developed, we call its nature, whether we are speaking of a man, a horse, or a family. Besides, the final cause and end of a thing is the best,[6] and to be self-sufficing is the end and the best.

[5] *Odyssey*, IX, 114.

[6] On Aristotle's theory of the final cause and end, see *Metaphysics*, p. 14, and Introduction. p. xxi.

Hence it is evident that the state is a creation of nature, and that man is by nature a political animal. And he who by nature and not by mere accident is without a state is either above humanity or below it; he is the

"Tribeless, lawless, heartless one,"

whom Homer [7] denounces—the outcast who is a lover of war; he may be compared to a bird which flies alone.

Now the reason why man is more of a political animal than bees or any other gregarious animals is evident. Nature, as we often say, makes nothing in vain, and man is the only animal whom she has endowed with the gift of speech. And whereas mere voice is but an indication of pleasure or pain, and is therefore found in other animals (for their nature attains to the perception of pleasure and pain and the intimation of them to one another, and no further), the power of speech is intended to set forth the expedient and inexpedient, and likewise the just and the unjust. And it is characteristic of man that he alone has any sense of good and evil, of just and unjust; and the association of living beings who have this sense makes a family and a state.

Thus the state is by nature clearly prior to the family and to the individual, since the whole is of necessity prior to the part; for example, if the whole body be destroyed, there will be no foot or hand, except in an equivocal sense, as we might speak of a stone hand; for when destroyed the hand will be no better than that. But things are defined by their working and power; and we ought not to say that they are the same when they are no longer the same, but only that they have the same name. The proof that the state is a creation of nature and prior to the individual is that the individual, when isolated, is not self-suffing; and therefore he is like a part in relation to the whole. But he who is unable to live in society, or who has no need because he is sufficient for himself, must be either a beast or a god: he is no part of a state.

---

[7] *Iliad*, IX. Classics Club edition, p. 129.

A social instinct is implanted in all men by nature, and he who first founded the state was the greatest of benefactors. For man, when perfected, is the best of animals, but, when separated from law and justice, he is the worst of all; since armed injustice is the more dangerous, and he is equipped at birth with the arms of intelligence and with moral qualities which he may use for the worst ends. Wherefore, if he have not virtue, he is the most unholy and the most savage of animals, and the most full of lust and gluttony. But justice is the bond of men in states, and the administration of justice, which is the determination of what is just, is the principle of order in political society.

CHAPTER 3. Seeing, however, that the state is made up of households, before speaking of the state, we must speak of the management of the household. The parts of the household are the persons who compose it, and a complete household consists of slaves and freemen. Now we should begin by examining everything in its least elements; and the first and least parts of a family are master and slave, husband and wife, father and children. We have therefore to consider what each of these three relations is and ought to be: I mean the relation of master and servant, of husband and wife, and, thirdly, of parent and child. And there is another element of a household, the so-called art of money-getting, which, according to some, is identical with household management, according to others, a principal part of it; the nature of this art will also have to be considered by us.

Let us first speak of master and slave, looking to the needs of practical life and also seeking to attain some better theory of their relation than exists at present. For some are of opinion that the rule of a master is a science, and that the management of a household, and the mastership of slaves, and the political and royal rule, as I was saying at the outset, are all the same. Others affirm that the rule of a master over slaves is contrary to nature, and that the distinction

between slave and freeman exists by law only, and not by nature; and being an interference with nature is therefore unjust.

CHAPTER 4. Property is a part of the household, and therefore the art of acquiring property is a part of the art of managing the household; for no man can live well, or indeed live at all, unless he be provided with necessaries. And as in the arts which have a definite sphere, the workers must have their own proper instruments for the accomplishment of their work, so it is in the management of a household. Now, instruments are of various sorts; some are living, others lifeless; in the rudder, the pilot of a ship has a lifeless instrument, in the look-out man, a living one; for in the arts the servant is a kind of instrument. Thus, too, a possession is an instrument for maintaining life. And so, in the arrangement of a family, a slave is a living possession, and property a number of such instruments; and the servant is himself an instrument, which takes precedence of all other instruments. For if every instrument could accomplish its own work, obeying or anticipating the will of others, like the statues of Daedalus, or the tripods of Hephaestus, which, says the poet,[8]

"of their own accord entered the assembly of the Gods";

if, in like manner, the shuttle would weave and the plectrum touch the lyre without a hand to guide them, foremen would not need laborers, nor masters slaves.

Here, however, another distinction must be drawn: the instruments commonly so called are instruments of production, whilst a possession is an instrument of action. The shuttle, for example, is not only of use, but something else is made by it, whereas of a garment or of a bed there is only the use. Further, as production and action are different in kind, and both require instruments, the instruments which they employ must likewise differ in kind. But life is action and not production, and therefore a slave is a minister of action [for

[8] *Iliad,* XVIII, Classics Club edition, p. 292.

he ministers to his master's life]. Again, a possession is spoken of as a part is spoken of; for a part is not only a part of something else, but wholly belongs to it; and this is also true of a possession. A master is only a master to his slave; he does not belong to him; whereas a slave is not only the slave of his master, but wholly belongs to him. Hence we see what is the nature and office of a slave; he who is by nature not his own but another's and is yet a man, is by nature a slave; and he may be said to belong to another who, being a human being, is also a possession. And a possession may be defined as an instrument of action, separable from the possessor.

CHAPTER 5. But is there anyone thus intended by nature to be a slave, and for whom such a condition is expedient and right? Or rather is not all slavery a violation of nature?

There is no difficulty in answering this question, on grounds both of reason and of fact. For that some should rule, and others be ruled is a thing not only necessary but expedient; from the hour of their birth, some are marked out for subjection, others for rule.

And whereas there are many kinds both of rulers and subjects, that rule is the better which is exercised over better subjects—for example, to rule over men is better than to rule over wild beasts. The work is better which is executed by better workmen; and where one man rules and another is ruled, they may be said to have such a work. In all things which form a composite whole and which are made up of parts, whether continuous or discrete, a distinction between the ruling and the subject element comes to light. Such a duality exists in living creatures, but not in them only; it originates in the constitution of the universe; even in things which have no life there is a ruling principle, as in musical harmony.

But we are wandering from the subject. We will, therefore, restrict ourselves to the living creature which, in the first place, consists of soul and body; and of these two, the one is by nature the ruler and the other the subject. Now we must look for the intentions of nature in things which retain their nature, and not in things

which are corrupted. And therefore we must study the man who is in the most perfect state both of body and soul, for in him we shall see the true relation of the two; although in bad or corrupted natures the body will often appear to rule over the soul, because they are in an evil and unnatural condition. First then we may observe in living creatures both a despotical and a constitutional rule; for the soul rules the body with a despotical rule, whereas the intellect rules the appetites with a constitutional and royal rule. And it is clear that both the rule of the soul over the body and of the mind and the rational element over the passionate are natural and expedient; whereas the equality of the two or the rule of the inferior is always hurtful. The same holds true of animals as well as of men; for tame animals have a better nature than wild, and all tame animals are better off when they are ruled by man; for then they are preserved. Again, the male is by nature superior, and the female inferior; and the one rules, and the other is ruled; this principle, of necessity, extends to all mankind.

Where then there is such a difference as that between soul and body, or between men and animals (as in the case of those whose business is to use their body, and who can do nothing better), the lower sort are by nature slaves, and it is better for them as for all inferiors that they should be under the rule of a master. For he who can be and therefore is another's, and who participates in reason enough to understand but not to have reason, is a slave by nature. Whereas the lower animals cannot even understand reason; they obey their instincts. And indeed the use made of slaves and of tame animals is not very different; for both with their bodies minister to the needs of life.

Nature would like to distinguish between the bodies of freemen and slaves, making the one strong for servile labor, the other upright and, although useless for such services, useful for political life in the arts both of war and peace. But the contrary sometimes happens: for some slaves have the souls and others have the bodies of freemen. Doubtless if men differed from one another in the mere forms of

their bodies as much as the statues of the gods do from men, all would acknowledge that the inferior class should be slaves of the superior. And where there is a difference in the body, how much more in the soul? But the beauty of the body is seen, whereas the beauty of the soul is not seen. It is clear, then, that some men are by nature free and others slaves, and that for these latter slavery is both expedient and right.

CHAPTER 6. But that those who take the opposite view have in a way right on their side, may be easily seen. For the words slavery and slave are used in two senses. There is a slave or slavery by law as well as by nature. The law of which I speak is a sort of convention, according to which whatever is taken in war is supposed to belong to the victors. But this right many jurists denounce, as they would an orator who brought forward an unconstitutional measure. They detest the notion that, because one man has the power of doing violence and is superior in brute strength, another shall be his slave and subject. Even among philosophers there is a difference of opinion. The origin of the dispute, and the reason why the arguments cross, is as follows: Virtue, when furnished with means, is deemed to have the greatest power of doing violence; and as superior power is only found where there is superior excellence of some kind, power is thought to imply virtue. But does it likewise imply justice?—that is the question.

To make the difference clearer, some assert that justice is benevolence; to which others reply that justice is nothing more than the rule of the stronger. If the two views are regarded as antagonistic and exclusive, still the alternative [viz, that no one should rule over others] has no force or plausibility, because it implies that not even the superior in virtue ought to rule, or be master. Some, clinging, as they think, to a principle of justice (for law and custom are a sort of justice), assume that slavery in war is justified by law, but they are not consistent. For what if the cause of the war be unjust? No one would ever say that he is a slave who does not deserve to be a slave.

Were this the case, men of the highest rank would be slaves and the children of slaves, if they or their parents chanced to have been taken captive and sold. Wherefore Greeks do not like to call themselves slaves, but confine the term to barbarians. In using this language, they really mean the natural slave of whom we spoke at first; for it must be admitted that some are slaves everywhere, others nowhere.

The same principle applies to nobility. Greeks regard themselves as noble everywhere, and not only in their own country, but they deem barbarians noble only when at home, thereby implying that there are two sorts of nobility and freedom, the one absolute, the other relative. The Helen of Theodectes [9] says:

"Who would presume to call me servant who am on both sides sprung from the stem of the Gods?"

What does this mean but that they distinguish freedom and slavery, noble and humble birth, by the two principles of good and evil? They think that as men and animals beget men and animals, so from good men a good man springs. But this is what nature, though she may intend it, cannot always accomplish.

We see then that there is some foundation for this difference of opinion, and that all are not either slaves by nature or freemen by nature, but also that there is in some cases a marked distinction between the two classes, rendering it expedient and right for the one to be slaves and the others to be masters: the one practicing obedience, the others exercising the authority which nature intended them to have. The abuse of this authority is injurious to both; for the interests of part and whole, of body and soul, are the same; and the slave is a part of his master, a living but separated part of his bodily frame. Where the relation between them is natural they are friends and have a common interest, but where it rests merely on law and force the reverse is true.

[9] Theodectes was a younger contemporary, perhaps a pupil of Aristotle, who quotes several times from his works. We have none of them.

CHAPTER 7. The previous remarks are quite enough to show that the rule of a master is not a constitutional rule, and therefore that all the different kinds of rule are not, as some affirm, the same. For there is one rule exercised over subjects who are by nature free, another over subjects who are by nature slaves. The rule of a household is a monarchy, for every house is under one head, whereas constitutional rule is a government of freemen and equals. The master is not called a master because he has science, but because he is of a certain character, and the same remark applies to the slave and the freeman. Still there may be a science for the master and a science for the slave. The science of the slave would be such as the man of Syracuse taught, who made money by instructing slaves in their ordinary duties. And such a knowledge may be carried further, so as to include cookery and similar menial arts. For some duties are of the more necessary, others of the more honorable sort; as the proverb says, "slave before slave, master before master." But all such branches of knowledge are servile.

There is likewise a science of the master, which teaches the use of slaves; for the master as such is concerned not with the acquisition but with the use of them. Yet this so-called science is not anything great or wonderful; for the master need only know how to order that which the slave must know how to execute. Hence those who are in a position which places them above toil have stewards who attend to their households, while they occupy themselves with philosophy or with politics. But the art of acquiring slaves, I mean of justly acquiring them, differs both from the art of the master and the art of the slave, being a species of hunting or war. Enough of the distinction between master and slave.

CHAPTER 8. Let us now inquire into property generally, and into the art of wealth-getting in accordance with our usual method [of resolving a whole into its parts]; for a slave has now been shown to be a part of property. The first question is whether the art of wealth-getting is the same as the art of managing a household, or a

part of it, or is instrumental to it; and if the last, whether in the way that the art of making shuttles is instrumental to the art of weaving, or in the way that the casting of bronze is instrumental to the art of the statuary. For they are not instrumental in the same way, but the one provides tools and the other material. By material I mean the substance out of which any work is made; thus wool is the material of the weaver, bronze of the statuary. Now it is easy to see that the art of household management is not identical with the art of wealth-getting, for the one uses the material which the other provides. And the art which uses household stores can be no other than the art of household management. There is, however, a question whether the art of wealth-getting is a part of household management or a distinct art. [They appear to be connected]; for the getter of wealth has to consider whence wealth and property can be procured.

But there are many sorts of property and wealth. There is farming and the care and provision of food in general; are these parts of the wealth-getting art or distinct arts? Again, there are many sorts of food, and therefore there are many kinds of lives both of animals and men; they must all have food, and the differences in their food have made differences in their ways of life. For of beasts, some are gregarious, others are solitary; they live in the way which is best adapted to sustain them, according as they are carnivorous or herbivorous or omnivorous; and their habits are determined for them by nature in such a manner that they may obtain with greater facility the food of their choice. But, as different species have different tastes, the same things are not naturally pleasant to all of them; and therefore the lives of carnivorous or herbivorous animals differ further among themselves.

In the lives of men too there is a great difference. The laziest are shepherds, who lead an idle life, and get their subsistence without trouble from tame animals; their flocks having to wander from place to place in search of pasture, they are compelled to follow them, cultivating a sort of living farm. Others support themselves by hunt-

ing, which is of different kinds. Some, for example, are brigands, others, who dwell near lakes or marshes or rivers or a sea in which there are fish, are fishermen, and others live by the pursuit of birds or wild beasts. The greater number obtain a living from the fruits of the soil. Such are the modes of subsistence which prevail among those whose industry is employed immediately upon the products of nature, and whose food is not acquired by exchange and retail trade. These are the shepherd, the farmer, the brigand, the fisherman, the hunter. Some gain a comfortable maintenance out of two employments, eking out the deficiencies of one of them by another; thus the life of a shepherd may be combined with that of a brigand, the life of a farmer with that of a hunter. Other modes of life are similarly combined in any way which the needs of men may require.

Property, in the sense of a bare livelihood, seems to be given by nature herself to all, both when they are first born, and when they are grown up. For some animals bring forth, together with their offspring, as much food as will last until they are able to supply themselves. Of these the vermiparous or oviparous animals are an instance; and the viviparous animals have up to a certain time a supply of food in themselves for their young, which is called milk. In like manner we may infer that, after the birth of animals, plants exist for their sake, and that the other animals exist for the sake of man, the tame for use and food, the wild—if not all, at least the greater part of them—for food, and for the provision of clothing and various instruments. Now if nature makes nothing incomplete, and nothing in vain, the inference must be that she has made all animals and plants for the sake of man. And so, in one point of view, the art of war is a natural art of acquisition, for it includes hunting, an art which we ought to practice against wild beasts, and against men who, though intended by nature to be governed, will not submit. For war of such a kind is naturally just.

Of the art of acquisition then there is one kind which is natural and is a part of the management of a household. For either the necessaries of life must exist previously, or the art of household manage-

ment must provide a store of them for the common use of the family or state. They are the elements of true wealth; for the amount of property which is needed for a good life is not unlimited, although Solon [10] in one of his poems says that

"No bound to riches has been fixed for man."

But there is a boundary fixed, just as there is in the arts; for the instruments of any art are never unlimited, either in number or in size, and wealth may be defined as a number of instruments to be used in a household or in a state. And so we see that there is a natural art of acquisition, which is practiced by managers of households and by statesmen, and what is the reason of it.

CHAPTER 9. There is another variety of the art of acquisition which is commonly and rightly called the art of getting wealth, and has in fact suggested the notion that wealth and property have no limit. Being nearly connected with the preceding, it is often identified with it. But though they are not very different, neither are they the same. The kind already described is natural, the other is learned by experience and art.

Let us begin our discussion of the question with the following considerations. Of everything which we possess there are two uses. Both belong to the thing as such, but not in the same manner, for one is the proper, and the other the improper or secondary use of it. For example, a shoe is used for wear, and is used for exchange; both are uses of a shoe. He who gives a shoe in exchange for money or food to him who wants one, does indeed use the shoe as a shoe, but this is not its proper or primary purpose, for a shoe is not made to be an object of barter. The same may be said of all possessions, for the art of exchange extends to all of them.

It arises at first in a natural manner from the circumstance that some have too little, others too much. Hence, however, we may infer

[10] The Athenian statesman and lawgiver, Solon, was also a poet, some of whose moralizing lines have come down to us in quotation, as here.

that retail commerce is not a natural part of the art of wealth-getting; had it been so, men would have ceased to exchange when they had enough. And in the first community, which is the family, this art is obviously of no use, but it begins to be useful when the society increases. For the members of the family had all things in common. When the family divided into parts, they still shared many things and had others too. Some of these they had to give in exchange for what they wanted, a kind of barter which is still practiced among barbarous nations. They exchange with one another the necessaries of life and nothing more; giving and receiving wine, for example, in exchange for corn and the like. This sort of barter is not part of the wealth-getting art and is not contrary to nature, but is needed for the satisfaction of men's natural wants.

The other or more complex form of exchange grew out of the simpler. When the inhabitants of one country became more dependent on those of another, and they imported what they needed, and exported their surplus, money necessarily came into use. For the various necessaries of life are not easily carried about; hence men agreed to employ in their dealings with each other something which was intrinsically useful and easily applicable to the purposes of life, for example, iron, silver, and the like. Of this the value was at first measured by size and weight, but in process of time they put a stamp upon it, to save the trouble of weighing and to mark the value.[11]

When the use of coin had once been discovered, out of the barter of necessary articles arose the other art of wealth-getting, namely, trade; which was at first probably a simple matter, but became more complicated as soon as men learned by experience whence and by what exchanges the greatest profit might be made. Originating in the use of coin, the art of wealth-getting is generally thought to be chiefly

[11] For Aristotle's earlier discussion of the importance of money as a standard of measurement in exchange, see *Ethics*, p. 163. Here he goes on to deplore the craze for heaping up large money fortunes by commercial operations, a very different thing, he says, from acquiring just what is needed for the life and comfort of the house.

concerned with it, and to be the art which produces wealth and riches, having to consider how they may be accumulated. Indeed, wealth is assumed by many to be only a quantity of coin, because the art of wealth-getting and retail commerce are concerned with coin. Others maintain that coined money is a mere sham, a thing not natural, but conventional only, which would have no value or use for any of the purposes of daily life if the users substituted another commodity for it. And, indeed, he who is rich in coin may often be in want of necessary food. How can that be wealth of which a man may have a great abundance and yet perish with hunger, like Midas in the fable, whose insatiable prayer turned everything that was set before him into gold?

Men seek after a better notion of wealth and of the art of wealth-getting than the mere acquisition of coin, and they are right. For natural wealth and the natural art of wealth-getting are a different thing. In their true form they are part of the management of a household; whereas trade is the art of producing wealth, not in every way, but by exchange. And it seems to be concerned with money, for money is the beginning of exchange and the end or limit of it. There is no bound to the wealth which springs from this art of money-making. As in the art of medicine there is no limit to the pursuit of health, and as in the other arts there is no limit to the pursuit of their several ends, for they aim at accomplishing their ends to the uttermost (but of means there is a limit, for the end is always the limit); so, too, in this art of money-making there is no limit to the end, which is wealth of a spurious kind, and acquisition of money. But the art of household management has a limit; the unlimited acquisition of money is not its business. And while, therefore, from one point of view, all wealth should have a limit, nevertheless, as a matter of fact, we find the opposite to be the case. For all money-makers increase their hoards of coin without limit.

The source of the confusion is the near connection between the two kinds of wealth-getting; in both, the instrument [i. e., wealth] is the same, although the use is different, and so they pass into one

another. For each is a use of the same property, but with a difference; accumulation is the end in one case, but there is a further end in the other. Hence some persons are led to believe that making money is the object of household management, and the whole idea of their lives is that they ought either to increase their money without limit, or at any rate not to lose it.

The origin of this disposition in men is that they are intent upon living only, and not upon living well. And, as their desires are un-limited, they also desire that the means of gratifying them should be without limit. Even those who aim at a good life seek the means of obtaining bodily pleasures; and, since the enjoyment of these ap-pears to depend on property, they are absorbed in making money. Thus arises the second species of wealth-getting. For, as their en-joyment is in excess, they seek an art which produces the excess of enjoyment; and, when they are not able to supply their pleasures by the art of money-making, they try other arts, using in turn every faculty in a manner contrary to nature. The quality of courage, for example, is not intended to make money, but to inspire confidence; neither is this the aim of the general's or of the physician's art; but the one aims at victory and the other at health. Nevertheless, some men turn every quality or art into a means of making money; this they conceive to be the end, and to the promotion of the end all things must contribute.

Thus, then, we have considered the art of money-making, which is unnecessary, and why men want it; and also the necessary art of wealth-getting, which we have seen to be different from the other, and to be a natural part of the art of managing a household, and concerned with the provision of food, not, however, like the former art, unlimited, but having a limit.

CHAPTER 10. And we have found the answer to our original question, whether the art of wealth-getting is the business of the manager of a household and of the statesman, or is not their busi-ness. It is an art which is of primary importance to them. As political

science does not make men, but takes them from nature and uses them, so nature provides them with food from the elements of earth, air, or sea. But at this stage begins the duty of the manager of a household, who has to order the things which nature supplies. He may be compared to the weaver, who has not to make but to use wool, and to know what sort of wool is good and serviceable or bad and unserviceable. . . .

Of the two sorts of wealth-getting one, as I have just said, is a part of household management, the other is commerce. The former is necessary and honorable, the latter a kind of exchange which is justly censured; for it is unnatural, and a mode by which men gain from one another. The most hated sort, and with the greatest reason, is usury, which makes a gain out of money itself, and not from the natural use of it.[12] For money was intended to be used in exchange, but not to increase at interest. And the term "interest," which means the birth of money from money, is applied to the breeding of money because the offspring resembles the parent. Wherefore of all modes of making money this is the most unnatural.

CHAPTER 11. Enough has been said about the theory of wealth-getting. We will now proceed to the practical part. The discussion of such matters is a liberal pursuit, but to be actively engaged in them is illiberal and irksome. The productive parts of wealth-getting are, first, knowledge of livestock—which are most profitable, and where, and how—as, for example, what sort of horses or sheep or oxen or any other animals are most likely to give a return. A man ought to know which of these pay better than others, and which pay best in particular places; for some do better in one place and some in another. Secondly, farming, which may be either tillage or planting, and keeping of bees or fish or fowls or any animals useful to

[12] The use of money as a standard of value and medium of exchange, as already explained, was to Aristotle its natural use. But the use of money as capital, especially the loaning of it at interest to get more money, a practice increasingly common in his time, seemed to him quite unnatural and wrong. Money was not a live thing. It did not naturally multiply, like flocks and herds.

man. These are the divisions of the true or proper art of wealth-getting and come first.

Of the other art, which consists of exchange, the first and most important division is commerce (of which there are three kinds—commerce by sea, commerce by land, and selling in shops—these again differing as they are safer or more profitable), the second is usury, the third service for hire. Of this last, one kind is employment in the mechanical arts, the other in unskilled bodily labor. There is still a third sort of wealth-getting, intermediate between this and the first or natural mode, which is partly natural, but is also concerned with exchange. This is industry that gets wealth from the earth and from products of the earth. This last, although it bears no fruit, is nevertheless profitable; for example, lumber cutting and mining. The art of mining, by which minerals are obtained, has many branches, for there are various kinds of things dug out of the earth.

Of the several divisions of wealth-getting I have now spoken generally. A minute consideration of them might be useful in practice, but it would be tiresome to dwell upon them at greater length now. Those occupations are most truly arts in which there is the least element of chance; they are the meanest in which the body is most deteriorated, the most servile in which there is the greatest use of the body, and the most illiberal in which there is the least need of excellence.

Works have been written on these subjects by various persons; for example, by Chares of Paros, and Apollodorus of Lemnos, who have treated of plowing and planting, while others have treated of other branches. Anyone who cares for such matters may refer to their writings. It would be well also to collect the scattered stories of the ways in which individuals have succeeded in amassing a fortune; for all this is useful to persons who value the art of getting wealth. There is the anecdote of Thales of Miletus [13] and his financial device, which involves a principle of universal application, but is attributed

[13] The first of the famous philosophers of Greece.

to him on account of his reputation for wisdom. He was reproached for his poverty, which was supposed to show that philosophy was of no use. According to the story, he knew by his skill in the stars while it was yet winter that there would be a great harvest of olives in the coming year; so, having a little money, he paid in advance for the use of all the olive-presses in Chios and Miletus, which he hired at a low price because no one bid against him. When the harvest time came, and many wanted them all at once and of a sudden, he rented them out at any rate he pleased, and made a quantity of money. Thus he showed the world that philosophers can easily be rich if they like, but that their ambition is of another sort. He is supposed to have given a striking proof of his wisdom, but, as I was saying, his device for getting money is of universal application, and is nothing but the creation of a monopoly. It is an art often practiced by cities when they are in want of money; they create a monopoly of provisions.

There was a man of Sicily, who, having money deposited with him, bought up all the iron from the iron mines. Afterwards, when the merchants from their various markets came to buy, he was the only seller, and without much increasing the price gained 200 per cent. Which when Dionysius [14] heard, he told him that he might take away his money, but that he must not remain at Syracuse, for he thought that the man had discovered a way of making money which was injurious to his own interests. He had the same idea as Thales; they both contrived to create monopolies for themselves. And statesmen ought to know these things; for a state is often as much in want of money and of such devices for obtaining it as a household, or even more so; hence some public men devote themselves entirely to finance.

CHAPTER 12. Of household management, we have seen, there are three parts. One is the rule of a master over slaves, which has

[14] The tyrant ruler of Syracuse in Sicily and the greatest Greek power in the West in the early fourth century, B.C. For more details about him see Books III, p. 316; V, p. 368.

been discussed already, another of a father, and the third of a husband. A husband and father rules over wife and children, both free; but the rule differs, the rule over children being a royal, over wife a constitutional rule. For although there may be exceptions to the order of nature, the male is by nature fitter for command than the female, just as the elder and full-grown is superior to the younger and more immature. In most constitutional states the citizens rule and are ruled by turns, for the idea of a constitutional state implies that the natures of the citizens are equal, and do not differ at all However, when one rules and the other is ruled we endeavor to create some difference of outward forms and names and titles of respect, which may be illustrated by the saying of Amasis about his foot-pan.[15] The relation of the male to the female is of this kind, but here the inequality is permanent. The rule of a father over his children is royal, for he receives both love and the respect due to age, exercising a kind of royal power. And therefore Homer has appropriately called Zeus "father of Gods and men," because he is the king of them all. For a king is the natural superior of his subjects, but he should be of the same kin or kind with them. Such is the relation of elder and younger, of father and son.

CHAPTER 13. It is clear that household management has to do more with men than with the acquisition of inanimate things, and with human excellence more than with the excellence of property which we call wealth, and with the virtue of freemen more than with the virtue of slaves. A question may indeed be raised, whether there is any excellence at all in a slave beyond merely the instrumental qualities of a servant—whether he can have the virtues of temperance, courage, justice, and the like; or whether slaves possess only the bodily qualities of a servant. Whichever way we answer the question, a difficulty arises; for, if they have virtue, in what will they differ from freemen? On the other hand, since they are men

[15] Amasis is said to have boasted he could make his foot-pan into a god as he himself had been made into a king. Herodotus, II, 172.

and share in reason, it seems absurd to say that they have no virtue. A similar question may be raised about women and children, whether they too have virtues: ought a woman to be temperate and brave and just, and is a child to be called temperate and intemperate, or not?

So in general we may ask about the natural ruler and the natural subject, whether they have the same or different virtues. For a noble nature is equally required in both; but if so, why should one of them always rule and the other always be ruled? Nor can we say that it is a question of degree, for the difference between ruler and subject is a difference of kind, and therefore not of degree. Yet how strange is the supposition that the one ought, and that the other ought not to have virtue! If the ruler is intemperate and unjust, how can he rule well? if the subject, how can he obey well? If he be licentious and cowardly, he will certainly not do his duty. It is evident, therefore, that both of them must have a share of virtue, but varying according to their various natures. The same principle is apparent to us in the constitution of the soul, in which one part naturally rules, and the other is subject. So the virtue of the ruler we maintain is different from that of the subject—the one being a virtue of the rational, and the other of the irrational part. It is obvious that the same principle applies generally, and therefore almost all things rule and are ruled according to nature.

But the kind of rule differs; the freeman rules over the slave after another manner from that in which the male rules over the female, or the man over the child. Although the parts of the soul are present in all of them, they are present in different degrees. For the slave has no deliberative faculty at all; the woman has, but it is without authority, and the child has, but it is immature. So it must necessarily be with the moral virtues also; all may be supposed to partake of them, but only in such manner and degree as is required by each for the fulfilment of his duty. Hence the ruler ought to have moral virtue in perfection, for his duty is entirely that of a master artificer, and the master artificer is reason; his subjects, on the other hand, require only that measure of virtue which is proper to each of them.

Clearly, then, some moral virtue belongs to all of them; but the temperance of a man and of a woman, or the courage and justice of a man and of a woman, are not, as Socrates maintained,[16] the same. The courage of a man is shown in commanding, of a woman in obeying. And this holds of all other virtues, as will be more clearly seen if we look at them in detail, for those who say generally that virtue consists in a good disposition of the soul, or in doing rightly, or the like, only deceive themselves. Far better than such definitions is the mode of speaking of those who, like Gorgias,[17] enumerate the virtues. All classes must be deemed to have their special attributes. The poet says of women,

> "Silence is a woman's glory," [18]

but this is not equally the glory of man. The child is imperfect, and therefore obviously his virtue is not relative to himself alone, but to a perfected man and to his teacher, and in like manner the virtue of the slave is relative to his master. Now we determined that a slave is useful for the wants of life, and therefore he will obviously require only so much virtue as will prevent him from failing in his duty through cowardice and intemperance.

Someone will ask whether, if what we are saying is true, virtue will not be required also in artisans, for they often fail in their work through misconduct. But is there not a great difference in the two cases? For the slave shares in his master's life; the artisan is less closely connected with him, and only attains excellence in proportion as he becomes a slave [i.e., is under the direction of a master]. The meaner sort of mechanic has a special and separate slavery; and whereas the slave exists by nature, not so the shoemaker or other artisan. It is manifest that the master ought to be a source of excellence in the slave; and not merely because he possesses the art which trains the slave in his duties. Wherefore they are mistaken who forbid us to

[16] In Plato's dialogue of *Meno,* 72-73, Socrates maintains this idea.

[17] In the same dialogue of *Meno,* 71-72, Gorgias argues against Socrates that there can be no general definition of virtue as a whole, only lists of separate virtues.

[18] Sophocles, *Ajax,* 293.

converse with slaves and say that we should employ command only, for slaves stand even more in need of admonition than children.

The further relations of husband and wife, parent and child, their several virtues, what in their intercourse with one another is good, and what is evil, and how we may pursue the good and escape the evil, will have to be discussed when we speak of the different forms of government.[19] For, inasmuch as every family is a part of a state, and these relationships are the parts of a family, and the virtue of the part must have regard to the virtue of the whole, women and children must be trained by education with an eye to the state, if the virtues of either of them are supposed to make any difference in the virtues of the state. And they must make a difference; for children grow up to be citizens, and half the free persons in a state are women.

Of these matters, enough has been said; of what remains, let us speak at another time. Regarding, then, our present inquiry as complete, we will make a new beginning. And, first, let us examine the various theories of a perfect state.

BOOK II

> *Ideal commonwealth and institutions. Criticisms of Plato's* Republic *and communism, and of Phaleas' plan for equalization of property. Discussion of the Spartan and other working constitutions.*

CHAPTER I. Our purpose is to consider what form of political community is best of all for those who are most able to realize their ideal of life. We must therefore examine not only this but other constitutions, both such as actually exist in well-governed states, and any theoretical forms which are held in esteem, so that what is good

---

[19] These questions are not answered in the *Politics*.

and useful may be brought to light. And let no one suppose that in seeking for something beyond we at all want to philosophize at the expense of truth. We only undertake this inquiry because all the constitutions with which we are acquainted are faulty.

We will begin with the natural beginning of the subject. Three alternatives are conceivable. The members of a state must either have (1) all things or (2) nothing in common, or (3) some things in common and some not. That they should have nothing in common is clearly impossible, for the state is a community, and must at any rate have a common place; one city will be in one place, and the citizens share in that one city. But should a well-ordered state have all things, as far as may be, in common, or some only and not others? For the citizens might conceivably have wives and children and property in common, as Socrates proposes in the *Republic* of Plato.[1] Which is better, our present condition, or the proposed new order of society?

CHAPTER 2.   There are many difficulties in a common ownership of wives. And the principle on which Socrates rests the necessity of such an institution does not appear to be established by his arguments. As a means to the end which he ascribes to the state, taken literally, it is impracticable, and how we are to interpret it is nowhere precisely stated. I am speaking of the premise from which the argument of Socrates proceeds, "that the greater the unity of the state the better." Is it not obvious that a state may at length attain such a degree of unity as to be no longer a state? The nature of a state is to be a plurality, but in tending to greater unity, from being a state it becomes a family, and from being a family, an individual; and the family may be said to be more one than the state, and the individual than the family. So that we ought not to attain this greatest unity even if we could, for it would be the destruction of the state. Again,

[1] Aristotle presents here his objections to the famous system of communism proposed in Plato's *Republic*, Book V, Classics Club edition, p. 332 ff. He is not, however always consistent in his criticisms or fair.

a state is not made up only of so many men, but of different kinds of men; for men all alike do not constitute a state. It is not as in a military alliance, the usefulness of which depends upon its quantity, even where there is no difference in quality. For there mutual protection is the end aimed at; and the question is the same as about the scales of a balance, namely, which is the heavier?

In like manner, a state differs from a nation; for in a nation the people are distributed into villages, and live scattered about, like the Arcadians; [2] whereas in a state a unity is to be formed out of elements differing in kind. . . . Again, from another point of view, this extreme unification of the state is clearly not good; for a family is more self-sufficing than an individual, and a city than a family, and a city comes into being when the community is large enough to be self-sufficing. If then self-sufficiency is to be desired, the lesser degree of unity is more desirable than the greater.

CHAPTER 3. But, even supposing that it were best for the community to have the greatest degree of unity, it is by no means proved that this unity will follow from the fact "of all men saying 'mine' and 'not mine' at the same instant of time," which, according to Socrates, is the sign of perfect unity in a state. For the word "all" is ambiguous. If the meaning be that each individual says "mine" and "not mine" at the same time, then perhaps the result at which Socrates aims may be in some degree accomplished; each man will call the same person his own son and his own wife, and so of his property and of all that falls to him. This, however, is not the way in which people would speak who had their wives and children in common; they would "all" say it, but not "each." In like manner, they would describe their property as belonging to them not severally but collectively. There is an obvious fallacy in the term "all"; like some

[2] To Aristotle, we must remember, the "nation" represented a lower state in political development than the compact Greek city state, which is what he has always in mind when he speaks of the "state." Arcadia was the most backward province of Greece.

other words, "both," "odd," "even," it is ambiguous, and in argument becomes a source of logical puzzles. That all persons call the same thing "mine" in the sense in which each man does so might be a fine thing, but it is impracticable. Or if the words are taken in the other sense, such a unity in no way conduces to harmony.

And there is another objection to the proposal. That which is common to the greatest number has the least care bestowed upon it. Everyone thinks chiefly of his own, hardly at all of the common interest; and only when he is himself concerned as an individual. For, besides other considerations, everybody is more inclined to neglect the duty which he expects another to fulfill; as in families many servants are often less useful than a few. Each citizen will have a thousand sons who will not be his sons individually, but anybody will be equally the son of anybody and will therefore be neglected by all alike. Further, upon this principle, everyone will call a boy "mine" or "not mine" according as he is doing well or not. However small a fraction he himself may be of the whole number, he may call every youth of the thousand, or whatever be the number in the city, "my son," or "so-and-so's son." Yet even about this he will not be positive; for it is impossible to know who chanced to have a child, or whether, if one came into existence, it has survived.

Then which is better, to say "mine" about every one of the two thousand or the ten thousand other citizens, or to use the word "mine" in the ordinary and more restricted sense? For usually the same person is called by one man his son and by another his brother or cousin or kinsman or blood relation or connection by marriage either of his own or of some relation of his; and these relationships he distinguishes from the tie which binds him to his fellow tribesman or neighbor. How much better it is to be the real cousin of somebody than to be a son after Plato's fashion! Nor is there any way of preventing brothers and children and fathers and mothers from sometimes recognizing one another; for children are born like their parents, and they will necessarily be finding indications of their relationship to one another. Geographers declare such to be the fact; they say that in Upper Libya,

where the women are common, nevertheless the children who are born are assigned to their respective fathers on the ground of their likeness. And some women, like the females of other animals—for example, mares and cows—have a strong tendency to produce offspring resembling their parents, as was the case with the Pharsalian mare called Honest. . . .

CHAPTER 4. . . . But in a state having women and children common, love will be watery; and the father will certainly not say "my son," or the son "my father." As a little sweet wine mingled with a great deal of water is imperceptible in the mixture, so, in this sort of community, the idea of relationship which is based upon these names will be lost; there is no reason why the so-called father should care about the son, or the son about the father, or brothers about one another. Of the two qualities which chiefly inspire regard and affection—that a thing is your own and that you love it—neither can exist in such a state as this. . . . Touching the community of wives and children, let this be our conclusion.

CHAPTER 5. Next let us consider what should be our arrangements about property: should the citizens of the perfect state have possessions in common or not? This question may be discussed separately from the enactments about women and children. Even supposing that the women and children belong to individuals, according to the custom which is at present universal, may there be an advantage in having and using possessions in common? Three cases are possible: (1) the soil may be divided up, but the produce may be thrown for consumption into a common stock; and this is the practice of some nations. Or (2), the soil may be common, and may be cultivated in common, but the produce divided among individuals for their private use. This is a form of common property which is said to exist among certain barbarians. Or (3), the soil and the produce may be alike common.

When the farmers are not the owners, the case will be different

and easier to deal with; but when those who till the ground also own it the problems involved will give a world of trouble. If they do not share equally in enjoyments and toils, those who labor much and get little will necessarily complain of those who labor little and receive or consume much. There is always a difficulty in men living together and having things in common, but especially in their having common property. The partnerships of fellow travelers are an example to the point; for they generally fall out by the way and quarrel about any trifle which turns up. So with servants: we are most liable to take offense at those with whom we most frequently come into contact in daily life.

These are only some of the disadvantages which attend the community of property. The present arrangement, if improved as it might be by good customs and laws, would be far better, and would have the advantages of both systems. Property should be in a certain sense common, but, as a general rule, private. For, when everyone has his separate interest, men will not complain of one another, and they will make more progress, because everyone will be attending to his own business. Yet among good men, and as regards use, "friends," as the proverb says, "will have all things common." Even now there are traces of such a principle, showing that it is not impracticable, but in well-ordered states exists already to a certain extent and may be carried further. For, although every man has his own property, some things he will place at the disposal of his friends, while of others he shares the use with them. The Spartans, for example, use one another's slaves, and horses, and dogs, as if they were their own; and when they happen to be in the country, they appropriate in the fields whatever provisions they want. It is clearly better that property should be private, but the use of it common; and the special business of the legislator is to create in men this benevolent disposition.

Again, how immeasurably greater is the pleasure, when a man feels a thing to be his own! For love of self is a feeling implanted by nature and not given in vain, although selfishness is rightly condemned. This, however, is not mere love of self, but love of self in

excess, like the miser's love of money; and all, or almost all, men love money, and other such objects in a measure. Furthermore, there is the greatest pleasure in doing a kindness or service to friends or guests or companions, which can only be done when a man has private property. These advantages are lost by the excessive unification of the state. Two virtues also are annihilated in such a state: first, temperance towards women (for it is an honorable action to abstain from another's wife for temperance sake); secondly, liberality in the matter of property. No one, when men have all things in common, will any longer set an example of liberality or do any liberal action; for liberality consists in the use a man makes of his own property.

Such legislation may have a specious appearance of benevolence. Men readily listen to it, and are easily induced to believe that in some wonderful manner everybody will become everybody's friend, especially when someone is heard denouncing the evils now existing in states, suits about contracts, convictions for perjury, flatteries of rich men and the like, which are said to arise out of the possession of private property. These evils, however, are due to a very different cause—the wickedness of human nature. Indeed, we see that there is much more quarreling among those who have all things in common, though there are not many of them when compared with the vast numbers who have private property. . . .

Let us remember that we should not disregard the experience of ages. In the multitude of years these things, if they were good, would certainly not have been unknown; for almost everything has been found out, although sometimes not put together. In some cases men do not use the knowledge which they have. Great light would be thrown on this subject if we could see such a form of government in the actual process of construction. The lawgiver could not form such a state at all without distributing and dividing the citizens into associations for common meals, and into clans and tribes. But all this legislation ends only in forbidding agriculture to the guardians, a prohibition which the Spartans try to enforce already.

Again, Socrates has not said, nor is it easy to decide, what in such a community will be the general form of the state. . . . One class will consist of the guardians, who are a sort of watchmen; another, of the farmers, and artisans and the rest, who are the real citizens. But [if so] the suits and quarrels, and all the evils which Socrates declares exist in other states, will exist equally among them. He says indeed that, having so good an education, the citizens will not need many laws, as, for example, laws about the city or about the markets; but then he confines his education to the guardians. . . .

Again, if Socrates makes the women common, and retains private property, the men will see to the fields, but who will see to the house? And what will happen if the agricultural class have both their property and their wives in common? Once more, it is absurd to argue, from the analogy of the animals, that men and women should follow the same pursuits; for animals have not to manage a household. . . . Again, he deprives the guardians of happiness, and says that the legislator ought to make the whole state happy. But the whole cannot be happy unless most, or all, or some of its parts enjoy happiness. In this respect happiness is not like the even principle in numbers, which may exist only in the whole, but in none of the parts; not so happiness. And if the guardians are not happy, who are? Surely not the artisans, or the common people. The Republic of which Socrates discourses has all these difficulties, and others quite as great. . . .

CHAPTER 7.   Other constitutions have been proposed; some by private persons, others by philosophers and statesmen, which all come nearer to established or existing ones than either of Plato's. No one else has introduced such novelties as the community of women and children, or public tables for women; other legislators begin with what is necessary. In the opinion of some, the regulation of property is the chief point, that being the question upon which all revolutions turn. This danger was recognized by Phaleas of

Chalcedon,[3] who was the first to affirm that the citizens of a state ought to have equal possessions. He thought that in a new colony the equalization might be accomplished without difficulty, but not so easily when a state was already established; that then the shortest way of reaching the desired end would be for the rich to give and not to receive marriage portions, and for the poor not to give but to receive them.

Plato in the *Laws* was of opinion that, to a certain extent, accumulation should be allowed, though he forbade, as I have already observed, any citizen to possess more than five times the minimum property qualification. But those who make such laws should remember what they are apt to forget—that the legislator who fixes the amount of property should also fix the number of children. For, if the children are too many for the property, the law must be broken. And, besides the violation of the law, it is a bad thing that many from being rich should become poor; for men of ruined fortunes are sure to stir up revolutions. That the equalization of property exercises an influence on political society was clearly understood by some of the old legislators. Laws were made by Solon and others prohibiting an individual from possessing as much land as he pleased. Other states have laws which forbid the sale of property; among the Locrians, for example, there is a law that a man is not to sell his property unless he can prove unmistakably that some misfortune has befallen him. . . .

Again, where there is equality of property, the amount may be either too large or too small, and the possessors may be living either in luxury or in penury. Clearly, then, the lawgiver ought to aim not only at the equalization of properties, but at moderation in their amount. And yet if he prescribe this moderate amount equally to all, he will be no nearer the mark; for it is not the possessions but the desires of mankind which require to be equalized. And this is impossible, unless a sufficient education is provided by the state. But

[3] Of this Phaleas, a writer on law and government, we know only what Aristotle tells us.

Phaleas will probably reply that this is precisely what he means; and that, in his opinion, there ought to be in states, not only equal property, but equal education. Still he should tell us what will be the character of his education; there is no use in having one and the same for all, if it is of a sort that predisposes men to avarice, or ambition, or both. Moreover, civil troubles arise, not only over inequalities of property, but over inequalities of honor, though in opposite ways. For the common people quarrel about the too great inequality of property, the higher class about the too great equality of honor; as the poet says,

"The bad and good alike in honor share." [4]

There are crimes of which the motive is want, and for these Phaleas expects to find a cure in the equalization of property, which will take away from a man the temptation to be a highwayman because he is hungry or cold. But want is not the sole incentive to crime; men also desire to gratify some passion which preys on them, or they are eager to enjoy pleasures unaccompanied with pain, and therefore they commit crimes. What is the cure for these three disorders? Of the first, moderate possessions and occupation; of the second, habits of temperance; as to the third, those who desire pleasures which depend on themselves will find the satisfaction of their desires in philosophy but nowhere else; for all other pleasures we are dependent on others. The fact is that the greatest crimes are caused by excess and not by poverty. Men do not become tyrants in order that they may not suffer cold. Hence great is the honor bestowed, not on him who kills a mere thief, but on him who kills a tyrant. Thus we see that the institutions of Phaleas avail only against petty crimes. . . .

CHAPTER 8. . . . To reward those who discover anything of use to the state is a proposal which has a specious sound, but cannot safely be enacted by law, for it may encourage informers, and

[4] *Iliad*, IX, Classics Club edition, p. 134.

perhaps even lead to political commotions. However, this question involves another. It has been doubted whether it is or is not expedient to make any changes in the laws of a country, even if another law be better. . . . And, since we have touched upon this subject, perhaps we had better go a little into detail; for, as I was saying, there is a difference of opinion, and it may sometimes seem desirable to make changes. Such changes in the other arts and sciences have certainly been beneficial; medicine, for example, and gymnastic, and every other art and science have departed from their traditional usage. And, if politics be an art, change must be necessary in this as in any other art.

The need of improvement is shown by the fact that old customs are exceedingly simple and barbarous. For the ancient Greeks went about armed and bought their wives of each other. The remains of ancient laws which have come down to us are quite absurd; for example, at Cumae there is a law about murder to the effect that if the accuser produce a certain number of witnesses from among his own kinsmen, the accused shall be held guilty. Again, men in general desire what is good, and not merely what their fathers had. And the primeval inhabitants, whether they were born of the earth or were the survivors of some destruction, may be supposed to have been no better than ordinary foolish people among ourselves. (Such is certainly the tradition concerning the earth-born men.) It would be ridiculous to rest contented with their notions.

Even when laws have been written down, they ought not to remain always unaltered. As in other sciences, so in politics, it is impossible that all things should be precisely set down in writing; for rules must be universal, but actions are concerned with particulars. Hence we infer that sometimes and in certain cases laws should be changed. But when we look at the matter from another point of view, great caution would seem to be required. For the habit of lightly changing the laws is an evil, and, when the advantage is small, some errors both of lawgivers and rulers had better be left; the citizen will not gain so much by the change as he will lose by the

habit of disobedience. The analogy of the arts is false; a change in a law is a very different thing from a change in an art. For the law has no power to command obedience except that of habit, which can only be given it by time, so that a readiness to change from old to new laws enfeebles the power of the law. Even if we admit that the laws are to be changed, are they all to be changed, and in every state? And are they to be changed by anybody who likes, or only by certain persons? These are very important questions; and therefore we had better reserve the discussion of them to a more suitable occasion.[5]

CHAPTER 9.   In the governments of Sparta and Crete, and indeed in all governments, two points have to be considered; first, whether any particular law is good or bad, when compared with the perfect state; secondly, whether it is or is not consistent with the idea and character which the lawgiver has set before his citizens. That in a well-ordered state the citizens should have leisure and not have to provide for their daily wants is generally stated, but there is a difficulty in seeing how this leisure is to be attained. [For, if you employ slaves, they are liable to rebel.] The Thessalian Penestae [6] have often risen against their masters, and the Helots in like manner against the Spartans, for whose misfortunes they are always lying in wait. Nothing, however, of this kind has as yet happened to the Cretans. The reason probably is that the neighboring cities, even when at war with one another, never form an alliance with rebellious serfs, rebellions not being for their interest, since they themselves have dependent populations. . . . Besides, if there were no other difficulty, the treatment or management of slaves is a troublesome affair; for, if not kept in hand, they are insolent, and think that they are as good as their masters, and, if harshly treated, they hate and conspire against them. Now it is clear that when these are the results, the citizens of a state have not found out the secret of managing their subject population.

[5] These questions are not discussed in the *Politics,* as it has come down to us.

[6] The Penestae in Thessaly, like the Helots in Sparta, were a subject population that had been enslaved by the conquerors.

Again, the license of the Spartan women defeats the intention of the Spartan constitution, and is adverse to the good order of the state. For husband and wife being each a part of every family, the state may be considered as about equally divided into men and women. Therefore, in those states in which the condition of the women is bad, half the city may be regarded as having no laws. And this is what has actually happened at Sparta. The lawgiver [7] wanted to make the whole state hardy and temperate, and he carried out his intention in the case of the men, but neglected the women, who live in every sort of intemperance and luxury. The consequence is that in such a state wealth is too highly valued, especially when the citizens fall under the dominion of their wives, after the manner of all warlike races, except the Celts and a few others who openly approve of male loves. The old mythologer would seem to have been right in uniting Ares and Aphrodite, [8] for all warlike races are prone to love, either of men or of women. This was exemplified among the Spartans, for even in the days of their greatness many things were managed by their women. But what difference does it make whether women rule, or the rulers are ruled by women? The result is the same. Even in regard to courage, which is not called for in daily life, but is needed in war, the influence of the Spartan women has been most mischievous. The evil showed itself in the Theban invasion, [9] when, unlike the women in other cities, they were utterly useless and caused more confusion than the enemy. . . .

But, when Lycurgus, as tradition says, wanted to bring the women under his laws, they resisted, and he gave up the attempt. They, and not he, are to blame for what then happened, and this defect in the constitution is clearly to be attributed to them. We are not, however, considering what is or is not to be excused, but what is right or wrong; and the disorder of the women, as I have already said, not

---

[7] Aristotle accepted the tradition that made Lycurgus the lawmaker of the Spartan military oligarchy.

[8] Ares was the Greek god of war, Aphrodite the goddess of love.

[9] Sparta had been invaded and defeated by the Theban army not forty years before Aristotle wrote.

only of itself gives an air of indecorum to the state, but tends in a measure to foster avarice.

The mention of avarice naturally suggests a criticism on the inequality of property there. While some of the Spartan citizens have quite small properties, others have very large ones; hence the land has passed into the hands of a few. And here is another fault in their laws; for, although the lawgiver rightly holds up to shame the sale or purchase of an inheritance, he allows anybody who likes to give or bequeath it away. Yet both practices lead to the same result. And nearly two fifths of the whole country are held by women, because of the number of heiresses and the large dowries which are customary. It would surely have been better to give no dowries at all, or, if any, but small or moderate ones. As the law now stands, a man may bestow his heiress on anyone whom he pleases, and, if he die intestate, the privilege of giving her away descends to his heir.[10] Hence, although the country is able to maintain 1500 cavalry and 30,000 infantry, the whole number of Spartan citizens [at the time of the Theban invasion] fell below 1000. The result proves the faulty nature of their laws respecting property; for the city sank under a single defeat; the want of men was their ruin. There is a tradition that, in the days of their ancient kings, they were in the habit of giving the rights of citizenship to strangers, and therefore, in spite of their long wars, no lack of population was experienced by them; indeed, at one time Sparta is said to have numbered not less than 10,000 citizens. Whether this statement is true or not, it would certainly have been better to have maintained their numbers by a better equalization of property. . . .

The charge which Plato brings, in the *Laws*, against the intention of the Spartan lawgiver, is likewise justified. The whole constitution aims at creating one kind of virtue only—the virtue of the soldier, which gives victory in war. And so long as they were at war, their power was preserved, but when they had attained empire they fell,

---

[10] The passage seems to mean that heiresses may be married by their relatives to rich men and so increase the concentration of land in the hands of a few.

for of the arts of peace they knew nothing, and had never engaged in any employment higher than war. There is another error, equally great, into which they have fallen. Although they truly think that the goods for which men contend are to be acquired by virtue rather than by vice, they err in supposing that these goods are to be preferred to the virtue which gains them.

Once more, the revenues of the state are ill-managed. There is no money in the treasury, although they are obliged to carry on great wars, and they are unwilling to pay taxes. The greater part of the land being in the hands of Spartans, they do not look closely into one another's contributions. The result which the lawgiver has produced is the reverse of beneficial; for he has made his city poor, and his citizens greedy. But enough respecting the Spartan constitution, of which these are the principal defects. . . .

[*Aristotle describes next the constitutions of the aristocratic governments of Crete and Carthage. The latter was, when he wrote, the strongest maritime power of the western Mediterranean. Not until the following century would she collide with the rising power of Rome. Aristotle seems to have known nothing of Rome.*]

CHAPTER 12. Of those who have treated of governments, some have never taken any part at all in public affairs, but have passed their lives in a private station; about most of them, what was worth telling has already been told. Others have been lawgivers, either in their own or in foreign cities, whose affairs they have administered; and of these some have made only laws, others have framed whole constitutions; for example, Lycurgus and Solon [11] did both. Of the Spartan constitution I have already spoken. As to Solon, he is thought by some to have been a good legislator, who put an end to the exclusiveness of the oligarchy, emancipated the people, established the ancient Athenian democracy, and harmonized the different elements

[11] Solon, the great ruler and lawgiver of Athens in the early sixth century B.C., started the city on the road to democracy.

of the state. According to their view, the council of Areopagus was an oligarchical element, the elected magistracy aristocratic, and the courts of law democratic.

The truth seems to be that the council and the elected magistracy existed before the time of Solon and were retained by him, but that he formed the courts of law out of all the citizens, thus creating the democracy, which is the reason why he is sometimes blamed. For in giving the supreme power to the law courts, which are elected by lot, he is thought to have ruined the non-democratic element. When the law courts grew powerful, to please the people, who were then playing the tyrant, the old constitution was changed into the existing democracy. Ephialtes and Pericles [12] curtailed the power of the Areopagus; they also instituted the payment of juries, and thus every demagogue in turn increased the power of the democracy until it became what we now see.

All this is true; it seems however to be the result of circumstances, and not to have been intended by Solon. For the people having been instrumental in gaining the empire of the sea in the Persian War, began to get a notion of themselves, and followed worthless demagogues, whom the better class opposed. Solon himself appears to have given the Athenians only that power of electing to offices and calling to account the magistrates which was absolutely necessary; for without it they would have been in a state of slavery and enmity to the government. . . .

Draco [13] has left laws, but he adapted them to a constitution which already existed, and there is no peculiarity in them which is worth mentioning, except the greatness and severity of the punishments.

Pittacus,[14] too, was only a lawgiver, and not the author of a constitution. He has a law peculiar to him, that if a drunken man strikes another, he shall be more heavily punished than if he were sober.

[12] Ephialtes and Pericles were in succession the leaders of the imperialist democracy of Athens in the fifth century B.C.

[13] The legendary author of the oldest written code of Athenian law.

[14] An elected dictator and lawgiver in the Ionian Greek city of Mitylene, of whom Aristotle speaks again. See pp. 312-313.

He looked not to the excuse which might be offered for the drunkard, but to expediency; for drunken men more often than sober commit acts of violence.

Androdamas [15] of Rhegium gave laws to the Chalcidians of Thrace. Some of them relate to homicide, and to heiresses; but there is nothing remarkable in them. Here then let us conclude our inquiry into the various constitutions which either actually exist, or have been devised by theorists.

BOOK III

> Definition of the citizen. Classification of governments by types: good types—monarchy, aristocracy, and constitutional commonwealth; bad types—tyranny, oligarchy, and extreme democracy. Aristocracy compared with the rule of the equal many. Forms of monarchy and dangers of absolutism.

CHAPTER 1.   He who would inquire into the nature of various kinds of government must first of all determine what is a state. At present this is a disputed question. Some say that the state has done a certain act; others, no, not the state, but the oligarchy or the tyrant. The lawmaker or statesman is concerned entirely with the state, for a constitution or government is an arrangement of the inhabitants of a state. The state then is composite, and, like any other whole, made up of many parts, which are the citizens who compose it. It is evident, therefore, that we must begin by asking, who is the citizen, and what is the meaning of the term.

Here again there may be a difference of opinion. A citizen in a democracy will often not be a citizen in an oligarchy. Leaving out

[15] Of this Androdamas we know nothing more than what Aristotle tells us here.

of consideration those who have been made citizens, or who have obtained the name of citizen in any other accidental manner, we may say, first, that a citizen is not a citizen because he lives in a certain place, for resident aliens and slaves share in the place. Nor is he a citizen who has no legal right except that of suing and being sued, for this right may be enjoyed under the provisions of a treaty. Resident aliens in many places possess such rights, although in an imperfect form; for they are obliged to have a patron. Hence they do but imperfectly participate in citizenship, and we call them citizens only in a qualified sense, as we might apply the term to children who are too young to be on the register, or to old men who have been relieved from state duties. Of these we do not say simply that they are citizens, but add in the one case that they are not of age, and in the other, that they are past age, or something of that sort; the precise expression is immaterial, for our meaning is clear. Similar difficulties to those which I have mentioned may be raised and answered in the case of deprived citizens and exiles.

But the citizen, whom we are seeking to define, is a citizen in the strictest sense, against whom no such exception can be taken. His special characteristic is that he shares in the administration of justice and in offices. Now some offices have a limit of time, and the same persons are not allowed to hold them twice, or can hold them again only after a fixed interval; others have no limit of time, as, for example, the office of dicast or ecclesiast.[1] It may, indeed, be argued that these men are not magistrates at all, and that their functions give them no share in the actual government. But surely it is ridiculous to say that those who have supreme power do not govern. Not to dwell further upon this, which is a purely verbal question, what we want is a common term including both dicast and ecclesiast. Let us, for the sake of distinction, call it "indefinite office," and we will

[1] A dicast was a member of one of the large popular juries, a body that acted as jury and judge in one, and from whose verdict there was no appeal. By such a jury Socrates was tried and condemned. An ecclesiast was a member of the ecclesia or political citizen assembly.

assume that those who share in such office are citizens. This is the most comprehensive definition of a citizen, and best suits all those who are generally so called. . . .

But the citizen of necessity differs under each form of government, and our definition is best adapted to the citizens of a democracy, but not necessarily to those of other states. For in some states the people are not acknowledged, nor have they any regular assembly but only extraordinary ones, and suits are distributed in turn among the magistrates. In Sparta, for instance, the Ephors [2] determine suits about contracts, which they distribute among themselves, while the elders are judges of homicide, and other cases are decided by other magistrates. A similar principle prevails at Carthage; there certain magistrates decide all cases. We should indeed modify our definition of the citizen so as to include members of these states. In them it is the holder of a definite, not of an indefinite office, who legislates and judges, and to some or all holders of definite offices is reserved the right of deliberating or judging about certain things or about all things.

The conception of the citizen now begins to clear up. He who has the power to take part in the deliberative or judicial administration of any state is said by us to be a citizen of that state. And speaking generally, a state is a body of citizens sufficing for the purposes of life.

CHAPTER 2.   But in practice a citizen is sometimes defined to be one whose parents are both citizens, though others insist on going further back, say to two or three or more ancestors. But there are some who raise the further question: How did this third or fourth ancestor come to be a citizen? Gorgias of Leontini, partly because he was in a difficulty, partly in irony, said: "Mortars are made by the mortar-makers, and the citizens of Larissa are also a manufactured article, made by the magistrates whose job it is to make Larissaeans." Yet the answer is really simple, for if according to the

---

[2] The Ephors were the chief magistrates in the Spartan state.

definition just given they shared in the government, they were citizens. The words, "born of a father or mother who is a citizen," cannot possible apply to the first inhabitants or founders of a state.

There is a greater difficulty in the case of those who have been made citizens after a revolution, as by Cleisthenes at Athens [3] after the expulsion of the tyrants, for he enrolled in the tribes a number of strangers and slaves and resident aliens. The doubt in these cases is not who is, but whether he who is ought to be a citizen. There will be a further doubt whether he who ought not to be a citizen is one really, for what ought not to be is false. So too, there are some who hold office and yet ought not to hold office, whom we call rulers, although they rule unjustly. But the citizen we defined by the fact of his holding some kind of rule or office; he who holds a judicial or legislative office fulfills our definition of a citizen. It is evident, therefore, that such citizens, even if doubt has arisen about them, must be called citizens. Whether they ought to be so or not is a question which is bound up with the previous inquiry.

CHAPTER 3.   A parallel question is raised respecting the state whether a certain act is or is not an act of the state; as, for example, in a time of transition from an oligarchy or a tyranny to a democracy. In such cases, some persons refuse to fulfill their contracts and other obligations on the ground that the tyrant and not the state contracted them. Others argue that the old constitutions were established by force, and not for the sake of the common good. But this would apply equally to the democracies, for they too may be founded on violence, and then the acts of the democracy will be neither more nor less legitimate than those of an oligarchy or of a tyranny. This question runs up into another. When shall we say that the state is the same and when different? It would be a very superficial view which considered only place and inhabitants; for the land and the

[3] The reforms of Cleisthenes at the end of the sixth century B.C. gave Athens a government based on the consent and participation of the whole body of male citizens.

population may be separated, and some of the inhabitants live in one place and some in another. This, however, is not a very serious difficulty. We need only remark that the word "state" is ambiguous, meaning both state and city.

The question is further asked when are men, living in the same place, to be regarded as a single city? What is the limit? Certainly not a city wall, for you might surround all Peloponnesus with a wall. But a city, having such vast circuit, would contain a nation rather than a state. It would be like Babylon, which, as they say, had been taken for three days before some of the inhabitants became aware of the fact. This problem may, however, with advantage be deferred to another occasion. A statesman has to consider the size of the state, and whether it should consist of more than one nation or not.[4]

Again, shall we say that while the race of inhabitants, as well as their place of abode, remain the same, the city is also the same, although the citizens are always dying and being born; as we call rivers and fountains the same, although the water is always flowing away and coming again? Or shall we say that the generations of men like the rivers are the same, but that the state changes? For, since the state is an association and an association of citizens under some one constitution, when the form of the government changes and becomes different, then it may be supposed that the state is no longer the same; just as a tragic differs from a comic chorus, although the members of both may be identical. In this manner we speak of every union or composition of elements as differing when the form of their composition alters; for example, a scale of the same sounds is said to be different, accordingly as the Dorian or the Phrygian mode [5] is employed. If this is true, it is evident that the sameness of the state consists chiefly in the sameness of the constitution, and it may or may not be called by the same name, whether the inhabitants are the same or entirely different. It is quite another question whether

---

[4] The size of the state is discussed in Book VII.
[5] The names of the two chief modes in Greek music.

a state ought or ought not to fulfill its engagements when the form of government changes.

CHAPTER 4. There is a point nearly allied to the preceding. Is the virtue of a good man and of a good citizen the same or not? But, before entering on this discussion, we must first obtain some general notion of the virtue of a citizen. Like the sailor, the citizen is a member of a community. Now sailors have different functions, for one of them is a rower, another a pilot, and a third a lookout-man, a fourth is described by some similar term. The precise definition of each individual's excellence applies exclusively to him, but there is, at the same time, a common definition applicable to them all. For they have all of them a common object, which is safety in navigation. Similarly, one citizen differs from another, but the salvation of the community is the common business of them all. This community is the state; the virtue of the citizen must therefore be relative to the state of which he is a member. If, then, there are many forms of government, it is evident that there cannot be one simple perfect virtue of all good citizens. But we say that a good man is he who has perfect virtue. Hence it is evident that the good citizen need not of necessity possess the virtue which makes a good man. . . . But all must have the virtue of a good citizen—thus, and thus only, can the state be perfect. But they will not have the virtue of a good man, unless we assume that in the good state all the citizens must be good. . . .

But will there be then no case in which the virtue of a good citizen and the virtue of a good man coincide? To this we answer that a good ruler is a good and wise man, and that a statesman must be a wise man. Some persons say that the education of the ruler too should be of a special kind; as the children of kings are instructed in riding and military exercises. Euripides says:

"No subtle arts for me, but what the state requires," [6]

[6] A line from the lost play, *Aeolus.*

as though there were a special education needed by a ruler. If now the virtue of a good ruler and that of a good man are the same and the citizens are subjects, the virtue of the good citizen and the virtue of the good man cannot be always the same, although in some cases they may; for the virtue of the ruler differs from that of the citizen. It was the sense of this difference which made Jason [7] say that he felt starved when he was not a tyrant, meaning that he could not endure to live in a private station. . . .

However, this is not the rule of which we are speaking; but there is a rule of another kind, which is exercised over freeborn and equals, a constitutional rule, which a ruler must learn by obeying, as he would learn the duties of a general of cavalry by being under the orders of a general of cavalry, or the duties of a general of infantry by being under the orders of a general of infantry, and by having had the command of a company or a regiment. It has been well said that he who has never learned to obey cannot be a good commander. The two are not the same, but a good citizen should be capable of both; he should know how to govern like a freeman, and how to obey like a freeman. These are the virtues of a citizen.

And although the temperance and justice of a ruler are distinct from those of a subject, the virtue of a good man will include both.[8] For the virtue of a good man, who is free and also a subject, will not be one virtue only—say justice—but will include distinct kinds of virtue, the one qualifying him to rule, the other to obey, and differing as the temperance and courage of men and women differ. For a man would be thought a coward if he had no more courage than a courageous woman, and a woman would be thought loquacious if she imposed no more restraint on her conversation than a good man. Indeed their part in the management of a household is different, for the duty of the one is to acquire, and of the other to

---

[7] This Jason was a Thessalian ruler, whom Aristotle quotes also in his *Rhetoric.*
[8] Earlier Aristotle drew a line between the good citizen and the good man. One was by no means the same as the other. Here the point of view has been shifted. The good man now, having all virtue, is both a good ruler and a good subject, even though the virtues required of each are different.

preserve. Prudence is peculiarly characteristic of the ruler; it would seem that all other virtues must belong equally to ruler and subject. Yet the virtue of the subject is certainly not wisdom, but only true opinion. He may be compared to the maker of the flute, while his ruler is like the flute player or user of the flute.

From these considerations may be gathered the answer to the question whether the virtue of the good man is the same as that of the good citizen, or different, and how far the same, and how far different.

CHAPTER 5.   There still remains one more question about the citizen: Is only he a true citizen who has a share of office, or is the craftsman to be included? If they who hold no office are to be deemed citizens, not every citizen can have the virtue of ruling and obeying which makes a citizen. But if none of the lower class are citizens, in which part of the state are they to be placed? For they are not resident aliens, and they are not foreigners. To this objection may we not reply that there is no more absurdity in excluding them than in excluding slaves and freedmen? [9] It must be admitted that we cannot consider all those citizens who are necessary to the existence of the state. For example, children are not citizens equally with grown-up men, who are citizens complete; children, not being grown up, are citizens only in a partial sense. Doubtless in ancient times, and among some nations, the artisan class were slaves or foreigners, and therefore the majority of them are so now. The best form of state will not admit them to citizenship. If they are admitted, then our definition of the virtue of a citizen will not apply to all citizens and freemen, but only to those who are free from the necessity of labor. The class to whom toil is a necessity are either slaves, who minister to the wants of individuals, or craftsmen and laborers, who are

[9] To Aristotle, as to Plato, it seemed that leisure for thought and education and political experience gained in holding office were essential requirements for citizenship in a well-conducted state. So those whose daily toil shut them out from such things could not be citizens. Those who made their living by trade were also undesirable as citizens. See p. 397.

servants of the community. These reflections carried a little further will explain their position; and indeed what has been said already is of itself explanation enough.

Since, however, there are many forms of government there must be many varieties of citizens, and especially of citizens who are subjects. Under some governments the craftsman and the laborer will be citizens, but not under others; for example, in an aristocracy or the so-called government of the best (if there be such a one), in which honors are awarded according to virtue and merit; for no man can practice virtue who is living the life of a craftsman or laborer. In oligarchies, the qualification for office is expensive, and therefore no laborer can ever be a citizen; but a craftsman may, for many of them are rich. At Thebes, there was a law that no man could hold office who had not retired from business for ten years. In many states, the law goes to the length of admitting aliens; for in some democracies a man is a citizen, even though only his mother is a citizen. A similar principle is applied at times to illegitimate children; the law is relaxed when there is a dearth of population. But when the number of citizens increases, first the children of a male or a female slave are excluded; then those whose mothers only are citizens. At last, the right of citizenship is confined to those whose fathers and mothers are both citizens.

Hence, as is evident, there are different kinds of citizens; and he is a citizen in the highest sense who shares in the honors of the state. In the poems of Homer [Achilles complains of Agamemnon treating him] "like some dishonored stranger"; for he who is excluded from honors of the state is no better than an alien. But when this exclusion is concealed, the object is to deceive the people. . . .

CHAPTER 6. Having determined these questions, we have next to consider whether there is only one form of government or many; and if many, what they are, and how many; and what are the differences between them.

A constitution is the arrangement of powers in a state, especially

of the supreme power, and the constitution makes the government. For example, in democracies the people are supreme, but in oligarchies, the few; therefore, we say that the two constitutions are different; and so in other cases.

First, let us consider what is the purpose of a state and how many forms of government there are by which human society is regulated. We have already said, earlier in this treatise, when drawing a distinction between household management and the rule of a governor, that man is by nature a political animal. And therefore men, even when they do not require one another's help, desire to live together all the same. They are in fact brought together by their common interests in proportion as they severally attain to any measure of well-being. Well-being is certainly the chief end both of individuals and of states. But also, for the sake of mere living, in which there is possibly some noble element, men meet together and maintain a political community, so long as the evils of existence do not heavily overbalance the good. Indeed, we all see that men cling to life even in the midst of misfortune, seeming to find in it a natural sweetness and happiness.

There is no difficulty in distinguishing the various kinds of authority; they have been often defined already in popular works. The rule of a master, although the slave by nature and the master by nature have in reality the same interests, is nevertheless exercised primarily with a view to the master's own interest, but incidentally considers the slave, since, if the slave perish, the rule of the master perishes with him. On the other hand, the government of a wife and children and household, which we have called household management, is exercised in the first instance for the good of the governed, or for the common good of both parties, but essentially for the good of the governed, as we see to be the case in medicine, gymnastics, and the arts in general, which are only incidentally concerned with the good of the artists themselves. There is no reason why the trainer may not sometimes practice gymnastics, and the pilot is always one of the crew. But the trainer or the pilot is considering the good of

those committed to his care, even though, when he is one of the persons taken care of, he incidentally participates in the advantage; for the pilot is also a sailor, and the trainer becomes one of those in training.

In politics, when a state is framed upon the principle of equality and likeness, the citizens think that they ought to hold office by turns. In the past naturally everyone would take his turn of service; and then somebody else would look after his interest, just as he, while in office, had looked after theirs. But nowadays, for the sake of the advantage which is to be gained from the public revenues and from office, men want to be always in office. One might imagine that our rulers were sickly men who were kept in health only while they continued in office; in that case we should be sure they would be hunting after places.

Our conclusion, however, is evident. Governments which have a regard to the common interest are constituted in accordance with strict principles of justice, and are therefore true forms; but those which regard only the interest of the rulers are all defective and perverted forms. For they are despotic, whereas a state is a community of free men.

CHAPTER 7.   Having determined these points, we have next to consider how many forms of constitution there are, and what they are; and in the first place what are the true forms, for when they are determined the perversions of them will at once be apparent. The words constitution and government have the same meaning; and the government, which is the supreme authority in states, is necessarily in the hands either of one, or of a few, or of many. The true forms of government, therefore, are those in which the one, or the few, or the many, govern with a view to the common interest; but governments which rule with a view to the private interest, whether of the one, or of the few, or of the many, are perversions. For the members of a state, if they are truly citizens, ought all to participate in the advantages of a state. We call that form of government in

which one rules, and which regards the common interest, kingship
or royalty; that in which more than one, but not many, rule, aristocracy [the rule of the best]. It is so called, either because the rulers
are the best men, or because they have at heart the best interests of
the state and of the citizens. When the citizens at large administer
the state for the common interest, the government is called by the
generic name of constitutional government. And there is a reason
for this use of language. One man or a few may excel in virtue; but
of virtue there are many kinds. As the number of rulers increases
it becomes more difficult for them to attain perfection in every kind,
though they may in military virtue, for this is found in the masses.
Hence, in a constitutional government the fighting men have the
supreme power, and those who possess arms are citizens.

Of the above-mentioned forms, the perversions are as follows:
of royalty, tyranny; of aristocracy, oligarchy; of constitutional government, democracy. For tyranny is a kind of monarchy which has in
view the interest of the monarch only; oligarchy has in view the interest of the wealthy; democracy, of the needy; none of them the
common good of all.

CHAPTER 8. But there are difficulties about these forms of
government, and it will therefore be necessary to state a little more
at length the nature of each of them. For he who would make a
philosophical study of the various sciences and is not regarding
practice only, ought not to overlook or omit anything, but set forth
the truth in every particular. Tyranny, as I was saying, is monarchy
exercising the rule of a master over political society; oligarchy is
when men of property have the government in their hands; democracy, the opposite, when the poor and not the men of property
are the rulers. And here arises the first of our difficulties, and it
relates to the definitions just given. For democracy is said to be the
government of the many. But what if the many are men of property
and have the power in their hands? In like manner, oligarchy is said
to be the government of the few; but what if the poor are fewer than

the rich, and have the power in their hands because they are stronger? In these cases the distinctions which we have drawn between these different forms of government would no longer hold good.

Suppose, however, we assign wealth to the few and poverty to the many and name the governments accordingly, and call an oligarchy a state in which the wealthy few, and a democracy one in which the many poor are the rulers, there will still be a difficulty. For, if the only known forms of government are the ones already mentioned, how shall we describe those other governments also just mentioned by us, in which the rich are the more numerous and the poor are the fewer, and both govern in their respective states?

The argument seems to show that, both in oligarchies and in democracies, the number of the governing body, whether greater, as in a democracy, or smaller, as in an oligarchy, is an accident due to the fact that the rich everywhere are few and the poor numerous. Then if so, there is a misapprehension of the causes of the difference between them. For the real difference between democracy and oligarchy is poverty and wealth. Wherever men rule by reason of their wealth, whether they be few or many, that is an oligarchy, and where the poor rule, that is a democracy. But as a fact the rich are few and the poor many; for few are well-to-do, and all are free. And wealth and freedom are the grounds on which the oligarchical and democratic parties respectively claim power in the state. . . .

CHAPTER 9. . . . But a state exists for the sake of a good life, and not for the sake of life only. If life only were the object, slaves and brute animals might form a state. But they cannot, for they have no share in happiness or in a life of free choice. Nor does a state exist merely for the sake of alliance and security from injustice, nor yet for the sake of trade and mutual intercourse; for then the Tyrrhenians and the Carthaginians, and all who have commercial treaties with one another, would be citizens of one state. True, they have agreements about imports, and compacts to do no wrong to one another, and written articles of alliance. But there are no magistrates common

to the contracting parties who will enforce their compacts; the different states have each their own magistrates. Nor does one state take care that the citizens of another are such as they ought to be, nor see that those who come under the terms of the treaty do no wrong or wickedness at all, but only that they do no injury to one another. Whereas, those who care for good government take into consideration [the larger questions of] virtue and vice in states. Whence it may be further inferred that virtue must be the serious care of a state which truly deserves the name. Otherwise the community becomes a mere alliance, which differs only in place from alliances of which the members live apart. And law is only a convention, "a surety to one another of justice," as the sophist Lycophron says,[10] and has no real power to make the citizens good and just.

This is obvious; for suppose distinct places, such as Corinth and Megara, to be united by a wall, still they would not be one city, not even if the citizens had the right to intermarry, which is one of the rights peculiarly characteristic of states. Again, if men dwelt at a distance from one another, though not so far off as to have no intercourse, and there were laws among them that they should not wrong each other in their trading, neither would this be a state. Let us suppose that one man is a carpenter, another a farmer, another a shoemaker, and so on, and that their number is ten thousand; nevertheless, if they have nothing in common but trade, alliance, and the like, that would not constitute a state. Why is this? Surely not because they live at a distance from one another; for even supposing that such a community were to collect in one place, and each man had a house of his own, which was in a manner his state, and they made a confederation with one another, but only against evil-doers; still an accurate thinker would not deem this a state, if their intercourse with one another was the same in character after as before their union.

Clearly then a state is not a mere society, having a common place,

---

[10] Lycophron, an obscure rhetorician, seems to have held the idea that the state was only a conventional device to ensure the safety of life and property.

established for the prevention of crime and for the sake of trade. These are conditions without which a state cannot exist; but all of them together do not constitute a state, which is a community of families and aggregations of families in well-being for the sake of a perfect and self-sufficing life. Such a community can only be established among those who live in the same place and intermarry. Hence arise in states family connections, brotherhoods, common sacrifices, amusements which draw men together. They are created by friendship, for friendship is the motive of society. But the end of the state is the good life, and these are the means toward it. And the state is a union of families and villages in a perfect and self-sufficing life, by which we mean a happy and honorable life.

Our conclusion then is that political society exists for the sake of noble actions, and not of mere companionship. And they who contribute most to such a society have a greater share in it than those who have the same or greater freedom or nobility of birth but are inferior in political virtue, or than those who exceed them in wealth, but are surpassed by them in virtue. From what has been said, however, it will be clearly seen that all the partisans of different forms of government speak of a part of justice only.[11]

CHAPTER 10.   There is also a doubt as to what is to be the supreme power in the state. Is it the multitude? Or the wealthy? Or the good? Or the one best man? Or a tyrant? Any of these alternatives seems to involve disagreeable consequences. If the poor, for example because they are more in number, divide among themselves the property of the rich, is not this unjust? No, by heaven (will be the reply), for the highest authority [i.e., the people] willed it. But if this is not injustice, pray what is? Then, when all has been taken, the majority will divide anew the property of the minority. And is it not evident, if this goes on, that they will ruin the state? Yet surely, virtue is not the ruin of those who possess her, nor is justice

[11] In the *Ethics* Aristotle made a careful distinction between what he called complete justice. that carried with it every virtue. and part justice or justice in a more limited sense, that meant only fairness in sharing and distributing of goods. See pp. 157-159.

destructive of a state; and therefore this law of confiscation clearly cannot be just. If it were, all the acts of a tyrant must of necessity be just; for he only coerces other men by superior power, just as the multitude coerce the rich. But is it just then that the few and the wealthy should be the rulers? What if they, in like manner, rob and plunder the people—is this just? If so, the other case [i.e., the case of the majority plundering the minority] will likewise be just. There can be no doubt that all these things are wrong and unjust.

Then ought the good to rule and have supreme power? But in that case everybody else, being excluded from power, will be dishonored. For the offices of a state are posts of honor; and if one set of men always hold them, the rest must be deprived of them. Then will it be well that the one best man should rule? Nay, that is still more oligarchic, for the number of those who are dishonored is thereby increased. Some may say that it is bad for any man, subject as he is to all the accidents of human passion, to have the supreme power, rather than the law. But what if the law itself be democratic or oligarchic, how will that help us out of our difficulties? Not at all; the same consequences will follow.

CHAPTER 11. Most of these questions may be reserved for another occasion. The principle that the multitude ought to be supreme rather than the few best is one that may be defended, and, though not free from difficulty, yet seems to contain an element of truth. For the mass, of whom each individual is but an ordinary person, when they meet together, may very likely be better than the few good, if regarded not individually but collectively, just as a feast to which many contribute is better than a dinner provided out of a single purse. For each individual among those many has his share of virtue and prudence; and when they meet together they become in a manner one man who has many feet and hands and senses. That is a symbol of their mind and disposition. Hence the many are better judges than a single man of music and poetry, for some understand one part, and some another, and among them they

understand the whole. There is a similar combination of qualities in good men, who differ from any individual of the many, as the beautiful are said to differ from those who are not beautiful, and works of art from realities. For in a portrait divergent features are brought into unity, although, if taken separately, an eye of one person or some other feature of another person would be fairer than in the picture.

Whether, however, this principle can apply to every democracy, and to all bodies of men, is not clear. Assuredly, by heaven, in some cases it cannot be right; for the same argument would equally hold about brutes; and wherein do some men differ from brutes? Nevertheless, there may be bodies of men about whom our statement is true. And if so, the problem which has been already raised, and also another which is akin to it, namely, what power should be assigned to the mass of freemen and citizens who are not rich and have no personal merit—are both solved. But there is a danger also in not letting them share, for a state in which many poor men are excluded from office will necessarily be full of enemies. The only solution is to assign them some deliberative and judicial functions. For this reason Solon and certain other legislators give them the power of electing to offices and of calling magistrates to account, but they do not allow them as individuals to hold office. When they meet together their perceptions are quite good enough, and combined with the better class they are useful to the state (just as impure food when mixed with what is pure sometimes makes the entire mass more wholesome than a small quantity of the pure would be), but each individual by himself forms an imperfect judgment.

On the other hand, a popular form of government involves certain difficulties. In the first place, it might be objected that he who can judge how well a sick man has been healed must be one who could himself heal the disease, and make him whole—that is, in other words, a physician, and so in all professions and arts. As, then, a physician ought to be judged by physicians, so ought men in general to be called to account by their peers. Now physicians are of three kinds.

There is the ordinary healer, and there is the physician of the higher class, and thirdly, the intelligent man who has studied the art. In all arts there is such a class and we attribute the power of judging to them quite as much as to professors of the art. Does not then the same principle apply to elections? For a right election can only be made by those who have knowledge. Geometricians, for example, will choose rightly another geometrician, and those who know how to steer, a pilot. Even if there be some occupations and arts with which private persons are acquainted, they certainly cannot choose an expert better than those who know. So, according to this argument, neither the election of magistrates, nor the calling of them to account, should be intrusted to the many.

Yet possibly even these objections are to a great extent met by our previous answer, that if the people are not utterly degraded, although individually they may be worse judges than those who have special knowledge, as a body they are as good or better. Moreover, there are some arts whose products are not judged solely or best by the artists themselves, but by those who do not possess the art. For example, the understanding of a house is not limited to the builder only. The user or in other words the master of the house will be even a better judge than the builder, just as the pilot will judge better of a rudder than the carpenter, and the guest will judge better of a feast than the cook.

This difficulty seems now to be sufficiently answered, but there is another akin to it. That inferior persons should have more authority in great matters than the good would appear to be a strange thing, yet the election and calling to account of magistrates is the greatest of all. And these, as I was saying, are functions which in some states are assigned to the people, since the assembly is supreme in all such matters. Yet persons of any age and having but a small property qualification sit in the assembly and deliberate and judge, although for the great officers of state, such as controllers and generals, a high qualification is required. This difficulty may be solved in the same manner as the preceding, and the present practice of democracies may be really defensible. For the power does not reside in the dicast

or the senator or the ecclesiast, but in the court and the senate and the assembly, of which the individual senators or ecclesiasts or dicasts are only parts or members. For this reason the many may claim to have a higher authority than the few; for the people and the senate and the courts consist of many persons, and their property collectively is greater than the property of one or of the few individuals holding great offices. But enough of this.

The discussion of the previous question shows nothing so clearly as that laws, when good, should be supreme; and that the magistrate or magistrates should regulate only those matters on which the laws are unable to speak with precision, owing to the difficulty of any general principle embracing all particulars. But what are good laws has not yet been clearly explained; the old difficulty remains. The goodness or badness, justice or injustice of laws depends of necessity on the constitutions of states. If so, true forms of government will of necessity have just laws, and perverted forms of government will have unjust laws.

CHAPTER 12. In all sciences and arts the end is a good, especially and above all in the highest science of all, which is the political science. Of this the good is justice, in other words, the common interest. All men think justice to be a sort of equality; and to a certain extent they agree in the philosophical distinctions which have been laid down by us in the *Ethics*.[12] For they admit that justice is a virtue involving relations to other persons, and that equals ought to have equality.

But there still remains the question, equality or inequality of what? This is a difficulty which the political philosopher has to resolve. For some persons are likely to say that offices of state ought to be unequally distributed, according to the superior excellence in any respect of each citizen, although there is no other difference between him and the rest of the community; for those who differ

[12] See the *Ethics*, Book V. pp. 156-170.

in any one respect have different rights and claims. But, surely, if this is true, the complexion or height of a man or any other distinction will be a reason for his obtaining a greater share of political rights! The error here lies on the surface, and may be illustrated by a comparison with other arts and sciences. When a number of flute players are equal in their art, there is no reason why those of them who are better born should have better flutes given to them. They will not play any better on the flute and the superior instrument should be reserved for him who is the superior artist. If what I am saying is still obscure, it will be made clearer as we proceed. For if there were a superior flute player who was far inferior in birth and beauty, even though either of these gifts may be a greater good than the art of flute playing and persons fortunate in these ways may excel the flute player for greater reasons than he excels them in his art, still he ought to have the best flutes given to him unless the advantages of wealth and birth contribute to excellence in flute playing, which they do not. . . .

Now the rival claims of candidates for office can be based only on the possession of elements which are essential to a state [such as wealth, virtue, etc.]. Therefore, the noble or the freeborn or the rich may with good reason claim office; for holders of offices must be freemen and taxpayers. A state can no more be composed entirely of poor men than entirely of slaves. But if wealth and freedom are necessary elements, justice and valor are equally so; for though without the former a state cannot exist at all, without the latter it cannot exist well.

CHAPTER 13.   If the existence of the state alone is to be considered, then it would seem that all, or some at least, of these claims are just, but if we are looking for a good life, as I have already said, education and virtue have superior claims. As, however, those who are equal in one thing ought not therefore to be equal in all, nor those who are unequal in one thing to be unequal in all, it is certain that all forms of government which rest on either of these principles

are perversions. All men have a claim in a certain sense, as I have already admitted, but none an absolute claim. The rich claim because they have a greater share in the land, and land is the common interest in the state. Also they are generally more trustworthy in contracts. The freeborn claim under the same title as the noble, for they are nearly akin. And the noble are citizens in a truer sense than the ignoble, for good birth is always valued in a man's own home and country. Another reason they have is that those who are sprung from better ancestors are likely to be better men, for nobility is excellence of race. Virtue, too, may be truly said to have a claim, for justice has been acknowledged by us to be a social virtue which implies all others.[13] Again, the many urge their claim against the few; for, when taken collectively, and compared with the few, they are stronger and richer and better. . . . But objections may be urged against all the claimants of political power. For those who found their claims on wealth or family have no basis of justice. On this principle, if any one person were richer than all the rest, it would appear that he ought to be their ruler. In like manner, he who is very distinguished by his birth ought to have superiority over all others who claim on the ground that they are freeborn. In an aristocracy or government of the best, a like difficulty occurs about virtues; for if one citizen be better than the other members of the government, however good they may be, he too, upon the same principle of justice, should rule over them. And if the people are to be supreme because they are stronger than the few, then if one man or more than one, but not a majority, is stronger than the many, they ought to rule, but not the many.

All these considerations go to show that none of the principles on which men claim to rule and hold all other men in subjection to them are strictly right. To those who claim to be masters of the state on the ground of their virtue or their wealth, the many might fairly answer that they themselves are often better and richer than the

13 See the *Ethics*, p. 157.

few—I do not say individually, but collectively. Another ingenious question which is sometimes put forward may be met in a similar manner. Some persons ask whether the lawgiver who desires to make laws that are truly right ought to legislate with a view to the good of the higher classes or of the many, when the case which we have mentioned occurs (that is, when the many collectively are better than the few). Now what is right is to be interpreted in the sense of what is equal; and what is equal and right is to be considered with reference to the good of the state and the common good of the citizens.

A citizen is one who shares in governing and being governed. He differs under different forms of government, but in the best state he is one who is able and willing to be governed and to govern with a view to the life of virtue. If, however, there is some one person, or more than one, although not enough to make up a whole class in a state, whose virtue is so outstanding that the virtues or the political ability of all the rest admit of no comparison with his or theirs, he or they can no longer be regarded as a part of a state. For justice will not be done to a superior man, if he is reckoned only the equal of those who are so far inferior to him in virtue and in political ability. Such a one may truly be deemed a god among men. Hence we see that legislation is necessarily concerned only with those who are equals in birth and in ability; and that for men of extraordinary virtue there is no law. They are themselves a law. Anyone would be ridiculous who attempted to make laws for them: they would probably retort what, in the fable of Antisthenes, the lions said to the rabbits ["Where are your claws?"], when in the council of the beasts the latter began haranguing and claiming equality for all.

For this reason democratic states have instituted ostracism. Equality is their aim above all things, and therefore they ostracize and banish from the city for a time those who seem to predominate too much through their wealth or the number of their friends or any other political influence. Mythology tells us that the Argonauts left Heracles behind for a similar reason; the ship Argo would not take him

because she feared he would be too much for the rest of the crew.[14] Wherefore those who denounce tyranny and blame the counsel which Periander gave to Thrasybulus cannot be held quite just in their censure. The story is that Periander, when the herald was sent to ask counsel of him, said nothing, but only cut off the tallest ears of corn till he had brought the field to a level.[15] The herald did not know the meaning of the action, but came and reported what he had seen to Thrasybulus, who understood that he was to cut off the principal men in the state. This is a policy not only expedient for tyrants and in practice confined to them, but equally necessary in oligarchies and democracies.[16] Ostracism is a measure of the same kind, which acts by disabling and banishing the most prominent citizens. Great powers do the same to whole cities and nations, as the Athenians did to the Samians, Chians, and Lesbians. No sooner had they obtained a firm grasp of their empire than they humbled their allies contrary to treaty. And the Persian king has repeatedly crushed the Medes, Babylonians, and other nations, when their spirit has been stirred by the recollection of their former greatness.[17]

The problem is a universal one, and concerns equally all forms of government, true as well as false; for, although perverted forms with a view to their own interests adopt this policy, those which seek the common interest do so likewise. The same principle may be observed in the arts and sciences. A painter will not allow his figure to have a foot which, however beautiful, is not in proportion, nor will a ship-builder allow the stern or any other part of his vessel to be unduly large. No more will the chorus-master allow anyone who sings louder or better than all the rest to sing in his choir. Monarchs, too, may

[14] According to the legend, the ship Argo spoke with a human voice, refusing to take Heracles on board.

[15] Herodotus in his history, V, 92, tells this story of Thrasybulus, tyrant of Miletus, and Periander, tyrant of Corinth. But according to Herodotus it was Thrasybulus who gave the answer to Periander's question.

[16] In the century before Aristotle ostracism had been a regular device of Athenian democracy to prevent the growth of too much disturbing influence by any one man. Once every year the citizens were asked if they wished to ostracize anyone. But in the fourth century, B.C., the practice had been dropped.

[17] Machiavelli advises a similar course in *The Prince*, ch. V.

practice such compulsion and still live in harmony with their cities, if their government is for the interest of the state. Where then there is an acknowledged superiority, the argument in favor of ostracism is based on a kind of political justice. It would certainly be better that the lawgiver should from the first so order his state as to have no need of such a remedy. But if the need arises, the next best thing is that he should endeavor to correct the evil by this or some similar measure.

The principle, however, has not been fairly applied in states; for, instead of looking to the public good, they have used ostracism for partisan purposes. It is true that under perverted forms of government, and from their special point of view, such a measure seems just and expedient, but it is also clear that it is not absolutely just. In a perfect state there would be great doubts about the use of it, not when applied to a man of excessive strength, wealth, and popularity or the like, but when used against someone outstanding in goodness. What is to be done with him? Mankind will not say that such a one is to be expelled and exiled. On the other hand, he ought not to be a subject. That would be as if men should claim to rule over Zeus and divide his empire among them. The only alternative is that all should joyfully obey such a man as their ruler according to what seems to be the order of nature, and that men like him should be kings in their states for life.

CHAPTER 14. The preceding discussion, by a natural transition, leads to the consideration of royalty, which we admit to be one of the true forms of government. Let us see whether in order to be well governed a state or country should be under the rule of a king or under some other form of government; and whether monarchy, although good for some, may be bad for others.

First we must determine whether there is one species of royalty or many. It is easy to see that there are many, and that the manner of government is not the same in all of them. Of royalties according to law, the Spartan is thought to answer best to the true pattern.

There the royal power is not absolute, except when the kings go on an expedition, and then they take the command. Matters of religion, too, are committed to them. The kingly office is in truth a kind of generalship, irresponsible and perpetual. The king has not the power of life and death, except when upon a campaign and in the field, after the manner of the ancients which is described in Homer. For Agamemnon is patient when they find fault with him in the assembly, but when the army goes out to battle he has the power of life and death. Does he not say: "When I find a man skulking apart from the battle, nothing shall save him from the dogs and vultures, for in my hands is death"? [18]

This then is one form of royalty—a generalship for life. Of such royalties, some are hereditary and others elective.

(2) There is another sort of monarchy not uncommon among the barbarians, which nearly resembles tyranny. But this is legal and hereditary. For barbarians, being more servile in character than Greeks, as Asiatics are than Europeans, do not rebel against a despotic government. Such royalties have the nature of tyrannies because the people are by nature slaves: but there is no danger of their being overthrown, for they are hereditary and legal. Wherefore also their guards are such as a king and not a tyrant would employ; that is to say, they are composed of citizens, whereas the guards of tyrants are mercenaries. For kings rule by law over voluntary subjects, but tyrants over involuntary. The former are guarded by their fellow citizens, the others are guarded against them.

These are two forms of monarchy, and there was a third (3) which existed in ancient Greece, called a dictatorship. This may be defined generally as an elective tyranny, which, like the barbarian monarchy, was legal, but differed from it in not being hereditary. Sometimes the office was held for life, sometimes for a term of years, or until certain duties had been performed. For example, the citizens of Mitylene elected Pittacus leader against the exiles, who were

[18] *Iliad.* II, Classics Club edition. p. 31.

headed by Antimenides and Alcaeus the poet. Alcaeus himself says in one of his banquet odes that they chose Pittacus tyrant, and reproaches his fellow citizens for "having made the low-born Pittacus tyrant of the spiritless and ill-fated city, with one voice shouting his praises." [19]

These forms of monarchy have always had the character of despotism, because they possess tyrannical power; but inasmuch as they are elective and acquiesced in by their subjects, they are kingly.

(4) There is a fourth species of kingly rule—that of heroic times —which was hereditary and legal, and was exercised over willing subjects. For the earliest chiefs were benefactors of the people in the arts or arms; they either gathered them into a community, or procured land for them. Thus they became kings of voluntary subjects, and their power was inherited by their descendants. They took command in war and presided over the sacrifices, except those which required a priest. They also decided cases either with or without an oath. When they swore, the form of the oath was the stretching out of their scepter. In ancient times, their power extended to all things whatsoever in city and country as well as in foreign parts. But at a later date they relinquished some of these privileges, and others the people took from them, until in some states nothing was left to them but the sacrifices. Even where they retained more of the reality, they had only the right of leadership in war beyond the border.

These then are the four kinds of royalty. First, the monarchy of heroic ages, which was exercised over voluntary subjects but limited to certain functions. The king was general and judge and had control of religion. The second is that of the barbarians, which is an hereditary, despotic government in accordance with law. A third is the power of the so-called dictator, which is an elective tyranny. The fourth is the Spartan, which is in fact a generalship, hereditary and perpetual. These four forms differ from one another in the manner I have described.

[19] Of the much-admired poet Alcaeus we have nothing left but fragments.

There is a fifth form of kingly rule in which one man has the disposal of everything, just as each tribe or each state has the disposal of public property. This form corresponds to control of a household. For as household management is kingly rule over a house, so this kingly rule is the household management of a city, or a nation, or many nations.

CHAPTER 15.   Of these forms we need consider only two, the Spartan and absolute royalty; for most of the others lie in a region between them, having less power than the last and more than the first. Thus the inquiry is reduced to two points: first, is it advantageous to the state that there should be a perpetual general, and if so, should the office be confined to one family or open to the citizens in turn? Secondly, is it well that a single man should have supreme power in all things? The first question falls under the head of laws rather than of constitutions; for a perpetual generalship might exist equally under any form of government, so that this question may be dismissed for the present.[20] The second kind of royalty is a matter of constitution. This we have now to consider, and briefly to run over the difficulties involved in it. We will begin by inquiring whether it is more advantageous to be ruled by the best man or by the best laws.

Advocates of royalty maintain that laws speak only in general terms, and cannot provide for special circumstances; and that for any science to abide by its written rules is absurd. In Egypt, the physician is allowed to alter his treatment after the fourth day, though, if sooner, he takes the risk. Hence it is argued that a government acting only according to written laws is plainly not the best. Yet surely the ruler cannot dispense with the general principle expressed in law. One too who is free from passion is better than he who is passionate. Yet whereas the law is passionless, passion must ever sway the heart of a man.

[20] It is not taken up again.

Yes, someone will answer, but then on the other hand an individual will be better able to decide particular cases. [To whom we in turn make reply.] There must be a legislator and laws must be passed, but these laws will have no authority when they miss the mark, though in other cases retaining their authority. But when the law cannot determine a point at all, or not well, should the one best man or should all decide? According to our present practice assemblies meet, sit in judgment, deliberate and decide, and their judgments relate to individual cases. Now any member of the assembly, taken separately, is certainly inferior to the wise man. But the state is made up of many individuals. And as a feast to which all the guests contribute is better than a banquet furnished by a single man, so a multitude is a better judge of many things than any individual.

Again, the many are more incorruptible than the few. They are like the greater quantity of water which is less easily poisoned than a little. The individual is liable to be overcome by anger or by some other passion, and then his judgment is necessarily perverted; but it is hardly to be supposed that a great number of persons would all get into a passion and go wrong at the same moment. Let us assume that they are freemen, and never act in violation of the law, but fill up the gaps which the law is obliged to leave. Or, if such virtue is scarcely attainable by the multitude, we need suppose only that the majority are good men and good citizens, and ask which will be more incorruptible, the one good ruler, or the many who are all good? Will not the many? But, you will say, there may be parties among them, whereas the one man is not divided against himself. To which we may answer that their character is as good as his. If we call the rule of many men, who are all good, aristocracy, and the rule of one man monarchy, then aristocracy will be better for states than monarchy, whether the government is supported by power or not, provided only that a number of men equal in virtue can be found.

The first governments were kingships, probably for the reason that of old, when cities were small, men of eminent virtue were few.

They were made kings because they were benefactors and benefits can be bestowed only by good men. But when many persons equal in merit arose, no longer enduring the predominance of one, they desired to have a commonwealth, and set up a constitution. But the ruling class soon deteriorated and enriched themselves out of the public treasury. Riches became the path to honor, and so oligarchies naturally grew up. These passed into tyrannies and tyrannies into democracies; for love of gain in the ruling classes was always tending to diminish their number, and so strengthen the masses, who in the end rose against their masters and established democracies. Since cities have increased in size, no other form of government appears to be any longer feasible.

However, supposing the principle to be granted that kingly power is the best thing for states, how about the family of the king? Are his children to succeed him? If they are no better than anybody else, that will be mischievous. But (says the lover of royalty) the king, though he might, will not hand on his power to his children. That, however, is hardly to be expected, and is too much to ask of human nature.

There is a difficulty too about the force he is to employ. Should a king have guards about him, by whose aid he may be able to coerce the refractory? If not, how will he administer his kingdom? Even if he is a lawful sovereign, who does nothing arbitrarily or contrary to law, still he must have some force wherewith to maintain the law. In the case of a limited monarchy, there is not much difficulty in answering this question; the king must have such force as will be more than a match for one or more individuals, but not so great as that of the people. The ancients followed this rule when they gave guards to anyone whom they appointed dictator or tyrant. Thus, when Dionysius asked the Syracusans to allow him guards, someone advised them to give him only a certain number.

CHAPTER 16. . . . Absolute monarchy or the arbitrary rule of a sovereign over all the citizens in a city which consists of equals

is thought by some to be quite contrary to nature. They argue that those who are by nature equals must have the same natural right and worth, and that for unequals to have an equal share, or for equals to have an unequal share in the offices of state, is as bad as for different bodily constitutions to have the same food and clothing. Wherefore it is thought just that among equals everyone should both be ruled and rule, and that all should have their turn. We thus arrive at a law; for an order of succession implies law. And the rule of law is preferable to that of any individual.

On the same principle, even when it is better for certain individuals to govern, they should be made only guardians and ministers of the law. For magistrates there must be; this is admitted. But men say that to give all authority to any one man when all are equal is unjust. There may indeed be cases which the law seems unable to determine, but in such cases can a man? Nay, it will be replied, but the law trains officers for this express purpose, and appoints them to determine matters which are left undecided by it to the best of their judgment. Further, it permits them to make any amendment of the existing laws which experience suggests. He who bids the law rule, may be deemed to bid God and Reason alone rule, but he who bids a man rule adds an element of the beast; for desire is a wild beast, and passion perverts the minds of rulers, even when they are the best of men. The law is reason unaffected by desire.

We are told that a patient should call in a physician; he will not get better if he is doctored out of a book. But the parallel of the arts is clearly not in point, for the physician does nothing contrary to the rule from motives of friendship; he only cures his patient and takes a fee. Whereas rulers do many things from spite and partiality. Indeed, if a man suspected his physician of being in league with his enemies to destroy him for a bribe, he would far rather consult a book. Even physicians, when they are sick, call in other physicians, and training-masters, when they are in training, other training masters, as if they could not judge truly about their own case and might be influenced by their feelings. Hence it is evident that when seeking

for justice men seek for a mean or a neutral, and the law is the mean.

Again, customary laws have more weight, and relate to more important matters, than written laws; and a man might be a safer ruler than a written law, but not safer than customary law. Again, it is by no means easy for one man to superintend many things; he will have to appoint a number of subordinates. What difference then does it make whether these subordinates always existed or were appointed by him because he needed them? . . . Matters of detail about which men deliberate cannot be put into laws. Nor does anyone deny that the decision of such matters must be left to men, but, they argue, there should be many judges and not one only. For every magistrate trained in law judges well; and it would surely seem strange that one person should see better with two eyes, or hear better with two ears, or act better with two hands or feet, than many with many. Indeed, it is already the practice even of kings to make for themselves many eyes and ears and hands and feet. For they make colleagues of those who are friends of themselves and their governments. They must be friends of the monarch and his government; for if not his friends, they will not do what he wants. But friendship implies likeness and equality; [21] and, therefore, if he thinks his friends ought to rule, he must think that persons equal to himself and like himself ought to rule. These are the principal problems relating to monarchy.

CHAPTER 17.   But may not all this be true in some cases and not in others? For there is a natural justice and expediency in the rule of a master over his servants, and also in that of a king over his subjects, and also in a constitutional government; whereas there is no justice or expediency in a tyranny or any other perverted form of government, which comes into being contrary to nature. From what has been said, it is manifest that, where men are alike and equal, it is neither expedient nor just that one man should be lord of all, whether there are laws or no laws but he himself in the place

---

21 See on this the *Ethics*, Book VIII, p. 196.

of law. Neither should a good man lord it over good men, or a bad man over bad; nor, even if he excels in virtue, should he have a right to rule, unless in the particular case which I have already mentioned, and to which I will once more recur.

I must now determine, first, what natures are suited for monarchies, then what for an aristocracy, and what for a constitutional government.

A people who are by nature capable of producing a line superior in the virtue that means political talent are fitted for kingly government. A people submitting to be ruled as freemen by men whose virtue renders them capable of political command are adapted for an aristocracy. A people among whom there naturally exists a warlike multitude, able to rule and to obey in turn, with a law that gives office to the well-to-do according to their deserts, are suited for constitutional freedom. However, when a whole family, or some individual, happens to be so pre-eminent in virtue as to surpass all others, then it is just that they should be the royal family and supreme over all, or that the one citizen should be king of the whole people. For, as I said before, to give him authority is not only right on general ground, which the founders of all states, whether aristocratic or oligarchic or democratic, habitually put forward (for these all recognize the claim of excellence, although not the same excellence), but accords with the principle already laid down. For it would not be right to kill or ostracize or exile such a man, or require him to take his turn in being governed. The whole is naturally superior to the part, and he who has this pre-eminence is like a whole to a part. If so, the only alternative is that he should have the supreme power, and that men should obey him, not in turn but always. These are the conclusions at which we arrive respecting monarchy and its various forms, and this is the answer to the question whether it is or is not advantageous to states, and to which, and how.

We maintain then that the true forms of government are three, and that the best must be that which is administered by the best, in which there is either one man or a whole family or many persons

excelling in virtue, and both rulers and subjects are fitted, the one to rule, the others to be ruled, in such a manner as to attain the most desirable life. We showed at the commencement of our inquiry that the virtue of a good man is necessarily the same as the virtue of a citizen in a perfect state. Clearly then, in the same manner and by the same means through which the man himself becomes truly good, he will frame the state, whether aristocratic or monarchical; and the same education and the same habits will be found to make a good man and a good statesman or king.

Having arrived at these conclusions, we must proceed to speak of the perfect state, and describe how it comes into being and is established. . . .

BOOK IV

> Discussion of existing and possible variations of democracy, oligarchy, and tyranny. Rule of the middle class as the best government under average conditions. Necessary branches of government—deliberative assembly, executive offices, courts of law.

CHAPTER 1. In all those arts and sciences that embrace the whole of any subject, and are not restricted to a part only, it is the province of each single art or science to consider all that appertains to its particular subject. For example, the art of gymnastics considers not only the suitableness of different modes of training to different bodies, but what sort is absolutely the best (for the absolutely best must suit the body that is by nature best and best furnished with the means of life), and also what common form of training is adapted to the great majority of men. And if a man does not desire the best habit of body or the greatest skill in gymnastics which might be attained by him, still the trainer or the teacher of

gymnastic should be able to impart some lesser degree of either. The same principle holds equally in medicine or shipbuilding or the making of clothes or the arts generally.

Hence it is obvious that government too is the subject of a single science, which has to consider both what kind of government would be best and most in accordance with our aspirations, if there were no outer impediments, and also what kind of government is adapted to particular states. For the best is often unattainable, and therefore the true lawmaker or statesman ought to be acquainted not only with (1) that which is best in the abstract but also with (2) that which is best considering the circumstances. We should be able further to say how a state may be constituted under any given conditions (3); both how it may be originally formed and, when formed, how longest preserved, when the supposed state is so far from the very best that it is without the conditions necessary for a good state, and is not even the best under the circumstances but an inferior type. He ought, moreover, to know (4) the form of government best suited to states in general; for political writers, although they have excellent ideas, are often unpractical.

We must consider then not only what form of government is best, but also what is possible and easily attainable by all. There are some who would have none but the most perfect; but for this many natural advantages are required. Others, again, speak of a more attainable form, and, although they reject the constitution under which they are living, extol some other one in particular, for example, the Spartan. Any change of government which has to be introduced should be one which men are both willing and able to adopt, since there is quite as much trouble in the reformation of an old constitution as in the establishment of a new one, even as to unlearn is as hard as to learn. And therefore, in addition to the qualifications of the statesman already mentioned, he should be able to find remedies for the defects of existing constitutions.

But this he cannot do unless he knows how many forms of government there are. It is often supposed that there is only one kind of

democracy and one of oligarchy.[1] But this is a mistake; so, in order
to avoid such mistakes, we must ascertain what differences there are
in the constitutions of states, and in how many ways they are combined. The same political insight will enable a man to know which
laws are best, and which are best suited to different constitutions; for
the laws are and ought to be adapted to the constitution, and not the
constitution to the laws. A constitution is the organization of offices
in a state; it determines what is to be the governing body, and what
's the end of each community. The laws are not to be confounded
with the principles of the constitution; they are the rules according
to which the magistrates should administer the state, and proceed
against offenders. So we must know the number and varieties of the
several forms of government, if only with a view to making laws.
For the same laws cannot be equally suited to all oligarchies or to
all democracies, since there is certainly more than one form both
of democracy and of oligarchy.

CHAPTER 2.   In our original discussion about governments,
we divided them into three true forms—monarchy, aristocracy, and
constitutional government—and three corresponding perversions—
tyranny, oligarchy, and democracy. Of monarchy and of aristocracy
we have already spoken, for the inquiry into the perfect state was
the same as the discussion of the two forms thus named,[2] since both
rest on a principle of virtue provided with external instruments. We
have already determined in what aristocracy and monarchy differ
from one another, and when the latter should be established. In
what follows we have to describe the so-called constitutional government, which bears the common name of all constitutions, and the
other forms, tyranny, oligarchy, and democracy.

It is obvious which of the three perversions is the worst, and which

---

1 Plato, for instance, describes only one kind of each of these forms of government.

2 Aristotle implies here that he has already described the ideal state and with it the
institutions of kingship and aristocracy at their best. But such a description, if he
ever wrote it, has been lost. His account in Book VII of how to build and organize
a perfect city is something different.

is the next in badness. That which is a perversion of the first and most divine government is necessarily the worst. And just as royal rule, if not a mere name, must exist by virtue of some great personal superiority in the king, so tyranny, which is the worst of governments, is necessarily the farthest removed from a well-constituted form. Oligarchy is a little better, but a long way from aristocracy, and democracy is the most tolerable of the three. . . .

Not to pursue this question further at present, let us begin by determining (1) how many varieties of states there are (since of democracy and oligarchy there are several); (2) what constitution is the most generally acceptable, and what is preferable next after the perfect; what other aristocratic or well-constituted form of government there is, which is at the same time adapted to states in general; (3) to whom each of the other forms of government is best suited. For democracy may meet the needs of some better than oligarchy, and conversely. In the next place (4) we have to consider in what manner a man ought to go about establishing some one among these various forms of democracy or oligarchy; [3] and lastly, (5) having briefly discussed these subjects to the best of our power, we will endeavor to ascertain the sources of the ruin or the preservation of states, both generally and in individual cases, and to what causes they are to be attributed.[4]

CHAPTER 3. The reason why there are many forms of government is that every state contains many elements. In the first place, we see that all states are made up of families. Then in the multitude of citizens there must be some rich and some poor, and some in a middle condition; the rich too are heavy-armed, and the poor not. Among the common people, some are farmers, and some traders, and some artisans. Among the upper classes also there are differences of wealth and property; for example, in the number of horses which they keep, for they cannot afford to keep them unless they are rich.

[3] This is done in Book V.
[4] For this see Book V.

Therefore in old times the cities whose strength lay in their cavalry were oligarchies. They used cavalry in wars against their neighbors, as was the practice of the Eretrians and Chalcidians, and also of the Magnesians on the river Maeander, and other people in Asia. Besides differences of wealth, there are differences of rank and merit. There are also other elements which we mentioned when treating of aristocracy and in enumerating the essentials of a state.[5] Of these elements, sometimes all, sometimes the lesser and sometimes the greater number, have a share in the government.

It is evident then that there must be many forms of government, differing in kind, since the parts of which they are composed differ from each other in kind. For a constitution is an organization of offices which the citizens all distribute among themselves, according to the power which the different classes possess, as, for example, the rich or the poor, or, by some principle of equality, both. There must therefore be as many forms of government as there are modes of arranging the offices, according to the superiorities and the differences in parts of the state.

There are generally thought to be two principal forms. As men say of the winds that there are but two—north and south—and that the rest are only variations of these, so of governments they say there are only two forms—democracy and oligarchy. For aristocracy is considered to be a kind of oligarchy, being the rule of a few, and the so-called constitutional government really a democracy; just as among the winds we make the west a variation of the north wind, and the east of the south. Similarly of modes in music there are said to be two, the Dorian and the Phrygian; the other arrangements of the scale are comprehended under one or other of these two. About forms of government this is a very favorite notion. But in either case the better and more exact way is to distinguish, as I have done, the one or two true forms, and to regard the others as perversions, either of the most perfectly attempered mode or of the best form of govern-

[5] These have not yet been enumerated. Later, in Book VII, chapter 8, they are mentioned.

ment. We may compare the oligarchic forms to the severe and more overpowering modes, and the democratic to the more relaxed and gentler ones.

CHAPTER 4. It must not be assumed, as some are fond of saying, that democracy is simply that form of government in which the greater number are sovereign, for in oligarchies, and indeed in every government, the majority rules. Nor again is oligarchy that form of government in which a few are sovereign. Suppose the whole population of a city to be 1300, and of these 1000 are rich, who do not allow the remaining 300, who are poor but free and in all other respects their equals, a share of the government. No one will say that this is a democracy. In like manner, if the poor were few and masters of the rich who outnumbered them, no one would ever call such a government, in which the rich majority had no share of office, an oligarchy. Therefore we should rather say that democracy is a form of government in which the free are rulers, and oligarchy one in which the rich rule. It is only an accident that the free are the many and the rich are the few. Otherwise a government in which offices were assigned according to stature, as is said to be the case in Ethiopia, or according to beauty, would be an oligarchy; for the number of tall or of good-looking men is small.

Still oligarchy and democracy are not sufficiently distinguished merely by these two characteristics of wealth and freedom. Both of them contain many other elements. Therefore we must carry our analysis further, and say that a government is not a democracy in which freemen who are few in number rule over many who are not free, as at Apollonia on the Ionian Gulf, and at Thera. In each of these states, the nobles, who were also the earliest settlers, were held in chief honor, although they were but few out of many. Neither is it a democracy when the rich have the government and exceed in numbers, as was the case formerly at Colophon, where the bulk of the inhabitants were possessed of large property before the Lydian War. But a government is a democracy when the free

who are also poor and a majority, govern, and an oligarchy when the rich and the noble govern and are at the same time few in number.

I have said there are many forms of government, and have explained to what cause the variety is due. Why there are more than those already mentioned, and what they are, and whence they arise, I will now proceed to consider, starting from the principle already admitted, that every state consists not of one but of many parts. If we were going to speak of the different species of animals, we should first of all find the organs that are indispensable to every animal, as, for example, organs of sense and of receiving and digesting food, such as the mouth and the stomach, also organs of locomotion.[6] Assuming now that there are only so many kinds of organs, but that there may be differences in them—I mean different kinds of mouths and stomachs and perceptive and locomotive organs—the possible combinations of these differences will necessarily furnish many varieties of animals. (For animals cannot be the same which have different kinds of mouths or of ears.) And when all the combinations are exhausted, there will be as many sorts of animals as there are combinations of the necessary organs.

So with the forms of government which have been described. States, as I have repeatedly said, are composed not of one but of many elements. One element is the food-producing class, who are called farmers; a second, the class of craftsmen, who practice the arts without which a city cannot exist—some of them are absolutely necessary, others contribute to luxury or to the grace of life. The third class is that of traders, and by traders I mean those who are engaged in buying and selling, either in commerce or retail trade. A fourth class is that of serfs or laborers. The soldiers make up the fifth class, and they are as necessary as any of the others, if the country is not to be the slave of every invader. For how can a state which has any title to the name be of a slavish nature? . . . Then, as the soul may be said to be more truly part of an animal

---

[6] This comparison of a state and its parts to an animal body and its organs was copied and developed by later writers for centuries after Aristotle.

than the body, so the higher parts of the state, that is to say, the warrior class and the class engaged in the administration of justice, and in deliberation, which is the special business of political intelligence—these are even more essential to the state than the parts which minister to the necessaries of life. . . .

There are also the wealthy who minister to the state with their property; these form a seventh class. The eighth class is that of magistrates and officers; for the state cannot exist without rulers. And therefore some must be able to take office and to serve the state, either always or in turn. . . . Different functions can be combined often in the same individual; for example, the warrior may also be a farmer, or an artisan, and the counselor a judge. All claim to possess political ability, and think that they are quite competent to fill most offices. But the same persons cannot be both rich and poor at the same time. For this reason the rich and the poor are regarded in a special sense as the parts of a state. Again, because the rich are generally few in number, while the poor are many, they appear to be antagonistic, and as the one or the other prevails they form the government. Hence arises the common opinion that there are but two kinds of government—democracy and oligarchy.

I have already explained that there are many differences in constitutions, and to what causes the variety is due. Let me now show that there are different forms of both democracy and oligarchy, as will indeed be evident from what has preceded. For within both the common people and the notables there are various classes. Within the common people, one class are farmers, another artisans, another traders, employed in buying and selling; another are the seafaring class, engaged either in war or in trade, as ferrymen or fishermen. (In many places some one of these classes forms quite a large population; as, for example, the fishermen at Tarentum and Byzantium the crews of triremes at Athens, the merchant seamen at Aegina and Chios, the ferrymen at Tenedos.) To the classes already mentioned may be added the day laborers, and those who, owing to needy circumstances, have no leisure, and those who are not of free

birth on both sides; and there may be other classes as well. The notables again may be divided up according to their wealth, birth, virtue, education, and similar differences.

Of the forms of democracy, first comes that which is said to be based strictly on equality. In such a democracy, the law calls it justice that the poor should have no more power than the rich, and that neither should be masters, but both equal. For if liberty and equality, as is thought by some, are the chief characteristics of democracy, they will be best attained when all persons alike share in the government to the utmost. And since the people are the majority, and the opinion of the majority is decisive, such a government must necessarily be a democracy. There is another in which the magistrates are elected according to a certain property qualification, but a low one. He who has the required amount of property has a share in the government, but he who loses his property loses his rights. Another kind is that in which all citizens who are not disqualified share in the government, and still the law is supreme. In another, everybody who is only a citizen is admitted to the government, and the law is supreme as before.[7] A fifth form of democracy, in other respects the same, is that in which not the law but the multitude have supreme power, and supersede the law by their decrees. This state of affairs is brought about by demagogues. For in democracies which are subject to the law the best citizens hold the first place, and there are no demagogues; but where the laws are not supreme, there demagogues spring up. The people become the monarch, and is many in one; and the many have the power in their hands, not as individuals, but collectively. Homer says "it is not good to have a rule of many," [8] though whether he means this corporate rule, or the rule of many individuals, is uncertain. And the people, now

[7] The distinction between this and the previous kind of democracy seems to be that in the first case a man's claim to be a citizen is sharply scrutinized and in the second any freeman is taken as a citizen without investigation. The latter had been the state of things in Athens before Pericles instituted strict rules for citizenship in the century before Aristotle.

[8] *Iliad*, II, Classics Club edition, p. 26.

being the monarch and no longer under the control of law, seeks to exercise monarchical sway, and grows into a despot; the flatterer is held in honor.

This sort of democracy is relatively to the other democracies what tyranny is to other forms of monarchy. The spirit of both is the same, and they alike exercise a despotic rule over the better citizens. The decrees of the populace correspond to the edicts of the tyrant; and the demagogue is to the one what the flatterer is to the other. Both have great power—the flatterer with the tyrant, the demagogue with democracies of the kind we are describing. The demagogues make the decrees of the people override the laws by referring all things to the popular assembly. And therefore they grow great, be-cause the people have all things in their power, and the demagogues hold in their hands the votes of the people, who are too ready to listen to them. Further, those who have any complaint to bring against the magistrates say, "let the people be judges." The people are too happy to accept the invitation; and so the authority of every office is undermined. Such a democracy is fairly open to the objec-tion that it is not a constitution at all; for where laws have no au-thority there is no constitution. Under a constitution the law must be supreme over all, and the magistrates judge only of particular cases. So that if democracy be a real form of government, the sort of system in which all things are regulated by popular decrees is clearly not a democracy in the true sense of the word, for decrees relate only to particulars.

CHAPTER 5. These then are the different kinds of democracy. Among oligarchies too there are different kinds. In one, the property qualification for any office is so high that the poor, although they form the majority, have no share in government; yet he who acquires the qualification may then get a share. Another sort is when there is a qualification for office, and a high one, and vacancies in the governing body are filled through elections by that body. If the candidate is chosen from all qualified persons, a constitution of this

kind inclines to an aristocracy; if only from a privileged class, to *n oligarchy. Another sort of oligarchy is when son succeeds father. There is a fourth form, likewise hereditary, in which the magistrates are supreme, and not the law. Among oligarchies this is what tyranny is among monarchies and the last-named form of democracy among democracies. In fact, this sort of oligarchy is called dynastic (or rule of powerful families).

These are the different sorts of oligarchies and democracies. It should however be remembered that in many states the constitution which is established by law, although not democratic owing to the education and habits of the people, may be administered democratically. Conversely in other states, the established constitution may incline to democracy, but may be administered in an oligarchical spirit. This most often happens after a revolution. For governments do not change at once; at first the dominant party are content with encroaching gradually upon their opponents. The laws which existed previously continue in force, but the authors of the revolution have the actual power in their hands.

CHAPTER 6. From what has been already said we may surely infer that there are many different kinds of democracies and of oligarchies. For it is evident that sometimes all the classes mentioned must share in the government, and again some only and not others. When the class of farmers and those of moderate means have the supreme power, the government is administered according to law. For the citizens, being compelled to live by their labor, have no leisure. So they set up the authority of the law and attend assemblies only when necessary. They all obtain a share in the government when they have acquired the qualification fixed by the law, and nobody is excluded. The absolute exclusion of any class would be a step towards oligarchy. But leisure cannot be provided for them unless there are revenues to support them. This is one sort of democracy, and these are the causes which give birth to it.

Another kind is based on a principle of election, which naturally

comes next in order. In this, everyone to whose birth there is no objection is a citizen and shares in the government if he can find time. In such a democracy the supreme power is vested in the laws, because the state has no means of paying the citizens. A third kind is when all freemen have a right to share in the government,[9] but do not actually share, for the reason which has already been given; so that in this form again the law must rule. A fourth kind of democracy is that which comes latest in the history of states. In our own day, when cities have far outgrown their original size and revenues have increased, all citizens have a place in the government, through the great preponderance of the masses. They all too, including the poor who receive pay and therefore have leisure to exercise their rights, share in the administration. Indeed, when they are paid, the common people have the most leisure, for they are not hindered by the care of property, which often fetters the rich, who are thereby prevented from taking part in the assembly or in the courts. In this way, the state is governed by the poor who are a majority, and not by the laws. So many kinds of democracies there are, and they grow out of these necessary causes.

Of oligarchies, one form is that in which the majority of citizens have some property, though not very much. This first form allows to anyone who obtains the required amount the right of sharing in the government. The sharers in the government being a numerous body, it follows that the law must govern and not individuals. For in proportion as they are further removed from a monarchical form of government, and have neither so much property as to be able to live without attending to business, nor so little as to need state support, they must admit the rule of law and not claim to rule themselves. But if the men of property in the state are fewer than in this first case and own more property, there arises the second form of oligarchy. For the stronger they are, the more power they claim, and having this object in view, they themselves select those of the other

* That is, the citizens here do not have to prove their free birth.

classes who are to be admitted to the government. But not being as yet strong enough to rule without law, they make the law represent their wishes. When this power is intensified by a further diminution of their numbers and an increase of their property, there arises the third and further stage of oligarchy, in which the governing class keep the offices in their own hands, and the law ordains that son shall succeed father. When, finally, the rulers have great wealth and numerous friends, this sort of dynastic despotism approaches a monarchy. Individuals rule and not the law. This is the fourth kind of oligarchy, and is analogous to the last sort of democracy.

CHAPTER 7. There are, however, still two forms besides democracy and oligarchy. One of them is universally recognized and included among the four principal forms of government, which are said to be (1) monarchy, (2) oligarchy, (3) democracy, and (4) the so-called aristocracy or government of the best. But there is also a fifth, which keeps the generic name of commonwealth or constitutional government. This is not common, and therefore has not been noticed by writers who attempt to enumerate the different kinds of government. Like Plato in his books about the state, they recognize only four.[10] . . .

CHAPTER 8. I have yet to speak of this so-called commonwealth and of tyranny. I put them in this order, not because a commonwealth or constitutional government is to be regarded as a perversion any more than the above-mentioned aristocracies. The truth is that they all fall short of the most perfect form of government, and so are reckoned among perversions, but the really perverted forms are perversions of these, as I said before. Last of all I will speak of tyranny, which I place last in the series because I am examining the constitutions of states, and this is the very reverse of a constitution.

Having explained why I have adopted this order, I will proceed

[10] See Plato's *Republic*, Books VIII and IX.

to consider constitutional government, the nature of which will be clearer now that oligarchy and democracy have been defined. For a constitutional government may be described generally as a fusion of oligarchy and democracy, though the name is usually applied to those forms of government which incline towards democracy and the name aristocracy to those which incline towards oligarchy, because birth and education are usually accompaniments of wealth. The rich too possess the material advantages the want of which is a temptation to crime, and hence are called noblemen and gentlemen. So, as aristocracy seeks to give predominance to the best citizens, people say also of oligarchies that they are composed of noblemen and gentlemen.

Now it appears impossible that a state which is governed by its best citizens should be ill governed, and equally impossible that a state which is governed by its worst should be well governed. But we must remember that good laws, if they are not obeyed, do not alone constitute good government. For there are two parts of a good government; one is the actual obedience of citizens to the laws, the other is the goodness of the laws which they obey. They may obey bad laws as well as good. And a further distinction is possible. They may obey either the best laws attainable to them, or the best absolutely. The distribution of offices according to merit is a special characteristic of aristocracy, for virtue is the principle of an aristocracy, as wealth is of an oligarchy, and freedom of a democracy. In all of them there of course exists the right of the majority; whatever seems good to the majority of those who share in the government has authority.

Generally, however, in a state of this kind there is a constitutional government [not an aristocracy], for the fusion goes no further than an attempt to unite the freedom of the poor and the wealth of the rich, who commonly take the place of the noble. Now there are three grounds on which men claim an equal share in the government—freedom, wealth, virtue (for the fourth, good birth, is the result of the two last, being only ancient wealth and virtue). It is clear that

an admixture or two elements, that is to say, of the free and the wealthy, is a commonwealth or constitutional government; and a union of all three an aristocracy or government of the best. And more than any other form of government, except the true and ideal, it has a right to this name.

Thus far I have described the different forms of states which exist besides monarchy, democracy, and oligarchy, and what they are, and in what aristocracies differ from one another, and commonwealths from aristocracies. That the two latter are not very unlike is obvious.

CHAPTER 9.   Next we have to consider how by the side of oligarchy and democracy the so-called commonwealth or constitutional government springs up, and how it should be organized. The nature of it will be at once understood from a comparison of oligarchy and democracy. We must ascertain their different characteristics, and taking a portion from each, put the two together, like the parts of an indenture. Now there are three methods by which fusions of government may be effected. In the first method, they combine the laws made by both governments, regarding, say, the administration of justice. In oligarchies, they impose a fine on the rich if they do not serve on juries, and give no pay to the poor; but in democracies they give pay to the poor and do not fine the rich. Now (1) a union of these two practices is a common or middle term between them, and is therefore characteristic of a constitutional government, for it is a combination of both. This is one method of uniting the two. Or (2) a mean may be taken between the statutes of the two. Thus democracies require no property qualification for members of the assembly or only a small one; oligarchies a high one. Here the common term is neither of these but a mean between them. (3) By a third method something is borrowed from the oligarchic and something from the democratic principle. For example, the appointment of magistrates by lot is democratic and the election of them oligarchic. The absence of a property qualification is democratic, the presence of one is oligarchic. In the constitutional state, one feature

will be taken from each—from oligarchy the rule of election to office, from democracy the disregard of property qualification. Such are the various methods of combination.

In a true union of oligarchy and democracy the same state may be termed either a democracy or an oligarchy; those who use both names evidently feel that the fusion is complete. Such a fusion there is in a mean; for both extremes appear in it. The Spartan constitution, for example, is often described as a democracy, because it has many democratic features. In the first place, the youth receive a democratic education. For the sons of the poor are brought up with the sons of the rich, who are educated in such a manner as to make it possible for the sons of the poor to be educated like them. A similar equality prevails in the following period of life, for when the citizens are grown up to manhood the same rule is observed; there is no distinction between rich and poor. In like manner they all have the same food at their public tables, and the rich wear only such clothing as any poor man can afford. Again, the people elect to one of the two greatest offices of state, and in the other they share; for they elect the senators and share in the ephoralty. Yet by other persons the Spartan constitution is called an oligarchy, because it has many oligarchic elements. All offices are filled by election and none by lot, which is one of the oligarchic characteristics. The power of inflicting death or banishment rests with a few persons, which is another; and there are others. In a well-balanced commonwealth there should appear to be both elements and yet neither. The government too should rely on itself, and not on foreign aid, nor on the good will of a large number of foreign states—they might be equally well disposed to a vicious form of government—but on the general willingness of all classes within the state to maintain the constitution.

Enough of the manner in which a constitutional government and in which the so-called aristocracies ought to be framed.

CHAPTER 10. Of the nature of tyranny I have still to speak, that it may have its place in our inquiry, since even tyranny we

reckon a form of government, although there is not much to be said about it. Already, in the former part of this treatise, I have discussed monarchy or kingship according to the most usual meaning of the term, and considered whether it is or is not advantageous to states, and what kind of monarchy should be established, and whence, and how.

When speaking of monarchy we spoke also of two forms of tyranny, which are both legal, and therefore easily pass into kingship. Among barbarians there are elected monarchs who exercise a despotic power. Despotic rulers were also elected in ancient Hellas, called dictators. These autocracies, when compared with one another, exhibit certain differences. And they are, as I said before, royal, in so far as the autocrat rules according to law and over willing subjects; but they are tyrannical in so far as he is despotic and rules according to his own fancy. There is also a third kind of tyranny, which is the most typical form, and is the opposite of the perfect monarchy. This tyranny is just that arbitrary power of an individual which is responsible to no one, and governs all alike, both equals and betters, with a view to its own advantage, not to that of its subjects, and therefore against their will. No freeman, if he can escape from it, will endure such a government. The kinds of tyranny are these and this many, for the reasons which I have given.

CHAPTER 11. We have now to inquire what is the best constitution for most states, and the best life for most men, neither assuming a standard of virtue which is above ordinary persons, nor an education which is exceptionally favored by nature and circumstances, nor yet an ideal state which is an aspiration only, but having regard to the life in which the majority are able to share, and to the form of government which states in general can attain. . . . If it was truly said in the *Ethics* that the happy life is the life according to unimpeded virtue [11] and that virtue is a mean, then the life which

[11] See the *Ethics,* Book VII, p. 191.

is a mean and a mean attainable by everyone must be best. And the same principles of virtue and vice are characteristic of cities and of constitutions; for the constitution is in pattern the life of the city.

Now within all states there are three elements; one class is very rich, another very poor, and a third in the mean. It is admitted that moderation and the mean are best, and therefore it will clearly be best to possess the gifts of fortune in moderation; for in that condition of life men are most ready to listen to reason. But he who greatly excels in beauty, strength, birth, or wealth, or on the other hand who is very poor, or very weak, or very much disgraced, finds it difficult to follow reason. Of these two kinds, the former grow into violent and great criminals, the latter into rogues and petty rascals. And two sorts of offenses correspond to them, the one committed by violence, the other by roguery.

Moreover, the middle class is least willing to hold office or over-eager for it, both of which dispositions are injurious to the state. But those who have too much of the goods of fortune, strength, wealth, friends, and the like, are neither willing nor able to submit to authority. The evil begins at home; for when they are boys, by reason of the luxury in which they are brought up, they never learn, even at school, the habit of obedience. On the other hand, the very poor, who are in the opposite extreme, are too degraded. So that the one class cannot obey, and can only rule despotically; the other knows not how to command and must be ruled like slaves. Thus arises a city, not of freemen, but of masters and slaves, the one despising, the other envying. Nothing can be more fatal to friendship and good fellowship in states than this; for good fellowship starts from friendship. When men are at enmity with one another, they would rather not even share the same path.

But a city ought to be composed, as far as possible, of equals and similars; and these are generally the middle classes. Wherefore a city which is composed of middle-class citizens is necessarily best constituted, as far as what we call the natural elements of a state. And this class of citizens is most secure in a state. For they do not,

like the poor, covet their neighbors' goods; nor do others covet theirs, as the poor covet the goods of the rich. So, as they neither plot against others nor are themselves plotted against, they pass through life safely. Wisely then did Phocylides [12] pray:

"Many things are best in the mean; I desire to be of a middle condition in my city."

Thus it is manifest that the best political community is formed by citizens of the middle class, and that those states are likely to be well administered in which the middle class is large, and if possible larger than both the other classes, or at any rate than either singly. For the addition of the middle class then turns the scale and prevents either of the extremes from being dominant. Great then is the good fortune of a state in which the citizens have a moderate and sufficient property. For where some possess much and the rest nothing, there may arise an extreme democracy, or a pure oligarchy; or a tyranny may grow out of either extreme—out of either the most rampant democracy or out of an oligarchy. But it is not so likely to arise out of a middle and nearly equal condition. I will explain the reason for this hereafter when I speak of the revolutions of states.

The mean condition of states is clearly best, since none is free from faction; but where the middle class is large, there are least likely to be factions and dissensions. For a similar reason large states are less liable to faction than small ones, because in them the middle class is large; whereas in small states it is easy to divide all the citizens into two classes, who are either rich or poor, and to leave nothing in the middle. Democracies are safer too and more permanent than oligarchies, because they have a middle class which is more numerous and has a greater share in the government. For when there is no middle class and the poor greatly exceed in number, troubles arise and the state soon comes to an end. A proof of the superiority of the middle class is that the best legislators have come from the middle rank; for example, Solon, as his own verses testify, and Lycurgus,

---

[12] An author of poetical maxims, who lived in the sixth century B.C. We have from him only a few fragmentary lines, like the ones quoted here.

for he was not a king, and Charondas, and almost all lawmakers. . . .

What then is the best form of government, and what makes it best is evident. Of other states, since we say there are many kinds of democracy and of oligarchy, it is not difficult to see which has the first and which the second or any other place in the order of excellence, now that we have determined which is best. For that which is nearest to the best must of necessity be the better, and that which is furthest from it the worse, if we are judging absolutely and not with reference to given conditions. I say "with reference to given conditions," since a particular government may be preferable in general, but another form may be better for some people.

CHAPTER 12. We have now to consider what and what kind of government is suited to what and what kind of men. I may begin by assuming, as a general principle common to all governments, that that element in a state which desires its permanence should be stronger than that which desires the reverse. Now every city is composed of quality and quantity. By quality I mean freedom, wealth, education, good birth, and by quantity, superiority of numbers. Quality may exist in one of the classes which make up a state, and quantity in another. For example, the meanly-born may be more numerous than the well-born, or the poor than the rich, yet they may not so much exceed in quantity as they fall short in quality. Where the number of the poor is proportionately greater than the wealth of the rich, there will naturally be a democracy, varying in form with the sort of people who compose it in each case. If, for example, the farmers preponderate in numbers, the first form of democracy will arise; if the artisans and laboring class, the last; and so with the intermediate forms. But where the rich and the notables exceed in quality more than they fall short in quantity, there oligarchy arises, likewise assuming various forms, according to the kind of superiority possessed by the oligarchs.

Now a lawgiver should always include the middle class in his government. If he makes his laws oligarchic, to the middle class let him

look; if he makes them democratic, he should equally try by his laws to attach this class to the state. Only there can the government ever be stable where the middle class exceeds one or both of the others, since in that case there will be no fear that the rich will unite with the poor against the rulers. For neither of those classes will ever be willing to serve the other. Though they look for some form of government more congenial to them both, they will find none better than this, for the rich and the poor will never consent to rule by turns, because they mistrust one another. The arbiter is always the one trusted, and the one in the middle is the arbiter. The more perfect the mixture of the political elements, the more lasting will be the state. Many of those who desire to form aristocratic governments make a mistake, not only in giving too much power to the rich but in attempting to overreach the people. . . .

CHAPTER 13. . . . In democracies they have counter devices. They pay the poor for attending assemblies and the law courts, and inflict no penalty on the rich for non-attendance. It is obvious that he who would duly mix the two principles should combine both practices, and provide that the poor should be paid to attend, and the rich fined if they do not attend, for then all will take part. If there is no such combination, power will be in the hands of one party only. The government should be confined to those who carry arms. As to a property qualification, no absolute rule can be laid down, but we must see what is the highest qualification sufficiently comprehensive to ensure that the number of those who have citizenship rights exceeds the number of those excluded. Still, even if they have no share in office, the poor, provided only that they are not outraged or deprived of their property, will be quiet enough. But to secure gentle treatment for the poor is not an easy thing, since a ruling class is not always humane. And in time of war the poor are apt to hesitate unless they are fed; when fed, they are willing enough to fight. In some states the government is vested not only

in those who are actually serving in the army but also in those who have served. Among the Malians, for example, the governing body consisted of the latter, while the magistrates were chosen from those actually on service. And the earliest government which arose among the Greeks, after the overthrow of the kingly power, grew up out of the warrior class and was originally taken from the knights (for strength and superiority in war at that time depended on cavalry). For without discipline infantry are useless, and in ancient times there was no military knowledge or tactics, and therefore the strength of armies lay in their cavalry. But when cities increased and the heavy-armed infantry grew in strength, more men had a share in the government. This is the reason why the states, which we call constitutional governments, were heretofore called democracies. Ancient constitutions, as might be expected, were oligarchic and royal. Their population being small they had no considerable middle class; the people were weak in numbers and organization, and were therefore more contented to be governed.

I have explained why there are various forms of government, and why there are more than is generally supposed, democracy, as well as other constitutions, having more than one form. I have told also what their differences are, and whence they arise, and what is the best form of government, speaking generally, and to whom the various forms of government are best suited. All this has now been explained.

CHAPTER 14. Having thus gained an adequate basis for discussion, we will proceed to speak of the points which follow next in order. We will consider the subject not only in general but with reference to particular constitutions. All contain three elements and a good lawmaker has to regard what is expedient for each. When they are well ordered, the constitution is well ordered, and as they differ from one another, the constitutions differ. There is, first (1) the organ which deliberates about public affairs; secondly (2) the system of magistrates, determining what they should be, over what

they should exercise authority, and what should be the mode of electing them; and thirdly (3) the judicial power.[13]

The deliberative element has authority in matters of war and peace, in making and unmaking alliances; it passes laws, inflicts death, exile, confiscation, elects magistrates, and audits their accounts. These powers must be assigned either to all the citizens or to some of them—for example, to one or more magistrates, or different ones to different magistrates, or some of them to all, and others of them to some only. That all things should be decided by all is characteristic of democracy; it is the sort of equality which the people desire. But there are various ways in which all may share in the government. They may deliberate, not all in one body, but by turns, as in the constitution of Telecles the Milesian. In other states the boards of magistrates meet and deliberate. They come into office by turns, and are elected out of the tribes and the smallest divisions of the state, until everyone has held office in turn. The citizens, as a body, on the other hand, are assembled only for the purposes of legislation, and to consult about the constitution, and to hear the edicts of the magistrates. . . . A fourth form of democracy is when all citizens meet to deliberate about everything, and the magistrates decide nothing, but make only the preliminary inquiries. That is the way in which the last and worst form of democracy, corresponding, as we said, to a close family oligarchy or a tyranny, is administered. All these methods are democratic.

On the other hand, for one group to deliberate about everything is oligarchic. This again is a method which, like the democratic, has many forms. When the deliberative class is constituted of those who have a moderate property qualification and so is numerous, and they respect and obey the law without altering it, and anyone who has the required qualification shares in the government, then,

---

[13] Aristotle makes here the distinction, so familiar to us, between the three branches of a constitutional government, the deliberative or what we call the legislative, the magisterial or executive, and the judicial. But there is, it will be noted, as yet no such sharp separation of functions as has become the rule in modern times.

because of their moderation, the oligarchy tends toward a constitutional government. But when only selected individuals and not the people as a whole share in the deliberations of the state, then, even though as in the former case, they observe the law, the government is a pure oligarchy. . . . These, then, are our conclusions respecting the deliberative, that is, the supreme element in states.

CHAPTER 15.   Next we will proceed to consider the distribution of executive offices, this too being a matter of politics over which many questions arise. What shall their number be? Of what shall they have charge, and what shall be their duration? Sometimes they last for six months, sometimes for less; sometimes they are annual, whilst in other cases offices are held for still longer periods. Shall they be for life or for a long term of years? Or, if for a short term only, shall the same persons hold them over and over again, or once only? Also about the elections to them: from whom are officials to be chosen, by whom, and how?

We should first attempt to say what are the possible kinds of offices, and then we may proceed to determine which are suited to different forms of government. Then what are to be included under the term "offices"? That is a question not so easily answered. For a political community requires many officers; and not everyone who is chosen by vote or by lot is to be regarded as a ruler. In the first place, there are the priests, who must be distinguished from political officers, as are the masters of choruses and heralds, and ambassadors, even though they are elected by vote. Some duties of superintendence again are political, covering either all the citizens in a single type of action, like the office of the general who superintends them when they are in the field, or only a section of them, like the inspectorships of women or of youth. But other offices deal with household economy, like that of the corn measurers who exist in many states and are elected officers. There are also menial offices which the rich have executed by their slaves. Speaking generally, those are offices of state to which are assigned the duties of deciding about certain

measures and of judging and commanding, especially the last; for to command is the especial duty of a magistrate. But the question is of no practical importance. No one has ever brought into court the meaning of the word, although such problems have a speculative interest.

What kinds of offices and how many are necessary to the existence of a state, and which, though not necessary, yet conduce to its well-being, are much more important considerations, for they affect all states, but especially small ones. For in great states it is possible and indeed necessary that every function should have its special official; where the citizens are numerous, many may hold office. And so it happens that some offices can be held a second time only after a long interval, or else held once only. Certainly every work is better done which receives the sole, not the divided, attention of the worker. But in small states it is necessary to combine many offices in a few hands, since the small number of citizens does not admit of many holding office; for who will there be to succeed them? And yet small states at times need the same offices and laws as large ones; the difference is that the latter want them often, the former only after long intervals. There is then no reason why the care of many offices should not be imposed on one person, for they will not interfere with each other. When the population is small, offices should be like the roasting spits which also serve to hold a lamp. So we must first ascertain how many magistrates are necessary in every state, and also how many are not exactly necessary, but are nevertheless useful, and then there will be no difficulty in judging what offices can be combined in one.

We should also know over which matters local tribunals are to have jurisdiction and when authority should be centralized; for example, should one person keep order in the market and another in some other place, or should the same person be responsible everywhere? Again, should offices be divided according to the subjects with which they deal, or according to the persons with whom they deal. I mean to say, should one person see to good order in general, or one look after the boys, another after the women, and so on?

Further, under different constitutions, should the magistrates be the same or different? For example, in democracy, oligarchy, aristocracy, monarchy, should there be the same magistrates, although they are elected, not out of equal or similar classes of citizens, but differently under different constitutions? In aristocracies, for example, they are chosen from the educated, in oligarchies from the wealthy, and in democracies from the free. Or are there different offices proper to different constitutions, and may the same be suitable to some, but unsuitable to others? For in some states it may be convenient that the same office should have a more extensive, in other states a narrower sphere. . . . A magistracy which controls the boys or the women, or any similar office, is suited to an aristocracy rather than to a democracy; for how can magistrates prevent the wives of the poor from going out of doors? Neither is it an oligarchic office; for the wives of the oligarchs are too fine to be controlled.

Enough of these matters. I will now inquire into the elections to offices. There are three questions to be answered, and the combinations of answers give all possible differences. First, who elects? Secondly, from whom? And thirdly, how? Each of the three answers may also differ in several ways. (1) All the citizens, or only some, may elect. (2) The magistrates are chosen either from all the people or from some who are distinguished either by a property qualification or by birth or merit, or for some special reason, as at Megara only those were eligible who had returned from exile and fought together against the democracy.[14] (3) They may be chosen either by vote or by lot. Again, these several variations may be combined. I mean that some officers may be elected by some, others by all, and some again from some group and others from all the people, and some by vote and others by lot. . . .

These are the different ways of constituting magistrates, and they correspond to the different forms of government. Which are proper

---

[14] The democracy at Megara seems to have been several times overthrown by those whom Aristotle called oligarchs, a clique of wealthy and powerful citizens. See Book V, p. 351.

to which, and how they ought to be established, will be evident when we determine the nature of their powers.[15] By powers I mean such power as a magistrate exercises over the revenue or in defense of the country. For there are various kinds of power. The power of a general, for example, is not the same as that which governs contracts in a market.

CHAPTER 16. Of the three parts of government, the judicial remains to be considered, and this we shall analyze on the same principle. There are three points on which the variations in law courts depend: namely, the persons from whom the judges are appointed, the matters with which they are concerned, and the manner of their appointment. I mean, (1) are the judges taken from all the people or from some only? (2) How many kinds of law courts are there? (3) Are the judges chosen by vote or by lot?

First, let me determine how many kinds of law courts there are. They are eight in number. One is the court of audits or scrutinies; the second takes cognizance of offenses against the state; the third is concerned with treason against the constitution; the fourth decides disputes respecting penalties, whether raised by magistrates or by private persons; the fifth decides the more important civil cases; the sixth tries cases of homicide, which are of various kinds, (1) premeditated, (2) unpremeditated, (3) cases in which guilt is confessed but the justice is disputed; and there may be a fourth court (4) in which murderers who have fled from justice are tried after their return; such as the Court of Phreatto is said to have been at Athens.[16] But cases of this sort rarely happen at all even in large cities. The different kinds of homicide may be tried either by the same or by different courts. (7) There are courts for foreigners, and of these there are two subdivisions: for the settlement of their disputes with one another, and for the settlement of disputes between them and

---

[15] Aristotle never does this in the *Politics* as we have it.

[16] An ancient court, about which Aristotle himself knew only by hearsay. In his time it was obsolete.

the citizens. Besides all these there must be (8) courts for petty suits about sums of a drachma [17] up to five drachmas, or a little more. These have to be settled but do not require many judges. . . .

Now if all the citizens serve as judges [18] in all the different cases which I have distinguished, they may be appointed by vote or by lot, or sometimes by lot and sometimes by vote. . . . Again, the modes of election may be combined. I mean that some may be chosen out of the whole people, others out of some, some out of both; for example, the same tribunal may be composed of some who were elected from all the people and of others who were elected from a group, either by vote or by lot or both.

In how many forms law courts can be established has now been considered. The first form, that in which the judges are taken from all the citizens, and in which all cases are tried, is democratic; the second, in which only a few judges try all cases, is oligarchic; the third, in which some judges are taken from all classes, and some from certain classes only, is aristocratic and constitutional.

BOOK V

Revolutions in states. Causes tending to produce revolutions under different types of government. Methods by which revolutions may be averted under all types.

CHAPTER I. The design which we proposed to ourselves is now nearly completed. Next in order we take up the causes of revolution in states, how many they are and what is their nature; what elements work ruin in particular states, and from what and into what

---

[17] The Greek silver coin, drachma, was worth about twenty cents.

[18] The reference is to the Athenian institution of great popular juries of five hundred more or less, chosen by lot from the citizen body, who tried all kinds of cases and, as judges, named the punishments. See p. 289, n. 1.

they mostly change; also what methods there are of preserving states generally, or a particular state, and by what means each state may be best preserved. These are questions that remain to be considered.

In the first place we must assume as our starting point that in the many forms of government which have sprung up there has always been some acknowledgment of justice and proportionate equality, although mankind fails in attaining them, as indeed I have already shown.[1] Democracy, for example, arises out of the notion that those who are equal in any respect are equal in all respects; because men are equally free, they claim to be absolutely equal. Oligarchy is based on the notion that those who are unequal in one respect are in all respects unequal; being unequal, that is, in property, the citizens suppose themselves to be unequal absolutely. The democrats think that, as they are equal, they ought to be equal in all things; while the oligarchs, under the idea that they are unequal, claim too much, which is more inequality. All these forms of government have a kind of justice, but, tried by an absolute standard, they are faulty. Therefore, both parties, whenever their share in the government does not accord with their preconceived ideas, stir up revolution.

Those who excel in virtue have the best right of all to rebel (for they alone can with reason be deemed absolutely unequal), but then they are of all men least inclined to do so. There is also the superiority claimed by men of rank, who are thought noble because they spring from wealthy and virtuous ancestors. Here then are opened the very springs and fountains of revolution, and hence arise two sorts of changes in governments. The first affects the constitution, when men seek to change from an existing form into some other, from democracy, for example, into oligarchy, and from oligarchy into democracy, or from either of them into constitutional government or aristocracy, and conversely. The other does not affect the constitution, when, without disturbing the form of government, whether oligarchy or monarchy or any other, the rebels try to get the adminis-

[1] See Book III, p. 297.

tration into their hands. There is besides a question of degree. An oligarchy, for example, may become more or less oligarchic, and a democracy more or less democratic. In like manner, the characteristics of other forms of government may be either more or less strictly maintained. Or, the revolution may be directed against a portion of the constitution only, for example, for the establishment or the overthrow of a particular office. . . . Everywhere inequality is a cause of revolution, an inequality in which there is no proportion, for instance, a perpetual monarchy among equals; and always it is a desire for equality which rises in rebellion. . . .

Still democracy appears to be safer and less liable to revolution than oligarchy. For in oligarchies there is the double danger of the oligarchs falling out among themselves and also with the people; but in democracies there is only the danger of a quarrel with the oligarchic party. No dissension worth mentioning arises among the people themselves. We may further remark that a government composed of the middle class more nearly approximates to democracy than to oligarchy, and is the safest of the imperfect forms of government.

CHAPTER 2. In considering how dissensions and political revolutions arise, we must first of all ascertain the beginnings and causes of them which affect constitutions generally. They may be said to be three in number; and we have now to give an outline of each We want to know (1) what is the feeling and (2) what are the motives of those who make them and (3) what causes political disturbances and quarrels. The universal and chief cause of revolutionary feeling has already been mentioned; namely, either the desire for equality, when men think that they are equal to others who have more than themselves; or, the desire for inequality and superiority, when they believe themselves superior and think they have not got more but the same or less than their inferiors, pretensions which may or may not be just. Inferiors revolt in order that they may be

equal, and equals that they may be superior. Such is the state of mind which creates revolutions.

The motives for making them are the desire for gain and for honor, or the fear of dishonor and loss. The authors of them want to divert punishment or dishonor from themselves or their friends. The causes and reasons of the motives and dispositions by which these men are excited about the things above mentioned, when viewed in one way, may be regarded as seven, and in another as more than seven. Two of them have been already noted; but they may act also in a different manner. For men are excited against one another by the love of gain and honor—not, as in the case I have just supposed, in order to get them for themselves, but at seeing others justly or unjustly monopolizing them. Other causes are insolence, fear, too much influence, contempt, disproportionate increase in some part of the state. Causes of another sort are election intrigues, carelessness, neglect about trifles, dissimilarity of elements.

CHAPTER 3.   What share insolence and avarice have in creating revolutions and how they work is plain enough. When the magistrates are insolent and grasping, they conspire against one another and also against the constitution from which they derive their power, making their gains either at the expense of individuals or of the public. It is evident too what an influence honor exerts and how it is a cause of revolution. Men who are themselves dishonored and see others obtaining honors rise in rebellion. The honor or dishonor when undeserved is unjust, though just when awarded according to merit. Again, superiority is a cause of revolution when one or more persons have an influence which is too much for the state and the power of the government. Out of such a condition of affairs rises a monarchy, or a family oligarchy. Therefore, in some places, as at Athens and Argos, they have recourse to ostracism.[2] But how much better to provide from the first that there should be no such

pre-eminent individuals, instead of letting them come into existence
and then finding a remedy!

Another cause of revolution is fear. Either men have committed
wrong, and are afraid of punishment, or they are expecting to suffer
wrong and are desirous of anticipating their enemy. Thus at Rhodes
the nobles conspired against the people through fear of the suits
that were being brought against them. Contempt is also a cause of
insurrection and revolution; in oligarchies, for example, when those
who have no share in the state are the majority, they revolt, because
they think they are the stronger. Or, again, in democracies, the rich
despise the disorder and anarchy of the state; at Thebes, for example,
where, after the battle of Oenophyta, the bad administration of the
democracy led to its ruin. At Megara the fall of the democracy was
due to a defeat occasioned by its disorder and anarchy. . . .

Political revolutions spring also from a disproportionate increase
in any part of the state. For a body is made up of many members, and
every member ought to grow in proportion, if symmetry is to be
preserved; but if the foot be four cubits long and the rest of the
body two spans, [3] the body loses its nature. Should the abnormal
increase be one of quality as well as quantity, it may even take the
form of another animal. Even so, a state has many parts, of which
some one may often grow on imperceptibly; the number of poor,
for example, in democracies and in constitutional states. And this
disproportion may sometimes happen by an accident. At Tarentum,
from a defeat in which many of the nobles were slain, in a battle with
the Iapygians just after the Persian War, the constitutional government in consequence became a democracy. . . .

Revolutions arise from this cause in democracies as well as in
other forms of government, but not to so great an extent. However,
when the rich grow numerous and wealth increases, the form of
government changes into an oligarchy or a government of families.
Forms of government also change—sometimes even without a revolu-

[3] The cubit was about twenty inches long, the span about nine.

tion, through election contests. . . . And again, a revolution may be accomplished by small degrees. I mean that a great change may sometimes slip into a constitution through neglect of a small detail. At Ambracia, for instance, the qualification for office, small at first, was eventually reduced to nothing. For the Ambraciots thought that a small qualification was much the same as none at all.[4]

Another cause of revolution is a difference between races, which do not at once acquire a common spirit; for a state is not the growth of a day, neither is it a multitude brought together by accident. Hence the admission of foreigners to colonies, either at the time of their foundation or afterwards, has generally produced a revolution. For example, the Achaeans who joined the Troezenians in the foundation of Sybaris, becoming later the more numerous, expelled them; hence the curse fell upon Sybaris. . . . The citizens of Apollonia on the Black Sea, after the introduction of a fresh body of colonists, had a revolution. The Syracusans, after the expulsion of their tyrants, having admitted foreigners and mercenaries to the rights of citizenship, quarreled and came to blows. The people of Amphipolis, having received Chalcidian colonists, were nearly all expelled by them.

In oligarchies then the masses make a revolution under the idea that they are unjustly treated, because, as I said before, they are equals and have not an equal share; and in democracies the nobles revolt, because they are not equals and yet have only an equal share.

Again, the situation of cities is a cause of revolution, when the country is not naturally adapted to preserve the unity of the state. . . . At Athens the inhabitants of the Piraeus are more democratic than those who live in the city.[5] Just as in war, when the impediment of a ditch, though ever so small, may break a regiment, so every cause of difference, however slight, makes a breach in a city. The

---

[4] For more about the revolution at Ambracia, see p. 354.

[5] Piraeus, the harbor of Athens, was, it will be remembered, about five miles from the main city. The sailors, who were the lowest class of citizens, congregated in the Piraeus.

greatest opposition is confessedly that of virtue and vice; but next comes that of wealth and poverty. There are other antagonistic elements, greater or less, of which one is this difference of place.

CHAPTER 4. In revolutions the occasions may be trifling, but great interests are at stake. Trifles are most important when they concern the rulers, as was the case of old at Syracuse; for the Syracusan constitution was once changed by a love-quarrel of two young men, who were in the government. The story is that while one of them was away from home, his beloved was won over by his companion, and the first to revenge himself seduced the other's wife. They then drew all the members of the government into their quarrel and broke the whole people up into parties. We learn from this story that we should be on our guard against the beginnings of such evils, and should put an end to the quarrels of chiefs and mighty men. The mistake lies in the beginning. As the proverb says, "Well begun is half done," so an error at the beginning, though itself very trivial, is proportionally half of the whole affair. In general, when the nobles quarrel, the whole city is involved, as happened in Hestiaea after the Persian War. The occasion then was the division of an inheritance. One of two brothers refused to give an account of their father's property and the treasure he had found. So the poorer of the two quarreled with him and enlisted the popular party in his cause, while the other, who was very rich, got the wealthy classes.

At Delphi, again, a quarrel about a marriage was the beginning of all the troubles which followed. In this case the bridegroom, imagining that some incident was of evil omen, came to the bride, but went away without taking her. Whereupon her relations, thinking he had insulted them, put some of the sacred treasure among his offerings while he was sacrificing, and then slew him, pretending that he had been robbing the temple. . . .

Governments change also into oligarchies or democracies or constitutional governments because the magistrates, or some other sec-

tion of the state, increase in power or renown. Thus, at Athens, the reputation gained by the court of the Areopagus [6] in the Persian War seemed to tighten the reins of government. On the other hand, the victory of Salamis, which was gained by the common people, who served in the fleet and won for the Athenians the empire of the sea, strengthened the democracy. At Argos, the nobles, having distinguished themselves against the Spartans in the battle of Mantinea, attempted to put down the democracy. . . . At Ambracia the people joined with the conspirators in expelling the tyrant Periander, and then transferred the government to themselves. And generally it should be remembered that those who have secured power for the state, whether private citizens or magistrates or tribes or any other part or section of the state, are apt to cause revolutions. For either envy of their greatness draws others into rebellion, or they themselves, in their pride of superiority, are unwilling to remain on a level with the others.

Revolutions break out also when opposite parties, such as the rich and the poor, are equally balanced, and there is little or no middle class; for if either party were manifestly superior, the other would not risk an attack upon them. This is why men eminent in virtue do not stir up insurrections, for they are always a minority. Such are the beginnings and causes of the disturbances and revolutions to which every form of government is liable.

Revolutions are accomplished in two ways, by force and by fraud. Force may be applied either at the time of making the revolution or afterwards. Fraud, again, is of two kinds; for (1) sometimes the citizens are deceived into accepting a change of government, and afterwards held in subjection against their will. . . . (2) In other cases the people are persuaded at first, and afterwards, by a repetition of the persuasion, their good will and allegiance are still retained. The revolutions which affect constitutions spring commonly from the above-mentioned causes.

[6] The old aristocratic council, whose power was reduced to a shadow as Athens grew more and more democratic.

CHAPTER 5. Now taking each constitution separately, we must see what follows from the principles already laid down. Revolutions in democracies are often caused by the intemperance of demagogues, who either in a private capacity report information against rich men until they compel them to combine (for a common danger unites even the bitterest enemies), or else come forward in public and stir up the people against them. The truth of this remark is proved by a variety of examples. At Cos the democracy was overthrown because wicked demagogues arose and the nobles combined. . . . Much in the same manner the democracy at Megara was overturned. There the demagogues drove out many of the nobles in order that they might be able to confiscate their property. At length the exiles, becoming numerous, returned, engaged and defeated the people, and established an oligarchy. . . .

Of old, the popular leader was also a general, and then democracies changed into tyrannies. Most of the ancient tyrants were originally demagogues. They are not so now, but they were then; and the reason is that they were generals and not orators, for oratory had not yet come into fashion. Whereas in our day, when the art of rhetoric has made such progress, orators lead the people. But their ignorance of military matters prevents them from usurping power; at any rate, instances to the contrary are few and slight. Formerly too tyrannies were more common than they now are, because great power was often placed in the hands of individuals. Thus a tyranny arose at Miletus out of the office of the Prytanis, who had supreme authority in many important matters. Moreover, in those days, when cities were not large, the people lived in the fields, busy at their work. Their chiefs, then, who possessed military talent, seized the opportunity, and winning the popular confidence by professing their hatred of the wealthy, succeeded in setting up a tyranny. . . . Dionysius, again, was thought worthy of his tyranny because he denounced Daphnaeus and the rich; his enmity to the nobles won for him the confidence of the people. . . . These are the principal causes of revolutions in democracies.

CHAPTER 6. There are two patent causes of revolutions in oligarchies [one coming from without, the other from within the government]. (1) First, when the oligarchs oppress the people, anybody is good enough to be their champion, especially if he be himself a member of the oligarchy, as Lygdamis was at Naxos, who afterwards came to be tyrant. . . . At Cnidos, again, the oligarchy underwent a great change. For the nobles fell out among themselves, because only a few shared in the government. There existed among them the rule already mentioned, that father and son could not hold office together, and, if there were several brothers, only the eldest was selected. The people took advantage of the quarrel, and choosing one of the nobles to be their leader, attacked and conquered the oligarchs, who were divided. Division is also a source of weakness. . . .

(2) One of the internal causes of revolutions in oligarchies is the personal rivalry of the oligarchs, which leads them to play the demagogue. Now, an oligarchic demagogue is of two sorts. Either (1) he practices on the oligarchs themselves (for, although the oligarchy are quite a small number, there may be a demagogue among them, as at Athens the party of Charicles predominated among the Thirty).[7] Or (2) the oligarch may play the demagogue with the people. . . . Oligarchies change whenever any attempt is made to narrow them, for then those who desire to keep their rights are compelled to call in the people. Changes occur also when the oligarchs waste their private property by extravagant living; for then they want to innovate, and either try to make themselves tyrants, or to install someone else in the tyranny. . . . Sometimes a party among the oligarchs try to create a political change. Sometimes they rob the treasury, and then, either the other oligarchs quarrel with the thieves, as happened at Apollonia in Pontus, or they with the other oligarchs. But an oligarchy which is at unity with itself is not easily destroyed from within. Of this we may see an example at

---

[7] The Thirty at Athens were the infamous group of unscrupulous oligarchs whom Sparta set up to govern the city after the Athenian defeats in the Peloponnesian War.

Pharsalus, for there, although the rulers are few in number, they govern a large city, because they have a good understanding among themselves. . . .

Oligarchy is liable to revolutions alike in war and in peace. In war because, not being able to trust the people, the oligarchs are compelled to hire mercenaries, and the general who is in command of them often ends in becoming a tyrant, as Timophanes did at Corinth. Or if there are more generals than one, they make themselves into a company of tyrants. Sometimes the oligarchs, fearing this danger, give the people a share in the government, because their services are so necessary to them. In time of peace, from mutual distrust, the two parties may hand over the defense of the state to the army or to an arbiter between the factions, who often ends the master of both. . . .

Changes in constitutional governments, and also in those oligarchies which limit the office of counselor, judge, or other magistrate to men having certain money qualification, often occur by accident. The qualification may have been originally fixed, according to conditions at the time, at such a sum as to include in the oligarchy only a few persons, or in the constitutional government just the middle class. But after a time of prosperity, arising from peace or some other good fortune, the same property swells to many times as large, and then everybody participates in every office. This happens sometimes gradually and insensibly, and sometimes quickly. These are the causes of changes and revolutions in oligarchies.

We must remark generally, both of democracies and oligarchies, that they sometimes change, not into the opposite forms of government, but only into another variety of the same class; I mean to say, from those forms of democracy and oligarchy which are regulated by law into those which are arbitrary, and conversely.

CHAPTER 7.   In aristocracies, revolutions are stirred up when only a few share in the honors of the state, a cause which we have already shown affects oligarchies. For an aristocracy is a sort of

oligarchy, and, like an oligarchy, is a government of the few, although the few here are the virtuous and not the wealthy. Hence the two are often confounded. Revolutions will be most likely to happen, and must happen, when the mass of the people are high-spirited, and have a notion that they are as good as their rulers. Thus at Sparta the so-called Partheniae, who were the [illegitimate] sons of the Spartan peers, attempted a revolution, and, being detected, were sent away to colonize Tarentum. Again, revolutions occur when great men who are at least equal to the best in merit are dishonored by those higher in office, as Lysander [8] was by the kings of Sparta; or when a brave man is excluded from the honors of the state; . . . or, again, when some are very poor and others very rich, a state of society which is most often the result of war, as at Sparta in the days of the Messenian War. . . .

Constitutional governments and aristocracies are frequently overthrown for some deviation from justice in the constitution itself. The cause of the downfall in the former is the ill-mingling of the two elements, democracy and oligarchy; in the latter, of the three elements, democracy, oligarchy, and virtue, but especially democracy and oligarchy. For to combine these is the endeavor of constitutional governments; and most so-called aristocracies have a like aim, but differ from commonwealths by the additional requirement of virtue. Hence some of them are more and some less permanent.

Those which incline more toward oligarchy are called aristocracies, and those which incline toward democracy constitutional governments. Therefore the latter are the safer of the two; for the greater the number, the greater the strength, and when men are equal they are contented. But the rich, if the government gives them power, are apt to be insolent and avaricious. In general, whichever way the constitution inclines, in that direction it is apt to change as one party gains more strength. A constitutional government be-

[8] The ambitious Spartan general, Lysander, after winning the victory over Athens and ending the Peloponnesian War, tried in vain to open the kingship at Sparta to citizens outside the two families to whom by tradition the office belonged.

comes a democracy, an aristocracy an oligarchy. But the process may be reversed, and aristocracy may change into democracy. This happens when the poor, under the idea that they are being wronged, force the constitution to take a contrary form. In like manner, constitutional governments change into oligarchies. The only stable principle of government is equality according to proportion, and every man to enjoy his own. . . .

I have already remarked that in all states revolutions are started by trifles. In aristocracies, above all, they are of a gradual and imperceptible nature. The citizens begin by giving up some part of the constitution, and so with greater ease change something else in the government which is a little more important, until they have undermined the whole fabric of the state. At Thurii there was a law that generals could be re-elected only after an interval of five years. Some high-spirited young men who were popular for their military prowess with the soldiers of the guard, despising the magistrates and thinking they would easily gain their purpose, set out to abolish this law, and allow their generals to hold perpetual commands. For they well knew that the people would be glad enough to elect them. Whereupon the magistrates who had charge of these matters, and who are called councilors, at first determined to resist; but afterwards consented, thinking that if only one law was changed, no further inroad would be made on the constitution. But other changes soon followed, which they in vain attempted to oppose. The state passed into the hands of the revolutionists, who established a dynastic oligarchy.

All constitutions are overthrown either from within or from without. The latter happens when some other government, close at hand, is interested in opposing them, or though distant, is powerful. This was exemplified in the old times by the Athenians and the Spartans. The Athenians everywhere put down oligarchies, and the Spartans democracies.

I have now explained the chief causes of revolutions and dissensions in states.

CHAPTER 8. We have next to consider what means there are of preserving states in general, and also particular cases. In the first place, it is evident that if we understand the causes which destroy states, we shall also understand the causes which preserve them; for opposites produce opposites, and destruction is the opposite of preservation.

In all well-organized governments there is nothing which should be more jealously maintained than the spirit of obedience to law, more especially in small matters. For lawlessness creeps in unperceived and at last ruins the state, just as the constant repetition of small expenses in time eats up a fortune. The change does not take place all at once, and therefore is not observed. The mind is deceived, as by the fallacy which says, "if each part is little, then the whole is little." This is true in one way, but not in another; for the whole and the all are not little, although they are made up of littles.

In the first place, men should guard against the beginnings of change, and in the second place they should not rely on the political devices of which I have already spoken, invented only to deceive the people,[9] for they are proved by experience to be useless. Further, we note that oligarchies as well as aristocracies may last not from any inherent stability in such forms of government, but because the rulers are on good terms both with the unenfranchised and with the governing classes, not maltreating those who are excluded from the government, but introducing into it the leading spirits from among the people. They should never wrong the high-spirited in a matter of honor, or the common people in a matter of money; and they should treat one another and their fellow citizens in a spirit of equality.

The equality which the friends of democracy seek to establish for the multitude is not only just but likewise expedient between equals. Hence, if the governing class are numerous, many democratic institutions are useful; as, for example, the restriction of the tenure of office to six months, so that all those who are of equal station may

[9] The reference is to the tricks by which oligarchs get power while posing as the people's friends.

share in them. Indeed, equals or peers, whenever they are numerous, become a kind of democracy, and therefore demagogues are very likely to arise among them, as I have already remarked. A short tenure of office prevents oligarchies and aristocracies from falling into the hands of families. It is not easy for a person to do any great harm when his tenure of office is short, whereas long possession begets tyranny in oligarchies and democracies. For the aspirants to tyranny are either the principal men of the state, who in democracies are demagogues and in oligarchies members of ruling houses, or those who hold great offices and have a long tenure of them.

States are preserved when their enemies are distant, and sometimes also when they are near, for the fear of them makes the government keep the state in hand. Wherefore the ruler who feels some concern for his state should invent terrors and bring distant dangers near, in order that the citizens may be on their guard and, like sentinels in a night-watch, never relax their attention. He should endeavor too by help of the laws to control the contentions and quarrels of the nobles, and to prevent those who have not hitherto taken part in them from being drawn in. No ordinary man can discern the beginning of evil, but only a true statesman. . . .

It is a principle common to democracy, oligarchy, and every other form of government, not to allow the disproportionate increase of any citizen, but to give moderate honor for a long time rather than great honor for a short time. For men are easily spoilt; not everyone can bear prosperity. But if this rule is not observed, at any rate the honors which have been given all at once should be taken away by degrees and not all at once. Especially should the laws provide against anyone having too much power derived from friends or from money; if he has, he and his followers should be sent out of the country. And since innovations creep in through the private behavior of individuals, there ought to be an office that will keep an eye on those whose life is not in harmony with the government, whether it be an oligarchy or a democracy or any other. For a like reason an increase of prosperity in any part of the state should be carefully watched. The

proper remedy for this evil is always to distribute the management of affairs and the offices of state among opposite elements; such opposites are the virtuous and the many, or the rich and the poor. Another way is to combine the poor and the rich in one body, or to increase the middle class. Thus an end will be put to the revolutions which arise from inequality.

But, above all, every state should be so administered and so regulated by law that its magistrates cannot possibly make money. In oligarchies, special precautions should be used against this evil. For the people do not take any great offense at being kept out of the government. Indeed they are rather pleased than otherwise at having leisure for their private business. But what angers them is to think that their rulers are stealing the public money. Then they are doubly enraged, for they are deprived of both honor and profit.

If offices brought no profit, then and then only could democracy and aristocracy be combined; for both nobles and people might have their wishes gratified. All would be able to hold office, which is the aim of democracy, but the nobles would be the magistrates, which is the aim of aristocracy. This result may be accomplished when there is no possibility of making money out of office-holding. For the poor will not want to have them when there is nothing to be gained from them. They would rather be attending to their own concerns. And the rich, who do not want money from the public treasury, will be able to take them. So the poor will keep to their work and grow rich, and the nobles will not be governed by the lower class. In order to prevent stealing of the public money, any transfer of the revenues should be made at a general assembly of citizens, and duplicates of the accounts deposited with the different brotherhoods, companies, and tribes. And honors should be given by law to magistrates who have the reputation of being incorruptible.

In democracies, the rich should be spared. Not only should their property not be divided, but their incomes, which in some states are taken from them imperceptibly, should be protected. It is a good thing too to prevent wealthy citizens, even when they are willing,

from undertaking expensive and useless public services, such as the giving of choruses, torch-races, and the like. In an oligarchy, on the other hand, great care should be taken of the poor, and lucrative offices should go to them. If one of the wealthy classes insults them, he should be punished more severely than if he had injured one of his own class. Provision should be made also that estates pass by inheritance and not by gift, and that no person should have more than one inheritance; for in this way properties will be equalized, and more of the poor rise to competency. It is also expedient, both in a democracy and in an oligarchy, to assign to those who have less share in the government (to the rich, that is, in a democracy and to the poor in an oligarchy) an equal share or a preference in all save the principal offices of state. The last should be entrusted chiefly or only to members of the governing class.

CHAPTER 9. Three qualifications are required of those who are to fill the highest offices: (1) first of all, loyalty to the established constitution; (2) great administrative capacity; (3) virtue and justice of the kind proper to the particular form of government. For, if what is just is not the same in all governments, the quality of justice must also differ. There may be a question, however, when all these qualities do not meet in the same person, how the selection is to be made. Suppose, for example, an able general is a bad man and not a friend to the constitution, and another man is loyal and just, which should we choose? In making the selection ought we not to consider two points—what qualities are common, and what are rare? Thus, in choosing a general, we should regard his skill rather than his virtue; for few have military skill, but many have virtue. In filling any office of trust or stewardship, on the other hand, the opposite rule should be observed; for more virtue than ordinary is required in the holder of such an office, but the knowledge needed is of a sort all men possess.

It may, however, be asked what a man wants with virtue, if he have political ability and is loyal, since these two qualities alone will

make him do what is right for the public interest. But may not men have both of them and yet be deficient in self-control? If, though they know and love their own interests, they do not always attend to them, may they not be equally negligent of the interests of the public?

Speaking generally, we may say that whatever laws are for the interest of states preserve the states. And the great preserving principle is the one we have repeatedly mentioned—to take care that loyal citizens outnumber the disloyal. Neither should we forget the middle course, which in these days is lost sight of under perverted forms of government. For many practices which are thought to be democratic are the ruin of democracies, and many which are thought to be oligarchic are the ruin of oligarchies. Those who think that all virtue is to be found in their own party principles push matters to extremes. They do not consider that disproportion destroys a state. A nose which varies somewhat from the ideal straightness to a hook or a snub may still be of good shape and agreeable to the eye. But if the variation be very great, all symmetry is lost, and the nose at last ceases to be a nose at all on account of its excessive size in one direction or defect in another. This is true of every other part of the human body. The same law of proportion holds equally in states. Oligarchy or democracy, although a departure from the most perfect form,[10] may yet be a good enough government; but if anyone attempts to push the principles of either to an extreme, he will begin by spoiling the government and end by having none at all. . . .

But of all the things I have mentioned that which most contributes to the permanence of constitutions is the adaptation of education to the form of government, and yet in our own day this principle is universally neglected. The best laws, though sanctioned by every citizen of the state, will be of no avail unless the young are trained by habit and education in the spirit of the constitution, if it is demo-

[10] The most perfect forms were listed far back as monarchy, aristocracy, and constitutional government. Aristotle has been showing how near the imperfect forms may actually be brought to the perfect.

cratic, democratically, or if it is oligarchic, oligarchically. For there may be a want of self-discipline in states as well as in individuals. Now, to have been educated in the spirit of the constitution is not to conduct oneself in any way oligarchs or democrats find agreeable, but in a way to make the existence of an oligarchy or of a democracy possible. Whereas, among ourselves, the sons of the ruling class in an oligarchy live in luxury, while the sons of the poor are hardened by exercise and toil and hence are both more inclined and better able to make a revolution.

In democracies of the more extreme type there has arisen a false idea of freedom which is contradictory to the true interests of the state. For two principles are characteristic of democracy, government by the majority and freedom. Men think that what is equal is just, and that equality is the supremacy of the popular will, and that freedom means doing what a man likes. In such democracies everyone lives as he pleases, or in the words of Euripides, "according to his fancy." But this is all wrong; men should not think it slavery to live by the rules of the constitution, for it is their salvation. I have now discussed generally the causes of the revolutions and destruction of states, and the means of their preservation and continuance.

CHAPTER 10. I have still to speak of monarchy and the causes of its destruction and preservation. What I have said already of other forms of government applies almost equally to royal and to tyrannical rule. For royal rule is in nature like an aristocracy, and a tyranny is a compound of oligarchy and democracy in their most extreme forms. It is therefore most injurious to its subjects, being made up of two wrong forms of government, and having the perversions and errors of both. These two forms of monarchy differ even in their origins. The appointment of a king is a device of the better classes against the people. He is elected by them out of their own number, because either he himself or his family excel in virtue and virtuous actions. Whereas a tyrant is chosen from the people to be their protector against the nobles, and to keep them from being injured.

History shows that almost all tyrants have been demagogues who gained the favor of the people by their accusation of the nobles. At any rate, this was the way in which tyrannies arose in the days when cities had increased in power. Others that were older originated in the ambition of kings wanting to overstep the limits of their hereditary power and become despots. Others again grew out of the class which were chosen to be chief magistrates; for in ancient times the people who elected them gave their magistrates, both civil and religious, a long tenure. Others arose out of the custom which oligarchies had of making some individual supreme over the highest offices. In any of these ways an ambitious man had no difficulty in creating a tyranny, if he desired, since he had the power in his hands already, either as a king or as one of the officers of state. . . .

But, as I was saying, royalty ranks with aristocracy; for it is based on the merit, of either the individual or his family, or on the benefits conferred by him, or on all these claims with power added besides. For all who have obtained kingly honor have benefited or had in their power to benefit their states and nations. Some, like Codrus,[11] have prevented their state from being enslaved in war. Others, like Cyrus,[12] have given their country freedom, or have settled or gained a territory, like the Spartan, Macedonian, and Molossian [13] kings. The idea of a king is to be a protector of the rich against unjust treatment, and of the people against insult and oppression. Whereas a tyrant, as has often been repeated, has no regard to any public interest, but only to his private ends. His aim is pleasure and the aim of a king, honor. So in their desires too they differ; the tyrant is desirous of riches, the king of what brings honor. And the guards of a king are citizens, but of a tyrant, mercenaries.

That tyranny has all the vices of both democracy and oligarchy is evident. As in an oligarchy so in a tyranny, the end is wealth; for

[11] Codrus, a legendary king of Athens, was said to have saved his country from being conquered by the sacrifice of his own life.

[12] Cyrus the Great delivered Persia from the Medes.

[13] The Molossians lived in the mountainous country of northwestern Greece.

only by wealth can a tyrant maintain either his guard or his luxury. Both oligarch and tyrant mistrust the people, and therefore deprive them of their arms. Both agree too in injuring the people and driving them out of the city and dispersing them. But from democracy tyrants have borrowed the art of making war on the nobles and destroying them secretly or openly, or exiling them, because they are rivals and stand in the way of their power; also, because plots against them are contrived by men of this class, who want either to rule or to escape subjection. Hence Periander advised Thrasybulus [14] to cut off the tops of the tallest ears of corn, meaning that he must always put out of the way the citizens who overtopped the rest. And as I have already intimated, the beginnings of change are the same in monarchies as in other forms of government. Subjects attack their sovereigns out of fear or contempt or because they have been unjustly treated by them. Of injustice, the most common form is insult, another is confiscation of property.

The ends sought by conspirators against monarchies, whether tyrannies or royalties, are the same as the ends sought by conspirators against other forms of government. Monarchs have great wealth and honor, which are objects of desire to all mankind. The attacks are made sometimes against their lives, sometimes against the office; where a sense of insult is the motive, against their lives. Any sort of insult (and there are many) may stir up anger, and when men are angry, they commonly act out of revenge, and not from ambition.

For example, the attack on the sons of Pisistratus [15] arose out of the public dishonor offered to the sister of Harmodius and the insult to himself. He attacked the tyrant for his sister's sake, and Aristogeiton joined in the attack for Harmodius' sake. . . . Many, too, infuriated by blows inflicted on their persons, which they deemed

[14] See note on the same story, told earlier, Book III, p 310, n. 15.
[15] The two sons of Pisistratus, tyrants at Athens, were killed in 510 B.C. by the two friends, Harmodius and Aristogeiton.

an insult, have either killed or attempted to kill the officers of state
or royal princes by whom they have been injured. . . .

Fear is another motive which has caused conspiracies both in
monarchies and in more popular forms of government. Thus Artapanes conspired against Xerxes and slew him, fearing that he would
be accused of hanging Darius without orders, for he thought that
Xerxes would forget what he had said in the middle of a meal, and
would forgive Darius' offense.[16]

Another motive is contempt, as in the case of Sardanapalus [17]
whom someone saw carding wool with his women, if the storytellers
say truly. The tale may be true, if not of him, of someone else. Dion
attacked the younger Dionysius [18] because he despised him, and saw
that he was equally despised by his own subjects and was always
drunk. Even the friends of a tyrant will sometimes attack him out
of contempt; for the confidence which he reposes in them breeds
contempt, and they think they will not be found out. The expectation of success is likewise a sort of contempt. The assailants are
ready to strike and think nothing of the danger, because they seem
to have the power in their hands. Thus generals of armies attack
monarchs; as, for example, Cyrus [19] attacked Astyages, despising the
effeminacy of his life, and believing that his power was worn out.
. . . Bold natures, placed by their sovereigns in a high military
position, are most likely to make the attempt in the expectation of
success; for courage is emboldened by power, and the union of the
two inspires them with the hope of an easy victory.

Attempts for motives of ambition are made in a different way.
There are men who will not risk their lives for riches and rewards
however great, but who regard the simple killing of a tyrant as an

---

[16] The meaning of this obscure sentence seems to be that Artapanes had hanged
Darius, son of Xerxes, king of Persia, for conspiring against his father, but was
afraid afterward that Xerxes would forget having told him to do so at dinner and
would forgive Darius' offense.

[17] On Sardanapalus, see *Ethics*, p. 89, n. 2.

[18] Son of the great Dionysius, tyrant of Syracuse in Sicily.

[19] Cyrus, founder of the Persian empire, to whom reference has already been made,
p. 366. As a young general, he attacked and slew his master, Astyages.

extraordinary action which will make them famous and honorable in the world; they wish to acquire, not a kingdom, but a name. It is rare, however, to find such men; he who would kill a tyrant must be prepared to lose his life if he fail. He must have the resolution of Dion, who, when he made war on Dionysius, took with him very few troops, saying that whatever measure of success he might attain would be enough for him, even if he were to die the moment he landed; such a death would be welcome to him. But this is a temper to which few can attain.

Tyrannies, like all other governments, are destroyed from without by some opposed and more powerful form of government. That such a government will have the will to attack them is clear when the two are opposed in principle, and everyone, if he can, does what he wills. Democracy is antagonistic to tyranny, on the principle of Hesiod, "potter hates potter," [20] because they are nearly akin. For the extreme form of democracy is tyranny. Royalty and aristocracy, on the other hand, are both alike opposed to tyranny because they are constitutions of a different type. And therefore the Spartans put down most of the tyrannies, and so did the Syracusans during the time when they were well governed. Tyrannies are destroyed also from within, when the reigning family are divided among themselves. . . . In the case of Dionysius, Dion, his own relative, attacked and expelled him with the assistance of the people. He afterward perished himself.

The two chief motives which induce men to attack tyrannies are hatred and contempt. Hatred of tyrants is inevitable, and contempt also is a frequent cause of their destruction. Thus we see that most tyrants who have won their power themselves, kept it, but those who inherited it lost it almost at once; for living in luxurious ease, they became contemptible, and offered many opportunities to their assailants. Anger, too, must be included under hatred and produces the same effects. It is oftentimes even more ready to strike. The

[20] *Works and Days*, 25.

angry are more impetuous in starting an attack, for they do not listen to reason. And men are very apt to give way to their passions when they are insulted. To this cause is to be attributed the fall of the sons of Pisistratus and many others. Hatred is more reasonable, but anger is accompanied by pain, which is an impediment to reason; whereas hatred is painless.

In a word, all the causes I mentioned as destroying the last and most unmixed form of oligarchy and the extreme form of democracy may be assumed to threaten tyranny. Indeed the extreme forms of them both are only tyrannies distributed among several persons. Kingly rule, however, is little affected by external causes, and is, therefore, lasting; it is generally destroyed from within. There are two ways in which its destruction may come about: (1) when the members of the royal family quarrel among themselves, and (2) when the kings attempt to administer the state too much after the fashion of a tyranny, and to extend their authority contrary to law. But there are no royalties in these days; one-man rulerships, where they exist, are tyrannies. For the rule of a king is over voluntary subjects, and he is supreme in all important matters, but in our own day men are more on an equality, and no one is so immeasurably superior to the others as to represent adequately the greatness and dignity of the office. Hence mankind will not, if they can help it, endure it, and anyone who obtains power by force or fraud is at once recognized as a tyrant.

In hereditary monarchies a further cause of destruction is the fact that kings too often fall into contempt and, although they possess no tyrannical but only royal power, are apt to outrage others. Their overthrow is then readily effected; for there is an end to a king when his subjects do not want to have him. A tyrant holds on, whether they like him or not. To these and the like causes the destruction of monarchies is to be attributed.

CHAPTER 11. They are preserved, to speak generally, by the opposite causes. Or, to consider them separately, royalty is preserved

by limitation of its powers. The more restricted the functions of kings, the longer their power will last unimpaired; for then they are more moderate and not so despotic in their ways, and are less envied by their subjects. This is why the kingly office has lasted so long among the Molossians. For a similar reason it has continued among the Spartans because there it was always divided between two men, and later was further limited by Theopompus [21] in various ways, particularly by the establishment of the Ephoralty. By diminishing the power of the king, he established on a more lasting basis the kingly office, which was thus made in a sense not less but greater. There is a story that when his wife once asked him whether he was not ashamed to leave to his sons a royal power which was less than he had inherited from his father, "No, indeed," he replied, "for the power I leave to them will be more lasting."

As to tyrannies, they are preserved in two altogether contrary ways. One of them is the old traditional method by which most tyrants administer their government. Of such arts Periander of Corinth is said to have been the great master, and many similar devices may be gathered from the Persians in their administration of government. There are also the rules already mentioned for the preservation of a tyranny, as far as possible, such as that the tyrant should lop off those who are too high, put to death men of spirit, allow no common meals, clubs, or education, or the like, be on his guard against anything likely to inspire either courage or confidence among his subjects, prohibit literary assemblies or other meetings for discussion, and take every means to prevent his people from knowing one another, for acquaintance begets mutual confidence. Further, he must compel the inhabitants of his city to appear in public and live at his gates; then he will know what they are doing. If they are always kept under, they will learn to be humble. In short, he should practice

---

[21] Theopompus was by tradition a Spartan king of the eighth century B.C. Aristotle here makes him the author of the institution of the Ephors, a board of elected overseers of the government, who were the real rulers of the state. But earlier he has spoken of Lycurgus as the founder of the Spartan constitution. Book II, p. 284.

these and the like Persian and barbaric arts, which all have the same object.

A tyrant should also endeavor to know what each of his subjects says or does, and should employ spies, like the female detectives at Syracuse and the eavesdroppers whom Hiero was in the habit of sending to any place of resort or meeting. For the fear of informers prevents people from speaking their minds, and, when they do, they are easily found out. Another art of the tyrant is to sow quarrels among the citizens; friends should be embroiled with friends, the people with the nobles, and the rich with one another. Also he should impoverish his subjects; he thus provides money for the support of his guards, and the people, having to keep hard at work, are prevented from conspiring. The Pyramids of Egypt afford an excellent example of this policy; also the offerings of the family of Cypselus [22] and the building of the temple of Olympian Zeus by the sons of Pisistratus; all these works were alike intended to occupy the people and keep them poor. Another practice of tyrants is to multiply taxes, after the manner of Dionysius at Syracuse, who contrived that within five years his subjects should bring into the treasury their whole property. The tyrant is also fond of making war in order that his subjects may have something to do and be always needing a leader. And whereas the power of a king is preserved by his friends, a characteristic of a tyrant is to distrust his friends because he knows that all men want to overthrow him, and they above all have the power.

Again, the evil practices of the last and worst form of democracy are all found in tyrannies. Such are the power given to women in their families in the hope that they will inform against their husbands, and the license allowed to slaves in order that they may betray their masters. For slaves and women do not conspire against tyrants; they are indeed friendly to tyrannies and also to democracies, since under them they have a good time. . . .

[22] A tyrant of Corinth.

Hence tyrants are always fond of bad men, because they love to be flattered, but no man having the spirit of a freeman in him will degrade himself by flattery. Good men love others, but do not flatter anybody. Moreover, bad men are useful for bad purposes. "Nail knocks out nail," as the proverb says. It is characteristic of a tyrant to dislike everyone who has dignity or independence. He wants to be alone in his glory, and anyone who claims a like dignity or asserts his independence encroaches on his prerogative, and is hated by him as an enemy to his power. Another mark of a tyrant is that he likes foreigners better than citizens, and lives with them and invites them to his table; for the citizens are enemies, but the foreigners enter into no rivalry with him. Such are the marks of a tyrant and the arts by which he preserves his power. There is no wickedness too great for him.

All that we have said may be summed up under three heads, which show the three aims of the tyrant. These are (1) the humiliation of his subjects, for he knows that a mean-spirited man will not conspire against anybody, (2) the creation of mutual mistrust among them, for a tyrant is not overthrown until men begin to have confidence in one another. This is why tyrants make war on the good; they have the idea that their power is endangered by them, not only because they will not be ruled despotically, but also because they are loyal to one another and to other men, and do not inform against one another or against other men. (3) The tyrant desires to keep his subjects incapable of action, for no one attempts what is impossible, and they will not attempt to overthrow his tyranny, if they are powerless. Under these three heads the whole policy of a tyrant may be summed up, and to one or the other of them all his ideas may be referred. (1) He sows distrust among his subjects; (2) he takes away their power; (3) he humbles them.

Such then is one of the two methods by which tyrannies are preserved. But there is another which proceeds on quite a different principle of action. The nature of this latter method may be gathered from a comparison of it with one way to destroy a kingdom. For one

mode of destroying kingly power is to make the office of king more tyrannical, and so the salvation of a tyranny is to make it more like the rule of a king. But of one thing the tyrant must be careful; he must keep power enough to control his subjects, whether they like him or not, for if he once gives this up he gives up his tyranny. But though the tyrant must retain his power as the foundation, in all else he should act or appear to act in the character of a king. In the first place, he should pretend a care of the public revenues, and not waste money in making presents of a sort at which the common people get excited, as when they see their scanty earnings taken from them and lavished on courtesans and foreigners and artists. He should give an account of what he receives and of what he spends (a practice which has been adopted by some tyrants); for then he will seem to be a steward of the public rather than a tyrant. Nor need he fear that, while he is lord of the city, he will ever be in want of money. Such a policy is certainly much more advantageous for the tyrant when he goes from home than to leave a great hoard behind him; for then the garrison who remain in the city will be less likely to attack his power. And a tyrant, when he is away from home, has more reason to fear the guardians of his treasure than the citizens, for the one accompany him, but the others remain behind.

In the second place, he should appear to collect taxes and to require public services for state purposes only, and to form a fund in case of war; and he ought to make himself the guardian and treasurer of that, as if it belonged, not to him, but to the public. He should appear not harsh but dignified, and when men meet him they should look upon him with respect but not with fear.

Yet it is hard for him to be respected if he inspires no respect, and therefore, whatever virtues he may neglect, at least he should maintain the character of an able soldier, and produce the impression that he is one.[23] Neither he nor any of his associates should ever be guilty

[23] It is interesting to compare this passage with the fifteenth and succeeding chapters of Machiavelli's *Prince*, in which the would-be tyrant is told how to use the appearance of virtue to build up his power. Machiavelli knew his Aristotle.

of the least offense against modesty towards the young of either sex
who are his subjects, and the women of his family should observe
a like self-control towards other women. The insolence of women
has ruined many tyrannies. In the indulgence of pleasures he should
be the opposite of our modern tyrants, who not only begin at day-
break and pass whole days in sensuality, but want other men to see
them, that they may admire their happy and blessed lot. In these
things a tyrant should be especially moderate, or at any rate should
not parade his vices to the world; for a drunken and drowsy tyrant
is soon despised and attacked. Not so one who is temperate and
wide awake.

His conduct then should be the very reverse of nearly everything
we have said before about tyrants. He ought to adorn and improve
his city, as though he were not a tyrant but a guardian of the state.
Also he should appear to be particularly earnest in the service of the
gods; for if men think a ruler is religious and has a reverence for
the gods, they are less afraid of suffering injustice at his hands, and
are less disposed to conspire against him, because they believe him
to have the very gods fighting on his side. At the same time his
religion must not be thought foolish. He should honor men of merit,
and make them believe they would be held in no more honor by
the citizens if they had a free government. Honors he should distribute himself, but punishments should be inflicted by officers and
courts of law. A precaution taken by all monarchs is not to make one
person great; but if one is promoted, then two or three should be
also, that they may look sharply after one another. If, after all, someone has to be made great, he should not be a man of bold spirit;
for such dispositions are ever most inclined to strike. And if anyone
is to be deprived of power, let it be diminished gradually, not taken
from him all at once.

The tyrant should abstain from all outrage; in particular from
personal violence and wanton conduct toward the young. He should
be especially careful of his behavior to men who are lovers of honor;
for as lovers of money are offended when their property is touched.

so are lovers of honor and good men when their honor is affected. Therefore a tyrant ought either not to use violence at all, or should seem to be employing only fatherly correction, and not trampling on others. His acquaintance with youth should be supposed to arise from affection, and not from the insolence of power. In general he should compensate any appearance of dishonor by an increase of honor.

Men who attempt his assassination are most dangerous, and require to be most carefully watched when they do not care to survive, if they achieve their purpose. Therefore special precaution should be taken against any who think that either they or their friends have been insulted. For when men are driven by their passion to assault others, they are regardless of themselves. As Heraclitus says, "It is difficult to fight against anger; for a man will buy revenge with his life." [24]

Since states are composed of two classes, poor men and rich, the tyrant should lead both to imagine that by his rule they are preserved and prevented from harming one another. Whichever of the two is stronger he should attach to his government; for, with this advantage, he has no need either to emancipate the slaves or to disarm the citizens. Either party, added to the force he already has, will make him stronger than his assailants.

But enough of these details. It is obvious what should be the tyrant's general policy. He ought to show himself to his subjects in the light, not of a tyrant, but of their steward and their king. He should not seize what is theirs, but should be their guardian. He should be moderate, not extravagant in his own way of life, a companion of the nobles and the hero of the multitude. For then his rule will of necessity be nobler and happier, because he will rule over better men, whose spirits are not crushed, over men to whom he himself is not an object of hatred, and of whom he is not afraid. His

[24] One of the fragmentary quotations we have from the works of the poet-philosopher, Heraclitus, of the sixth century B.C.

power too will be more lasting. His behavior will be virtuous, or at least half virtuous, and he will not be wicked, but only half wicked.

CHAPTER 12.   Yet no forms of government are so short-lived as oligarchy and tyranny. The tyranny which lasted longest was that of Orthagoras and his sons at Sicyon.[25] That continued for a hundred years. The reason was that they treated their subjects with moderation, to a great extent observed the laws, and in various ways gained the favor of the people by the care which they took of them. Cleisthenes, in particular, was respected for his military ability. If report may be believed, he crowned the judge who decided against him in the games. Some say the sitting statue in the market place of Sicyon is a likeness of him. . . . But in fact, tyrannies generally have been of quite short duration.

I have now gone through all the causes by which constitutional governments and monarchies are either destroyed or preserved. . . .

[There follows a criticism of Plato's account of the causes and invariable course of revolutions in states as given in the Republic, VIII, Classics Club edition, pp. 432-3, 437-8, 443-5, 451-6. Aristotle argues that Plato over-simplifies the process, that there are many more causes of revolution than he mentions and that they follow no invariable rule of passage from one form of government to another, for instance, a democracy may change into an oligarchy instead of into a tyranny, etc.]

[25] Orthagoras and his descendants, one of whom was the Cleisthenes mentioned below, were tyrants of Sicyon, in the Peloponnesus during the sixth century, B.C.

BOOK VI

Further study of characteristics of democracies and oli-garchies and how best to organize and preserve them.

CHAPTER I. . . . I have shown now what forms of democracy are suited to particular cities, and what forms of oligarchy to particular peoples, and to whom each of the other forms of government is suited. Continuing, we must show which of these governments is best for each state, and also briefly proceed to consider how these and other forms of government are to be established.[1]

First of all, let us speak of democracy, since that will also shed light on the opposite form of government, commonly called oligarchy. For the purposes of this inquiry we must enumerate all the elements and characteristics of democracy, since from various combinations of these the varieties of democratic government arise. There are several of these, differing from each other, and the difference is due to two causes. One has been already mentioned, namely, differences in population. The popular element may consist of farmers or craftsmen or laborers; and if the first of these be added to the second, or the third to the two others, not only does the democracy become better or worse, but its very nature changes. A second cause is yet to be mentioned. Differences in combination of the various properties and characteristics of democracy make a difference in the democracy. One democracy will have few and another will have more, and another will have all of these characteristics. There is an advantage in knowing them all, whether a man wishes to establish some new form of democracy, or only to remodel an

---

[1] Book VI is in great part a discussion of the same topics that have been already treated in Books IV and V. It differs chiefly in detail and, occasionally, in point of view. An ancient editor evidently joined on here something originally separate.

existing one. The founders of states try to bring together all the elements which accord with the ideas of their particular constitutions. This, however, is a mistake of theirs, as I have already remarked when speaking of the destruction and preservation of states.[2] But we will now set forth the principles, characteristics, and aims of such a state.

CHAPTER 2.   The basis of a democratic state is liberty, which, according to the common opinion of men, can be enjoyed only in such a state. This they affirm to be the great end of every democracy.[3] One principle of liberty is for all to rule and be ruled in turn, and indeed democratic justice is the application of numerical not proportionate equality. Whence it follows that the majority must be supreme, and that whatever the majority approves must be the end and just. Every citizen, it is said, must have equality; and therefore in a democracy the poor have more power than the rich, because there are more of them, and the will of the majority is supreme. This, then, is one sign of liberty which all democrats affirm to be a principle of their state. Another is that a man should live as he likes. This, they say, is the privilege of a freeman. On the other hand, not to live as a man likes is the mark of a slave. This is a second characteristic of democracy, whence has arisen the claim of men to be ruled by none, or, this being impossible, to rule and be ruled in turn. It adds to the freedom based on equality [which was the first characteristic].

Such being our foundation and such the principles of democracy, its characteristics are as follows. Officers should be elected by all out of all. All should rule over each, and each in his turn over all. Appointments to all offices, or to all but those which require experience and skill, should be made by lot. No property qualification should

[2] See Book V, pp. 364-365.
[3] Plato has a lively, ironical description of the liberty to be found in a democracy. See the *Republic,* Book VIII. Classics Club edition, pp. 445-446.

be required for office, or only a very low one. No man should hold the same office twice, or often, except in the case of military offices. The tenure of all offices, or of as many as possible, should be brief. All men should sit in judgment, or judges selected out of all should judge all cases, or most, or the greatest and most important—such as the examination of accounts, cases involving the constitution, and private contracts. The assembly should be supreme over all matters, or at any rate over the most important, and the magistrates over none or only over a very few. Of all governing institutions, a council is the most democratic when there is not the means to pay all the citizens, but when they are paid even this is robbed of its power; for then the people take over cases themselves, as I said in the previous discussion.[4]

The next characteristic of democracy is payment for services; assembly, law courts, magistrates, everybody receives pay, when it is to be had. When it is not to be had for all, then it is given to the law courts and to the stated people's assemblies, to the council, and to the magistrates, or at least to those who are compelled to take their meals together.[5] And whereas oligarchy is characterized by birth, wealth, and education, the marks of democracy appear to be the opposite of these—low birth, poverty, mean employment. Another mark is that no office is for life; but if any such have survived the changes in the ancient constitution, it should be stripped of its power, and the holders should be elected by lot and no longer by vote. Such points are common to all democracies; for democracy and popular power in their truest form are based upon the recognized principle of democratic justice, that all should count equally. Equality implies that the rich should have no more share in the government than the poor, and should not be the only rulers, but that all should rule equally according to their numbers. In this way men think that they will secure equality and freedom in their state. . . .

---

[4] See Book IV, p. 345.
[5] That is, the chief magistrates in the state.

CHAPTER 4. Of the four kinds of democracy we listed earlier in our discussion, the best is that which came first in order.[6] It is also the oldest of them all. I shall speak of them also as naturally classified by their inhabitants. For the best material of democracy is an agricultural population. There is no difficulty in forming one where the mass of the people live by agriculture or the tending of cattle. Being poor, they have no leisure, and therefore do not often attend the assembly, and not having the necessaries of life, they are always at work and do not covet the property of others. Indeed, they find their employment pleasanter than the cares of government or office, where no great gains can be made, for the many are more desirous of gain than of honor. A proof is that even the ancient tyrannies were patiently endured by them, even as they still endure oligarchies, if they are allowed to work and not deprived of their property. Some of them grow rich quickly and the others are well enough off. Yet they have the power of electing magistrates and calling them to account; their ambition, if they have any, is thus satisfied. In some democracies, they do not all share in appointment to offices, except through representatives elected in turn out of the whole people, as at Mantinea. Still, if they have the right to deliberate, the many are contented. Even this form of government may be regarded as a democracy, and was such at Mantinea.

Hence, in such a democracy, it is both expedient and customary that all should elect to offices, and conduct scrutinies of accounts, and sit in the law courts, but that the great offices should be filled by election from persons having a property qualification, the greater offices requiring a higher qualification. Or, if there be no offices for which a qualification is required, then those who are marked out by special ability should be appointed. Under such a form of government the citizens are sure to be governed well, for the offices will always be held by the best persons. The people are willing enough to elect them and are not jealous of the good. The good and the notables

[6] See Book IV, p. 326.

will then be satisfied, for they will not be governed by men who are their inferiors, and the persons elected will rule justly, because the rest will call them to account. Every man should be responsible to the others, nor should anyone be allowed to do just as he pleases; for where absolute freedom is allowed there is nothing to restrain the evil inherent in every man. But the principle of responsibility secures what is the greatest good in states; the right persons rule and are prevented from doing wrong, and the people have their due. Evidently this is the best kind of democracy, and why? Because the people are drawn from that particular class. The ancient laws of many states aimed at making the people farmers and were excellent. They provided either that no one should possess more than a certain quantity of land, or that, if he did, the land should not be within a certain distance from the town or the acropolis. Formerly in many states there was a law forbidding anyone to sell his original allotment of land. . . .

Next best to an agricultural people and in many respects similar, are a pastoral people, who live by their flocks. They are the best trained of any for war, robust in body and able to camp out. The people of whom other democracies consist are far inferior to these country people for their life is inferior. There is no room for moral excellence in any of their employments, whether they be craftsmen, traders, or laborers. Besides, people of this class can readily come to the assembly, because they are continually moving about in the city and the market; whereas the farmers are scattered over the country and do not meet or equally feel the need of meeting together. Where the territory of the state extends far beyond the city, there is no difficulty in making an excellent democracy or constitutional government; for the people have to settle in the country. Even if there is a town population, the assembly of a democracy ought not to meet when the country people cannot come. We have thus explained how the first and best form of democracy should be constituted. It is clear that the other or inferior sorts will deviate in a regular order, and

the population which is included will at each stage be of a lower kind.

The last form of democracy, that in which all share alike, is one which cannot be borne by all states, and will not last long unless well-regulated by laws and customs. The more general causes which tend to destroy this or other kinds of government have been already considered. In order to constitute such a democracy and strengthen the people, its leaders have the habit of including as many as they can, and making citizens not only of those who are legitimate, but even of the illegitimate, and of those who have only one parent a citizen, whether father or mother; for everything comes natural to such a democracy. In this way the demagogues proceed. Whereas the right thing would be to make no more additions to the common class of citizens, when the number of them exceeds that of the nobles or of the middle class—beyond this not to go. When they go beyond this point, the state becomes disorderly, and the nobles grow excited and impatient of the democracy, as in the insurrection at Cyrene. For no notice is taken of a little evil, but when it increases too much it strikes the eye. . . . However, such a government will have many supporters, for most persons would rather live in a disorderly than in a sober manner.

CHAPTER 5. The mere establishment of a democracy is not the sole or the principal business of the lawgiver, or of those who wish to create such a state; for any state, however badly constituted, may last one, two or three days. A far greater task is the preservation of it. The lawgiver should therefore endeavor to lay a firm foundation according to the principles already described of the preservation and destruction of states. He should guard against the destructive elements, and make laws, written or unwritten, that will contain all the measures preservative of states. He must not think that the truly democratic or oligarchic measure is whatever will give the greatest amount of democracy or oligarchy, but what will make them last longest. . . .

Now, in the last and worst form of democracy the citizens are very numerous, and can hardly be made to assemble unless they are paid; and to pay them when there are no revenues presses hardly upon the upper class, for the money must be obtained by property taxes and confiscations and corrupt practices of the courts, things which have before now overthrown many democracies. So wherever, I say, there are no revenues, the government should hold few assemblies, and the law courts should consist of many persons, but sit for a few days only. This system has two advantages. First, the rich do not fear the expense, even though they are unpaid themselves when the poor are paid. Secondly, cases are better tried, for wealthy persons, although they do not like to be long absent from their own affairs, do not mind going for a few days to the law courts. Where there are revenues, the demagogues should not be allowed after their fashion to distribute the surplus. The poor are always receiving and always wanting more and more, for such help is like water poured into a leaky cask. Yet a true friend of the people should see that they be not too poor, for extreme poverty lowers the character of the democracy. Measures should also be taken to give them lasting prosperity. Since this is equally to the interest of all classes, the proceeds of public revenues should be accumulated and distributed among the poor, if possible, in such quantities as may enable them to purchase a little farm, or, at any rate, make a beginning in trade or agriculture. And if this benevolence cannot be extended to all, money should be distributed in turn by tribes or other divisions. Meantime the rich should pay the fees for the attendance of the poor at the necessary assemblies, and should in return be excused from useless public services.

By administering the state in this spirit, the Carthaginians retain the affections of their people. Their policy is from time to time to send some of them into their dependent towns, where they grow rich. It is worthy too of a generous and sensible nobility to divide the poor amongst them, and give them the means of going to work. The example of the people of Tarentum also is well deserving of imita-

tion; for, by sharing the use of their property with the poor, they gain their good will. . . .

CHAPTER 6.   Enough has been said of the manner in which democracies ought to be constituted.

From these considerations there will be no difficulty in seeing what should be the constitution of the oligarchies. We have only to reason from opposites and compare each form of oligarchy with the corresponding form of democracy.

The first and best organized oligarchy is akin to a constitutional government. In this there should be two standards of property qualification, one high, the other low—the lower qualifying for the humbler yet indispensable offices and the higher for the superior ones. Whoever acquires the prescribed qualification should have the rights of citizenship. The nature of those admitted should be such as to make the entire governing body stronger than those who are excluded, and all new citizens should be taken out of the better class of people. The same principle, narrowed a little, gives another form of oligarchy. Going on so, at length we reach the most cliquish and tyrannical of them all, answering to the extreme democracy, which, being the worst, requires vigilance proportionate to its badness. For as healthy bodies and ships well provided with sailors may undergo many mishaps and survive them, but sickly constitutions and rotten, ill-manned ships are ruined by the very least mistake, so the worst forms of government require the greatest care. The populousness of democracies generally preserves them, for number in a democracy takes the place of justice based on proportion. But the preservation of an oligarchy clearly depends on an opposite principle, namely, its good order. . . .

CHAPTER 8.   . . . The necessary offices in a state may be summed up as follows: offices concerned with religion, with war, with revenue and expenditure, with the market, with the city, with

the harbors, with the country; also with the courts of law, with records of contracts, with execution of sentences, with custody of prisoners, with audits and scrutinies and accounts of magistrates; lastly, those which preside over the public deliberations of the state. There are likewise offices characteristic of such states as are peaceful and prosperous and at the same time have a regard to good order: such as the offices of the guardians of women, guardians of the laws, guardians of children, and directors of gymnastics; also superintendents of gymnastic and Dionysiac contests,[7] and of other similar spectacles. Some of these are clearly not democratic offices; for example, the guardianships of women and children. The poor, who have no slaves, must employ both their women and children as servants. . . .

BOOK VII

The ideal aim of men as individuals and as associated in states. The life of virtue as including both thought and action. Neither war nor political power the highest good. How to build and organize an ideal city. Education of children for citizenship.

CHAPTER I. He who would duly inquire about the best form of a state ought first to decide which is the most desirable life.[1] While this remains uncertain, the best form of a state must also be uncertain; for, in the natural order of things, those may be expected to lead the best life who have the best form of government that their circumstances allow. We ought therefore to ascertain, first of all,

[7] The festival of Dionysius was the occasion for great competitions in athletics, chariot racing, production of new plays, musicianship, etc.

[1] Books VII and VIII, on the building and organization of an ideal city, are quite different in style from those that precede them and mingle new ideas with others that have already been stated. some more than once.

which is the most generally desirable life, and then whether the same life is or is not best for a state and for individuals.

Assuming that enough has been already said about the best life in popular discussions, we will now only repeat the statements contained in them. Certainly no one will dispute the propriety of that partition of goods which separates them into three classes, namely, external goods, goods of the body, and goods of the soul, or deny that the happy man must have all three.[2] For no one would maintain that he is happy who has not in him a particle of courage or temperance or justice or prudence, who is afraid of every insect which flutters past him, and will commit any crime, however great, in order to gratify his lust of meat and drink, who will sacrifice his dearest friend for the sake of half-a-farthing, and is as feeble and false in mind as a child or a madman.

These propositions are universally admitted as soon as uttered, but men differ about the degree or relative superiority of this or that good. Some think that a very moderate amount of virtue is enough, but set no limit to their desires of wealth, property, power, fame, and the like. To whom we reply by an appeal to facts, which easily prove that men do not acquire or preserve virtue by the help of external goods, but external goods by the help of virtue, and that happiness, whether consisting in pleasure or in virtue or in both, is more often found with those who are most highly cultivated in mind and character and have only a moderate share of external goods, than among those who possess external goods to a useless extent but are deficient in higher qualities. Nor is this only a fact of experience, but, if reflected upon, it will easily appear to accord with reason. For, whereas external goods have a limit, like any other instrument, and all the things we use are of such a nature that where there is too much of them they must either do harm or at any rate be useless to their possessors, every good of the soul, the greater it is, is also of greater use—if the epithet useful as well as noble is appropriate to such

---

[2] Aristotle had made this same division in his *Ethics*. See p. 93.

subjects. . . . Again, it is for the sake of the soul that goods external and goods of the body are desirable at all, and all wise men ought to choose them for the sake of the soul, and not the soul for the sake of them.

Let us acknowledge then that each one has just so much of happiness as he has of virtue and wisdom, and of good and wise action. God is a witness to us of this truth,[3] for he is happy and blessed, not by reason of any external good, but in himself and by reason of his own nature. And herein must lie the difference between good fortune and happiness. For external goods come of themselves, and chance is the author of them, but no one is just or temperate by or through chance.

In like manner, and by a similar train of argument, a happy state may be shown to be that which is best and acts rightly. And rightly it cannot act without doing right acts, and neither an individual nor state can do right acts without virtue and wisdom. Thus the courage, justice, and wisdom of a state have the same form and nature as the qualities which give an individual who possesses them the name of just, wise, or temperate. . . .

Let us assume then that the best life, both for individuals and states, is the life of virtue, with external goods enough for the performance of good actions. If any dispute our assertion, we will in this treatise pass them over, and consider their objections hereafter.

CHAPTER 2.   The question remains to be discussed whether the happiness of the individual is the same as that of the state, or is different. Here again there can be no doubt; no one denies that they are the same. For those who hold that the well-being of an individual consists in his wealth, think also that riches make the happiness of a whole state; and those who value most highly the life of a tyrant, deem that city the happiest which rules over the greatest number; while those who esteem an individual by his virtue say that the more virtuous a city is, the happier it is. . . .

[3] See *Ethics*, Book X. p. 284.

Now it is evident that that form of government is best in which every man, whoever he is, can act for the best and live happily. But even those who agree in thinking that the life of virtue is the most desirable raise a question, whether the life of business and politics is or is not more desirable than one which is wholly independent of external goods, I mean than a contemplative life, which by some is maintained to be the only one worthy of a philosopher. For these two lives—the life of the philosopher and the life of the statesman —appear to have been preferred by those who have been most keen in the pursuit of virtue, both in our own and in other ages. . . . Yet to a reflecting mind it must appear very strange that a statesman should be always considering how he can dominate and tyrannize over others, whether they will or not. How can that which is not lawful be the business of the statesman or the lawmaker? Unlawful it certainly is to rule without regard to justice, for there may be might where there is no right. The other arts and sciences offer no parallel; a physician is not expected to persuade or coerce his patients, nor a pilot the passengers in his ship. Yet many appear to think that a despotic government is a true political form; and what men affirm to be unjust and inexpedient in their own case they are not ashamed of practicing towards others. They demand justice for themselves, but where other men are concerned they care nothing about it. Such behavior is irrational, unless one party is born to command and the other born to serve, in which case men have a right to command, not indeed all their fellows, but only those who are intended to be subjects; just as we ought not to hunt men, either for food or for sacrifice, but only the animals which are intended for food or sacrifice, that is to say, such wild animals as are eatable. . . .

A good lawgiver should inquire how states and races of men and communities may participate in a good life, and in the happiness which is attainable by them. His rules will not always be the same. Where there are neighbors he will have to deal with them according to their characters, and see what duties are to be performed towards

each. The end at which the best form of government should aim may be properly made a matter of future consideration.

CHAPTER 3. But let us now address those who, while they agree that the life of virtue is the most desirable, differ in the manner of practicing it. For some renounce political power, and think the life of the free citizen is different from the life of the statesman and best of all; but others think the life of a statesman best. The argument of the latter is that he who does nothing cannot do well, and that virtuous activity is identical with happiness. To both we say: "You are partly right and partly wrong." The first are right in affirming that the life of a free citizen is better than the life of a despot; for there is nothing grand or noble in employing slaves, in so far as they are slaves; or in issuing commands about necessary things.

But it is an error to suppose that every sort of rule is despotic, like that of a master over slaves, for there is as great a difference between the rule over free men and the rule over slaves as there is between slavery by nature and freedom by nature, about which I said enough at the commencement of this treatise.[4] And it is equally a mistake to place inactivity above action, for happiness is activity, and the actions of the just and wise are the realizations of much that is noble.

But perhaps someone, accepting these premises, may still maintain that supreme power is the best of all things, because the possessors of it are able to perform the greatest number of noble actions. If so, the man who is able to rule, instead of yielding any power to his neighbor, ought rather to take it away; and the father should not make way for his son, nor the son for his father, nor friend for friend. They should bestow not a thought on one another in comparison with this higher object; for the best is the most desirable and acting well is the best. There might be some truth in such a view, if we assume that robbers and plunderers attain the chief

4 See Book I, chapters 4-7.

good. But this can never be; and hence we infer the view is false. For the actions of a ruler cannot really be noble, unless he is as much superior to other men as a husband is to a wife, or a father to his children, or a master to his slaves. And therefore he who violates the law can never recover by any act, however great, what he has already lost in departing from virtue. . . . If, however, there is anyone superior both in virtue and in the power of performing the best actions, him we ought to follow and obey; but he must have the capacity for action and virtue.

If we are right in our view, and happiness is assumed to be virtuous activity, the active life will be best both for the city collectively and for individuals. Not that a life of action must necessarily be action with other people, as some persons think; nor are only those ideas to be regarded as practical which are pursued for the sake of practical results, but rather the thoughts and contemplations which are independent and complete in themselves. For virtuous activity, and therefore action of that kind, is an end in itself. Even in the midst of external action the directing mind is said most truly to act. Neither, too, is it necessary that states, which are cut off from others and choose to live alone, should be inactive; for there may be activity in the parts of the state. There are many ways in which members of a state act on one another. The same thing is equally true of each individual. If it were otherwise, God and the universe, who have no external actions over and above their own energies, would be far from perfection. Hence it is evident that the same life is best for the individual and for states and for mankind collectively.

CHAPTER 4. Thus far by way of introduction. In what has preceded I discussed various forms of government. In what remains the first point to be considered is what should be the material conditions of an ideal or perfect state; for a perfect state cannot exist without a due supply of the means of life. Therefore we shall presuppose many purely imaginary conditions, though nothing impossible. There will be a certain number of citizens, a country in

which to place them, and the like. As the weaver or shipbuilder or any other artisan must have the material proper for his work (and in proportion as this is better prepared, so will the result of his art be nobler), so the statesman or lawgiver must also have the materials suited to him.

First among the materials required by the statesman is population. He will consider what should be the number and character of the citizens, and then what should be the size and character of the country. Most persons think that a state in order to be happy ought to be large; but even if they are right, they have no idea what is a large and what a small state. For they judge of the size of a city by the number of the inhabitants; whereas they ought to regard, not their number, but their power. A city too, like an individual, has a work to do; and the city which is best adapted to the fulfillment of its work is to be deemed greatest, in the same sense of the word in which Hippocrates [5] could be called greater, not as a man, but as a physician, than someone else who was taller. And even if we reckon greatness by numbers, we ought not to include everybody, for there must always be in cities a multitude of slaves and travelers and foreigners. We should count only those who are members of the state and form an essential part of it. Their number is a proof of the greatness of a city; but a city which produces numerous artisans and comparatively few soldiers cannot be great; for a great city is not to be confounded with a populous one.

Experience shows, moreover, that a very populous city can rarely, if ever, be well governed; since all cities which have a reputation for good government have a limited population. We may argue on grounds of reason too and reach the same conclusion. For law is order, and good law is good order; but a very great multitude cannot be orderly. To introduce order into the unlimited is the work of divine power, a power such as holds together the universe. Beauty

[5] The so-called father of Greek scientific medicine, who had died about fifty years before Aristotle wrote.

is realized in number and magnitude; therefore the city which combines magnitude with good order must be thought the fairest. But to the size of cities there is a limit, as there is to other things—plants, animals, tools. None of these retain their natural power when they are too large or too small, but they either lose their nature altogether or are spoiled. For example, a ship which is only a span 6 long will not be a ship at all, nor a ship a quarter of a mile long. And there may be a ship of a certain size, either too large or too small, which will still be a ship, but bad for sailing. In like manner, a state when composed of too few is not as a state ought to be, self-sufficing; when of too many, though self-sufficing in all mere necessaries, it is a nation and not a state, being almost incapable of constitutional government. For who can be general of such a vast multitude, or who herald, unless he have the voice of a Stentor? 7

A state then only begins to exist when it has attained a population sufficient for a good life in a political community. It may indeed somewhat exceed this number, but, as I was saying, there must be a limit. What the limit should be will be easily ascertained by experience. For both governors and governed have duties to perform. The special functions of governors are to command and to judge. But if the citizens of a state are to judge and distribute offices according to merit, then they must know each other's characters. Where they do not possess this knowledge, both the election to offices and the decision of lawsuits will go wrong. When the population is very large they are manifestly settled at haphazard, which clearly ought not to be. Besides, in an over-populous state, foreigners and foreign-born will readily acquire the rights of citizens, for who will find them out? Clearly then the best limit of the population of a state is the largest number which suffices for the purposes of life and can be taken in at a single view. Enough concerning the size of the state.

6 Nine inches.
7 Stentor was a Greek warrior at the siege of Troy who, according to Homer, had a voice as loud as the voices of fifty men. *Iliad*, V, Classics Club edition, p. 85.

CHAPTER 5. Much the same principle will apply to the territory of the state. Everyone would agree in praising the state that is most entirely self-sufficing; and that must be the state which is all-producing, for to have all things and want nothing is sufficiency. In size and extent it should be such as may enable the inhabitants to live temperately and liberally in the enjoyment of leisure. Whether we are right or wrong in laying down this limit, we will inquire more precisely hereafter, when we have occasion to consider the right uses of property and wealth—a matter much disputed, because men are inclined to rush into one of two extremes, some into meanness, others into luxury.

It is not difficult to determine the general character of the territory required. There are, however, some points on which military authorities should be heard; they tell us that it should be difficult of access for the enemy, and easy of exit for the inhabitants. Further, we require that the land, as well as the inhabitants of whom we spoke just now, should be taken in at a single glance, for a country which is easily seen can be easily protected. As to the position of the city, if we could have what we wish, it should be well situated in regard to both sea and land. These are the principles—that it should be a convenient center for the protection of the whole country, and that it should be suitable for receiving the fruits of the soil, and also for bringing in of timber and any other products that can be transported.

CHAPTER 6. Whether communication with the sea is beneficial to a well-ordered state or not is a question which has often been asked. It is argued that the introduction of strangers brought up under other laws, and the increase of population, will be adverse to good order (for a maritime people will always have a crowd of merchants coming and going); and that such increase is inimical to good government. Apart, however, from these considerations, it would be undoubtedly better, both with a view to safety and to the provision of necessaries, that the city and territory should be con-

nected with the sea. The defenders of a country, if they are to maintain themselves against an enemy, should be where they can be easily relieved both by land and by sea. If they are not able to attack by sea and land at once, they will have less difficulty in doing mischief to their assailants on one element, if they themselves can use both. Moreover, it is necessary that they should import from abroad what is not found in their own country, and export what they have in excess; for a city ought to be a market, not indeed for others, but for herself. . . .

Undoubtedly the possession of a moderate naval force is advantageous to a city. The city should be formidable not only to its own people but also to neighbors in certain cases, and when necessary, able to assist them by sea as well as by land. The proper number or magnitude of this naval force depends on the character of the state. If her function is to take a leading part in politics, her naval power should be commensurate with the scale of her enterprises. The population of the state need not be much increased, since there is no necessity that the sailors be citizens. The marines who have control and command will be freemen, and belong to the infantry; and wherever there is a dense population of peasants and farmers, there will always be sailors more than enough. Of this we see instances at the present day. The city of Heraclea, for example, although small in comparison with many others, can man a considerable fleet. Such are our conclusions as to the territory of the state, its harbor, its towns, its relations to the sea, and its maritime power.

CHAPTER 7.   Having spoken of the number of the citizens, we will now speak of what should be their character. The subject can be easily understood by anyone who casts his eye on the more celebrated states of Greece, and generally on the distribution of races in the habitable world. Those who live in a cold climate and in [northern] Europe are full of spirit, but wanting in intelligence and skill. Accordingly they keep their freedom, but have no political

organization and are incapable of ruling over others. Whereas the natives of Asia are intelligent and inventive but wanting in spirit, and therefore they are always in a state of subjection and slavery. But the Greek race, which is situated between them, is intermediate too in character, being both high-spirited and intelligent. Hence it continues free, and is the best-governed of any nation, and, if it could be formed into one state, would be able to rule the world. There are also similar differences among the different tribes of Greece; for some of them are of a one-sided nature and either intelligent or courageous, while in others there is a happy combination of both qualities. And clearly those whom the lawmaker will most easily lead to virtue will be both intelligent and courageous. . . .

CHAPTER 8. . . . We must see next how many things are indispensable to the existence of a state, for what we call the parts of the state will be found among them. Let us then enumerate the functions of a state, and we shall easily elicit what we want. First, there must be food; secondly, arts, for life requires many implements; thirdly, there must be arms, for the members of a community need them to maintain authority both against disobedient subjects and against external enemies; fourthly, there must be a certain amount of revenue, both for internal needs, and for purposes of war; fifthly, or rather first, there must be the service of religion which they call ritual; sixthly, and most necessary of all, there must be a power to decide what is for the public interest, and what is just in men's dealings with one another.

These are the things which every state may be said to need. For a state is not a mere aggregate of persons, but a union of them, sufficient for the purposes of life; and if any of these things are wanting, it is impossible for the community to be self-sufficing. A state then should be framed with a view to the fulfillment of these functions. There must be farmers and artisans, and a warlike and a wealthy class, and priests, and judges to decide what is just and expedient.

CHAPTER 9. Having determined these points, we have in the next place to consider whether all ought to participate in every sort of occupation. Shall every man be at once farmer, artisan, councilor, judge, or shall we suppose the several occupations just mentioned assigned to different persons? Or, thirdly, shall some employments be assigned to individuals and others common to all? The arrangement is not the same in every state. As we were saying, all occupations may be shared by all, or not all by all but only by some. Hence arise the differences between states; for in democracies all share in all, in oligarchies the opposite practice prevails. But we are speaking here of the best form of government and that under which the state will be most happy, and happiness, as has been already said, cannot exist without virtue. It is clear that in such a state, which possesses citizens who are absolutely and not merely relatively just, they must not lead the life of craftworkers or tradesmen,[8] for such a life is ignoble and inimical to virtue. Neither must they be farmers, since leisure is necessary both for the development of virtue and the performance of political duties.

Again, there must be in a state a class of warriors and another of councilors, to advise about the expedient and determine matters of law; and these seem in a special manner parts of the state. Now, should these two classes be distinguished, or are both their functions to be assigned to the same persons? Here again there is no difficulty in seeing that both functions will in one way belong to the same, in another, to different persons. To different persons in so far as their occupations are suited to different ages of life, for one requires wisdom, and the other strength. But on the other hand, since those who are able to use or to resist force can never be willing to remain always in subjection, from this point of view the persons are

[8] In Book III Aristotle has already excluded craftsmen and laborers from citizenship. See p. 296. For his opinion of trading and usury as occupations, see Book I p. 266. Plato had already pronounced retail trade an illiberal occupation and dishonorable for the citizen, who should live off his land. See Plato, *Laws*, XI, 919. In this part of the *Politics*, Aristotle takes many suggestions from Plato, with whom he has hitherto steadily disagreed.

the same; for those who carry arms can always determine the fate of a constitution. Therefore, by an ideal constitution both functions would be entrusted to the same persons, not, however, at the same time, but in the order prescribed by nature, who has given to young men strength and to older men wisdom. Such a distribution of duties will be expedient and also just; it is founded on a principle of proportion to ability. In addition, this ruling class should be owners of property, for they are citizens, and the citizens of a state should be in good circumstances; whereas the craftsmen or any other class, whose art is not an art producing virtue, have no share in the state. This follows from our first principle; for happiness cannot exist without virtue, and a city is not termed happy with regard to a portion of its citizens, but with regard to them all. And clearly property should be in their hands, since the farmers will of necessity be slaves or barbarians or peasants.

Of the classes above enumerated there remain only the priests, and the manner in which their office should be regulated is obvious. No farmer or craftworker should be appointed to it; for the gods should receive honor from citizens only. Now since the body of the citizens is divided into two classes, warriors and councilors, and it is seemly both that the worship of the gods should be duly performed, and a rest provided in service for those who in old age have given up active life, to the old men of these two classes should be assigned the duties of priesthood.

We have shown what are the necessary conditions, and what the parts of a state; farmers, craftsmen, and laborers of all kinds are necessary to the existence of states, but the parts of the state are the warriors and councilors. And these are distinguished severally from one another, the distinction being in some cases permanent, in others not. . . .

CHAPTER 10. . . . I have already remarked that the land should belong to those who bear arms and those who have a share in the government and that the farmers should be a class distinct

from them. I have determined too what should be the extent and nature of the territory. Let me proceed to discuss the distribution of the land, and the character of the agricultural class; for I do not think that property ought to be common, as some maintain, but only that by friendly consent there should be a common use of it; and that no citizen should be in want of subsistence.

As to common meals, there is a general agreement that a well-ordered city should have them. We will hereafter explain what are our own reasons for taking this view. They ought, however, to be open to all citizens. Yet it is not easy for the poor to contribute the requisite sum out of their private means, and to provide also for their own households. The expenses of religious worship should likewise be a public charge. The land must therefore be divided into two parts, one public and the other private, and each part should be subdivided, half of the public land being appropriated to the service of the gods, and the other half used to defray the cost of the common meals; while of the private land, half should be near the border, and the other near the city, so that, each citizen having two lots, they may all of them have land in both places.[9] There is justice and fairness in such a division, and it tends to inspire unity among the people in their border wars. Where there is not this arrangement, some of them are too ready to come to blows with their neighbors, while others are so cautious that they quite lose their sense of honor. Wherefore there is a law in some places which forbids those who dwell near the border to take part in public deliberations about wars with neighbors, on the ground that their interests will pervert their judgment.

For the reasons already mentioned then, the land should be divided in the manner described. The best thing of all would be that the farmers should be slaves, not all of the same race and not spirited; for if they have no spirit they will be better suited for their work, and there will be no danger of their making a revolution. The

[9] Plato had advocated such a distribution of land and described the method in considerable detail in his *Laws*, V, 745.

next best thing would be that they should be peasants or of foreign stock, and of like inferior nature. Some of them should be slaves of individuals, and employed on private estates of men of property; the remainder should be the property of the state and employed on the common land. I will hereafter explain what is the proper treatment of slaves, and why it is expedient that liberty should be always held out to them as the reward of their services.[10]

CHAPTER 11.   We have already said that the city should be open to the land and to the sea, and to the whole country as far as possible. As to the spot itself, our wish would be to find a situation fortunate in four things. The first is health—this is a necessity. Cities which lie toward the east, and are blown upon by winds coming from the east, are the healthiest. Next, they should be sheltered from the north wind, to have a milder winter. The site of the city should be convenient too, both for political administration and for war. With a view to the latter it should provide easy exit for the citizens, and at the same time be inaccessible and difficult of capture for enemies. There should be a natural abundance of springs and fountains in the towns; or, if there is a deficiency of them, great reservoirs may be established for the collection of rain-water, such as will not fail when the inhabitants are cut off from the country by war. Special care should be taken of the health of the inhabitants, which will depend, chiefly, on the healthfulness of the locality and of the quarter to which they are exposed and, secondly, on the use of pure water. This latter point is by no means a minor consideration. For the elements which we use most and oftenest for the support of the body contribute most to its health; and among these are water and air. So, in all wise states, if there is any lack of pure water and the supply is not all equally good, the drinking water should be separated from that which is used for other purposes.

10 This subject is never reached in our *Politics*. It is interesting to remember that in his will Aristotle directed that some of his slaves be freed.

As to fortresses, there is a difference between what is suitable for different forms of government. Thus a high citadel is suited to an oligarchy or a monarchy, but one on a plain to a democracy; neither one to an aristocracy but rather a number of strong places. The arrangement of private houses is considered to be more agreeable and generally more convenient, if the streets are regularly laid out after the modern fashion which Hippodamus [11] introduced. But for the security in war the antiquated mode of building, which made it difficult for strangers to get out of a town and for invaders to find their way in, is preferable. A city should therefore adopt both plans of building. Houses can be arranged irregularly, as farmers plant their vines, in what are called "clumps." The whole town should not be laid out in straight lines, but only certain quarters and regions. Thus security and beauty will be combined.

As to walls, those who say that cities making any pretension to military valor should not have them, are quite out of date in their notions.[12] They may see the cities which prided themselves on this notion confuted by facts. True, there is little courage shown in skulking for safety behind a rampart, when an enemy is similar in character and not much superior in number; but when the besiegers are superior, they may be and often are beyond ordinary power to resist, and too much for the valor of a few. If the city is to be saved and escape defeat and outrage, the strongest wall will be the best weapon of the warriors, more especially now that missiles and siege engines have been brought to such perfection. To have no walls would be as foolish as to choose a site for a town in an exposed country and level the heights; or as if an individual were to leave his house unwalled, lest the inmates should become cowards. Nor must we forget that those who have their cities surrounded by walls

[11] Hippodamus of Miletus is said to have been the architect of the city of Rhodes and of a part, at least, of the buildings of the Athenian port of Piraeus. He designed his cities in straight streets, a novelty in Greece at the time.

[12] Here Aristotle is differing again from Plato, even calling him old-fashioned. Plato had thought that city walls had a bad effect on the health and morale of the citizens. *Laws*, VI, 778-779.

may either take advantage of them or may not; but cities which are unwalled have no choice. . . .

CHAPTER 12. As the walls will be marked off by guard-houses and towers built at suitable intervals, and the body of citizens must be distributed at common tables, the idea will naturally occur that we should establish some of the common tables in the guardhouses. The arrangement might so be made. The principal common tables of the magistrates would occupy a suitable place. There too would be the buildings appropriated to religious worship, except those dedicated to the rites which the law or the Pythian oracle [13] restricts to a special locality.[14] The site should be a spot seen far and wide, to give due elevation to virtue and tower over the neighborhood. Near the spot should be established a forum like that the Thessalians call the "freemen's forum." From this all trade should be excluded, and no craftsman, farmer, or any such person allowed to enter, unless he is summoned by the magistrates. . . . There should also be a traders' market place, distinct and apart from the forum, in a situation convenient for the reception of goods both by sea and land.

But in speaking of magistrates, we must not forget another section of the citizens, namely, the priests, for whom public tables should likewise be provided in their proper place near the temples. The magistrates who deal with contracts, indictments, summonses, and the like, and those who have care of the public places and of the city respectively, ought to be established near the spot and in some public place of meeting. The neighborhood of the traders' market place will be a suitable spot. The upper forum we devote to the life of leisure, the other is intended for the necessities of trade. The same order should prevail in the country, for there too the magistrates, called by some "inspectors of forests," and by others "wardens of the country," must have guardhouses and common tables while they are

[13] The oracle of Apollo at Delphi.
[14] This arrangement of buildings is found in Plato's Laws, VI, 778.

on duty. Temples also should be scattered throughout the country, dedicated some to gods and some to heroes.

But it would be a waste of time for us to linger over details like these. The difficulty is not in imagining but in carrying them out. We may talk about them as much as we like, but the execution of them will depend upon fortune. Wherefore let us say no more about these matters for the present. . . .

CHAPTER 14. Since every political society is composed of rulers and subjects, let us consider whether the relations of one to the other should interchange or be permanent. For the education of the citizens will necessarily vary with the answer given to this question. Now, if some men excelled others in the same degree in which gods and heroes are supposed to excel mankind in general, being in the first place far more perfect even in their bodies, and, also, in their minds, so that the superiority of the governors over subjects was patent and undisputed, it would clearly be better that one class should rule and the others serve. But since this is impossible, and kings have no marked superiority over their subjects, such as Scylax [15] affirms to be the case among the Indians, it is obviously necessary on many grounds that all citizens alike should take their turn at governing and being governed. Equality consists of the same treatment given to similar persons; and no government can stand which is not founded on justice. For, if the government is unjust, everyone in the country unites with the governed in a desire to have a revolution, and the members of the government cannot be so numerous as to be stronger than all their enemies put together. Yet that the governors should excel their subjects is undeniable.

How all this is to be effected, and in what way they will respectively share in the government, the lawgiver has to consider. The subject has been already mentioned.[16] Nature herself furnished one

[15] An ancient traveler and writer on geography, whose writings Aristotle apparently knew.
[16] See pp. 397-398.

principle of choice when she made a difference between old and young of the same kind. Of these she fitted the one to govern and the other to be governed. No one takes offense at being governed when he is young, nor does he think himself better than his governors, especially if he will enjoy the same privilege when he reaches the required age.

We conclude that from one point of view governors and governed are identical, and from another different. Therefore their education must be the same and also different. For he who would learn to command well must, as men say, first of all learn to obey. As I observed in the first part of this treatise, one kind of government rules for the sake of the rulers and another rules for the sake of the ruled.[17] The former is a despotic, the latter a free government. Some commands too differ not in the thing commanded, but in the intention with which they are imposed. Wherefore many apparently menial offices are an honor to the free youth by whom they are performed; for actions do not differ in themselves so much as honorable or dishonorable as in the end and intention of them. But since we say that the virtue of a citizen and a ruler is the same as that of a good man, and that the same person must be a subject and a ruler, the lawgiver has to see that he becomes a good man, and know by what means this may be accomplished, and what is the end of the perfect life.

Now the soul of man is divided into two parts, one of which has reason in itself, and the other, though not having reason in itself, is able to obey reason.[18] And we call a man good because he has the virtues of these two parts. In which of them man's end is more likely to be found is no matter of doubt to those who adopt our division. In the world both of nature and of art, the inferior always exists for the sake of the better or superior, and the better or superior is that which has reason. . . .

The whole of life is further divided into two parts, business and

[17] See Book III, p. 298.
[18] See the *Ethics*, Book I, p. 100.

leisure, war and peace, and all actions into those which are necessary and useful and those which are honorable. And the preference given to one or the other class of actions must necessarily be like the preference given to one or the other part of the soul and its actions over the other's. War must be for the sake of peace, business for the sake of leisure, things useful and necessary for the sake of things honorable. All these points the statesman must keep in view when he frames his laws; he should consider the parts of the soul and their functions, and, above all, the better part and the goal. He must also remember the diversities of human lives and actions. For men must engage in business and go to war, though leisure and peace are better; they must do what is necessary and useful, though what is honorable is better.

By such principles children and persons of every age which requires education should be trained. Yet even the Greeks of the present day, who are reputed to be best governed, and the lawmakers who gave them their constitutions, do not appear to have framed their governments with a regard to the best end, or to have given them laws and education with a view to all the virtues, but in a vulgar spirit to have fallen back on those which promised to be more useful and profitable. Many modern writers have taken a similar view; they commend the Spartan constitution, and praise the lawgiver for making conquest and war his sole aim.[19] . . . But surely they are not a happy people now that their empire has passed away, nor was their lawgiver right. How preposterous is the result, for although they continued in the observance of his laws and no one interfered with them, yet they have lost the better part of life!

These writers err further about the sort of government which a lawmaker should approve; for the government of free men is noble, and implies more virtue than despotic government. Neither is a city to be deemed happy or a lawmaker to be praised because he trains

[19] Plato was not among these "modern writers." "War," he said in his *Laws*, I. 628, "whether external or civil, is not the best and the need of either is to be deplored; but peace with one another and good will are best."

his citizens to conquer and obtain dominion over their neighbors, for there is great evil in this. On a similar principle any citizen who could, would obviously try to seize power in his own state—a crime which the Spartans accuse King Pausanias of attempting, although he had so great honor already.[20] No such principle and no law making this an object is either statesmanlike or useful or right. For the same things are best both for individuals and for states, and these are the things which a lawmaker ought to implant in the minds of his citizens. Neither should men study war with a view to the enslavement of those who do not deserve to be enslaved. First of all they should provide against their own enslavement, and in the second place obtain empire for the good of the governed, and not to exercise a despotism. In the third place, they should seek to be masters only over those who deserve to be slaves. Both the facts and the arguments prove that a lawmaker should direct all his military and other measures to the provision of leisure and the establishment of peace. For most military states are safe only while they are at war, but fall when they have acquired their empire; like unused iron, they rust in times of peace. And for this the lawmaker is to blame, if he never has taught them how to lead a life of peace.

CHAPTER 15. Since the end of individuals and of states is the same, the end of the best man and of the best state must also be the same; it is therefore evident that there ought to exist in both of them the virtues of leisure. For peace, as we have often repeated, is the end of war, and leisure of toil. But leisure and culture may be promoted not only by those virtues that are practiced in leisure but also by some that are useful in toil. For many necessaries of life have to be supplied before we can have leisure. Therefore a city must be temperate and brave, and be able to endure. For truly, as the proverb says, "there is not leisure for slaves," and those who cannot face danger like men are the slaves of any invader. Courage and

[20] Pausanias had won great glory by his victory over the Persian army at Plataea in 479 B.C., before he was accused of trying to make himself dictator in Sparta.

endurance are required for toil and wisdom for leisure, temperance and justice for both. The last is especially needed in times of peace and leisure; for war compels men to be just and temperate, whereas the enjoyment of good fortune and the leisure which comes with peace tend to make them insolent. Those then who seem to be best off and in possession of every good have special need of justice and temperance, for instance, those (if such there be, as the poets say) who dwell in the Islands of the Blest. They above all need wisdom and temperance and justice, the more the more leisure they have, living in the midst of abundance.

It is not hard then to see why a state that would be happy and good ought to have these same virtues. If it be disgraceful in men not to be able to use the goods of life, it is peculiarly disgraceful not to be able to use them in time of peace, to show excellent qualities in action and war, and when they have peace and leisure, to be no better than slaves. Wherefore we should not practice virtue after the manner of the Spartans. For they, while agreeing with other men in their idea of the highest good, differ from them in thinking that it may be obtained by the practice of a single virtue. . . .

But we have still to consider whether the training of early life is to be that of reason or of habit. The two, however, should accord, and when in accord will then form the best of harmonies. . . . But as the body is prior in order of growth to the soul, so the irrational is prior to the rational. The proof is that anger and will and desire are implanted in children from their very birth, but reason and understanding develop as they grow older. Wherefore, the care of the body ought to precede that of the soul, and the training of the appetites should follow. None the less, our care of them must be for the sake of the reason, and our care of the body for the sake of the soul.

CHAPTER 16. Since then a lawgiver should begin by considering how the bodies of the children whom he is rearing may be as sound as possible, his first care will be about marriage. At what

age should his citizens marry, and who are fit to marry? In legislating on this subject he ought to consider the persons and their relative ages, that there be no disproportion in them, and that they may not differ in bodily powers, as will be the case if the man is still able to beget children while the woman is unable to bear them, or the woman able to bear while the man is unable to beget; for from these causes arise quarrels and differences between married persons. Secondly, he must consider the time at which the children will succeed to their parents. There ought not to be too great an interval of age, for then the parents will be too old to derive any pleasure from their affection, or to be of any use to them. Nor ought they to be too nearly of an age. To youthful marriages there are many objections; the children will be wanting in respect to their parents, who will seem to be their contemporaries, and disputes will arise in the management of the household. Thirdly, and this is the point from which we digressed, the lawgiver must mold to his will the bodies of the children new-born.

Almost all these objects may be secured by attention to one point. Since the time of generation does not commonly last beyond the age of seventy years in the case of a man, and fifty in the case of a woman, the commencement of their union should take account of these periods. The union of male and female when too young is bad for the procreation of children. In all other animals too the off-spring of the young are small and ill-developed, and tend to be of the female sex. So also in man, as is proved by the fact that in those cities in which men and women are accustomed to marry young, the people are small and weak. In childbirth also younger women suffer more, and more of them die. . . . Women should marry when they are about eighteen years of age, and men at thirty-seven: [21] then they are in the prime of life, and the decline in the powers of both will coincide. Further, the children, if their birth takes place

[21] Plato in the *Republic*, V, Classics Club edition, p. 348, sets up the prime of life for women at from twenty to forty years, and for men at from about twenty-five to fifty-five.

at the time that may reasonably be expected, will succeed in their prime, when the fathers are already in the decline of life, and have nearly reached their term of three-score years and ten. . . .

What constitution in the parent is most advantageous to the off-spring is a subject which we will hereafter consider [22] when speaking of the education of children. We will make only a few general remarks at present. The temperament of an athlete is not suited to the life of a citizen, or to health, or to the procreation of children, any more than a sickly or exhausted constitution. One should be in a mean between them. A man's constitution should be inured to labor, but not to labor which is excessive or of one sort only, such as is practiced by athletes; he should be capable of all the actions of a free man. These remarks apply equally to both parents.

Women who are with child should be careful of themselves; they should take exercise and have a nourishing diet. The first of these prescriptions the lawgiver will easily carry into effect by requiring them to take a walk daily to some temple, where they can worship the gods who preside over birth.[23] Their minds, however, unlike their bodies, they ought to keep unexercised. Offspring derive their natures from their mothers as plants do from the earth.

As to the exposure and rearing of children, let there be a law that no deformed child shall live. But where there are too many children (for in our state population has a limit) they must not be exposed solely for that reason. When couples have children in excess, let abortion be procured before sense and life have begun. What may or may not be lawfully done in these cases depends on the state of life and sensation. . . .

CHAPTER 17. After the children are born, the manner of rearing them is supposed to have a great effect on their bodily strength. It would appear from the example of animals, and of those nations who desire to foster the military habit, that the food which

[22] Nothing more is said on this matter.
[23] Plato has something to say on this in his *Laws*. VII. 789.

has most milk in it is best suited to human beings. The less wine, however, the better, if they would escape diseases. Also all the motions which children can be taught at an early age are very useful. But to preserve their tender limbs from distortion, some nations use mechanical appliances, which straighten their bodies. To accustom children to the cold from their earliest years is also an excellent practice, which greatly conduces to health and hardens them for military service. Hence many barbarians have a custom of plunging their children at birth into a cold stream; others, like the Celts, clothe them in a light wrap only. For human nature should be early taught to endure all that by habit it can be made to endure; but the process must be gradual. And children, from their natural warmth, may be easily trained to bear cold. Such care should attend them in the first stage of life.

The next period lasts to the age of five. During this time no demand should be made on the child for study or labor lest its growth be impeded; but there should be sufficient motion to prevent the limbs from being inactive. This can be secured, among other ways, by amusement, but the amusement should not be vulgar or tiring or riotous. The directors of education, as they are termed, should be careful what tales or stories the children hear; [24] for the sports of children are designed to prepare the way for the business of later life, and should be for the most part imitations of the occupations they will hereafter pursue in earnest. Those are wrong who [like Plato] in the Laws attempt to check the loud crying and screaming of children, for these contribute towards their growth, and, in a manner, exercise their bodies.[25] Straining the voice has an effect similar to that produced by the retention of the breath in violent exertions.

Then besides other duties, the directors of education should have

[24] Plato was very emphatic on this point. See the *Republic*, II, Classics Club edition, pp. 278-280.

[25] Plato advises simply that the child be protected as much as possible from sorrow and fear, the things that make him cry, so that his soul may grow gentle and cheerful. *Laws*, VII, 792.

an eye to their bringing up and take particular care that they are left as little as possible with slaves. Until they are seven years old they must live at home, but even at this early age they may acquire traits that are mean and low from what they see and hear. Indeed, there is nothing which a lawmaker should be more careful to forbid than indecency of speech; for the light utterance of shameful words leads soon to shameful acts. The young especially should never be allowed to repeat or hear anything of the sort. A freeman who is found saying or doing something forbidden, if he be too young as yet to have the privilege of a seat at the public tables, should be disgraced or beaten; an elder man should be degraded, as his slavish conduct deserves. And since we do not allow improper language, clearly we should also banish pictures and stage plays which are indecent. Let the rulers see that there is no image or picture representing unseemly actions, except in the temples of those gods at whose festivals the law permits ribaldry, and whom the law also orders shall be worshiped by persons of mature age on behalf of themselves, their children, and their wives. But the lawgiver should not allow youth to be spectators of comedy until they are of an age to sit at the public tables and drink strong wine. By that time education will have armed them against the evil influences of such representations. . . .

BOOK VIII

Subjects of the ideal education for children. Education for utility and for enjoyment in leisure.

CHAPTER I. No one will doubt that a lawgiver should direct his attention above all to the education of youth, or that the neglect of education does harm to states. The citizen should be molded to suit the form of government under which he lives. For

each government has a peculiar character, which originally formed and still continues to preserve it. The character of democracy creates democracy, and the character of oligarchy creates oligarchy. The better the character, always the better the government.

Now for the exercise of any faculty or art, previous training and practice are required. Clearly then they are required for the exercise of virtue. And since the entire state has one end, manifestly education should be one and the same for all, and should be public, and not private. It should not be as at present, when everyone looks after his own children separately, and gives them separate instruction of the sort he thinks best. The training in things of common interest should be the same for all. Neither must we suppose that any one of the citizens belongs to himself, for they all belong to the state, and are each of them a part of the state, and the care of each part is inseparable from the care of the whole. In this particular the Spartans are to be praised, for they take the greatest pains about their children, and make education the business of the state.

CHAPTER 2. That education should be regulated by law and should be an affair of state is not then to be denied; but what should be the character of this public education, and how young persons should be educated, are questions yet to be considered. For men are by no means agreed about the things to be taught, whether we aim at virtue or the best life. Neither is it clear whether education should be more concerned with intellectual or with moral virtue. Existing practice is perplexing; no one knows on what principle we should proceed. Should the useful in life, or should virtue, or should higher knowledge, be the aim of our training? All three opinions have been entertained. Again, about method there is no agreement; for different persons, starting with different ideas about the nature of virtue, naturally disagree about the practice of it.

Undoubtedly children should be taught those useful things that are really necessary, but not all useful things. For occupations are divided into liberal and illiberal, and to young children should be imparted only such kinds of knowledge as will be useful to them

without vulgarizing them. Any occupation, art, or science, which makes the body or soul or mind of the freeman less fit for the practice or exercise of virtue, is vulgar. Therefore we call those arts vulgar which tend to deform the body, and likewise all paid employments; they absorb and degrade the mind. There are some liberal skills quite proper for a freeman to acquire, but only to a certain degree; if he attend to them too closely, in order to attain perfection in them, the same evil effect will follow. The object also which a person sets before him makes a great difference. If he does or learns anything for his own sake or for the sake of his friends or with a view to excellence, the action will not appear illiberal; though if done for the sake of others, the very same action will appear menial and servile. The received subjects of instruction, as I have already remarked, are partly of a liberal and partly of an illiberal character.

CHAPTER 3. The customary branches of an education are four, namely, (1) reading and writing, (2) gymnastic exercises, (3) music, to which is sometimes added (4) drawing. Of these, reading, writing, and drawing are regarded as useful for the purposes of life in a variety of ways, and gymnastic exercises are thought to infuse courage. As to music a question may be raised. In our own day most men cultivate it for pleasure, but originally it was included in education, because nature herself, as has been often said, requires that we should be able, not only to work well, but to use our leisure well. For, as I must repeat once again, the prime end of all action is leisure. Both are necessary, but leisure is better than labor.

Hence now the question must be asked in good earnest, what ought we to do when at leisure? Clearly we ought not to be always amusing ourselves, for then amusement would be the end of life. But if this is inconceivable, still amid serious occupations amusement is needed even more than at other times. For he who is hard at work has need of relaxation, whereas work is always accompanied with exertion and effort. So at suitable hours we should introduce amusements, and they should be our medicines; for the emotion

they create in the soul is a relaxation, and from that pleasure we obtain rest. And leisure of itself gives pleasure and happiness and enjoyment of life; they are experienced not by the busy man but by those who have leisure. For a man at work has in view some end which he has not yet attained; but happiness is an end, since all men know it is attended by pleasure and not by pain. Pleasure, however, is taken differently by different persons, and varies according to the habit of the individual. The pleasure of the best man is the best, and springs from the noblest sources.

Apparently then there are branches of learning and education which we should study solely with a view to the enjoyment of leisure, and these are to be valued for their own sake; whereas the kinds of knowledge which are useful in business are necessary, and exist for the sake of other things. Therefore our fathers admitted music into education, not on the ground of either its necessity or its utility; for it is not necessary, nor even useful in the same way that reading and writing are useful in wealth getting, in the management of a household, in the acquisition of knowledge, and in political life. Nor is it, like drawing, useful for a more correct judgment of the works of artists, nor again, like gymnastics, does it give health and strength, for neither of these is to be gained from music. There is, however, a use of music for intellectual enjoyment in leisure, which seems indeed to have been the reason of its introduction into education. For music is one of the ways in which, it is thought, a freeman might pass his leisure. As Homer says,

"But only he should be called to the pleasant feast," [1]

and then describes those whom he would invite,

"The bard who would delight them by his song."

And in another place Odysseus says there is no better way of passing life than when

---

[1] This line is not in our text of Homer. In Aristotle's text it evidently came close to the one he quotes next, which is from the *Odyssey*, XVII, 385.

"Men's hearts are merry and the banqueters in the hall, sitting in order, hear the voice of the musician." [2]

Evidently, then, there is a sort of education in which parents should train their sons, not because it is useful or necessary, but because it is liberal or noble. Whether this is of one kind only, or of more than one, and if so, what those are, and how they are to be imparted, must hereafter be determined. This much we are able to say, the ancients witness to us; for their opinion may be gathered from the fact that music is one of the received and traditional branches of education. Further, it is clear that children should be instructed in some useful things, for example, in reading and writing, not only for their usefulness, but also because many other sorts of knowledge are acquired through them. For a like purpose they should be taught drawing, not to prevent their making mistakes in their own purchases, or to save them from being imposed upon in the buying or selling of articles, but rather because it makes them judges of the beauty of the human form. But to be always seeking after the useful does not become free and exalted souls. It is clear too that in education habit must go before reason, and the body before the mind. Therefore boys should be handed over to the trainer, who creates in them the proper habit of body, and to the wrestling-master, who teaches them their exercises.

CHAPTER 4. Of those states which in our own day seem to take the greatest care of children, some aim especially at producing in them an athletic habit; but they only injure their forms and stunt their growth. Although the Spartans have not fallen into this mistake, yet they brutalize their children by laborious exercises which they think will make them courageous. But in truth, as we have often repeated, education should not be exclusively directed to this or to any other single end. . . . And parents who devote their children to gymnastics while they neglect their necessary education in

---

[2] *Odyssey,* IX, 7.

reality vulgarize them; for they make them useful to the state in one quality only, and even in this our argument proves them to be inferior to others. We should judge the Spartans not from what they have been, but from what they are; for now they have rivals who compete with them in education and formerly they had none.

It is an admitted principle that some gymnastic exercises should be employed in education, but that for children they should be of a lighter kind, avoiding severe regimen or painful toil, lest the growth of the body be impaired. The evil of excessive training in early years is strikingly proved by the example of the Olympic victors; for not more than two or three of them have won a prize both as boys and as men. Their early training and severe gymnastic exercises exhausted their constitutions. When boyhood is over, three years should be spent in other studies. The period of life which follows that may then be devoted to hard exercise and strict regimen. Men ought not to labor at the same time with their minds and with their bodies; [3] for the two kinds of labor are opposed to one another. The labor of the body impedes the mind, and the labor of the mind the body. . . .

[3] See Plato, *Republic*, VII, Classics Club edition, p. 423.

POETICS

POETICS

BY NOW we have seen something of Aristotle as a critic in the fields of science, philosophy, and morals. In the following selections we find him quite as much at home as a critic of literature, in particular of that type of poetic literature that was then most admired in Greece, and in the production of which Athenians had shown surpassing genius. The first book of the *Poetics*—which is all we have—is a study of tragic drama. The second book, we are told, dealt with comedy, but it has long since disappeared.

Determined, as always, to mark out first a clear outline of his subject, Aristotle begins by drawing distinctions between tragedy and comedy on the one hand and tragedy and epic poetry on the other, as regards origin, style, and material. He then proceeds to list the elements that together, in his opinion, make up a good play—plot, characters, thought, diction, scenic effect, and music. In his time, we may remember, all serious Greek drama was spoken in blank verse, with interludes between the acts of choruses sung to music. It was impressively produced, on a low stone stage, against a stately architectural background, in an open air theater, cut out of a rocky hillside. The actors were few but each part was intensely significant. A choir below the stage played the rôle of interested onlookers and between the acts sang the lyrics of joy, compassion, awe, or resignation that the situation called for. But on the matters of setting, costuming, music, and performance Aristotle, so far as our text goes, has almost nothing to say. To him the plot is the thing, with characters, thought, and diction following next after. His idea of a truly tragic plot is a disastrous reversal of fortune, coming, through his own fault, to a man of essentially noble quality, accompanied by the

discovery that some other person or persons are not what they had seemed. His test of a great tragedy is its power to cleanse the beholders' emotions through the pity and fear which it awakens in them.

To many of us the plays Aristotle cites as models of fine tragedy, Sophocles' *Oedipus Tyrannus* and Euripedes' *Medea* and *Iphigenia in Tauris,* are merely names, if that. They may, however, be read in English translations by Gilbert Murray and others, and occasionally one is performed in a college theater with sensational effect. For sheer, concentrated tragedy and thrill nothing outdoes the masterpieces of the Athenian stage. But it is possible to read the *Poetics* with only Shakespeare's tragedies in mind. By Shakespeare's time the musical choruses had vanished, the shape of the stage had altered, and the actors swarmed over it in what would have seemed to a Greek an ungoverned, disorderly crew. Nor did Shakespeare attempt to follow Aristotle's recommendation to keep the action of the play within the time limit of one day's circuit of the sun. But to Aristotle, as we have said, these were not the things that mattered most. What mattered were what Shakespeare kept—the tragic plot, the noble characters, the lofty thought and poetic diction. Lear, Hamlet, Othello, Macbeth, and Richard II, all men of innate dignity and high position, have their eyes opened to things in themselves and others to which they had been blind and plunge therewith from greatness down to misery. The spectacle of their downfall creates in us for the moment a sense of being cleansed from the trivial and the mean.

On today's stage the poetic language of Shakespeare has gone the way of the Greek choruses. Our tragic playwrights are more apt than either the Greeks or Shakespeare to choose for theme a catastrophe caused by conflicts of ideas and social classes, and to take for hero a person whom both Aristotle and the Elizabethan dramatist would have regarded as too humble to be heroic. Nevertheless, in plays like Chekhov's *Cherry Orchard,* Galsworthy's *Skin Game,* O'Neill's *Beyond the Horizon,* St. John Ervine's *John Ferguson* and

Maxwell Anderson's *Winterset* there are the elevation of character and thought, the shock of recognition of truths previously unperceived about oneself and others, and the resulting suffering, which Aristotle called the essential stuff of tragedy, and beholding which we still feel something of his cleansing sense of pity and of awe.

I PROPOSE to treat of Poetry in itself and of its various kinds, noting the essential quality of each; to inquire into the structure of the plot required for a good poem; into the number and nature of the parts of which a poem is composed; and similarly into whatever else falls within the same inquiry. Following, then, the order of nature, let us begin with the principles which come first.

Epic poetry and tragedy, comedy also and dithyrambic [1] poetry, and the music of the flute and of the lyre in most of their forms, are all in their general conception modes of imitation. They differ, however, from one another in three respects—their mediums, their objects, their manner or mode of imitation being in each case distinct.

For as there are persons who, by conscious art or mere habit, imitate and represent various objects through the medium of color and form, or, again, by the voice; so in the group of arts above mentioned, taken as a whole, the imitation is produced by rhythm, language, or harmony, either singly or combined.

Thus in the music of the flute and of the lyre, harmony and rhythm alone are employed; also in other arts, such as that of the shepherd's pipe, which are essentially similar to these. In dancing, rhythm alone is used without harmony; for even dancing imitates character, emotion, and action, by rhythmical movement. . . .

There are, again, some arts which employ all the means above mentioned—namely, rhythm, tune, and meter. Such are dithyrambic and nomic [2] poetry, and also tragedy and comedy; but between them the difference is that in the first two cases these means are all em-

[1] For dithyrambic poetry the ordinary English reader may understand what we call lyric poetry. More strictly defined the dithyramb was a hymn or ode in rapturous style, such as were sung at the festivals of the god, Dionysus.

[2] Nomic poetry is instructive poetry, maxims or wise sayings in the form of verse.

ployed in combination, in the latter, now one means is employed, now another.

Such, then, are the differences of the arts with respect to the medium of imitation.

II

Since the objects of imitation are men in action, and these men must be either of a high or a low type (for moral character mainly answers to this division, goodness and badness being the distinguishing marks of moral differences), it follows that we must represent men either as better than in real life, or as worse, or as they are. It is the same in painting. Polygnotus depicted men as nobler than they are, Pauson as less noble, Dionysius drew them true to life.[3]

Now it is evident that each of the arts of imitation above mentioned will exhibit these differences, and itself become a distinct kind in imitating objects that are thus distinct. Such diversities may be found even in dancing, flute playing, and lyre playing. So again in language, whether prose or verse, unaccompanied by music. Homer, for example, makes men better than they are; Cleophon as they are; Hegemon of Thasos, the inventor of parodies, worse than they are.[4] The same distinction marks off tragedy from comedy; for comedy aims at representing men as worse, tragedy as better than in actual life.

III

There is still a third difference—the manner in which each of these objects may be imitated. For the medium being the same, the objects the same, the poet may imitate by narration—in which case he can either take another personality as Homer does, or speak in his own person, unchanged—or he may present all his characters as living and moving before us.

[3] Unfortunately no work by any of these famous Greek painters has come down to us.
[4] The writings of Cleophon and Hegemon are also lost.

These, then, as we said at the beginning, are the three differences which distinguish artistic imitation—the medium, the objects, and the manner. So that from one point of view, Sophocles [5] is an imitator of the same kind as Homer—for both imitate higher types of character; from another point of view, he is of the same kind as Aristophanes [6]—for both imitate persons acting and doing. Hence, some say, the name of "drama" is given to such plays, as representing action. . . .

IV

Poetry in general seems to have sprung from two sources, each of them lying deep in our nature. First, the instinct of imitation is implanted in man from childhood, one difference between him and other animals being that he is the most imitative of living creatures, and through imitation learns his earliest lessons. And no less universal is the pleasure he takes in seeing things imitated. We have evidence of this in the facts of experience. Objects which in themselves we view with pain, we delight to contemplate when reproduced with minute fidelity: such as the forms of the most ignoble animals and of dead bodies. The cause of this, again, is that to learn gives the liveliest pleasure, not only to philosophers but to men in general, although their capacity of learning is more limited. Thus the reason why men enjoy seeing a likeness is that in contemplating it they find themselves learning or inferring, and saying perhaps, "Ah, that is he." If they happen not to have seen the original, their pleasure will be due not to the imitation as such, but to the execution, the coloring, or some such other cause.

Imitation, then, is one instinct of our nature. Next there is the instinct for harmony and rhythm, meters being manifestly sections

---

[5] Sophocles was one of the great trio of fifth century Athenian tragedians, the other two being Aeschylus and Euripides. Seven of Sophocles' tragedies have been preserved.

[6] The famous satirical comedy writer of the end of the fifth century B.C.

of rhythm. Persons, therefore, starting with this natural gift developed by degrees their special aptitudes, until their rude im-
provisations gave birth to poetry.

Poetry now diverged in two directions, according to the individual
character of the writers. The graver spirits imitated noble actions
and the actions of good men. The more trivial sort imitated the
actions of meaner persons, at first composing satires, as the former
did hymns to the gods and praises of famous men. A poem of the
satirical kind cannot indeed be put down to any author earlier than
Homer; though there were probably many such writers. But from
Homer onward, instances can be cited—his own *Margites*,[7] for example, and other similar compositions. The appropriate meter was
also here introduced; hence the measure is still called the iambic [8] or
lampooning measure, being that in which people lampooned one
another. Thus the older poets were distinguished as writers either
of heroic or of lampooning verse.

As in the serious style Homer is pre-eminent among poets, for he
alone combined dramatic form with excellence of imitation, so he
too first laid down the main lines of comedy, by dramatizing the
ludicrous instead of writing personal satire. His *Margites* bears the
same relation to comedy that the *Iliad* and *Odyssey* do to tragedy.
And when tragedy and comedy appeared, the two classes of poets
still followed their natural bent: the lampooners became writers of
comedy, and the epic poets were succeeded by tragedians, since the
drama was a larger and higher form of art. . . . Tragedy advanced
by slow degrees; each new element that showed itself was in turn

[7] The mock battle epic that went by the name of *Margites* has long been lost.
Whether it was really the work of the author of the *Iliad,* as Aristotle thought, we
cannot judge.

[8] The pattern of the iambic meter was a line composed of a series of pairs of
syllables, a short syllable, followed by a long one. We in English still use its equivalent, an unaccented syllable followed by an accented, both in comic verse, such as
"O oysters, come and walk with us,
The walrus did beseech,"
and also in grand and serious poetry, such as *Paradise Lost.*

developed. Having passed through many changes, it found its natural form, and there it stopped.

Aeschylus first introduced a second actor;[9] he diminished the importance of the chorus, and assigned the leading part to the dialogue. Sophocles raised the number of actors to three, and added scene painting. It was not till late that the short plot was discarded for one of greater compass, and the grotesque diction of the earlier satiric form for the stately manner of tragedy.

V

Comedy is, as we have said, an imitation of characters of a lower type—not, however, in the full sense of the word bad, the ludicrous being merely a subdivision of the ugly. It consists of some defect or ugliness which is not painful or destructive. To take an obvious example, the comic mask is ugly and distorted, but does not imply pain.

The successive changes through which tragedy passed, and the authors of these changes, are well known, whereas comedy has had no history, because it was not at first treated seriously. . . .

Epic poetry agrees with tragedy in so far as it is an imitation in verse of characters of a higher type. They differ in that epic poetry admits but one kind of meter[10] and is narrative in form. They differ, again, in their length: for tragedy endeavors, as far as possible, to confine itself to a single circuit of the sun, or but slightly to exceed this limit; whereas the epic action has no limits of time. This, then, is a second point of difference; though at first the same freedom was admitted in tragedy as in epic poetry. . . .

[9] Before Aeschylus' time the embryonic Greek tragedy consisted of speeches by a single actor or narrator telling the chorus what had happened and a series of songs, dances, and responses by the chorus, expressing their wonder, joy, or grief at the news.

[10] To a Greek the only meter admissible in an epic poem was the meter of the *Iliad* and the *Odyssey*, or what was called hexameter verse. Virgil used the same meter for the *Aeneid*. In English a well known example of hexameter verse is Longfellow's *Evangeline:*

"This is the forest primeval: the murmuring pines and the hemlocks"—

VI

Tragedy, then, is an imitation of an action that is serious, complete, and of a certain magnitude; in language embellished with every kind of artistic ornament, the several kinds being found in separate parts of the play; in the form of dramatic action, not of narrative; through pity and fear effecting the proper purification of these emotions.[11] By "language embellished," I mean language into which rhythm, harmony, and song enter. By "the several kinds in separate parts," I mean that some parts are rendered through the medium of verse alone, others again with the aid of song.

Now as tragic imitation implies persons acting, it necessarily follows, in the first place, that spectacular equipment will be a part of tragedy. Next, song and diction, for these are the medium of imitation. By diction, I mean the metrical arrangement of the words: as for song, it is a term whose sense everyone understands.

Again, tragedy is the imitation of an action, and an action implies personal actors, who necessarily possess certain distinctive qualities of character and thought; for it is by these that we form our estimate of their actions and these two—thought and character—are the natural causes from which their actions spring, and on their actions all success or failure depends. Now, the imitation of the action is the plot; by plot I here mean the arrangement of the incidents. By character I mean that because of which we ascribe certain qualities to the actors. Thought is needed whenever they speak to prove a statement or declare a general truth. Every tragedy, therefore, must have six parts, which parts determine its quality—namely, plot, character, diction, thought, spectacle, song. . . .

But most important of all is the structure of the incidents. For tragedy is an imitation, not of men, but of action and life, of happi-

[11] Note that an unhappy or what we call a tragic ending was not one of the Greek requirements for a tragedy, though Aristotle thought it the perfect ending. See p. 433. Many tragedies ended with a solemn reconciliation after a conflict or quiet after pain, to please the audience, Aristotle says.

ness and misery. And life consists of action, and its end is a mode of activity,[12] not a quality. Now character determines men's qualities, but it is their action that make them happy or wretched. The purpose of action in the tragedy, therefore, is not the representation of character: character comes in as contributing to the action. Hence the incidents and the plot are the end of the tragedy; and the end is the chief thing of all. So without action there cannot be a tragedy; there may be one without character. . . .

Again, you may string together a set of speeches expressive of character, and well finished in point of diction and thought, and not produce the essential tragic effect nearly so well as with a play which, however deficient in these respects, yet has a plot and artistically constructed incidents. Besides which, the most powerful elements of emotional interest in tragedy—reversal of the situation and recognition scenes[13]—are parts of the plot. A further proof is that novices in the art attain to finish of diction and precision of portraiture before they can construct the plot. It is the same with almost all the early poets.

The plot, then, is the first principle, and, as it were, the soul of a tragedy: character holds the second place. A similar statement is true of painting. The most beautiful colors, laid on confusedly, will not give as much pleasure as a simple chalk outline of a portrait. Thus tragedy is the imitation of an action, and of actors mainly with a view to the action. . . .

The spectacle is, indeed, an attraction in itself, but of all the parts it is the least artistic, and connected least with the art of poetry. For the power of tragedy is felt even apart from representation and actors. Besides, the production of scenic effects is more a matter for the property man than for the poet.

[12] See the *Ethics*, p. 92.
[13] These two admired features of many old dramatic plots Aristotle explains further on.

VII

These principles being established, let us now discuss the proper structure of the plot, since this is the first and most important thing in tragedy.

Now, according to our definition, tragedy is an imitation of an action that is complete and whole and of a certain magnitude; for there may be a whole that is wanting in magnitude. A whole is that which has a beginning, a middle, and an end. A beginning is that which does not have to follow anything else, but after which something else naturally takes place. An end, on the contrary, is that which itself naturally follows something else, either by necessity or as a general rule, but has nothing coming after it. A middle is that which follows something else as some other thing follows it. A well-constructed plot must neither begin nor end at haphazard, but conform to these principles.

Again, a beautiful object, whether it be a living organism or any whole composed of parts, must not only have an orderly arrangement of parts, but must also be of a certain magnitude; for beauty depends on magnitude and order. Hence a very tiny creature cannot be beautiful; for the view of it is confused, the object being seen in an almost imperceptible moment of time. Nor, again, can one of vast size be beautiful; for as the eye cannot take it all in at once, the unity and sense of the whole is lost for the spectator; as it would be if there were a creature a thousand miles long. As, therefore, in the case of living bodies and organisms, a certain magnitude is necessary, and a magnitude which may be easily embraced in one view; so in the plot, a certain length is necessary, and a length which can be easily embraced by the memory. . . . And to state the matter roughly, we may say that the proper length is such as to allow for a sequence of necessary or probable events that will bring about a change from calamity to good fortune, or from good fortune to calamity.

VIII

Unity of plot does not, as some persons think, consist of having a single man as the hero. For infinitely various are the incidents in one man's life which cannot be reduced to unity; and so, too, there are many actions of one man out of which we cannot make one action. Hence the error, as it appears, of all poets who have composed a Heracleid, a Theseid,[14] or other poems of the kind. They imagine that as Heracles was one man, the story of Heracles must also be a unity. But Homer, as in all else he is of surpassing merit, here too—whether from art or natural genius—seems to have happily discerned the truth. In composing the *Odyssey* he did not include all the adventures of Odysseus—such as his wound on Parnassus, or his feigned madness at the mustering of the host[15]—incidents between which there was no necessary or probable connection: but he made the *Odyssey* and likewise the *Iliad* center around an action that in our sense of the word is one. As therefore, in the other imitative arts, the imitation is one when the object imitated is one, so the plot, being an imitation of an action, must imitate one action and that a whole, the structural union of the parts being such that, if any one of them is displaced or removed, the whole will be disjointed and disturbed. For a thing whose presence or absence makes no visible difference is not an organic part of the whole.

IX

It is, moreover, evident from what has been said that it is not the function of the poet to relate what has happened but what may happen—what is possible according to the law of probability or necessity. The poet and the historian differ not by writing in verse or in prose. The work of Herodotus[16] might be put into verse, and it would still

[14] That is, a long-drawn narrative of all the exploits of a Heracles or a Theseus.
[15] Incidents said to have occurred before the opening of the *Iliad*.
[16] The first of the great Greek historians, who wrote the story of the world, as he knew it, down through the Persian wars.

be a species of history, with meter no less than without it. The true difference is that one relates what has happened, the other what may happen. Poetry, therefore, is a more philosophical and a higher thing than history: for poetry tends to express the universal, history the particular. . . .

But even if a poet chances to take an historical subject, he is none-theless a poet; for there is no reason why some events that have actually happened should not conform to the law of the probable and the possible, and in virtue of that aspect of them he is their poet or maker.

Of all plots and actions the episodic are the worst. I call a plot "episodic" in which the episodes or acts succeed one another without probable or necessary sequence. Bad poets compose such pieces by their own fault, good poets, to please the players; for, as they write show pieces for competition, they stretch the plot beyond its capacity, and are often forced to break the natural continuity.

But again, tragedy is an imitation not only of a complete action, but of events inspiring fear or pity. Such an effect is best produced when the events come on us by surprise and when, at the same time, they follow as cause and effect. The wonder will then be greater than if they happened of themselves or merely by accident; for co-incidences too are most marvelous when they have a look of design. We may instance the statue of Mitys at Argos, which fell upon his murderer while he was watching a festival, and killed him. Such events seem the result of more than chance. Plots, therefore, con-structed on these principles are necessarily the best.

X

Plots are either simple or complex, for the actions in real life, of which they are an imitation, are obviously either one or the other. An action which is one and continuous in the sense above defined, I call simple, when the change in the hero's fortune takes place without reversal of the situation and without recognition.

A complex action is one in which the change is accompanied by such a reversal, or by recognition, or by both. These all should arise from the internal structure of the plot, so that what follows should be the necessary or probable result of what went before. It makes a great difference whether the event is caused by or simply happens after the previous action.

XI

Reversal of the situation is a change by which conditions in the play are transformed into their opposite, keeping always to our rule of probability or necessity. Thus in the Oedipus,[17] the messenger comes to cheer Oedipus and free him from his alarms about his mother, but by revealing who Oedipus really is produces the opposite effect. . . .

Recognition, as the name indicates, is a change from ignorance to knowledge, producing love or hate between the persons destined by the poet for good or bad fortune. The best form of recognition is coincident with a reversal of the situation, as in the Oedipus.[18]

Even inanimate things of the most trivial kind may in a sense be objects of recognition. Again, we may recognize or discover whether a person has done a thing or not. But the recognition which is most intimately connected with the plot and action is, as we have said, the recognition of persons. This recognition, combined with a re-

[17] The *Oedipus Tyrannus* of Sophocles is a tragedy which Aristotle much admired and which happily has come down to us. At its opening, Oedipus is the prosperous king of Thebes, with a wife, Jocasta, whom he dearly loves. In the course of the play he discovers that instead of being, as he supposed, a shepherd's son, he is the child of Jocasta and her former husband, the late King of Thebes, exposed to die in infancy because of an ominous prophecy and rescued by the shepherd who brought him up. He learns also that an arrogant old man he killed in a roadside quarrel was the late king, his father. He is therefore the unwitting murderer of his own father and for years has lived in incest with his own mother. At the news, Jocasta hangs herself and Oedipus puts out his eyes and goes blinded and accursed into banishment.

[18] Shakespeare frequently uses these classical dramatic devices of reversal of situation and recognition. The tragedy of *King Lear* is an outstanding illustration of the first. The themes of disguise, mistaken identity, and revelation or recognition occur again and again; notably in *As You Like It, Twelfth Night, Winter's Tale* and *The Tempest*.

versal, will produce either pity or fear; and actions producing these effects are those which, by our definition, tragedy represents. Moreover, it is upon such situations that the issue of good or bad fortune will depend. Recognition, then, being between persons, it may happen that one person only is recognized by the other—when the latter is already known—or it may be necessary that the recognition should be on both sides. Thus Iphigenia is revealed to Orestes by the sending of the letter; but another act of recognition is required to make Orestes known to Iphigenia.[19]

Two parts, then, of the plot—reversal of the situation and recognition—turn upon surprises. A third part is the scene of suffering. The scene of suffering is a destructive or painful action, such as a death on the stage, bodily agony, wounds, and the like. . . .

XIII

As a sequel to what has already been said, we must proceed to consider what the poet should aim at, and what he should avoid in constructing his plots; and by what means the specific effect of tragedy will be produced.

A perfect tragedy should, as we have seen, be arranged not on the simple but on the complex plan. It should, moreover, imitate actions which excite pity and fear, this being the distinctive mark of tragic imitation. It follows plainly, in the first place, that the change of fortune presented must not be the spectacle of a virtuous man brought

---

[19] The reference here is to Euripides' play of *Iphigenia in Tauris*. Aristotle summarizes briefly the story of Iphigenia on p. 437. As the young daughter of King Agamemnon, she was brought from her home to the port of Aulis to be sacrificed, that her father and his fleet might have a favorable wind to sail to Troy. She was snatched from the altar by the goddess Artemis and disappeared. Years later she is a priestess serving in the savage country of Tauris. Her brother Orestes, whom she left at home, a little child, is now a maddened wanderer, seeking absolution for his crime of killing his mother, Clytemnestra, in revenge for her murder of his father, Agamemnon. When Iphigenia finds Orestes on the shore at Tauris, neither, of course, knows the other. In fact, he has no idea that his long lost sister is alive. Through a letter which she gives him he learns who she is, but meanwhile by a law of the country he is condemned to die as a sacrilegious intruder. Through some words of his at the last moment she discovers that he is Orestes and saves him.

from prosperity to adversity: for this moves neither pity nor fear: it merely shocks us. Nor, again, that of a bad man passing from adversity to prosperity: for nothing can be more alien to the spirit of tragedy; it possesses no single tragic quality; it neither satisfies the moral sense nor calls forth pity or fear. Nor, again, should the downfall of an utter villain be exhibited. A plot of this kind would, doubtless, satisfy the moral sense, but it would inspire neither pity nor fear; [20] for pity is aroused by unmerited misfortune, fear by the misfortune of a man like ourselves. Such an event, therefore, will be neither pitiful nor terrible.

There remains, then, the character between these two extremes— that of a man extraordinarily good and just, who yet brings misfortune on himself not by vice or depravity, but by some error or frailty.[21] He must be one who is highly renowned and prosperous, a personage like Oedipus, Thyestes, or other illustrious men of great families.

The best constructed plot should, therefore, be single in its issue, rather than double, as some maintain. The change of fortune should be not from bad to good, but, reversely, from good to bad. It should come about as the result not of vice, but of some great error or frailty, in a character either such as we have described, or better rather than worse. . . . A tragedy, to be perfect according to the rules of art, should be of this construction. Hence they are in error who censure Euripides just because he follows this principle in his plays, many of which end unhappily. It is, as we have said, the right ending. The best proof is that on the stage and in dramatic competition, such plays, if well worked out, are the most tragic in effect; and Euripides, faulty though he may be in the general management of his subject, yet is felt to be the most tragic of the poets.

In the second rank comes the kind of tragedy which some place

[20] Shakespeare's tragedy of *Richard III* is sometimes cited in disproof of this statement. Richard is an "utter villain" but we take a keen interest in his bold struggle to master fate.

[21] Two notably brave and generous tragic heroes, whose downfall is due to one shortcoming in character or judgment, are, of course, Lear and Othello. Some readers would include Hamlet.

first. Like the Odyssey, it has a double thread of plot, and also an opposite ending for the good and for the bad actors. It is accounted the best only because of the weakness of the spectators; for the poet is guided in what he writes by the wishes of his audience. The pleasure, however, thence derived is not the true tragic pleasure. It is proper rather to comedy, where those who, in the piece, are the deadliest enemies—like Orestes and Aegisthus [22]—quit the stage as friends at the close, and no one slays or is slain.

XIV

Fear and pity may be aroused by spectacular means; but they may also result from the inner structure of the piece, which is the better way, and indicates a superior poet. For the plot ought to be so constructed that, even without the aid of the eye, he who hears the tale told will thrill with horror and melt to pity at what takes place. This is the impression we should receive from hearing the story of Oedipus. But to produce this effect by the mere spectacle is a less artistic method, and dependent on extraneous aids. Those who employ spectacular means to create a sense not of the terrible but of the merely monstrous are strangers to the purpose of tragedy; for we must not demand of tragedy any and every kind of pleasure, but only that which is proper to it. And since the pleasure the tragic poet should offer is that which comes from pity and fear through imitation, it is evident that this quality must be impressed on the incidents.

Let us then determine what circumstances strike us as terrible or pitiful.

Actions of this sort must happen between persons who are either friends or enemies or indifferent to one another. If an enemy kills an enemy, there is nothing to excite pity either in the act or the intention —except in so far as the suffering itself is pitiful. So too with indif-

---

[22] In the tragic story of Agamemnon and his son Orestes, Aegisthus is the paramour of Agamemnon's wife, Clytemnestra, who influences her to murder her husband on his return from Troy. Orestes, her son, kills Aegisthus as well as his mother when he finally avenges his father.

ferent persons. But when the tragic incident occurs between those who are near or dear to one another—if, for example, a brother kills, or intends to kill, a brother, a son his father, a mother her son, a son his mother, or any other deed of the kind is done—these are situations to be looked for by the poet. He may not indeed destroy the framework of the received legends—the fact, for instance, that Clytemnestra was slain by Orestes . . . but he ought to show invention of his own, and skillfully handle the traditional material. . . .

Enough has now been said concerning the structure of the incidents and the right kind of plot.

XV

With regard to the characters there are four things to be aimed at. First, and most important, they must be good. Now any speech or action that manifests some kind of moral purpose will be expressive of character: the character will be good if the purpose is good. The goodness is possible in every class of persons. Even a woman may be good, and also a slave, though the one is liable to be an inferior being, and the other quite worthless. The second thing to aim at is appropriateness. There is a type of manly valor, but manliness in a woman, or unscrupulous cleverness, is inappropriate. Thirdly, a character must be true to life: which is something different from goodness and appropriateness, as here described. The fourth point is consistency: for even though the person being imitated, who suggested the type, is inconsistent, still he must be consistently inconsistent.

As in the structure of the plot, so too in the portraiture of character, the poet should always aim at either the necessary or the probable. Thus a person of a given character should speak or act as it is necessary or probable that he would; just as this event should follow that as a necessary or probable consequence. It is therefore evident that the unraveling of the plot, no less than the complication, must arise out of the plot itself; it must not be brought about by

supernatural interference—as in the *Medea*.[23] The supernatural should be employed only for events outside the drama—for past or future events, beyond the range of human knowledge, which need to be reported or foretold; for to the gods we ascribe the power of seeing all things. Within the action there must be nothing improbable. If the improbable cannot be excluded, it should be outside the field of the tragedy, as is the improbable element in the *Oedipus* of Sophocles.

Again, since tragedy is an imitation of persons above the common level, the example of good portrait painters should be followed. They, while reproducing the distinctive features of the original, make a likeness true to life and yet more beautiful. So too the poet, in representing men hot tempered or indolent or with other defects of character, should preserve the type and yet ennoble it. In this way Agathon and Homer have portrayed Achilles.[24]

These, then, are rules the poet should observe. Nor should he neglect those appeals to the eye, which, though not among the essentials, are the concomitants of poetry; for here too there is much room for error. But of this enough has been said in our published treatise.[25] . . .

XVII

In constructing the plot and working it out with the proper diction, the poet should put the scene, as far as possible, before his eyes. In this way, seeing everything with the utmost vividness, as if he were an actual eyewitness, he will discover what is in keeping with it, and be most unlikely to overlook inconsistencies. . . .

[23] In Euripides' play of *Medea*, the heroine, who out of indignation at her wrongs has killed her two children and brought about the death of her husband's new bride, escapes from his fury into the sky in a magic chariot.

[24] We have nothing left of any work by Agathon. We know only that he was a playwright who promised to rival Euripides but who left Athens for some reason at the age of forty and died disappointed in a foreign land. At the banquet celebrated in Plato's dialogue of the *Symposium* he was the happy and admired host. See Classics Club edition of *Plato*, pp. 159-216. For Homer's noble treatment of Achilles, see especially the *Iliad*, Books IX, XIX, XXIV.

[25] Aristotle wrote a dialogue *On Poets*, now lost.

Again, the poet should act out his own play to the best of his power, with the gestures that go with it; for those with a sympathetic nature, who themselves feel the emotion, are most convincing; and one who is grieved himself despairs, one who is angry rages with the most lifelike reality. Hence poetry implies either a special gift of nature or a strain of madness. In the one case a man can take the mold of any character; in the other, he is lifted out of his proper self.

As for the story, whether the poet takes it ready-made or constructs it for himself, he should first sketch its general outline and then fill in the episodes and amplify in detail. The general plan may be illustrated by the *Iphigenia*.[26] A young girl is sacrificed; she disappears mysteriously from the eyes of those who sacrificed her; she is transported to another country, where the custom is to offer up all strangers to the goddess. To this ministry she is appointed. Some time later her own brother chances to arrive. The fact that the oracle for some reason ordered him to go there is outside the general plan of the play. The purpose, again, of his coming is outside the action proper. However, he comes, he is seized, and, when on the point of being sacrificed, reveals who he is. The mode of recognition may be either that of Euripides or of Polyidus,[27] in whose play he exclaims very naturally: "So it was not my sister only, but I too who was doomed to be sacrificed"; and by that remark he is saved.

After this, the names being once given, it remains to fill in the episodes. We must see, however, that they are relevant to the action. In the case of Orestes, for example, there is the madness which led to his capture and his deliverance by means of the purificatory rite. In a play the episodes are short, but in epic poetry they lengthen out the tale. Thus the story of the *Odyssey* can be stated briefly. A certain man is absent from home for many years; he is jealously watched by Poseidon, and quite alone. Meanwhile his home is in a wretched plight—suitors are wasting his substance and plotting against his son. At length, tempest-tossed, he arrives and makes himself known; he

---

[26] On the story of Iphigenia see p. 432, n. 19.
[27] We have no plays of Polyidus.

attacks the suitors with his own hand, and is himself preserved while he destroys them. This is the essence of the plot; the rest is episode.

XVIII

Every tragedy falls into two parts—complication and unraveling or *dénouement*. Incidents before the play opens and often others within the play itself form the complication; the rest is the unraveling. By the complication I mean all that extends from the beginning of the action to the part which marks the turning point to good or bad fortune. The unraveling is that which extends from the beginning of the change to the end. . . .

Again, the poet should remember what has been often said, and not make an epic structure into a tragedy. By an epic structure I mean one with a multiplicity of plots—as if, for instance, you were to make a tragedy out of the entire story of the *Iliad*. In the epic poem, owing to its length, each part can assume its proper magnitude. In the drama the result is far from answering to the poet's expectation. The proof is that the poets who have dramatized the whole story of the fall of Troy, instead of selecting portions, like Euripides; or who have taken the whole tale of Niobe, and not a part of her story, like Aeschylus, either fail utterly or meet with poor success on the stage. . . .

XXIII

As for that poetry which is narrative in form and imitates in meter, the plot manifestly ought, as in a tragedy, to be constructed on dramatic principles. It should have for its subject a single action, whole and complete, with a beginning, a middle, and an end. It will thus resemble a living organism in all its unity, and produce the pleasure proper to it. It will differ in structure from historical compositions, which of necessity present not a single action, but a single period, and all that happened within that period to one person or to many, however little connected together the events may be. For as the sea fight at Salamis and the battle with the Carthaginians in

Sicily took place at the same time but did not tend to any one result, so in the ordinary course of events one thing sometimes follows another, and yet no single end is thereby produced. Such is the way, we may say, most poets write.

Here again, then, as has been already observed, the transcendent excellence of Homer is manifest. He never attempts to make the whole war of Troy the subject of his poem, though that war had a beginning and an end. It would have been too vast a theme, and not easily embraced in a single view. If not that, it would have been over-complicated by the variety of the incidents in it. As it is, he detaches a single portion, though he admits as episodes many events from the general story of the war—such as the Catalogue of Ships [28] and others —thus diversifying the poem. . . . For this reason the *Iliad* and the *Odyssey* each furnish the subject of but one tragedy, or, at most, of two. . . .

XXIV

Again, epic poetry may have as many kinds as tragedy: it may be simple, or complex, a tale of character or of suffering. The parts also, with the exception of song and spectacle, are the same; for it requires reversals of the situation, recognitions, and scenes of suffering. Moreover, the thought and the diction must be artistic. In all these respects, Homer is our earliest and sufficient model. Indeed each of his poems has a twofold character. The *Iliad* is at once simple and a tale of suffering, and the *Odyssey* complex (for recognition scenes run through it), and at the same time a tale of character. Moreover, in diction and thought they are supreme.

Epic poetry differs from tragedy in the scale on which it is constructed, and in its meter. As regards scale or length, we have already laid down an adequate limit: the beginning and the end must be capable of being brought within a single view. This condition will be satisfied by poems on a smaller scale than the old epics, and an-

---

[28] In the second half of Book II of the *Iliad*, Homer interrupts the course of his story to insert a catalogue of the ships that came to Troy and their leaders. See Classics Club edition. pp. 33-42.

swering in length to the group of tragedies presented at a single sitting.[29]

Epic poetry has, however, a great—a special—capacity for enlarging its dimensions, and we can see the reason. In tragedy we cannot imitate several lines of action carried on at one and the same time; we must confine ourselves to the action on the stage and the part taken by the players. But in epic poetry, owing to the narrative form, many events simultaneously transacted can be presented; and these, if relevant to the subject, add mass and dignity to the poem. The epic has here an advantage, and one that conduces to grandeur of effect, to diverting the mind of the hearer, and relieving the story with varying episodes. For sameness of incident soon produces satiety, and makes tragedies fail on the stage. . . .

Homer, admirable in all respects, has the special merit of being the only poet who rightly appreciates the part he should take himself. The poet should speak as little as possible in his own person, for it is not this that makes him an imitator. Other poets appear themselves upon the scene throughout, and imitate but little and rarely. Homer, after a few prefatory words, at once brings in a man or woman or other personage, none of them wanting in characteristic qualities, but each with a character of his own.

The element of the wonderful is required in tragedy. But the improbable, on which the wonderful depends for its chief effects, has wider scope in epic poetry, because there the person acting is not seen. Thus, the pursuit of Hector would be ludicrous if placed upon the stage—the Greeks standing still and not joining in the pursuit, and Achilles waving them back.[30] But in the epic poem the absurdity passes unnoticed. Now the wonderful is pleasing, as may be inferred from the fact that everyone tells a story with some addition of his own, knowing that his hearers like it. . . .

---

[29] Greek dramatists of the great period used to produce their plays in groups of four, three more or less connected tragedies followed by a comic or satiric play, all seen by the audience in one sitting.

[30] Achilles' pursuit of Hector is described in the *Iliad*, Book XII.

But the poet should prefer probable impossibilities to improbable possibilities. The tragic plot must not be composed of improbable parts. Everything improbable should, if possible, be excluded; or, at all events, it should lie outside the action of the play itself. . . .

But once the improbable has been introduced and an air of likelihood imparted to it, we must accept it in spite of the absurdity. Take even the incidents in the *Odyssey* where Odysseus is left upon the shore of Ithaca.[31] How intolerable even these might have been would be apparent if an inferior poet were to treat the subject! As it is, the absurdity is veiled by the poetic charm with which the poet invests it.

The diction should be elaborated in the pauses of the action where there is no expression of character or thought. For, conversely, character and thought are merely obscured by a diction that is over brilliant.

XXV

With respect to problems and their solutions, the number and nature of the sources from which they spring may be thus set forth.

The poet being an imitator, like a painter or any other artist, must of necessity imitate one of three objects: things as they were or are, things as they are said or thought to be, or things as they ought to be. This he does in language—using either current expressions or, it may be, rare words or metaphors. There are also many modifications of language, which we concede to the poets. Add to this, that the standard of correctness is not the same in poetry and in politics, any more than in poetry and in any other art. Within the art of poetry itself there are two kinds of faults—those which touch its essence, and those which are accidental. If the poet intended to describe something right, but described it incorrectly through lack of ability to express himself, his art is faulty. But if his failure was due to a wrong intention—if, for instance, he represented a horse as throwing out both his off legs at once, or introduced technical inaccuracies in medicine

[31] *Odyssey*, Book XIII. 116 ff.

or some other science—the error was not in the essentials of his art. These are the points of view from which we should consider and answer the questions raised in the problems.

First as to questions which concern the poet's own art. If he describes the impossible, he is guilty of an error; but the error may be justified, if the end of the art be thereby attained (the end being that already mentioned)—if, that is, the effect of this or any other part of the poem is thus rendered more striking. A case in point is the pursuit of Hector. If, however, the end might have been as well or better attained without violating the rules of poetic correctness, the error is not justified; for every kind of error should, if possible, be avoided.

Again, does the error touch the essentials of the poetic art or some accident of it? For example, not to know that a hind has no horns is a less serious matter than to paint it inartistically.

Further, if it be objected that a description is not true to fact, the poet may perhaps reply, "But the objects are as they ought to be", just as Sophocles said that he drew men as they ought to be, Euripides as they are. In this way the objection may be met. If, however, the description is neither true nor of the thing as it should be, the poet may answer, "This is how men say the thing is." This dictum applies to the tales about the gods. It may well be that these stories are not loftier than the facts nor yet true to fact; they are, very possibly, what Xenophanes [32] says of them. But anyhow, "this is what is said."

XXVI

The question may be raised whether the epic or tragic form of imitation is the higher. If the more refined art is the higher, and the more refined in every case is that which appeals to the better sort of audience, the art which addresses itself to any and everyone is manifestly most unrefined. The audience then is supposed to be too

[32] Xenophanes of Colophon, who lived almost two hundred years before Aristotle, seems to have been remembered largely for his attacks on and ridicule of the popular polytheism of Greece.

dull to comprehend unless the performers throw in something of their own, who therefore indulge in perpetual movements.

So we are told that epic poetry is addressed to a cultivated audience, who do not need gestures, tragedy to an inferior public. Being then unrefined, it is evidently the lower of the two.

Now, in the first place, this censure attaches not to the poetic but to the actors' art; for gesticulation may be equally overdone in epic recitation. . . . Next, all action is not to be condemned—any more than all dancing—but only that of bad performers. . . . Again, tragedy, like epic poetry, produces its effect even without action; it reveals its power by mere reading. If, then, in all other respects it is superior, this fault, we say, is not inherent in it.

And superior it is, because it has all the epic elements—it may even use the epic meter, with music and spectacular effects as important accessories; and these produce the most lively of pleasures. Further, it creates a vivid impression when read as well as when acted. Moreover, the art in it attains its end within narrower limits; and the concentrated effect is more pleasurable than one which is spread over a long time and so diluted. What, for example, would be the effect of the *Oedipus* of Sophocles, if it were cast into a form as long as the *Iliad?* Once more, the epic imitation has less unity; as is shown by this, that any epic poem will furnish subjects for several tragedies. . . .

If, then, tragedy is superior to epic poetry in all these respects and, moreover, fulfills its specific function better as an art—for each art ought to produce, not any chance pleasure, but the pleasure proper to it, as already stated—it plainly follows that tragedy is the higher art, as attaining its end more perfectly.

Thus much may suffice concerning tragic and epic poetry in general; their several kinds and parts, with the number of each and their differences; the causes that make a poem good or bad; the objections of the critics and the answer to their objections.